# EMERGENT COMMERCIAL TRENDS AND AVIATION SAFETY

For Ayush, in hope

# EMERGENT COMMERCIAL TRENDS AND AVIATION SAFETY

RUWANTISSA I.R. ABEYRATNE

Routledge
Taylor & Francis Group
LONDON AND NEW YORK

First published 1999 by Ashgate Publishing

Reissued 2018 by Routledge
2 Park Square, Milton Park, Abingdon, Oxon, OX14 4RN
711 Third Avenue, New York, NY 10017

*Routledge is an imprint of the Taylor & Francis Group, an informa business*



A Library of Congress record exists under LC control number: 99020600

Typeset in Great Britain by Manton Typesetters, Louth, Lincolnshire.

ISBN 13: 978-1-138-62516-7 (hbk)
ISBN 13: 978-0-429-46010-4 (ebk)

# Contents

# Foreword

Telecommunications, air transport and electronic data processing will be recognized as the landmark contributions of the twentieth century towards globalization. Among them, aviation has become an indivisible and vital part of the world economy and international interaction thanks to its ability to shrink intercontinental travel times for passengers and cargo to mere hours, whereas only two generations earlier, weeks or months were required.

International air navigation and air transport create a complex web of social relations on the global scale – relations which require regulation to harmonize the conflicting social interests and to assure safe, orderly and economic air transport. Technology, politics and economic interests are closely interwoven in the regulatory web, and protectionist traditions compete with modern ideas of liberalization and globalization. Safety of flight is one of the commonly recognized maxims in air navigation, although the level of implementation of safety standards is not uniform among States at different stages of economic and technical development. While statistically aviation is by far the safest mode of transport, the complex technology and its demands on the controlling human element will never be able to completely avoid accidents; issues of liability require a modern, global regulatory framework and rejection of the antiquated current systems rooted in the infancy of aviation.

R.I.R. Abeyratne presents in this book a lucid, penetrating and original picture of the evolving concepts of traffic rights and the trends towards liberalization and globalization of air transport, competition and safeguards required to preserve the right of all States to operate an airline. He uses analytical and critical methods for his legal argument, and does so in remarkably simple and comprehensible language – a gift rather rare in the legal profession. The strength of his analysis lies in his vision of the inter-relation of aviation economy and aviation safety, and his observations on international safety oversight and liability of air carriers are fully up to date and convincing.

R.I.R. Abeyratne is an exceptional aviation practitioner, scholar and prolific publicist who has to his credit numerous books and studies on air law and related disciplines. Educated as a lawyer at Colombo University, Sri Lanka, he received his postgraduate education (LLM degree) at Monash University, Australia, and McGill University, Canada; he obtained a doctoral degree in law from McGill University and from the University of Colombo, and has been honoured by membership of several learned societies. His practical experience stems from his earlier senior position with Air Lanka and his current position as a senior international civil servant in the Secretariat of ICAO in Montreal. The quality and usefulness of his publications is assured by his impressive knowledge of the inner workings of airlines, as well as of the wide international contexts and needs of the global aviation community.

This book will prove useful not only for lawyers, but also for the governments, airlines, economists, social scientists, politicians, journalists and the general public.

Professor Dr Michael Milde
Director
Institute of Air and Space Law
McGill University
Montreal
Canada

# Preface

It is incontrovertible that the pre-eminent concern of the air transport industry and aircraft manufacturers at present is aviation safety. It is also the foremost priority of the International Civil Aviation Organization (ICAO), which called an International Conference for Directors General of Civil Aviation World-wide in November 1997 to review ICAO's Safety Oversight Programme and to consider its expansion. The findings of this conference were being addressed by ICAO at the time of writing, and the strategic objective of the ICAO Strategic Action Plan, which was adopted by the ICAO Council on 7 February 1997, is to promote the safety, security and efficiency of international civil aviation.

This book discusses the factors which may compromise the safety of civil aviation, and analyses the regulatory process which has been formulated by ICAO and the regional civil aviation bodies – AFCAC, ECAC and LACAC – to address these concerns.

The rapid commercialization of air transport in recent times has had an inevitable impact on aviation safety. Part I of this book traces the history of the Chicago Convention of 1944, which set some commercial goals, but failed to set other important ones. It then traces the fifty-year history of commercial aviation, and examines current commercial trends such as franchising of the airline product, outsourcing and the virtual airline, the millennium bug, and the use of smart cards in customs and immigration procedures as possible threats to aviation safety if they are overused.

Part II explores the enormity of the problems faced by the international community in ensuring aviation safety, and discusses the management of safety into the next millennium, and Part III seeks to draw together some general conclusions about the issues addressed in the book.

### Strategic Alliances of Airlines

Today's commercial competition has transcended the past era, where dominant markets protected their established market shares. Most mega-commercial activity was then the purview of governmental control under instrumentalities of State which were mostly cumbersome bureaucracies at best. Perhaps the best analogy is the biggest commercial market – the United States – which had until recently extensively regulated larger commercial activities pertaining to energy, transportation and telecommunications.

Happily, over the past decade, commercial air carriers have broken the shackles of rigid regulation to form strategic alliances among themselves. These alliances have been formed as a result of the realization that the performance of an airline can be affected by two factors: the average performance of all competitors in the airline industry, and whether the airline concerned is a superior or inferior performer in the industry. Michael Porter[1] encapsulates these two factors in the single premise that any business achieves superior profitability in its industry by attaining either higher prices or lower costs than rivals. Curiously, in the airline industry, it is the latter – lower costs – which has been the cornerstone of strategic alliances.

The reason for airlines banding together is to share an otherwise wasted market which is still regulated by bilateral governmental negotiations. This unfortunate state of affairs has been brought about by a lacuna in the Convention of International Civil Aviation[2] (Chicago Convention) which leaves the absolute prerogative of allowing air carriers to carry passengers, cargo and mail into and out of their territories to States.[3] This privilege has encouraged the protective instincts of States to ensure that their national carriers obtain optimum market share 'belonging' to them, based on a now antiquated belief that all passengers, cargo and mail destined to a particular State or leaving that State are the birth right of the national carrier of that State. This stifling phenomenon has encouraged airlines to think more strategically over the past two decades, resulting in the pursuit of improved operational effectiveness in their activities.

The seminal response of most strategic airlines to the interference of governments was to 'share' each others' resources, including air traffic rights, thus gaining access to what was disallowed under bilateral governmental agreement. Recently, airlines have become more aware than ever that theirs is becoming an increasingly capital-intensive industry, and that there is a compelling need to reduce costs in order to survive. The end result has been an array of commercial arrangements between airlines, from statements of common interests to block space arrangements, code-sharing and co-ordination of frequent flyer programmes, to name just a few.[4]

*The Philosophy of Strategic Alliances*

Arguably the most spectacular strategic airline alliance so far is the Star Alliance, which was launched in 1997 by Lufthansa, SAS, United Airlines, Thai Airways International and Air Canada. Brazilian carrier Varig joined later, and it is expected that Ansett Australia and Air New Zealand will join the alliance in 1999. Recently, Singapore Airlines signed a commercial agreement with SAS – one of the Star Alliance members – which will bring Singapore Airlines inextricably close to the alliance itself.[5] It is evident that the carriers of North America, Europe and the Asia-Pacific regions which form the Star Alliance have skilfully manoeuvred their dominance of the regions they represent. The direction in which the alliance is heading, with the possible future membership of Japan's All Nippon Airways (ANA), is incontrovertibly to assert its presence in the burgeoning Asia-Pacific market, in particular the Pacific Region.

The underlying philosophy of the airline alliances typified by a Star Alliance is not so much an emphasis on the more effective use of resources such as labour, capital and national resources (which are inevitably important factors), but rather an overall reliance on the strategy of location, where the sharing of locations represented by the various airlines has enabled them to produce their goods and services in a consistent manner, thus achieving a status equivalent to a cartel while still retaining their individual identities.

Airlines have developed both a corporate strategy and a competition strategy to cope with competition. Both these strategies are becoming increasingly complementary rather than being mutually exclusive, which they were at the inception of airline competition fifty years ago. As airlines began to compete with each other across borders, they acquired the ability to locate themselves overseas, creating a compelling need for commercial airlines to be fully acquainted with locational strategy and competitive advantages of various locations. Very early in the game, giants such as PanAm and TWA began to realize that even the strongest companies with an established position in the airline industry unthreatened by competition from new entrants or smaller airlines would start losing business if they faced a better or cheaper product. The threat of new entrants, the bargaining power of suppliers and customers and the superior quality or low cost of substitute products were arguably the underlying reasons why established airlines began experiencing a downturn in the 1960s, which was exacerbated through the 1970s and 1980s. These threats could not be effectively circumvented or overcome by the established carriers, partly because of the sustained circumscription of market entry imposed by Article 6 of the Chicago Convention.

The genesis of airline alliances was therefore a contrived symbiosis or coexistence between the new entrants or new competitors – which had the clout of resources but not the dimensions of a larger carrier – and the larger carriers themselves which had an established product to offer. Together, these two types of carrier could eradicate such obstacles as product differentiation (which was a distinct disadvantage to carriers which did not have an established brand), capital requirements (which again was a disadvantage faced by smaller carriers), economies of scale (which forced a smaller carrier to compete on a large scale) and government policy (which affected both types of carrier – particularly larger carriers which had the resources to operate air services, but not the market access to a given region).

Another type of commercial alliance is the mega-alliance referred to earlier, typified by the Star Alliance. The precursor to this type of alliance could have been the modest 'pool agreement' between two carriers operating Third and Fourth Freedom traffic (traffic purely originating and ending in each others' territories). The pool agreement was written into a bilateral air services agreement between two States in order to ensure equal enjoyment of market share between their carriers in the route between their States' territories. This notion gave rise to an extension of the principle of pooling, which was to share locational traffic on a Fifth Freedom (traffic which is picked up at intermediate or beyond points on services between two States), and more importantly, Sixth Freedom basis (traffic to which a carrier had no right, but could operate under the air traffic rights of another carrier, through a commercial arrangement such as a code-sharing agreement signed by and between the carriers).

*Some Types of Strategic Alliances*

Airline alliances, particularly code-sharing agreements, add destinations to a route network and offer more frequent services to customers. With such arrangements, an airline can add flights using its code-sharing partner's flight entitlements and operate to additional destinations without adding any resources. Of course, such an arrangement would create a duopoly, depriving customers of the benefit of competition, pricing, etc. if the airlines concerned were in competition on a given route. Code-sharing not only affects passenger traffic, but influences the consolidation of cargo carriage as well, as was seen in the Swissair-Delta Airlines cargo alliance across the Atlantic.[6]

In Europe, the 'open skies' concept introduced by the European Union as legislator in 1977 was meant to open competition between European carriers in Europe in order to offer competitive airline services to customers. However, this has not had the desired effect, mainly due to airlines forming alliances under the umbrella of the 'open skies' legislation. In particular, the four alliances, headed by British Airways, Lufthansa, KLM and Swissair, have vigorously entered into alliances with smaller carriers under franchising agreements in order to gain access to markets they have not obtained in their air services agreements.

There are approximately 1,200 scheduled air carriers in the world. It is estimated that there are approximately 10,000 aircraft in the air at any given moment. Excluding China and the countries of the former Soviet Union, approximately 380,000 civil aircraft are registered in ICAO States. Of these, 45,000 are used by commercial operators.[7] Forecasts of the number of passengers carried on scheduled services in nine intercontinental route groups show the transpacific and Europe-Asia markets as the fastest-growing at 8 per cent and 7.5 per cent per annum respectively for the forecast period through to the year 2003.[8] International scheduled passenger traffic is forecast to grow at an average rate of 6.5 per cent per annum, compared with 4 per cent per annum for domestic traffic.[9] These rapidly evolving trends will no doubt be accommodated by equally rapidly developing technology and economic norms in the airline industry. Incontrovertibly, code-sharing and computer reservation systems (CRSs) are at the forefront of this process.

Although technically code-sharing and the functions of computer reservations systems are two different activities of the air transport industry, they become inextricably linked to each other when two air carriers which share each other's codes wish to have their shared flights displayed in each other's CRSs. Displaying a code-shared flight in the CRS of one code-sharing partner differently from the system of the other makes no commercial sense to both the air carrier concerned and the consumer. Thus, multiple listings of the same flight may appear in CRS and airline schedules, often misleading the potential passenger, but certainly drawing an identifiable link between the two systems. Therefore, both activities, which have undergone significant growth over the past few years, warrant close analysis in view of their inextricable link to each other and joint quest for commercial credibility and consistency. An inexorable implication of this symbiosis is the impact the two activities may bring to bear on the principles of the law of contract.

## Notes

1 Michael E. Porter, *On Competition*, Harvard Business Review Series, 1996, at 4.
2 Convention on International Civil Aviation, signed Chicago, 7 December 1944. See ICAO Doc. 7300/7 (7th edn), 1997.
3 Article 6 of the Chicago Convention provides: 'No scheduled international air

service may be operated over or into the territory of a Contracting State, except with the special permission or other authorization of that State, or in accordance with the terms of such permission or authorization.'

4 See Russel Miller, 'International Airline Alliances: A Review of Competition Law Aspects', *Air & Space Law*, 1998, Vol. XXIII, No. 3, at 125.

5 ITA Press, 16–31 October 1998, at 4.

6 Robert Koenig, 'Swissair, Delta Raise Trans-Atlantic Cargo Status', *Journal of Commerce*, 2 June 1998, at 8A.

7 *Outlook for Air Transport to the Year 2003*, ICAO Circular 252-AT/103, 1995, Chapter 2, at 5.

8 Id., Chapter 1, at 2.

9 Id., Chapter 5, at 37.

# PART I
# HISTORY AND COMMERCIAL TRENDS

# 1 Competition Rules in Commercial Aviation

## Introduction

The perceived inadequacy of the Chicago Convention[1] of 1944 to provide multilateral guidelines on air traffic rights for commercial air carriers has led to the need for bilateral negotiations between contracting States regarding the exchange of air traffic rights between their national carriers. Article 6 of the Convention provides that no scheduled international air service may be operated over or into the territory of a contracting State except with the special permission or other authorization of that State, and in accordance with the terms of such permission or authorization. This provision explicitly requires a scheduled commercial air carrier of a State to obtain special permission or authorization from the State over which the carrier flies or into which it operates air services. This permission usually takes the form of a bilateral air services agreement or at least an operating permit granted as an interim measure until the formalization of such an agreement.

The significance of this ambivalence of the Chicago Convention is that for the fifty years since the Convention was adopted, scheduled commercial carriers have had to refrain from free commercial competition, and subject themselves to States' assessment of whether awarding particular traffic rights to a carrier from a third State would adversely affect the operation of air services by their own carriers. Unlike shipping lines operating by sea, there is no free competition among scheduled commercial carriers in the operation of air services.

One of the corollaries to the air traffic rights debate has been debate over whether the present bilateral regime adequately serves the current needs of commercial aviation. As an alternative, some have suggested that air services should be considered a trade in service, and that this subject should be brought within the purview of the General Agreement on Trade in Services (GATS) under the umbrella of the World Trade Organization (WTO).

This chapter will analyse the reasons behind the air traffic rights protectionism which has resulted from Article 6 of the Chicago Convention, and examines competition rules, both in commercial aviation and those of the WTO.

## The Genesis of Air Traffic Rights

### *The Chicago Conference*

The foundation for the Chicago Conference of 1944 was laid by President Roosevelt of the United States. In his inaugural message to the conference on 1 November 1944, President Roosevelt, referring to the Paris Conference of 1919 which was designed to open Europe to air traffic but unfortunately took years to implement, stated:

> I do not believe that the world today can afford to wait several years for its air communications. There is no reason why it should.
>
> Increasingly, the airplanes will be in existence. When either the German or Japanese enemy is defeated, transport planes should be available for release from military work in numbers sufficient to make a beginning. When both enemies have been defeated, they should be available in quantity. Every country has its airports and trained pilots; practically every country knows how to organize airlines.
>
> You are fortunate to have before you one of the great lessons of history. Some centuries ago, an attempt was made to build great empires based on domination of great sea areas. The lords of these areas tried to close the areas to some, and to offer access to others, and thereby to enrich themselves and extend their power. This led directly to a number of wars both in the Eastern and Western Hemispheres. We do not need to make that mistake again. I hope you will not dally with the thought of creating great blocs of closed air, thereby tracing in the sky the conditions of future wars. I know you will see to it that the air which God gave everyone shall not become the means of domination over anyone.[2]

Thus President Roosevelt urged States to eschew protectionism, while encouraging them to avoid dominance over one another. Ever since, the economic regulation of international air transport has remained an obdurate dilemma: how can States avoid being dominated by others without protecting themselves? The solution is still being sought, as this chapter will show.

The Chairman of the conference, US delegate Adolf A. Berle Jr, endorsed the President's comments by observing:

> There are many tasks which our countries have to do together, but in none have they a clearer and plainer common interest than in the work

> of making the air serviceable to mankind. For the air was given to all; every nation in the world has access to it. To each nation there is now available a means of friendly intercourse with all the world, provided a working basis for that intercourse can be found and maintained.[3]

At the conference, the United States took the position that the use of the air and the use of the sea were both common, in that they were highways given by nature to all. They were different in that mankind's use of the air is subject to the sovereignty of nations over which such use is made. The United States was therefore of the opinion that nations ought to arrange among themselves for its use in such manner as would be of the greatest benefit to all humanity, wherever situated. The United States further asserted the rule that each country has a right to maintain sovereignty of the air which is over its lands and its territorial waters. There was no question of alienating or qualifying this sovereignty. This absolute right, according to the United States, had to be qualified by the subscription by States to friendly intercourse between nations, and the universal recognition of the natural rights of States to communicate and trade with each other. This right could not be derogated by the use of discriminatory measures.[4] The fact that the United States required States to exchange air traffic rights reciprocally is clearly evident in the statement:

> It is therefore the view of the United States, that, without prejudice to full rights of sovereignty, we should work upon the basis of exchange of needed privileges and permissions which friendly nations have a right to expect from each other.[5]

According to the United States, the privilege of communication by air with friendly countries was not a right to wander at will throughout the world. In this respect, it was contended that traffic by air differed materially from traffic by sea, where commerce need have no direct connection with the country from which the ship may have come. Air routes were analogous to railroad lines, and the right to connect communication links between States was to establish a steady flow of traffic, thereby opening economic routes between countries. According to the United States, it was too early to go beyond this concept, and States should accept the fact that all the Chicago Conference would accomplish was to adopt a Convention that would establish communication between States.[6]

With regard to the establishment of an international organization, the United States was of the view that in the purely technical field, considerable power could be wielded by such an organization, while in the economic and political fields, only consultative, fact-gathering and fact-finding functions should be performed by it. The United States concluded:

> ... the United States will support an international organization in the realm of air commerce having power in technical matters and having consultative functions in economic matters and the political questions which may be directly connected with them under a plan by which continuing and collected experience, widening custom, and the growing maturity of its counsel may establish such added base as circumstances may warrant for the future consideration of enlarging the functions of the consultative group.[7]

It is worthy of note that in 1944, the United States Government had envisioned greater scope in economic issues for the proposed international organization.

In its position statement, the United Kingdom strongly advocated a plan that would provide the services needed between States, serve the interests of the travelling public, and be equitable. It was further recognized that each State had a fair share in the operation of air services and carriage by air of traffic, giving as an example the pre-war proposals by the United Kingdom and the United States to open a transatlantic service on a fifty-fifty basis. The United Kingdom further contended:

> While recognizing national interests we want to encourage enterprise and efficiency which are indeed themselves a national as well as an international interest. And we want therefore to encourage the efficient and to stimulate the less efficient ... only by common action on some such lines as indicated can we reduce and gradually eliminate subsidies, thereby putting civil aviation on an economic footing and incidentally very considerably relieving the tax payer. Unrestricted competition is their most fruitful soil.[8]

The United Kingdom seemed to have adopted a balanced approach that supported the establishment of air services to meet the needs of the travelling public while not unduly affecting the rights of States to have a fair share of traffic for themselves.

Canada suggested the establishment of an international air authority to plan and foster the organization of air services. This authority would, according to Canada, ensure, *inter alia,* that so far as possible, international air routes and services were divided freely and equitably between the various member States, and ensure to every State the opportunity of participating in international airline operations, in accordance with its need for an air transportation service and its industrial and scientific resources.[9]

India, while believing that it was essential for air services to develop rationally, with a certain degree of freedom of the air being the inherent right of every State, went on to say:

> We believe that the grant of commercial rights – that is to say, the right to carry traffic to and from another country – is best negotiated and agreed to on a universal reciprocal basis, rather than by bilateral agreements. We think that only such an arrangement will secure to all countries the reciprocal rights which their interests require. But the grant of any such freedoms and rights must, in our opinion, necessarily be associated with the constitution of an authority which will regulate the use of such freedoms. It will be the function of such authority ... to ensure that the interests of the people, both of the most powerful and of the smaller countries, are secured.[10]

India's position has therefore been to recommend a liberal approach of universal reciprocity within the parameters of control by an authority which could ensure that the smaller nations were protected from being swamped by larger States.

France also strongly supported the establishment of an international organization which could act as a 'watchdog' against predatory practices by States in the operation of international air services. In its position statement, France stated:

> As the President of the United States of America recommended yesterday in his message, we must endeavour to avoid the future formation of rival blocs.
>
> To escape this danger, of which we were so justly warned, all the nations invited here must have a reasonable share in air transportation. The international organization, which we are to consider, seems to us the only means of reaching this goal and of affording to international air transportation the unlimited development to which it is entitled.[11]

The incontrovertible fact that emerges from the views of the States cited above is that there had been general consensus that competition for air traffic rights, based on the concept of State sovereignty, should be fair and equitable. It is for this reason that some States even went to the extent of suggesting the creation of an 'umpire' to determine and rule on whether fair competition was being practised when States began to operate commercial air services between each other's territory.

The spirit of international civil aviation is therefore one of sharing air services and giving every country an opportunity not merely to indulge in trade in air services, but also to operate air services. The Government of the United States concluded:

> Worldwide development of civil aviation is a powerful force for world unity and world peace;
>
> A general system of rights for planes to travel and to carry international commerce should be set up, becoming the established custom

> of commerce by air, as similar arrangements have become the settled law of commerce by sea;
> These rights of transit and commerce should be available to all nations, permitting equal opportunity and reasonable competition ...[12]

Adolf A. Berle Jr, the US delegate to the Chicago Conference, referring to plurilateralism, or sharing the international airways among a few nations, had this to say in 1944:

> It may be noted that this movement necessarily includes some of the features of the old mercantile trading companies which became colonial empires. But it short-circuits the period within which those huge concerns were private monopolies run for private enrichment. Moreover, it fails to answer the problems of all peoples, unless all peoples are assigned a place in the scheme of things. A naked division of air commerce among, let us say, Britain, the Soviet Union, China and the United States – which was actually proposed by Senator Brewster, who is a recognized spokesman for Pan American Airways in the United States Senate – necessarily means wiping all other countries out of the international air. Other countries intensely dislike the idea. What is more, they can cite chapter and verse for their protests – the Atlantic Charter states as one of the joint war aims of President Roosevelt and Prime Minister Churchill: 'To further the enjoyment by all States, great or small, victor or vanquished, of access on equal terms to the trade and to the raw materials of the world which are needed for their economic prosperity.' This they consider a necessary premise of the following article of the Charter, which calls for the fullest collaboration between nations in the economic sphere, looking toward improved labour standards, economic advancement, and social security.
> It is easy for critics to assume that the advocates of economic collaboration in the air – as in other fields – are merely endeavouring to find a new form of words to justify economic imperialism. Yet the criticism is by no means necessarily just. Like any plan which rests on governmental power, the result will be liberation or oppression, depending on whether the plan is fair to all or whether it favours some at the expense of others ...[13]

There is a certain irony in this statement, reflecting the overall spirit of the Chicago Convention, which includes the regulatory framework that applies to air traffic rights. There is no doubt that if air traffic rights are brought within the purview of GATS under the overall GATT umbrella, the total liberalization of international air services that would result would in turn lead to free competition in the world, leaving a few mega-carriers to enjoy the total aviation market. In this scenario, the rights of others who are prevented from operating air services for their States would indeed be a thing of the past.

*The Chicago Convention*

Fifty-two States signed the Chicago Convention on 7 December 1944. The Convention came into force on 4 April 1947, on the thirtieth day after it was deposited with the Government of the United States. In its Preamble, the Chicago Convention records the fact that the signatory States agree on certain principles and arrangements in order that international civil aviation may be developed in a safe and orderly manner, and that international air transport services may be established on the basis of equality of opportunity and operated soundly and economically. *Ex facie*, this pronouncement blends the need for order in civil aviation with the need for equality of opportunity and the economical operation of air services.

As a first measure, the contracting States to the Convention recognize the complete and exclusive sovereignty of every State over the air space above its territory[14] – a pre-eminent tenet of international air law that has been recognized from the time of the Roman Empire[15] and carried over to the Paris Convention of 1919.[16] While each contracting State agrees that aircraft of the other parties which are not engaged in scheduled international air services shall have the right, subject to the observance of the terms of the Convention, to make flights into or transit non-stop across its territory, and make landings for non-traffic purposes without having to obtain permission of the grantor State for such operations, such aircraft are also generally given the right to take on or discharge passengers, mail and cargo, provided the aircraft are engaged in the carriage of such traffic and the rights of a State concerned are not derogated by such operations.[17]

The most contentious provision of the Chicago Convention in relation to commercial air transport is Article 6, according to which a scheduled international air service may not operate air services into the territory of a contracting State, except with the special permission or other authorization of that State, and in accordance with the terms of such permission or authorization. Pursuant to the inability of contracting States to reach multilateral agreement on uniformity in the award of air traffic rights, two agreements emerged that attempted to group States into accepting a limited common base on commercial aviation. The first – the Transit, or Two Freedoms Agreement – was signed by 32 States, and admitted of aircraft of those States being able to fly across each other's territories or land in them for non-traffic purposes without having to obtain permission from the grantor State concerned. The second – the Five Freedoms, or Transport Agreement – was signed by 20 States which granted each other the Five Freedoms of the Air, as they are known today, which their carriers could use freely in each other's territories.[18] Those States which did not sign any of these agreements were required to sign bilateral air services agreements with each other if their aircraft were to operate commercial air services involving taking on or discharging passengers, mail and cargo in each other's territories. In addition, cabotage was introduced in Article 7 of the Convention, giving States the right to prohibit aircraft from one State picking up or discharging passengers, mail and cargo destined from one point of a foreign State to another.

*Post-Chicago Convention Trends*

The economic significance of the Chicago Convention lies entirely in its main theme – meeting the needs of the peoples of the world for economical air transport while preventing waste through unfair competition and providing for a fair opportunity for all States concerned to operate air services. In order to accomplish this goal, the Convention, through ICAO, has to consider all aspects of economic implications posed by the operation of international air services by commercial air transport enterprises of the world, particularly those of the member States of ICAO.

In August 1945, at the first meeting of the Opening Session of the Interim Council of the Provisional International Civil Aviation Organization (PICAO), the Hon. C.D. Howe, Canadian Minister of Reconstruction, said :

> We [Canada] believe that there must be greater freedom for development of international air transport and that this freedom may best be obtained within a framework which provides equality of opportunity and rewards for efficiency.[19]

Dr Edward Warner, Representative of the United States of America (later the first President of the ICAO Council) said at the same meeting:

> Our first purpose will be to smooth the paths for civil flying wherever we are able. We shall seek to make it physically easier, safer, more reliable, more pleasant; but I believe it will be agreed also that we should maintain the constant goal that civil aviation should contribute to international harmony. The civil use of aircraft must so develop as to bring the peoples closer together, letting nation speak more understandingly unto nation.[20]

Dr Warner notably stressed that the purpose of civil aviation was to promote international harmony and dialogue between nations. He also made it clear that the seminal task of civil aviation is to bring the people of the world together through understanding and interaction. It is clear that, at this stage at least, civil aviation was recognized as a social necessity, rather than a mere economic factor. In addition, through the statements of Minister Howe and Dr Warner, one can glean the attitude of the international community towards aviation at that time:

- civil aviation was based on equality of opportunity;
- it was a social need, rather than a fiscal tool.

The First Interim Assembly of the Provisional International Civil Aviation Organization (PICAO) was held in May 1946. This session set the scene for identifying issues that had culminated in the provisions of the Chicago Convention. In the period that followed the First Interim Assembly Session, PICAO commissioned a group of experts called Commission 3 to draft a multilateral agreement on commercial rights for aircraft, which culminated in a Draft Multilateral Agreement on Commercial Rights. The Draft Agreement contained three basic elements:

1 a grant of the right to operate commercially to a reasonable number of traffic centres serving as conveniently as is practicable each State's international traffic;
2 a basic regulatory provision dealing with the amount of capacity to be provided, with subsidiary provisions designed to prevent abuses;
3 a provision for the settlement of differences between contracting States through arbitral tribunals with power to render binding decisions.[21]

The only provisions of the draft on which unanimous agreement was not reached were those concerning routes and airports and capacity.

Commission No. 3 also carried out an inquiry into the distinction between scheduled and non-scheduled services, as they appeared in Article 5 and 6 of the Chicago Convention. As a result, at the 17th Session of the ICAO Council in 1952, the Air Transport Committee examined a Secretariat study on regulations in international non-scheduled aviation. The study found that, at the time, national policies with respect to foreign non-scheduled aircraft taking on or discharging traffic in their territories had assumed a variety of forms. There were 13 States which required prior permission for each individual flight or series of flights, where the granting of permission was based on the circumstances of each case. Ten States required that permission for non-scheduled flights should be granted for each flight or series of flights subject to prescribed regulations. Some States required specific bilateral agreements, while others demanded reciprocal treatment for their carriers.[22] Five European States were known to have made arrangements by means of formal bilateral arrangements for the regulation of non-scheduled commercial flights between their territories.[23]

The Committee also noted that the Council had expressed the view that a 'stop for non-traffic purposes', as referred to in Article 5 of the Convention, should be taken to include the freedom to load and unload passengers or goods not carried for remuneration or hire. The Council had also considered 'remuneration or hire' to mean something received for the act of transportation from someone other than the operator. This interpretation would mean that flights carried out on the business of the operator would receive the freedom granted by the first paragraph of Article 5.[24] The Council's analysis of Article 5 also indicated that the State flown over must not consider its right to require landing a matter of course, and that this right, as granted in the provision, must not be exercised too restrictively. Consideration was also given to the fact that although Article 3 of the Chicago Convention precludes its application to State aircraft, most States may be prepared to agree that civilian State aircraft should be given the type of free passage described in the first paragraph of Article 5.[25] The same right may be given to emergency operations, taxi-type flights and all-inclusive charter tours.[26]

An analysis containing the above views of the ICAO Council, together with a definitive report by the Council to contracting States of scheduled international air services[27] as referred to in Article 6 of the Chicago Convention, was adopted by Council at its Fifteenth Session on 28 March 1952. This report stipulated that a scheduled international air service must in the first instance consist of a series of flights – a single flight by itself could not constitute a scheduled international air service. Article 6 therefore requires that in order to constitute a scheduled national air service, a series of flights must be performed through the air space over the territory of more than one State, and must be performed by aircraft for the transport of passengers, cargo or mail for remuneration. The service must be performed so as to serve traffic between the same two or more points, either according to a published timetable, or with flights so regular or frequent that they constitute a recognizably systematic series.[28] The word 'remuneration' in the provision has the same application and meaning as in Article 5.

Meanwhile, in 1946, the United States and the United Kingdom, as a compromise between the 'free market' approach of the former and the somewhat more cautious and conservative approach of the latter, entered into a bilateral agreement for air services between their two territories called 'Bermuda I'. The Bermuda I agreement was typified by its restrictive pricing regime and its liberal capacity arrangements and route descriptions. Under the agreement, while the United States compromised by withdrawing its opposition to the international regulation of fares, and agreed that primary fare-setting functions should devolve upon the International Air Transport Association (IATA), the United Kingdom agreed to retract its earlier position that capacity should be regulated, and recognized that airlines should be allowed to regulate capacity by determining their frequency on a given route, provided that governments were the ultimate arbiters of the control of capacity on the routes that were relevant to their territories. Accordingly, Bermuda I determined that capacity should bear a strong and close relationship to the requirements of the public for air transport.

### *The Influence of Bermuda I*

As a result of the dichotomy between liberalization on the one hand and protectionism on the other, States were impelled to couch their positions on commercial air traffic rights in the words of Article 6 of the Convention, thereby inhibiting their carriers' commercial freedom to operate air services wherever they considered profitable without first obtaining permission from the grantor State. In other words, protectionism had won over liberalization. A corollary to this debate was the polarization of two groups of States: one which required capacity to be controlled, and the other which required tariffs to be subject to some degree of control. The resultant Bermuda I Agreement, between the United States of America and the United Kingdom also provided a model bilateral air services agreement for States, where the Five Freedoms of the air were defined, capacity control between two points was brought under the purview of the air carriers concerned (subject to the approval of their States), and the task of tariff-setting was given to the International Air Transport Association (IATA).

Many other States followed the Bermuda model in their air services agreements for nearly thirty years following its conclusion. One of the advantages of the Bermuda model lay in the IATA tariff-setting clause, which achieved a certain multilateralism through bilateralism, while one of its main disadvantages has been that it gave governments a basis on which to formulate their own civil aviation policies and sometimes adopt an unduly restrictive stance on their sovereignty in airspace, leading to the frequent withdrawal by States of air traffic rights that were being enjoyed by airlines. Owing to these shortcomings, Bermuda I predictably collapsed after thirty years.[29]

One of the ways the international aviation community attempted to circumvent the veneer of absolute protectionism reflected in Article 6 of the Chicago Convention was by introducing to the Bermuda principles the concept of fair and equal opportunity. According to this principle, each bilateral air service agreement between two States, if it follows the Bermuda pattern, should include a clause which provides that there shall be fair and equal opportunity for the designated airlines of both contracting parties to operate the agreed air services on the specific routes between their respective territories. In operating the agreed services, the airlines of each contracting party are required to take into account the interests of the airlines of the other contracting party so as not to affect unduly the services which the latter provide on the whole or part of the same routes. The factors taken into account in ensuring fair and equal opportunity for each carrier are:

- the requirements of the public for transportation on the same routes;
- the capacity, at a reasonable load factor, that each carrier may offer.

In addition to emphasis being laid on ensuring fair and equal opportunity for each carrier, the air services agreement also insists that no carrier should unduly affect the operation of air services of the other. Capacity determination at a reasonable load factor to fulfil the requirements of the public is usually a requirement, although the main thrust of the clause is to ensure that some protection is being afforded to the carrier which is less fortunate than the other, so that both carriers obtain a fair deal on their operations on the same route. Therefore, it is arguable that all operational factors have to be taken into consideration to ensure that one carrier does not unduly affect the operations of the other. This is dealt with in more detail in Chapter 2.

*The Role of ICAO*

ICAO was established on 4 April 1947. The first ICAO Assembly in 1947 followed the development of a Multilateral Agreement on Commercial Rights in International Civil Air Transport that was commenced by PICAO. At this assembly, the United Kingdom felt that certain general principles should govern route agreements.[30] The concern of the US Government was that in matters of frequencies, capacity route exchanges and Fifth Freedom traffic rights, there would be disorder in operating on a general multilateral basis.[31] At this meeting, the Canadian delegate clarified the reason for seeking multilateralism in air services by stating:

> So we looked at the matter basically and said, 'Why do we want Multilateralism?' and the feeling that I had, speaking for Canada, was

> not that we wanted uniformity, although that is desirable, in as much as I see no end result in uniformity for its own sake. We had a much loftier purpose in mind, and that was the idea of creating a set of conditions that all nations who wanted to fly could use so that they would know in advance what their opportunities were, what the conditions were that they would be up against, so that it would not be possible for one nation to discriminate against another, and grant to another nation privileges that they would not be willing to grant to others equally entitled to them, so that these things would not lead to friction between nations and quarrels and eventually be the seed from which might spring a war. For this reason, it was said we wanted multilateralism, not merely uniform clauses.[32]

The views of the developing world were placed before the assembly by the Peruvian delegate:

> The multilateral agreement is a high ideal for which we have already fought and must continue to fight, but a firm fighting spirit should not allow eagerness to obscure reality. The latter, as we Peruvians see it, places grave difficulties in the way of an absolute and universal multilateral agreement. Those difficulties emanate from the different stages of development in commercial aviation among various nations, from the different aeronautical potential of each country, from the variations found when considering each country in international air transport, according to its climatic or geographical conditions and lastly, what is more important, the substantial differences between the countries already in commercial aeronautics, and those countries, such as ours, which can only look to the future.[33]

At its Second Session, held in Geneva in June 1948, the ICAO Assembly adopted Resolution A2–16, which called for further action on a Multilateral Agreement on Commercial Rights, and resolved that contracting States should study and consider the above elements.[34]

## Recent Trends

### *The Air Transport Colloquium*

Following a decision taken by the ICAO Council on 11 June 1991, a World-wide Air Transport Colloquium was held at ICAO on 6–10 April 1992. The Colloquium discussed the strengths and weaknesses of the bilateral system, possible complementary and alternative multilateral regulatory structures, air service regulatory relationships between groupings of States on the one hand and between individual States and groupings of States on the other, the applicability or inapplicability to air transport of international trade concepts such as market access, non-discrimination, transparency and increasing participation of developing States, foreign and multinational ownership of national airlines, nationality of aircraft, and access to domestic traffic by foreign airlines.[35]

The overall commercial considerations of the Colloquium – such as market access, foreign and multinational ownership of airlines, transparency, non-discrimination and cabotage – were directly or indirectly linked with the award of air traffic rights to airlines, which was the primary concern of the Colloquium. At the conclusion of the Colloquium, there appears to have been the general view that caution should be applied in considering a multilateral approach to the award of air traffic rights. The positive aspects of a bilateral system were identified as:

1 its capacity to fill a multilateral void;
2 its symbiosis with the multilateral system of airline co-operation that exists now;
3 the ability of bilateralism to provide much of the legal basis for the world's international air transportation system;
4 the way in which it applies fair and equal opportunity for the airlines of negotiating States;
5 the high degree of protection that the bilateral system offers national airlines of all nations of the world;
6 the manner in which bilateralism appears to protect weaker airlines against their more powerful foreign competitors;
7 the way in which the bilateral system of negotiation for air traffic rights has created a regulatory system that treats international air transport as a special case among service industries.

The disadvantages of the bilateral system were said to be:

1 the way in which it is being challenged by many who believe air transport is not 'special';
2 the perceived disadvantages the system imposes upon airports (which lose valuable revenue when air services are restricted by bilateral negotiations), cities and consumers, in particular by imposing regulatory limitations on growth and opportunity;
3 the failure of the system to adapt to changing market and political systems;
4 the fact that costs are incurred in maintaining the bilateral system, as opposed to a free market system, which would run by itself;
5 the proliferation of bilateral agreements that airlines have to contend with in operating their air services.[36]

The Colloquium identified the following advantages of a multilateral system:

1 it was rapidly growing in popularity among some nations, owing to its timely emergence in a period of rapid transnationalization of ownership and globalization in service industries;
2 it was commended by some as a path to liberalization of the air services agreement;
3 it would better serve the fiscal interests of airports, while giving the consumer a wider choice of product.[37]

However, the disadvantages of multilateralism were manifold:

1 a consensually acceptable global multilateral structure has yet to be conceived, and even if it is eventually designed, it may not succeed in protecting national carriers and ensuring their continued presence in the international scene;
2 a multilateral system may not be able to ensure fully adequate air service links for all concerned States;
3 there is consensus that a multilateral air services structure has to be approached very cautiously, making it unforeseeable in the near future;
4 multilateralism may not be a complete replacement for existing bilateral arrangements between some States, thus requiring a dual structure;
5 a multilateral structure would be very difficult (if not impossible) to design, in view of the many safeguards that are built into bilateral air services agreements at present.[38]

As expected, the Colloquium emerged as a forum for collecting points of view of experts in the field, and did not align itself either way – towards bilateralism or multilateralism.[39]

*Post-Colloquium Trends*

The role of ICAO in furthering and implementing the economic goals of the Chicago Convention and the efficient and thorough manner in which the ICAO executed its objectives were emphasized by the Colloquium. *Avmark Aviation Economist* reported immediately after the conclusion of the meeting:

> ICAO's Secretariat had taken much trouble to try to focus the delegates' thinking on the relevant topics, maintain quality in the debate and avoid the long political ramblings that tend to characterise meetings attended by government representatives. The comprehensive

> background material provided included long lists of questions that needed answering, compilations of expert views on the subjects, definitions and examples illustrating the key concepts, excerpts from relevant pieces of legislation, and details of agreements, industry groupings and organizations.[40]

Some of the recent bilateral air services negotiations between States provide an insight into the current thinking in the debate over multilateralism, plurilateralism and bilateralism. For example, the United States and the United Kingdom have made known the philosophy behind their air transport policies:

> The aim ... is to replace the restrictions in the current air services agreement with a regime that enables airline managements to determine the price and supply of air services ... both governments want to see vigorous but fair competition, offering the public an even wider choice of airlines, routes and fares.[41]

Immediately after this statement was made, however, talks between the States ended in deadlock due to the fact that the United Kingdom was negotiating for curbs on foreign ownership of US airlines to be lifted, and the US had required the UK to give free access to London Heathrow airport before any more concessions were given to UK carriers such as Virgin Atlantic and British Airways.[42]

At the same time, a similar situation had developed between the United States and Japan, where Japan required the bilateral agreement with the United States to be reworked so that capacity in the marketplace and extensive further rights enjoyed by the US carriers would be curtailed. Japan contended that bilateral agreements should reflect market conditions accurately, and claimed that US carriers had a far greater share of the US–Japan capacity, and operated far more flights beyond Japan than could be justified by by Americans' demand for travel to the Asia-Pacific region.[43]

The debate over whether air traffic rights should operate under a liberal trading environment or whether the present system of regulation should prevail continues, despite tendencies in both the developed and developing world towards regulation and protectionism. This was evident at a gathering of senior aviation officials from throughout the world in June 1993, where Singapore Airlines strongly urged the United States to take a lead in the effort to bring about a more liberal aviation trading environment through the gradual building of a multilateral regime, only to be opposed vigorously by Air France.[44] One journalist observed:

> One commentator described the differences that undermined efforts to arrive at a multilateral air transport agreement at Chicago as fol-

lows: 'while the U.S. delegation sought to use a multilateral convention essentially to "codify" a free market ethic, other nations saw a multilateral agreement as a way to ensure that the robust U.S. airline industry would not monopolize international civil aviation'. This comment equally describes the situation today. Then, as now, the different degrees of economic development and associated economic policies of countries make it unrealistic to expect agreement on a universal set of rules to govern international air transport.[45]

*The Fourth Air Transport Conference*

As a result of a review of the findings of the Colloquium, the ICAO Council decided in June 1992 that there was a compelling need to explore new regulatory arrangements for international air transport, and announced the Fourth World-wide Air Transport Conference, to be held on 23 November–6 December 1994 at ICAO Headquarters in Montreal. Since a period of intensive examination of international air transport regulation in the 1940s after the Chicago Conference was convened, ICAO had held only three air transport conferences, in 1977, 1980 and 1985. Those conferences were by no means comprehensive in their deliberations, and had only addressed specific issues.

As a preparatory measure in September 1992, ICAO appointed the Study Group of Experts on Regulatory Arrangements for international transport (GEFRA), which assisted the ICAO Secretariat with preparations for the conference. In 1993, 12 GEFRA members representing government, air carrier and airport expertise from all regions of the world undertook a comprehensive exploration of seven topics that would be discussed at the conference. The Air Transport Conference would examine the core issues identified and analysed by the GEFRA Group in its role as a 'trail-blazer' in commercial aviation. Its main consideration has been succinctly expressed by the President of the ICAO Council:

> Today, as we stand at the crossroads and see but dimly the avenues which may be opening up to us, we must decide what our attitude is to be towards preparing adequately for change. There are but two possibilities. One is to take a protective stance, to sink roots even deeper into familiar soil, yet to risk ultimately being uprooted as the world continues to change all around us. The other possibility is a dynamic one: it is to trust human creativity and to employ it to the fullest and in a cooperative way to bring about a better future.[46]

At the 29th Session of the ICAO Assembly in September/October 1992, the South American States submitted that since the signing of the Chicago Convention in 1944, international air transport had not been regulated from a commercial standpoint, which had led to fundamental changes in the structure of the air transport industry being influenced by unilateral decisions taken by one State or groups of States. Accordingly, there was a compelling need to establish a new set of international rules governing international air transport.[47] *A fortiori*, the South American States claimed that such a need was strongly felt in the prevailing environment of mega-carriers and computer reservation macro-systems within a concept of globalization in the marketing and presentation of international air transport services. The proposing States expressed the wish that the new regulatory structure should address the following issues:

- a new international airline profile (legal, economic, operative and administrative);
- bases for the designation of airlines, taking into account the corporate structure (company mergers, integration of markets);
- new criteria regarding substantial ownership and effective control of airlines, as a function of their designation;
- new ideas with respect to traffic rights;
- new principles related to non-scheduled flights and charter flights;
- elaboration of a code of conduct on commercial competition.[48]

They also wanted these issues to be discussed extensively in a forum chosen by the States themselves, whether through an Extraordinary Assembly with powers to issue resolutions or through an air transport conference with limited competence, not later than 1994, in order to establish the bases for international air transport in the third millennium.

The Economic Commission of the Assembly, while recognizing that there was support for the general proposal above, decided in favour of the latter proposal – that a conference, adequately prepared, be convened in the latter part of 1994.[49] The meaning and purpose of the conference was succinctly summed up in a commentary at the time:

> ... the initiative to organize a conference where the future of economic regulation will be the central focus is not only a laudable idea but a logical one following the WATC [World Air Transport Colloquium], the ongoing economic liberalization policies and developments within and outside the air transport sector. The conference is not intended to establish binding legal decisions nor amend the Chicago Convention but merely to exchange ideas on the impact of macro and micro level developments on the economic regulation of international air transportation.[50]

*Some Interim Global Issues*

In early 1993, Sir Collin Marshall of British Airways reportedly confirmed the willingness of the airline to support deregulation and, *inter alia*, global partnerships that would result in British Airways gaining greater access to the principal markets of the world.[51] At the same time, the UK–US bilateral air services agreement was being renegotiated, wherein the United States claimed that the agreement was unfair to the United States.[52] Earlier, the Canadians had levelled a similar accusation against the United States, where the air services agreement for scheduled air services between Canada and the United States gave rise to transborder air services on 83 city-pairs, of which Canadian operators operated exclusively on 26 routes and US carriers operated exclusively on 35. An official Canadian report claimed that one of the reasons for the imbalance in market shares was the imbalance in the number of bilateral routes awarded to the airlines of each country, plus certain structural competitive advantages that had enabled US carriers to maintain their dominance and improve their market share.[53]

Meanwhile, in the Asia-Pacific region, a three-cornered dispute had erupted wherein Australia had sought independent international arbitration on its air transport agreement with the United States and the bilateral air services agreement between the US and Japan, claiming that the exercise of Fifth Freedom traffic rights by United States carriers between Sydney and Tokyo gave those carriers an unfair commercial advantage. Meanwhile, reportedly, concerns were being expressed by Hong Kong, Japan and South Korea on an alleged imbalance of the exercise of Fifth Freedom traffic rights by US carriers in their favour.[54] These concerns emerged at a time when the French had already renounced their bilateral air services agreement with the United States, and Japan had restricted Fifth Freedom traffic rights for US carriers.[55] In the same region, the single Australasian aviation market in which both Australia and New Zealand participated was terminated by Australia on the grounds that New Zealand had benefited unequally from the total liberalization of the exercise of air traffic rights between the two countries.[56]

At its hearings in June 1993, the Airline Commission appointed by President Clinton of the United States agreed that the bilateral system of international aviation agreements had run its course, but had found no consensus on what sort of regime should succeed it.[57] It was generally the opinion of the Commission that the emergence of strong airline alliances would finally break the back of the bilateral system. *Avmark Aviation Economist* has since examined this view with interest, and observed that the growth in cross-border investment and strategic alliances, helped by the lifting of foreign ownership restrictions, will make the bilateral negotiating process obsolete. According to the *Avmark* study, the growth of multinational airlines would make it difficult for government negotiators to decide whose interests they were supposed to represent.[58]

Meanwhile, the Comité des Sages of the European Community (EC) stressed the need for the EC to adopt a common external aviation policy by 30 June 1995 that would deal with non-European States and airlines. In the eyes of the Comité, the proposed policy would, on the one hand, dispel concerns about discriminatory treatment and, on the other, would form a basis for increased reciprocal market access across Europe as a whole. The Comité hastened to add that such a policy should be consonant with the provisions of the Chicago Convention and any decisions taken within the purview of ICAO.[59]

Recognizing that it was not possible to annul bilateral air services agreements of member States and adopt a common multilateral policy, the Comité suggested that a step-by-step external policy with the following requisites be examined:

- transparency of all bilateral air services agreements;
- preservation of all existing traffic rights of bilateral air services agreements;
- ensuing compatibility of provisions of new air services agreements with EC legislation;
- establishment of a policy for discussion with non-EC States regarding the modalities of a new multilateral external agreement.

The overall principles of the policy are expected to achieve a liberal aviation trading regime, to be consistently applied to all non-European Community States, to be phased over a number of years, and, *inter alia,* provide the basis for co-operation in the application of competition rules and other conditions for conducting business.[60]

Just before the commencement of the ICAO Fourth World-wide Air Transport Conference, the United States made public its new international aviation policy, which established free trade in aviation services with nine unidentified European nations. In addition, under the new policy, the United States proposed to renew efforts to liberalize existing bilateral agreements with the United Kingdom and Canada, and seek unrestricted market-based agreements with any country that could offer 'strategic benefits' to the US carriers.[61] Although it was not a new strategy, the new policy required the United States to enhance existing bilateral air services agreements and vigorously defend its existing bilateral rights. It also recognized that most States may not be willing to exchange air traffic rights unconditionally. The new policy also promoted phased liberalization of air traffic rights with any State that would be prepared to enter into such agreements with the United States, and sought the strengthening of aviation relationships between the United States and new growth areas such as South America, Asia and Central America.[62]

*Objectives of the Fourth Conference*

GEFRA assisted the ICAO Secretariat throughout the preparatory stage of the Fourth Conference. In the period that followed the Colloquium, the 12 GEFRA members, representing government, air carrier and airport expertise from all regions of the world, undertook a comprehensive exploration of present regulation, future regulatory content, and future regulatory process and structure, all of which were summarized. The deliberation of future regulatory content covered the following subjects:

- **objectives** – the basic goals of States against which possible new regulatory arrangements for the future can be evaluated; GEFRA saw these objectives as *participation* (the reliable and sustained involvement by a State in the international air transport system), *adaptation* (the adjustment of air transport regulation to the broader dynamic environment in which international air transport operates), *enhancement* (the growth and improvement in the quantity and quality of the international air services received by a State to and from its territory for the benefit of users, service providers, communities and others), *simplification* (the elimination of complex and detailed management that characterizes most existing regulatory arrangements, with the resultant reduction of time and monetary costs to governments, service providers and users) and *flexibility* (the design of new regulatory arrangements for international air transport in ways that permit air carriers to maximize opportunities);[63]
- **market access** – route rights (e.g. points of origin, intermediate stops, destinations, beyond points); traffic rights (e.g. for Fifth Freedom and Sixth Freedom traffic, connecting/stop-over traffic, cabotage); operational rights (air carrier designation and aircraft use, e.g. dry and wet leases, blocked space, code-sharing, change of gauge, intermodal);
- **air carrier ownership and control** – ownership and control criteria for licensing of foreign designated air carriers and their possible elimination, replacement or modification; implications of privatization; inward (foreign) investment in national air carriers and the right of establishment; nationality of aircraft;

- **safeguards** – need, nature and purposes (price/capacity/other); elements, forms and specific kinds (including dispute resolution mechanisms); participation of developing countries;
- **structural impediments** – subsidies and other State aids; physical restraints on access (slot allocation);
- **the broader regulatory environment** – the need to relate air transport regulation to competition laws (including impacts on tariff co-ordination/interlining); environmental laws; taxes on air traffic; trade agreements and arrangements;
- **'doing business' matters** – air carrier ground handling arrangements at airports; currency conversion and remittance of earnings; non-national personnel; the sale , marketing and distribution of air service products including distribution through computer reservation systems.[64]

Future regulatory process and structure involved the consideration of ways States can interact and the kinds of agreements they can reach bilaterally, especially between a State and a group of States (or between two groups of States), and in their ongoing quest for multilateralism in the global regulation of commercial air transport services.[65]

The GEFRA exercise proved to be a comprehensive exploration of new regulatory arrangements which would be applicable to the many subjects and areas that are now covered by air transport agreements. Some of the more notable subjects relating to air traffic rights that were examined by GEFRA were market access (route, operational and traffic rights), progressive liberalization (phased approaches to the introduction of new regulatory arrangements) and the need for safeguards to prevent or react to specific instances of unfair competition, as well as a 'safety net' to ensure continuing participation in the air transport system. GEFRA also examined two 'structural impediments' – State aids/subsidies to airlines and physical limitations (at airports) to market access with a view to instigating new regulatory arrangements which would ensure that neither of these impediments would affect competition adversely nor impede market access unfairly. GEFRA also considered a regulatory process and structure for the future: the ways States could interact, and the kinds of agreements they could reach bilaterally, especially between a State and a group of States (or between two groups of States).

Given GEFRA's work, it was expected that the ICAO Fourth World-Wide Air Transport Conference would harmoniously blend the elements of liberalization and regulation to adapt to changes within the air transport industry. In an information paper published in the *ICAO Journal* prior to the conference, Dr Assad Kotaite, President of the ICAO Council, summed up the spirit of the conference:

> What both regional regulation and more broadly based multilateralism share is a focus on liberalization. Whether we wish to confront it or merely adjust to it, liberalization will be at the very core of regulatory change. Yet nowhere has liberalization taken place by the elimination of regulation. Rather, liberalization has occurred with changes to regulation: changes best undertaken or accommodated with adequate preparation.
>
> Today as we stand at the crossroads and see but dimly the avenues which may be opening up to us, we must decide what our attitude is to be towards preparing adequately for change. There are but two possibilities. One is to take a protective stance, to sink roots even deeper into familiar soil, yet to risk ultimately being uprooted as the world continues to change all around us. The other possibility is a dynamic one: it is to trust in human creativity and to employ it to the fullest and in a co-operative way to bring about a better future.[66]

The conference also bore in mind that although international air transport is a vibrant, high-technology and capital-intensive service industry which has grown and expanded rapidly for the past fifty years with a well-designed legal, economic regulatory and industrial framework as set down in the Chicago Convention, the conference was being held at a time of grave financial concern for the air transport industry. Although overcapacity and depressed yields in markets, increasing costs of participation, disparity in resources and growing infrastructural constraints and costs were some of the more significant factors that had caused difficult times for the air transport industry, there was also uncertainty and complexity in many aviation relations between States. These problems were further compounded by widespread concerns about the future direction and stability of both the regulatory and operating environment, and the evolving structural changes in the industry. There were compelling external forces, such as increasing competition, globalization of the world economy, transnationalization of business, privatization of service industries, regionalization and liberalization (including a reduction in many countries of the regulation of service industries) which had already had a noticeable effect on regulatory approaches to international air transport. The conference had the daunting task of focusing on the tools or regulatory content needed for a less restricted industry in an increasingly competitive global environment, in conformity with the general trends of changing regulatory needs in most other service industries.[67]

The task of the conference was therefore to review the present regulatory content of international air transport, examine and discuss proposed future regulatory arrangements as contained in the subjects examined by GEFRA, and consider future regulatory processes and structures. It then had to consolidate conclusions and develop recommendations on further action by ICAO and/or by States.[68] It was hoped that this process would enable States to use some of the conclusions of the conference immediately, while the ICAO Council could either publish or otherwise disseminate a consolidated recommendation that could be developed from these recommendations, or undertake a further study or other action that would facilitate progress in considering future regulatory arrangements in international air transport.[69]

*Examination of Issues*

The conference recognized *in limine* that the present system of economic regulation of international air transport was a corollary to the failure to achieve a widely accepted and comprehensive multilateral agreement on the exchange of economic rights at the Chicago Conference of 1944. The corresponding absence of regulatory provisions for multilateral regulation of market access of air transport in the Chicago Convention had led to the evolution over many years of a system of bilateral regulation of air traffic rights. The conference therefore had to consider both the status quo and the rapidly changing environment for commercial air transport.

One of the most significant issues facing commercial aviation under the bilateral system of negotiation was the resultant imbalance in the distribution of international traffic. As an example, the conference considered the statistics, which showed that, with respect to international passengers (scheduled and non-scheduled) embarked and disembarked at airports in 1993, 25 airports in 17 countries accounted for 44 per cent of the total international passengers embarked and disembarked at over 1,000 airports in 182 countries. In terms of tonnes of international cargo loaded and unloaded at airports, 15 airports in 12 countries accounted for 50 per cent of the total amount of international cargo loaded and unloaded worldwide.[70] Over the same year, 30 air carriers from 25 countries accounted for 76 per cent of total international passenger-kilometres performed worldwide by 365 air carriers. The market share of the largest 30 carriers had increased slightly over a ten-year period from 1982 to 1993, while the market share of the largest 10 carriers had increased by 2 per cent. This tendency towards concentration of international passenger services in a few air carriers also manifested itself in international cargo, where 30 scheduled service air carriers from 26 States were responsible for transporting 75 per cent of the total tonne-kilometres performed in 1993.[71] Many air carriers had concluded bilateral agreements relating to special commercial arrangements, such as those relating to code-sharing, pooling, block space, yield management and schedule co-ordination, making themselves stronger in the market place.

Although these arrangements had the ability to strengthen the commercial potential of air carriers, they would also be calculated to obtain indirect market access for them, thus causing concern among those air carriers which depended entirely on their bilateral air services agreements for the carriage of commercial traffic between States.

Another consideration that influenced the deliberations of the conference was the ICAO traffic forecast up to the year 2003, according to which, total world airline scheduled passenger traffic in terms of passenger-kilometres is expected to grow at an annual rate of 5 per cent during the period 1992–2003, compared with 5.6 per cent per year during 1982–1992. Freight traffic growth during 1992–2003 is forecast to be stronger, at 6.5 per cent per year in terms of freight tonne-kilometres. International traffic is expected to continue to grow faster than total traffic – 6.5 per cent per year for passenger-kilometres, and 7 per cent per year for freight tonne-kilometres.[72] During 1992–2003, the annual total number of domestic and international aircraft departures on scheduled services is forecast to rise by nearly 25 per cent (to 18 million), the number of passengers carried is expected to rise by over 50 per cent (to 1,835 million) and the number of freight tonnes carried is also projected to increase by over 50 per cent (to 27 million).[73]

One of the future regulatory arrangements proposed at the conference was that parties would grant each other full market access (unrestricted route, operational and traffic) rights for use by designated air carriers, with the option to exchange cabotage and so-called Seventh Freedom rights. Of course, each party would have the right to impose a time-limited capacity freeze as an extraordinary measure and in response to a rapid and significant decline in that party's participation in a country pair market. This measure, called the 'safety net' was intended to form a buffer against a total swing towards favouring unregulated commercial operations of air carriers. The market access and 'safety net' principle was designed to award to each party's air carrier unrestricted basic market access rights to the other party's territories for services touching the territories of both parties (to the exclusion of cabotage rights, i.e. rights to operate commercial air services within points in the territory of another party), optionally, for so called Seventh Freedom services (i.e. services touching the territory of the granting party without touching the territory of the designating party), and/or optionally, with cabotage rights. To these rights, the 'safety net' brought in the caveat that each party would have the right to impose a capacity freeze as an extraordinary measure, under six conditions that called for such a freeze. They were:

1 to be implemented only in response to a rapid and significant decline in that party's participation in a country-pair market;

2 to be applied to all scheduled and non-scheduled fights by the air carriers of each party and any third State which directly serve the affected country-pair market;
3 to be intended to last for a maximum finite period of, for example, one year, two years, or one year, renewable once;
4 to require close monitoring by the parties to enable them to react jointly to relevant changes in the situation (e.g., an unexpected surge in traffic);
5 to be responsible for creating a situation in which any affected party may employ an appropriate dispute-resolution mechanism to identify and seek to correct any underlying problem;
6 to be aimed at requiring mutual efforts to ensure the earliest possible correction of the problem and removal of the freeze.[74]

It is worthy of note that the above framework of future regulatory arrangements was intended to function in different structures and relationships, e.g. bilaterally between two States, between a State and a group of States, between two groups of States, and multilaterally among a small or large number of States. It was expected that this structure would also respect all rights, existing and newly granted.[75]

*Positions of States*

Some States and groups of States made their positions on the traffic rights issue known at the conference. Some African States, while observing that the current participation of developing States in international air transport was marginal, with no foreseeable improvement in the future, maintained that Africa's position reflected a downward trend in market access in respect of African carriers. To improve the status quo, the African States suggested that new regulations in air transport should enshrine 'preferential measures', so that the current inequalities with respect to air transport market access could gradually be eliminated.[76] The African States further contended that the world order requires a new system of ethics which could be reflected in the form of preferential measures, taking into account the economic conditions of developing countries. These preferential measures would have to be applied to States with equity and fair distribution of world resources. According to the recommendation, they would have to bring into play social considerations, such as solidarity and equality with regard to opportunities. In practice, according to the proposing States, such preferential measures would have to provide for a transfer of wealth, not in the form of aid provided by those who remain in the market to those excluded from it, but through a new understanding of some basic principles such as reciprocity, which need to be rethought and reformulated. The African States which submitted this proposal to the conference requested that ICAO be entrusted with the task of developing such preferential measures.[77]

The States of Latin America and the Caribbean reaffirmed the principles and objectives contained in the Chicago Convention, but noted that the State parties to the Convention had different levels of development, so any proposal aimed at establishing future air transport regulation must take cognizance of that reality. The Latin American and Caribbean States did not believe that the proposals on market access, as formulated, would not guarantee consistency with the principles of the Chicago Convention, which, in their view, admitted of the co-existence of markets which are organized differently. They therefore recommended an approach that allowed direct participation and adaptation by developing countries, such as one that allowed effective access by those countries to funding and advanced technologies under reasonable financial and economic conditions.[78] Citing the Andean Group of States in Latin America as an example of progressive economic integration and co-operation, the proposing States reaffirmed that the development of air transport in Latin America and the Caribbean is crucial to the socio-economic progress of the region, and that in this context, the 'safety net', safeguards, and dispute-resolution mechanisms proposed did not offer adequate guarantees to ensure effective participation or adaptation by the region's airlines in the future arrangements. The States requested that ICAO, as the governing body for the development of air transport, continue its in-depth studies in such a way that any future air transport regulation would take into account the potential for participation and adaptation by all States, and in particular by developing States.[79]

The Arab States' position was that future arrangements for the regulation of international air transport should largely depend on the scope of co-operation among States. They also believed that while these arrangements may be necessary, any new regulations should be cautiously thought out and thoroughly considered before they replace existing ones. The proposed market access principles and 'safety net' solution, together with ownership and control clauses, were in this context inadequate, and must be subject to deeper study and consideration. While the Arab States endorsed progressive deregulation of international air transport, they observed that the present bilateral system of market access aimed to facilitate air transport operations by air carriers of States, and that serious consideration should be given to these facts by the conference in formulating future regulatory arrangements.[80]

The Russian Federation proposed regionally based regulation as the most acceptable form for States with compatible levels of economic development. The rationale for this view was that levels of economic development vary from country to country, and States would not be able to enter into multilateral arrangements for the worldwide regulation of commercial air transport. According to the view of the Russian Federation, regional arrangements between groups of States which share similar levels of economic development could eventually lead to liberalized market access and a multilateral 'open skies' agreement.[81] The Russian Federation also believed that if a mechanism for liberalization of international air transport was formulated, there would arise a compelling and urgent need to study the legal consequences of such a formulation. It therefore recommended that the ICAO Legal Committee study the legal implications of such regulation, so that the ICAO Secretariat could develop recommendations which would include definitions of a legal content of the terms and concepts, such as 'market access', 'access right', etc.[82]

Several States also recorded their views on the subject of regulation of air transport. Algeria suggested that air services agreements should be revised on the basis of an equitable sharing of capacity according to the traffic generation of each party, up to a 65 per cent/ 35 per cent division, and any combination beyond this limit should be negotiated multilaterally. Brazil recommended that a multilateral arrangement should relate only to technical and administrative clauses, and Hungary focused attention on the importance of air law and aviation economics in future international air transport, calling for a sustained programme of training of personnel in these subjects to meet future challenges. The Kingdom of the Netherlands suggested a compromise between bilateralism and multilateralism, and recommended regional co-operation as the appropriate measure. Japan cautioned the conference against the possible adverse effects of regulatory liberalization, and suggested that a careful study be conducted that would reflect the effects of liberalization.[83]

On the general principle that all rights, existing and newly granted, should be fully respected, the conference concluded that bilateralism and multilateralism could co-exist, and could each accommodate different approaches to international air transport regulation. The conference also felt that liberalization at the sub-regional or regional level provided valuable experience as regards content, process and structure of regulatory change. One of the factors the conference considered critical for the development and efficient growth of air transport was the training of personnel, *inter alia*, in the fields of aviation law, economics and management. Accordingly, the conference arrived at the conclusion that ICAO should continue to play a role in facilitating, *inter alia*, the evolution of future regulatory arrangements for international air transport, and should, in particular and within available resources, proceed with studies on a number of important issues, including safeguards, 'safety nets' and other measures to ensure fair competition; code-sharing, and computer reservations systems.[84]

The conference also adopted a recommendation which, *inter alia*, recognized that fifty years after the signing of the Chicago Convention, international air transport was going through a period of dynamic change, and that in this context a general goal was the achievement of the gradual, progressive, orderly and safeguarded liberalization of international air transport regulation. The recommendation called for ICAO to take effective action to exert a leadership role in the economic regulation of international civil aviation.[85] It recognized that ICAO should continue to play a role in facilitating the evolution of future regulatory arrangements for international air transport on a bilateral, regional and global basis – taking into account at all times the importance to States of effective participation in international air transport – and proceed with studies and develop recommendations as appropriate on a number of important issues. One of these issues was the further development and refinement of the safeguard mechanism and 'safety net' arrangement presented to the conference, along with other appropriate preventive measures to ensure safe and orderly development of international air transport and fair competition.[86]

The Fourth World-wide Air Transport Conference was successful in eliciting from some States and groups of States their respective positions on the award of air traffic rights to air carriers. They were diverse – from a cry for regionalism to a request for sustained adherence to bilateralism until a viable and overall alternative is agreed upon. There was also the view that any new regulatory regime should be embarked upon with caution. In addition to this new-found wisdom, the international air transport industry has also had the benefit of knowing how air carriers of the developed and the developing world have conducted themselves in sharing air traffic rights with each other between the Colloquium and the conference. Under these circumstances, there is seemingly no way that in the near future a worldwide multilateral regulatory regime would gain universal acceptance. One alternative seems to be regionalism, although the idea has gained a mixed reception from such blocs as Europe and North America.

The only remaining measure is to revisit the liberalized market access concept with a closer look at the 'safety net' philosophy. Since the Fourth World-wide Air Transport Conference was held, the ICAO Council has decided that studies on the following four topics should be referred to a Panel:

- development and refinement of the safeguard mechanism and 'safety net' arrangement presented to the conference;

- review of the traditional air carrier ownership and control criteria;
- development into more formalized structures of some regulatory arrangements on 'doing business' matters
- possible development into more formalized structures of some regulatory arrangements on 'hard rights'.

The Air Transport Regulation Panel (ATRP), which carried out regulatory work arising from the air transport conferences in 1977 and 1980, was reactivated with revised membership and new terms of reference for this task. The ATRP undertook the work concerned as a matter of high priority during 1996–1998, and reported its findings to the Air Transport Committee.

*Some Recent Developments*

Despite the many attempts by the international community to find common ground in the field of air traffic rights, there still seems to be a pronounced tendency by both the developed and developing nations towards protecting the established market share of their carriers in given routes. At the time of writing, the Chairman of United Airlines was reported to have accused UK aviation regulators of being too protectionist. The contentious issue in this context was the US–UK bilateral air services negotiations, where US carriers have been demanding more access to London's Heathrow Airport. Under prevailing regulations, only two US carriers are permitted to operate air services into Heathrow, and the United States claims that the number of flights and destinations departing from London granted to US carriers is limited.[87]

At the same time, the European Commission, which is attempting to take over the negotiation of air traffic rights on behalf of member States of the European Union (EU), has commenced legal action against member States which have signed individual deals with the United States. The EU believes that there would be benefits to all its member States if there was an EU-wide agreement with the United States on air transport services. The EU believes that such an agreement would balance reciprocal levels of market access with an adequate framework of safeguards and other provisions to ensure free and fair competition. Transport Commissioner Neil Kinnock has observed:

> I do not believe that this balance can be achieved on the basis of the bilateral 'open skies' agreements between the US and some member States of the European Union. The cumulative effects of those agreements would undermine the system of conditional access on which

the EU internal market is based and they would establish an unwelcome precedent for future negotiations.[88]

The United States has also been involved in protracted bilateral air services negotiations with Japan, where, in the summer of 1995, the two States decided on what each thought was a mutually beneficial air services agreement.[89] Meanwhile, in the Asia-Pacific region, Hong Kong and Australia had given each other six months to find a solution to the dispute between QANTAS and Cathay Pacific Airways over the Australian carrier's Fifth Freedom rights at Kai Tak to Singapore and Bangkok. Cathay Pacific Airways has alleged that QANTAS has taken undue advantage of those rights. The bilateral air services agreement between the two countries, which expired in the summer of 1995, was extended in its existing form until the end of 1995, to allow negotiators adequate time to consider the two carriers' accusations of unfair competition against each other.[90] Since then, the two authorities concerned have reached bilateral arrangements with regard to the operation of air services between the territories of their countries.

A new dimension to the air traffic rights debate is reflected in the position taken by airports in Europe which are increasingly disturbed by delays in opening up more air service opportunities. Airports Council International (ACI), the worldwide association of airports, has claimed that States have so far listened only to the views of their national airlines in negotiating air services agreements with other States, and that airports should also be consulted on the basis that an increase or decrease in the use of air traffic rights by carriers would have a direct impact on the workload of the airports concerned.[91] Although the position taken by ACI is logical and justifiable, an additional lobby would make any move towards liberalization of commercial air services in the future a more complex issue than it already is.

The 31st session of the ICAO Assembly, which held its deliberations from 19 September to 4 October 1995, adopted a resolution which recognizes ICAO as the multilateral body in the United Nations system competent to deal with air transport and develop, *inter alia*, policy guidance on a continuing basis regarding the regulation of international air transport for contracting States. The thrust of this resolution is that ICAO is charged to recommend policy on a continuing basis covering the economic regulation of air transport.[92] It remains to be seen how this mandate would be affected by the conservatism which still afflicts commercial air transport.

## Competition Rules in the World Trade Organization

### *Air Transport Services within GATS*

There has been sustained interest in the world of commerce at the prospect of bringing international air services within the General Agreement on Trade in Services (GATS) under the umbrella of the General Agreement on Tariffs and Trade (GATT). The resolution of the 31st session of the ICAO Assembly addresses this issue by recognizing that ICAO has actively promoted an understanding by all parties concerned of the provisions of the Chicago Convention and of ICAO's particular mandate and role in international air transport. The resolution also requests the World Trade Organization and its member States to accord due consideration to the fact that ICAO has a constitutional responsibility to international air transport which could be discharged through the results of ICAO's World-wide Air Transport Conference and ICAO's continuing work on economic regulation of international air transport.[93]

In the process of its deliberations, the ICAO Colloquium of 1992 considered the views of experts on whether air traffic rights should be considered trade in services and brought within the purview of GATT – a proposal that had been included on the agenda of GATT under GATS. There has been sustained debate in the aviation world over whether air services performed by commercial airlines – operating both scheduled and unscheduled flights – should be included in GATS.[94] GATS seeks to establish a multilateral framework of principles and rules for trade in services, with a view to expansion of such trade under conditions of *transparency*,[95] national treatment,[96] and *progressive liberalization*.[97] The fundamental principle of GATT is its Most Favoured Nation (MFN) Treatment clause,[98] whereby each party to the agreement immediately and unconditionally accords to services and service providers of any other party treatment no less favourable than that it accords to like services and service providers of any other country. These provisions reflect the basic philosophy of GATS, and play a vital role in affecting the decision of the international community on whether or not air transport services should be brought under its purview. Other features of GATS which have attracted discussion in relation to air services are provisions relating to increasing participation of developing countries within GATS,[99] and dispute settlement.[100]

The issue of trade in services in general was discussed in GATT's round of multilateral trade negotiations launched by ministers of GATT contracting States who met in September 1986 in Punta del Este, Uruguay. The Uruguay Round was the eighth round of multilateral trade negotiations held by GATT so far,[101] and by far one of the most complex. This round of negotiations was assisted by the Group of Negotiators on Services (GNS) which GATT established in 1986 to follow the services negotiations. The GNS had drafted a detailed agreement comprising 35 articles and five annexes, where one of the annexes comprises provisions on air transport services. The Annex on Air Transport Services applies both to scheduled and unscheduled air services and generally excludes its application to the following:

- air traffic rights covered by the Chicago Convention, including the Five Freedoms of the air[102] and bilateral air services agreements;
- directly related activities which would limit or affect the ability of parties to negotiate, grant or to receive traffic rights, or which would have the effect of limiting their exercise.[103]

Notwithstanding the above provisions, however, GATS applies, *inter alia*, to computer reservations systems in air transport, the selling or marketing of air transport services, and transactions in aircraft maintenance.[104] The proposition that GATS would not apply to air traffic rights covered by the Chicago Convention, but would apply to the selling or marketing of air transport services creates *in limine* a dichotomy that must be resolved. Air traffic rights that result from the Chicago Convention's provisions allow the selling or marketing of air transport services, and the two are inextricably linked. The confusion is confounded to a greater degree by Article 1 of GATS, which defines trade in services as, *inter alia*, the supply of a service from the territory of one party into the territory of another party. The application of this definition to the provision of air transport services by an air transport enterprise would lead one to the inexorable conclusion that the definition of trade in services provided in GATS refers implicitly to the exercise of air traffic rights – which are obtained by virtue of the Chicago Convention. The explicit exclusion of air traffic rights in GATS is therefore ambivalent.

For the present, the overall purpose of including air transport services in GATS seems to be to apply the broad principles of market access and the MFN philosophy to the selling or marketing of air traffic services. The purview of GATS in controlling air transport services would therefore be considered only in situations where air traffic rights are exercised multilaterally or plurilaterally. GATS would not apply in instances where States elect to use Article 6 of the Chicago Convention which governs all bilateral air services agreements and requires that the permission of a grantor State is necessary for a commercial air transport enterprise to operate air services into or out of a State. In any event, the Annex on Air Transport Services in

GATS does not reflect confidence in itself by providing in Article 6 that the operation of the Annex shall be reviewed periodically, or at least every five years.

There are two provisions in the Annex on Air Transport Services in GATS which are also worthy of mention. One covers the access to and use of publicly available services offered by a party on reasonable and non-discriminatory terms,[105] and the other sets out dispute settlement procedures which could only be invoked where settlement procedures provided for in bilateral air services agreements or under the Chicago Convention itself have been exhausted.[106]

The regulation of air transport services lies within the purview of ICAO, whose Legal Bureau maintains a register of all bilateral air transport agreements. The bilateral air transport agreement usually includes a reciprocal agreement between States for their carriers to have fair and equal opportunity in operating air services between their territories without unduly affecting the air services operated by each other. Under a bilateral agreement, capacity offered by carriers must bear close relationship to the needs of the people using air transport.[107] These regulatory provisions have so far succeeded in protecting carriers of lesser developed States by obtaining for them fair and equal opportunity to operate air services in routes that are shared by more established carriers of wealthier nations.[108]

Since GATS cannot sustain air transport services within a bilateral framework, it now remains to be seen whether the aviation community will move in future towards placing air traffic rights in a multilateral or plurilateral system. If so, GATS would doubtless redouble its efforts seeking to include air transport services within its purview under liberalized market access and the MFN treatment clause. In this context, the role played by ICAO – the guardian and mentor of international civil aviation – becomes relevant.

ICAO has the mandate (under the Convention on International Civil Aviation signed in Chicago in 1944), experience and expertise to regulate a wide range of air transport matters – technical, economic and legal. Issues of operating arrangements, market access, pricing and capacity for the designated airlines of each State are the subject of bilateral air transport agreements between States, except for arrangements within the European Union for mutual relations between member States. International air transport is, in effect, conducted under an extensive network of some 3,000 separate bilateral agreements or treaties. ICAO has taken the position that international air transport is an economic activity in which there is a strong national interest and involvement, as well as a long-established, comprehensive and detailed structure of standards, principles and operating arrangements.

ICAO believes it important to draw to the attention of GATS and its member States certain critical features of international air transport which are relevant to any present or future consideration of how air transport should be treated in the context of the trade in services negotiations. The main consideration that impels ICAO to maintain steadfastly its position as the guiding force behind air transport services is that it feels that bilateralism at the operating level has over the decades proved to be a flexible system which allows States to pursue their own objectives, whether these be open and competitive, or more protective and restrictive regimes for their airlines. ICAO strongly maintains that any external multilateral framework which sought general or limited application would need to recognize and be compatible with this existing structure of air transport regulation.

Nevertheless, multilateralism in the form of a broad-based consensus on principles and guidance to States in the conduct of their air transport activities has excited renewed interest within ICAO in recent years. While seeking to progressively develop positions and guidance to assist States in their regulatory/economic activities, ICAO recognizes the sovereignty of States in pursuing their own national air transport policies and objectives. ICAO's role in this sphere is therefore merely consultative and recommendatory, without being incompatible with liberalization in this sector. ICAO has also expressed its resolve to continue to co-operate with GATT and the GNS in its trade-in-services discussions to ensure that ICAO's views and concerns and the particular features of the international air transport sector are properly taken into account by these bodies.

ICAO's position on the regulation of air transport services was formally adopted at its 7th Assembly, held in June/July 1953, where Assembly Resolution A7-15 resolved that there was no prospect at the time of achieving a universal multilateral agreement, although ICAO acknowledged that the achievement of multilateralism in commercial rights remained one of its objectives. This Resolution is still in force, and reflects ICAO's commitment to achieving an acceptable multilateral basis for air transport services.

Later, at its 26th Session, in September/October 1986, the ICAO Assembly adopted Resolution A26-14, which reaffirmed that ICAO was the multilateral body in the United Nations system competent to deal with international air transport, and urged contracting States which participated in any multilateral negotiations on trade in services where international air transport was included to ensure that their representatives were fully aware of potential conflicts with the existing legal system for the regulation of international air transport. The resolution also requested the ICAO Council to actively promote a full understanding by international bodies involved with trade in services of the role of ICAO in international air transport and the existing structure of international agreements regarding air transport. This resolution helped sensitize States and GATT regarding the air transport sector, and although it is no longer in force, it reflects ICAO's philosophy on the subject. However, in view of the significant recent and possible future developments in the trade-in-service negotiations, the question arises whether this policy is adequate to continue to serve the interests of ICAO and international air transport over the next few years, or whether it requires reassessment and additional directives from the Assembly.

Assembly Resolution A26-14 gave guidance to States and the Council, and expressed certain concerns, but it did not set out an organizational view on the inclusion of international air transport in a multilateral agreement on trade in services. A future session of the Assembly may consider developing such a view for transmission to GATT and the GNS, as well as to contracting States.

One view the Assembly may consider is that air transport should not be included in a services agreement. The adoption of such a position by ICAO could be grounded on two of the concerns found in Resolution A26-14: one is ICAO's concern about its role as the United Nations specialized agency responsible for air transport matters; the other is ICAO's concern for the integrity of the Chicago Convention principles and arrangements, and the widespread bilateral air transport agreements that are a consequence of those principles.

At ICAO's Air Transport Colloquium in April 1992, at least two speakers expressed the need to exercise caution on the subject of handing over air transport services to GATS. The International Air Transport Association's Director General, Dr Gunter Esez, informed the Colloquium that most international airlines categorically opposed the inclusion of air transport services in GATS. While recognizing that national interests clearly exist in air traffic rights issues, Dr Esez drew the attention of the Colloquium to the economic concerns of the airline industry. He saw the need for a balance between economic regulations and a free market, on the basis that bilateralism *per se* cannot exist on its own in view of multilateral practices in such areas as tariff co-ordination, which have proven that plurilateralism has a distinct edge over bilateralism in commercial air transport.[109] Dr Esez's assessment was that any such plurilateralism would be best developed by ICAO and not a trade institution such as GATT.[110]

Another speaker at the Colloquium, Vijay Poonoosamy, said:

> The underlying premise of GATT is that free trade in the air transport sector will promote economic growth and development. I beg to differ. To enable international air transport to deliver its many and varied goods in a safe and orderly manner we must steer a common sense and enlightened course between regulatory overkill and destructive laissez-faire for more than 45 years. ICAO has provided a means for

> governments to co-operate in the development and maintenance of an effective trading environment for international air transport. Today ICAO provides the proper forum for charting such a vital course for survival.[111]

Gary Sampson, Director of the GNS Division of GATT, expressed the view that over the last decade the airline industry had changed dramatically, moving towards reduced administrative regulation of airlines and the promotion of competition through greater reliance on market forces as opposed to government fiat in determining service levels such as fares, capacities and frequencies. Sampson further stated that although there was clear distinction between 'hard rights' such as air traffic rights and 'soft rights' such as as marketing and sales rights, the application of GATS both to hard and soft rights would enable participants to concentrate their efforts on doing business without restraint under the GATS agreement.[112] David Buckingham, the Australian delegate to the Colloquium, was of the view that what the international community needed was not a simplistic affirmation of the relevance to aviation of the GATT principles of free trade, but a broad-based agreement that liberalized trade in aviation rights.[113] The author Daniel M. Kasper stressed that fundamental GATT principles such as the unconditional MFN and market access clauses were likely to impede rather than advance liberalization.[114] Instead, he advocated a conditional MFN treatment scenario under a plurilateral system, where only those parties willing and able to accede to terms of the said agreement would be required to comply.[115]

The main strength of the GATT approach to air transport services lies in its commitment to liberalization within a defined time scale. The discipline of GATT in accomplishing its objectives also acts as a positive factor. In a general sense, GATT is viewed with favour by those who see some merit in its role as custodian and guide of air transport services, for two reasons:

1. the modern trend of aviation towards globalization, privatization and cross-border alliances and Computer Reservations System (CRS) conglomerates, and the overall tendency of air transport operators to seek market access have made bilateralism obsolete; the changing structure of international civil aviation needs to consider multilateralism, which is the ideal of GATT;
2. the Uruguay Round which intends to envelope air transport services in the GATT concept, advocates a process of gradual liberalization (firstly only of soft rights), negotiated market access and an efficient dispute-settlement system.[116]

Arguments against GATT's role in air transport services are more compelling, however, the most basic being that aviation issues must essentially come within the purview of an organization which specializes in international civil aviation, such as ICAO. The strongest objection is aimed at the principles of GATT, for instance the unconditional MFN treatment philosophy which is calculated to lead to competitive imbalances between airlines, and the long and tedious process of GATT which would take some time to resolve disputes, whereas under the existing bilateral system more expeditious measures are available.[117] To overcome this problem, experts have suggested that GATT's MFN rule should apply only to soft trading rights in aviation (such as ground handling, CRS and sales), and hard rights should be included in a multilateral agreement outside GATT.[118] Kasper opposes the application of the MFN philosophy to air services:

> ... unconditional MFN would deprive air service negotiators of essential flexibility. Trade barriers in air services vary widely in form and impact across markets, forcing even liberal nations to discriminate when granting traffic rights in order to counteract the sometimes severe restraints their carriers encounter in foreign markets. Due to the nature of this non-tariff barriers and to the fact that they often arise in ancillary markets, a universal solution, such as the elimination of the ancillary restraints by all signatories, would be exceedingly difficult to negotiate and to enforce.
>
> Under these circumstances, adopting unconditional MFN would undermine the ability of governments to tailor packages of economic rights that offset the mix of restraints in particular foreign markets. It would be especially troubling for those markets characterised by a high degree of cooperation between the national airline and the government.[119]

There is also the disturbing thought that unlike in a bilateral negotiation for air traffic rights, where two States can readily analyse the economic implications of sharing air traffic rights between points within the two States, the MFN principle would create a free-for-all, the consequences of which would not be capable of being economically assessed or controlled.

IATA has suggested that ICAO adopts GATT principles with regard to all aspects of the air services agreement, except in the area of air traffic rights and frequency of operations of aircraft. This suggestion has been strongly resisted by the International Chamber of Commerce (ICC), which argues that the aviation field should retain its purity of having characteristics and attributes that are susceptible to negotiation, although air traffic rights should be negotiated under a more efficient system than the prevailing bilateral system. Kasper shares a compatible view:

> To achieve true liberalization in air services, a new approach will be required, one that focuses on securing agreement among a relatively small group of liberal trading partners willing to abide by a strict condition on a reasonably level playing field.[120]

Although GATS does not seek control over air traffic rights, it is appropriate to consider this subject as a future element of the overall GATT philosophy. It is evident that the principles of GATT are inconsistent with the present legal regime that applies to air traffic rights. The Chicago Convention is the sole legal document that governs the principle of air traffic rights, and it explicitly recognizes the principles of State sovereignty in Article 1. The sovereignty of a State reserves for that State the right to control activities within its territory, and *a fortiori*, the Convention strengthens this concept by requiring that special permission of a State must be obtained for the operation of air services into and out of its territory by an air transport operator of another State.

The foregoing discussion reflects the fact that ever since the question of commercial air traffic rights arose as a corollary to the principle of sovereignty as recognized in the Paris Convention, and later in the Chicago Convention, air transport has been viewed as a social need, run on a principle of equality of opportunity that is not a mere theoretical concept, but one that can be practically enjoyed by States.[121] To these qualities have been added the view of Dr Wassenbergh, that State policy in civil aviation must protect the integrity and identity of the national society.[122] In its Preamble, the Chicago Convention, calls for co-operation between nations and peoples so that international air transport services may be established on the basis of equality of opportunity, and operated soundly and economically. The Chicago Convention further charges ICAO with the task of ensuring the prevention of economic waste caused by unreasonable competition,[123] ensuring that the rights of contracting States are fully respected, and that every contracting State has a fair opportunity to operate international airlines.[124] Therefore, the critical question is whether multilateral liberalization of the bilateral air services agreement would preclude some States from having a fair opportunity to operate international airlines on an equal-opportunity basis. It is only logical to conclude that the answer to the question of whether multilateralism should ultimately replace bilateralism would stem from a clear perception of what is meant by the term 'multilateralism' in this context, and whether multilateralism would interfere with the States' right to the practical enjoyment of fair and equal opportunity in the operation of air services.

## Notes

1 *Convention on International Civil Aviation,* ICAO Doc. 7300/7 (7th edn), 1997.
2 *Proceedings of the International Civil Aviation Conference, 1 November–7 December 1944,* Chicago, Illinois: US Department of State, at 423.
3 Id., at 43.
4 Id., at 55.
5 Id., at 56.
6 Id., at 57.
7 Id., at 61.
8 Id., at 65.
9 Id., at 69.
10 Id., at 76.
11 Id., at 82.
12 Adolf A. Berle Jr, *Freedoms of the Air, Blueprint for World Civil Aviation,* US Government Printing Offices, 1945, at 1.
13 Id., at 5.
14 *Convention on International Civil Aviation,* 15 UNTS 295; ICAO Doc. 7300/6, 7 December 1944, Article 1.
15 For a discussion of the legal foundation of sovereignty and air traffic rights see R.I.R. Abeyratne, 'The Air Traffic Rights Debate: A Legal Study', *Annals of Air & Space Law,* 1993, Vol. XVIII, Part I, 3, at 16.
16 *Convention Relating to the Regulation of Aerial Navigation,* 13 October 1919, Article 1.
17 Id., Article 5.
18 See Shawcross and Beaumont, *Air Law* (4th edn), Vol. I, London: Butterworths, 1977, paras 207–9. There are three other freedoms of the air that have been added since the Chicago Convention was signed: The Sixth Freedom provides that an airline has the right to carry traffic between two foreign States via its own State or registry. This freedom can also be considered a combination of Third and Fourth Freedoms secured by the State of registry from two different States producing the same effect as the Fifth Freedom *vis-à-vis* both foreign States; the Seventh Freedom allows an airline operating air services entirely outside the territory of its State of registry, to fly into the territory of another State and there discharge, or take on, traffic coming from, or destined for, a third State or States, and the Eighth Freedom is cabotage, as referred to in Article 7 of the Chicago Convention. See Paul Stephen Dempsey, *Law and Foreign Policy in International Aviation,* New York: Transnational Publishers, 1987, at 50.
19 *PICAO Documents,* Montreal, 1945, Vol. 1, Doc. 1, at 3.
20 Id., Doc. 2, at 2.
21 *Views of Commission No. 3,* Doc. 4023, A-1–P/3, 1/4/47. See also C-WP/369, 22/6/49, for a detailed discussion of the Commission's work on the Agreement.
22 AT-WP/295, 15/12/52, at 5.
23 Ibid.
24 See AT-WP/296, 15/12/52, at 9.
25 Ibid.
26 AT-WP/296 op. cit., at 10.
27 At its Second Session held in Geneva in June 1948, the ICAO Assembly adopted Resolution A2-18, which called for the adoption by Council of a definition of the term 'scheduled international air service'. See *Resolutions and Recommendations of the Assembly 1–9th Sessions,* 1947–55, Part II, Doc. 7670, at 79-80.

28 See *Report by the Council to Contracting States on the Definition of a Scheduled International Air Service and the Analysis of the Rights Conferred by Article 5 of the Convention*, Doc. 7278, C/841, 10/5/52.
29 The Bermuda II Agreement, which was signed in 1977, contained a system of multiple designation of airlines by one State and other liberal provisions that toned down the harshness of capacity and route designation of its predecessor.
30 ICAO Doc. 4510, A1-EC/72, May 1947, at 12–13.
31 Id., at 23.
32 Id., at 35
33 Id., at 45–6.
34 *Resolutions and Recommendations of the Assembly 1–9th Sessions*, 1947–55, Part II, Doc. 7670, at 78.
35 *ICAO Council to Convene World-wide Air Transport Colloquium*, ICAO News Release PIO 9/91, at 1.
36 ICAO WATC-5.1, 6/4/92, at 1.
37 ICAO WATC-5.1, 6/4/92, at 2.
38 Ibid.
39 For a detailed discussion of the Colloquium, see Abeyratne, op. cit.
40 'The Tortuous Path to Plurilateralism', *Avmark Aviation Economist*, May 1992, 14, at 17.
41 Carol A. Shifrin, 'U.S., U.K Seek New Air Services Pact', *Aviation Week & Space Technology*, 26 April 1993, at 30.
42 *Air Transport*, 14 December 1993, No. 12,894, at 3.
43 *Aviation Daily*, 25 May 1993, at 305.
44 *Aviation Daily*, 4 June 1993, at 358.
45 Bruce Stockfish, 'Opening Closed Skies: The Prospects For Further Liberalization of Trade in International Air Transport Services', *Journal of Air Law & Commerce*, Spring 1992, Vol. 57, No. 3,599, at 639–40.
46 Dr Assad Kotaite, 'New Regulatory Concepts Expected to Emerge at World-wide Air Transport Conference Late Next Year', *ICAO Journal*, May 1993, 20, at 21.
47 A 29-WP/163, EX/49 EC/38, 30/9/92, at 1.
48 Id., at 2.
49 A 29-Min EC/4, 3/10/92, at 3.
50 Dr B.D.K. Henaku, 'ICAO: Fourth Air Transport Conference: An Examination of the Underlying Objectives', *Zeitschrift für Luft- und Weltraumrecht*, September 1994, 247, at 256.
51 *World Airline News*, 26 April 1993, at 3.
52 See *Interavia Air Letter*, 20 April 1993, at 2.
53 *Open Skies: Meeting the Challenge*, Report of the Special Committee on Canada–United States Air Transport Services, House of Commons, Canada, January 1991, at 7.
54 'Passage and Rights', *Flight International*, 21–27 April 1993, Vol. 143, No. 4,366, at 3.
55 *Interavia Air Letter*, 23 April 1993, No. 12,730, at 2. See also *Aviation Daily*, 25 May 1993, at 305, where Japan Airlines is reported to have claimed that the bilateral air services agreement between the United States and Japan had to be restructured as it awarded an unequally higher market share to US carriers on the US–Japan route. See also *Interavia Air Letter*, 18 January 1994, No. 12,913, at 3, where Cathay Pacific accused the United States of calling for liberalization of air traffic rights from Asian carriers while maintaining protectionism in the US market.
56 See 'New Zealand Seeks to Resolve Australia Dispute', *Air Letter*, 8 November

1994, No. 13,118, at 162. See also *Air Letter*, 14 November 1994, No. 13,122, at 1.
57 *Aviation Daily*, 25 June 1993, at 479.
58 Heini Nuutinen, 'Bermuda 3 – or the End of Bilateralism', *Avmark Aviation Economist*, May 1993, 5, at 7.
59 *Aviation Daily*, 17 February 1994, at 275.
60 Id., at 276.
61 See *Aviation Daily*, 2 November 1994, at 179.
62 Ibid.
63 See *Seminar Programme of the World-wide Air Transport Conference on International Air Transport Regulation: Present and Future*, 25/10/94, at Attachment 2.
64 See AT Conf/4-WP/1, 13/5/94, at 1.
65 Id., at 2.
66 Kotaite, op. cit., at 21.
67 See AT Conf/4-WP/4, 13/5/94, at 1–3.
68 Id., at 5.
69 Ibid.
70 AT Conf/4-WP/5, 8/8/94, at 5.
71 Ibid.
72 ICAO News Release, PIO 10/94, at 1.
73 Ibid.
74 AT Conf/4-WP/7, 14/4/94, at 3.
75 See generally AT Conf/4-WP16, 23/6/94.
76 AT Conf/4-WP/80, 23/11/94, at 2.
77 Ibid.
78 AT Conf/4-WP/90, 30/11/94, at 1.
79 Id., at 2.
80 AT Conf/4-WP/89, 30/11/94, revised, 1/12/94, at 1-2.
81 AT Conf/4-WP/78, 23/11/94, at 1.
82 AT Conf/4-WP/79, 23/11/94, at 1-2.
83 AT Conf/4-WP/93, 2/12/94, at 3-1. It is also noteworthy that the International Air Transport Association (IATA) declared that a sensible course should be steered between excessive regulation and destructive *laissez-faire*, while the Airports Council International (ACI) stated that liberalization was welcome in principle but such liberalization should not threaten airline competition. The ACI believed that, in such an eventuality, government action should be considered, and that on an overall basis, airports should be involved in the regulatory process and airport interests should be reflected in regulations emanating from such a process. Id., at 3-2.
84 Id., at 3-4.
85 AT Conf/4-WP/94, 6/12/94, at A-4.
86 Ibid.
87 *Aviation Daily*, 21 September 1995, at 3.
88 Malory Davies, 'Battle for the Open Skies', *Global Transport*, Autumn 1995, at 45.
89 *ITA Press*, 1–31 August 1995, at 2.
90 Ibid.
91 Jeff Apter, 'Airports Demand Voice at Air Service Negotiations', *Airport Forum*, 5 September 1995, at 8.
92 A31-WP/224, P/57, *Report on Agenda Item 36.1-5*.
93 Ibid.
94 GATT was a multilateral body established in Geneva on 1 January 1948 on coming into force of the General Agreement on Tariff and Trade (GATT) negotiated and signed by 23 countries. GATT functions as the principal inter-

national body concerned with negotiating reduction of trade barriers and with international trade relations. While being an organization to which member States belong, where they could use it as a forum in which they can discuss and overcome their problems and negotiate to enlarge world trading opportunities, GATT is also a code of rules which is calculated to liberalize world trade. GATS is an Annex to the Final Act of the Uruguay Round agreement and has a special segment on air transport services as trade in services. One of the agreements contained in the Final Act of the Uruguay Round) establishes the World Trade Organization to serve as single institutional framework for GATT as well as all the agreements and arrangements concluded under the Uruguay Round. This permanent organizational framework, which replaces the GATT structure, will be headed by a Ministerial Conference at least once every two years and will include a General Council to oversee the operation of the Agreement and to act as both a dispute-settlement body and a trade policy review mechanism. Therefore, all references to GATT in this chapter will refer to the World Trade Organization.

95 Article III of GATS requires each party to publish promptly all relevant laws, regulations, administrative guidelines and all other decisions, rulings or measures of general application, by the time of their entry into force.

96 GATT's national treatment philosophy provides foreign services and services suppliers with treatment no less favourable than that accorded to a country's own services and service suppliers.

97 Since GATS is an Annex to the GATT agreement it should be noted that the provisions of GATS are governed by those of GATT, and that both documents incorporate the same basic principles.

98 Article II of GATS. Article XVI extends the MFN principle to market access.

99 Article IV of GATS provides that the increasing participation of developing countries in world trade shall be facilitated through negotiated specific commitments by different parties. It also requires developed member States to establish contact points within two years from the entry into force of the GATS agreement to facilitate the access of developing States' service providers to information related to their respective markets concerning: commercial and technical aspects of the supply of services; registration, recognition and obtaining of professional qualifications; and the availability of service technology. The provision also states that special priority shall be given to the least developed States in the implementation of Article IV, and particular account will be taken of the difficulties experienced by developing States in accepting negotiated commitments in view of their special economic situation and their development, trade and financial needs.

100 Article XXIII on dispute settlement is considered to be well balanced and equitable, and provides that if any Party should consider that another Party fails to carry out its obligations or commitments under the agreement, it may make written representations or proposals to the other Party or Parties concerned, and the latter should give sympathetic consideration to the representations or proposals so made. If no satisfactory settlement can be arrived at, the GATT agreement provides for a formal dispute settlement procedure in Articles XXII and XXIII.

101 There have been seven earlier rounds of trade agreements: 1947 in Geneva; 1949 in Annecy, France; 1951 in Torquay, United Kingdom; 1960–1962 in Geneva (the Dillon round); 1964–1967 in Geneva (the Kennedy round); 1973–1979 in Geneva (the Tokyo round), where negotiations were launched at a ministerial meeting in September 1973 in Tokyo. The Tokyo round produced the most comprehensive agreements, where 99 member States participated. Negotiations of the Tokyo round were concluded in November 1979 with agreements

covering: an improved legal framework for the conduct of world trade (including recognition of tariff and non-tariff treatment in favour of and among developing countries as a permanent legal feature of the world trading system; non-tariff measures (subsidies and countervailing measures); technical barriers to trade; government procurement; customs valuation; import licensing procedures; a revision of the 1967 GATT anti-dumping code; bovine meat; dairy products; tropical products, and an agreement on free trade in civil aircraft. The agreements contained special and more favourable treatment for developing countries.

102 The Five Freedoms of the Air were created at the Chicago Conference of 1944 and comprise the following:

1 the right to fly over the territory of a State without landing;
2 the right to land in the territory of a State for non-traffic purposes;
3 the right to put down passengers, mail and cargo taken on in the territory of the State whose nationality the aircraft possesses;
4 the right to take on passengers, mail and cargo destined for the territory of the State whose nationality the aircraft possesses;
5 the right to take on passengers, mail and cargo destined for the territory of any other contracting State, and the right to put down passengers, mail and cargo coming from any such territory.

103 Annex on Air Transport Services, *General Agreement on Trade in Services*, MTN TNG/W/FA, Article 2.
104 Id., Article 3.
105 Id., Article 4.
106 Id., Article 5.
107 These conditions are the result of an agreement reached on 11 February 1946 by the United States and the United Kingdom in Bermuda. For a clear analysis of the Bermuda Agreement, see Ramon de Murias, *The Economic Regulation of International Air Transport*, North Carolina: McFarland, 1989, 52–72.
108 See generally Abeyratne, op. cit., at 3.
109 ICAO WATC-1.10, 6/4/92, at 1. See also *Airline Business*, June 1992, at 37; Ron Katz, 'ICAO Montreal Colloquium: The Future of Air Transport Regulation', *IFALPA International Quarterly Review*, June 1992, No. 10, 13–15.
110 *Aviation Daily*, 9 April 1992, at 56.
111 ICAO Doc. WATC-3.11, 8/4/92, at 4.
112 ICAO Doc. WATC-3.13, 8/4/92, at 4.
113 ICAO Doc. WATC-3.15, 8/4/92, at 5.
114 See Daniel M. Kasper, *Deregulation and Globalization: Liberalizing International Trade in Air Services*, Massachusetts: Balinger, 1988.
115 ICAO Doc. WATC-3.17, 8/4/92, at 5.
116 Geoffrey Lipman, 'Is GATT Just Another Four Letter Word?', *Aerospace World*, September 1990, Vol. IV, 97, at 98. See also Daniel M. Kasper, 'The GATT Approach – Applying the GATT to Air Services – Will it Work?', *ITA Magazine*, November/December 1989, 5, at 9-12.
117 Kathryn B. Creedy, 'Should Air Transport be in or out of GATT?', *Interavia*, 1990, Vol. 9, 716, at 717.
118 Ibid.
119 See Kasper, op. cit., at 96.
120 Id., Preface.
121 See John C. McCarrol, 'The Bermuda Capacity Clauses in the Jet Age', *Journal of Air Law and Commerce*, Spring 1963, Vol. 29, No.2, 115, at 119, where the author says: 'fair and equal opportunity ... to operate should mean ... equality

of practical capability to operate'. See also P. Van Der Tuuk Adriani, 'The Bermuda Capacity Clauses', *Journal of Air Law & Commerce*, Autumn 1955, Vol. 22, No. 406, at 413.

122 Dr H.A. Wassenbergh lists seven objectives of a State's policy in respect of modern civil aviation. They are:

1 to contribute to the functioning of the international community of States as a total legal order by upholding and further developing the rule of international law;
2 to protect the integrity and identity of the national society;
3 to promote the nation's participation in man's activities in the air and space;
4 to create the best possible conditions and opportunities for use by the public of aviation and space activities;
5 to increase the benefits to be derived from the use of the air and outer space for its nationals;
6 to promote the further development of technology and the knowledge of man;
7 to co-operate with other States on the basis of equal rights in order to bridge conflicting national interests and achieve the aims mentioned above.

See H.A. Wassenbergh, 'Reality and Value of Air and Space Law', *Annals of Air & Space Law*, 1978, Vol. III, 323, at 352.

123 Chicago Convention, Article 44(e).

124 Id., Article 44(f).

# 2 Free Trade in Air Traffic Rights and Preferential Measures for Developing Countries

## Introduction

Unlike in other modes of transport, such as shipping, rail and road transport (where operators of ships, trains and road vehicles may conduct commercial international transportation without obtaining permission of the host country), the landing rights of commercial aircraft must be stringently and diligently negotiated: an aircraft of country A cannot carry passengers, mail and cargo on a scheduled basis into and out of country B without country A signing an air services agreement with country B to that effect, or at least obtaining an operating permit to do so. This situation has prevailed since 1944, when the Convention on International Civil Aviation (Chicago Convention)[1] was signed. As stated earlier, Article 6 of the Chicago Convention stipulates that no scheduled air service may be operated over and into the territory of a contracting State except with the special permission or other authorization of that State, and in accordance with the terms of such permission or authorization.

The commercial anomaly of bilateral negotiations between States for air traffic rights for their national carriers has resulted in a steady evolutionary process of unique competition among carriers. At present, air traffic rights are negotiated by States both bilaterally and multilaterally, with an attempt by some to introduce a policy of 'open skies', whereby free exchange of air traffic rights between carriers of consenting States would be practised. Two practical obstacles have prevented the introduction of an 'open skies' policy between those States which profess to promote it:

1 sustained competition between air carriers for what they con-

sider their 'rightful market share' in air traffic, and their insistence that an absolute 'open' skies policy would be to their disadvantage;
2 the apprehension that an 'open skies' policy, if fully implemented, would create cartels between mega-carriers, or at best an oligopoly, where limited competition between a few mega-carriers would effectively preclude participation in air transport by carriers from developing countries.

This chapter will examine these two factors, and discuss measures taken by the international aviation community under the aegis of the International Civil Aviation Organization[2] to ensure that emerging trends in commercial air transport do not erode the competitiveness of carriers from developing countries.

## The 'Open Skies' Policy

At the time of writing, the United States and the United Kingdom were discussing deregulating air transport between the countries. The talks aimed to replace the UK–USA bilateral air services agreement with an 'open skies' agreement, which would allow the market to determine prices, routes and scheduling. The United States has already signed 'open skies' agreements with the Netherlands and Germany, although an agreement for 'open skies' with the United Kingdom would be on a much larger scale, considering the frequency of air services between the two countries. One of the problem areas that was being ironed out at the discussions was the reported apprehension of the UK authorities that an 'open skies' policy between the United Kingdom and the United States, if fully implemented, would give US carriers access to countries beyond the United Kingdom with full commercial traffic rights (i.e. the right to carry passengers between the United Kingdom and third countries), whereas UK carriers would have no rights to fly between destinations in the United States.[3]

According to a study carried out in the United States, a liberalized 'open skies' agreement with the United Kingdom would provide a $108 billion boost to the US economy and create 152,000 new jobs over a five-year period of steady growth, leading to an estimated 9.4 million new passengers a year who would take advantage of the 86 per cent increase in air services between the two countries[4] and help introduce US–UK air services from 12 new US cities.[5] American Airlines chairman Robert Crandall summed up the view of the US carriers on an 'open skies' policy between the two countries:

> This study confirms what we have been saying for some time – open skies with the UK will be good for passengers, shippers and communities across the country by providing new service, more competition and lower fares in the transatlantic market.[6]

Earlier, in June 1996, Japan rejected a proposal by the United States for an 'open skies' agreement on somewhat similar grounds to the UK – that US carriers would have unlimited rights to fly beyond Japan under the current bilateral air services agreement which was signed in 1952 by the two countries, whereas in return, Japan Airlines, the only Japanese airline at that time, would enjoy no comparable benefit.[7] Japan has openly claimed that it does not support the US version of 'open skies' for two reasons:

1. Japan would not have access to the large US domestic market;
2. 'open skies' does not take into account inconsistencies created by capacity constraints in airports such as Narita and Kansai.[8]

The United States, on the other hand, maintains that the Japanese authorities seem more intent on protecting intra-Asian air service markets for Japanese carriers by blocking out US carrier competitors than opening the US–Japan aviation market.[9]

In their defence, the US carriers have consistently advocated an 'open skies' policy throughout the world. In May 1996, Delta Airlines' Chief Executive Ronald Allen called upon the European Union to enter into an 'open skies agreement' with the United States. Allen contended that 'open skies' are useful because they remove government restrictions on every aspect of aviation except for safety and predatory market behaviour, and concluded that an 'open skies' policy would result in a more vibrant marketplace where consumers were allowed to select among the best, most efficient and most competitive operators.[10]

The United States has also sought 'open skies' agreements with some Asian countries. In September 1995, US authorities signed a Memorandum of Understanding with the authorities of Hong Kong which to a large extent liberalized existing arrangements for the carriage of cargo by air between the two countries.[11] Singapore Airlines has been a staunch supporter of the 'open skies' policy, and has openly called for its implementation between Asia and the United States. According to Singapore Airlines' Chairman, Cheong Choong Kong:

> The US and Singapore agree that liberalizing aviation is in the best interests not only of the consumers but of the economy generally through the stimulation of trade ... I hope therefore that the US will

> extend its open skies to cover the Asia-Pacific region, which, based on traffic forecasts, is going to be the largest aviation market within 15 years.[12]

Later, in December 1996, Cheong was critical of the stance taken by the United States in response to the offer of 'open skies' by Singapore and Malaysia. He said:

> ... it was 'no secret' that open skies bilaterals with Singapore and Malaysia were attainable right away ... but unfortunately it was all or nothing with them [the USA]; they insisted on a critical mass of willing countries before they would proceed. Apparently, Malaysia and Singapore did not constitute such a critical mass.[13]

He has also extended his comments on liberalization to Australia and New Zealand, claiming that those countries should open their markets so that tourists could fly in and out of – and, more importantly, within – their territories more conveniently,[14] thus suggesting that such markets should not be protected and reserved for the national carriers of Australia and New Zealand.

In this context, the suggestion made by the Prime Minister of Malaysia in October 1995, that Asia-Pacific nations must adopt a common stand in talks with the United States, is significant. The key contention of Asian countries against most developed countries in the West is that the latters' enthusiasm for 'open skies' is tainted by their refusal to lay open their domestic markets within the 'open skies' package, reflecting an imbalance between those countries which do not have extensive domestic markets and those – such as the United States – which do. Prime Minister Mohamad said:

> Asia-Pacific nations must be prepared to act in concert and adopt a co-ordinated stance in negotiating with the EU and the US ... the consequence of not doing so will likely be the domination of the aviation industry by the mega carriers from the US and Europe.[15]

In January 1997, officials from the United States and Singapore reached an 'open skies' deal, making Singapore the first Asian country to sign such an agreement with the United States.[16] The US–Singapore deal followed a preliminary meeting in October 1996 which included South Korea, Taiwan, Malaysia and Brunei. On 10 January 1997, the United States reopened negotiations with Japan, expecting to seek progress towards an 'open skies' agreement in 1997. This was finally achieved in 1998.

In view of these developments, it is difficult to deny that the 'open skies' policy advocated by the various proponents is overprotective. Most nations still give an unusually high priority to the marketing policies of their airlines, which are naturally geared to world protectionism and exploitation. An ideal 'open skies' policy would resemble Dubai's, where, irrespective of reciprocity, unlimited access to air traffic rights is given to anyone who wishes to operate air services. Maurice Flanagan, Group Managing Director of Emirates (the airline of Dubai) wrote:

> Open skies describes the situation in which a country allows unlimited traffic rights to the airlines of other countries, almost always on a reciprocal basis and is not all common. Open skies usually results from bilateral negotiation. Singapore, however, places open skies on the table immediately, and, if the other side reciprocates, there the negotiations end. Holland is much the same. But Dubai grants open skies unconditionally, i.e. without requesting reciprocity, which is unique for a place which has its own airline.[17]

Whichever way the 'open skies' policy is interpreted, and whatever its nature in practice is, it is inevitable that liberalization would affect market forces and airlines in different ways. Given the free market competition expanding around the globe in recent times the emergence of free trade agreements such as NAFTA (North American Free Trade Agreement) EFTA (European Free Trade Agreement), free market forces within the European Union, the collapse of the communist economy in most countries, including the former USSR, and increasing consumer demands in Japan, protectionism in commercial aviation should give way to some degree of liberalization in the least.

We are therefore faced with the prospect of commercial aviation being controlled by a group of air carriers which may serve whole global regions, operated by a network of commercial and trade agreements. Regional carriers would predominate, easing out niche carriers and small national carriers, which would be unable to compete with the larger carriers' lower unit costs and joint ventures. It is arguable that a perceived justification for 'open skies' or unlimited liberalization exists even today in bilateral air services agreements between two countries, where fair and equal opportunity to operate air services is a *sine qua non* for both national carriers. This has been reinterpreted to mean 'fair and equal opportunity to compete', and later still, 'fair and equal opportunity to effectively participate' in international air transportation as agreed.[18] Of course, there has been no universal acceptance of this evolving interpretation, and the carriers and States have stubbornly maintained their own positions.

## Fair and Equal Opportunity to Operate Air Services

As stated earlier, a typical bilateral air services agreement requires the airlines operating the services for each contracting party to take into account the interests of the airlines of the other contracting party, to avoid undermining the services their competitor provides on all or part of the same routes. The factors taken into account in ensuring fair and equal opportunity for each carrier are:

- the requirements of the public for transportation on the same routes;
- the capacity at a reasonable load factor that each carrier may offer.

However, such factors as determining capacity at a reasonable load factor to fulfil the requirements of the public are subservient to the main consideration: affording some protection to a less fortunate carrier to allow both carriers to obtain a fair deal in their operations on the same route, So it is arguable that *all* operational factors must be taken into account to avoid one carrier unduly affecting the operations of the other.

Capacity considerations have always undermined the meaning and purpose of the 'fair and equal opportunity' clause, and predetermination of capacity has often been considered the primary objective of the provision.[19] This insistence on the part of most contracting States on capacity as the sole criterion in interpreting the 'fair and equal opportunity clause' has deprived developing nations of the opportunity to inaugurate new air routes and foster already existing ones. Besides, capacity is always determined by uncorroborated statistics of uplift and discharge of passengers, mail and cargo furnished by both contracting parties, which often contradict each other. It is an incontrovertible fact that the capacity consideration has proven an effective tool in the hands of any contracting State which does not intend to grant traffic rights to another on a particular route.

Needless to say, this approach has left developing countries in a hapless situation, lacking any bargaining ability. In addition to the fact that capacity statistics can seldom be authenticated, the parochial vision of many contracting States has perverted the purpose for which the 'fair and equal opportunity clause' was introduced in 1944 by the Chicago Convention.[20] By no means is the capacity consideration unimportant, but to place sole reliance upon it is unfair.

*Genesis of the Clause*

Any country which ratifies the Chicago Convention becomes bound by the provision which states that:

> no scheduled international air service may be operated over or into the territory of a contracting States, except with the special permission or other authorization of that State, and in accordance with the terms of such permission or authorization.

In other words, a country has to obtain operating permission from a contracting State into whose territory its national carrier wishes to operate air services through the air services agreement, whose various provisions pertaining to exclusive sovereignty of States and the conditions they may impose on foreign carriers operating air services over their territorial air space have been derived from the Chicago Convention.[21] Under the Convention, ICAO is designated the tasks of:

- ensuring the safe and orderly growth of international civil aviation throughout the world;[22]
- ensuring that the rights of contracting States are fully respected, and that every contracting State has a fair opportunity to operate international airlines;[23]
- promoting the development of all aspects of international civil aeronautics.[24]

These three considerations are interlinked, and cannot be considered in isolation. The perplexing dichotomy which pervades any negotiations for air traffic rights is that on the one hand the derivative norms of Article 44 of the Chicago Convention are not considered in relation to 'the fair and equal opportunity' clause of the air services agreement, and on the other, insistence on the single aspect of capacity regulation stultifies the growth and development of international civil aviation. For example, by insisting on capacity being commensurate with traffic demand, the contracting states require carriers to prove before even operating on a given route that capacity would justify demand. Traffic demand statistics are often unreliable for two reasons:

- they may not be authentic, and the figures of each State are often disputed by the other;
- traffic demand is not static, but variable, and future demand would depend on how each carrier marketed its product and developed a given air route.

This vicious circle defeats the Chicago Convention's aim of insuring the growth and development of international civil aviation throughout the world. Such problems as the allocation of capacity and the eventual observance of the use of capacity are often found to be impracticable measures in the implementation of the 'fair and equal opportunity clause'.[25] There have been attempts to avoid rigid adherence to capacity criteria in determining the rights of individual carriers, on the basis that a rigid allocation of capacity or an insistence on specific capacity in relation to an imaginary demand is undesirable.[26]

Whatever the motivations behind the attempt to circumvent the spirit of the 'fair and equal opportunity clause', the ICAO functions in controlling this aspect of growth and equality have seldom been exercised.

The 'fair and equal opportunity' clause acts to the detriment of developing countries mainly due to its interpretation, and the insistence on capacity as the main criterion is heavily influenced by commercial factors, since air services negotiations involve hard bargaining for commercial rights. In this context, developing countries are faced with four distinct problems:

1 their unequal bargaining power;
2 lack of reciprocity from foreign national carriers operating air services to them;
3 the refusal of some contracting States to recognize air services agreements and their provisions
4 differing interpretations of provisions of air services agreements, and the lack of arbitration.

Of the four problems, perhaps (3) and (4) are the more serious. However, (1) and (2) are the causes of problems (3) and (4). For instance, since most air traffic to many developing countries comprises tourists, but some developing countries send few tourists abroad, most countries' national carriers have refused to recommend to their aeronautical authorities any additional routes or increased frequency of operation for developing countries' national carriers even though traffic could be developed on such routes.

The absence of an effective body to enforce international agreements and arbitration clauses seems to give contracting States the liberty and flexibility to interpret the 'fair and equal opportunity' clause to their advantage. Reprehensible as this may seem, negotiations for air traffic rights concern trading rights, and so it is justifiable for anyone to try to gain an advantage if the opportunity arises.

A serious malady which seems to afflict the 'fair and equal opportunity' clause is that most contracting States do not pay attention to the *language* of Article 44 of the Chicago Convention. As one commentator has said:

> The creative and comprehending power of language is of special importance to the law. There is practically no existence of legal notions outside language.[27]

It is indisputable that the primary motive and purpose of Article 44 is to promote and develop the growth of international civil aviation through fair and equal opportunity afforded to all carriers. To subvert this policy in preference to commercial exigencies and considerations is to relegate the importance of the language of the law to the background.[28]

In the above context, it is arguable that when States propose the implementation of an 'open skies' policy, and refuse to give regard to the real meaning of Article 44 in their negotiations for air services, such an act highlights the inequality of bargaining power of developing States together with the economic and geographic impediments they suffer in the field of international civil aviation. This need not be so, since *pari passu* if fair and equal opportunities are afforded to developing countries in operating their air services, such constraints may be alleviated to a considerable extent. This is especially so in instances where new routes are envisaged. Awarding air traffic rights to burgeoning carriers for a trial period would fulfil the spirit of Article 44 in the Chicago Convention.

The above discussion reflects the difficulties in applying the 'fair and equal opportunity' clause although it demonstrates that it is the only measure which can aid developing countries' airlines in a global free-for-all. If liberalization and multilateralism eventually lead to an 'open skies' philosophy being implemented, a similar clause would be needed to assist the developing countries in a more practical manner.

### *Preferential Measures*

In 1994, ICAO focused the attention of its member States on the changing aero-political environment by convening the Fourth ICAO World-wide Air Transport Conference. More than 800 delegates from 138 States and 28 international and regional organizations attended this conference in order to assess and review past and present issues relating to air transport, and to examine its future regulation. One of the landmarks of the conference was the presentation by ICAO of future regulatory arrangements, which had been prepared prior to the conference by a group of ICAO experts on future regulatory arrangements for international air transport (GEFRA).[29]

The conference addressed, *inter alia*, safeguards and a 'safety net' as a basis for regulatory arrangement, and concluded that future international regulation initiatives should have due regard to the objective participation of all stakeholders in international air transport, and their interests should be taken into account equitably and in all deliberations.[30]

The 'safety net' envisaged by the conference pertains to a measure or measures that would be calculated to ensure continued participation by air carriers in the event of unforeseen or temporary circumstances, irrespective of their size, capacity and efficiency. The conference also addressed the issue of preferential measures for carriers of developing countries, which would ensure that they would not be at a disadvantage when competing with carriers of developed countries which were greater in size.[31]

This initiative emerged from the general view that developing countries would be in favour of liberalization of air transport if the conditions of competition included such preferential measures for their carriers. At ICAO's 31st Assembly held in 1995, the African States insisted that the success of developing countries in international air transport could only be achieved if equality of States, non-discrimination, interdependence, harmonization and global co-operation among States, which were recognized as abiding principles of economic regulation of air transport at the 1994 Conference, were accompanied by genuine equality of opportunity for developing countries in the face of competition introduced as a result of future regulation of international air transport.[32]

The African States were of the view that preferential measures were not privileges, aids or other forms of moral reparation, but rather represented an attempt to obviate economic disparities among nations which go beyond the framework of air transport regulation. According to the African States, these economic factors create an unbalanced situation which distorts the principle of equality or opportunity.[33] However, they did not feel that this precluded future regulatory arrangements, nor that preferential measures would cure all ills and defects identified in the current system, but that these should be binding commitments on States, not mere voluntary arrangements between airlines.

The measures suggested by the African States reflect the fundamental need to address market access. In capacity management, particular emphasis was given to the notion of reciprocity by coefficients based on the gross national product of countries which were State parties to a bilateral or multilateral arrangement. Some of the areas of commercial conduct in air transport identified for preferential measures were ground handling, remittance of earnings and currency conversion, and computer reservation systems.

### *Definition of a Developing Country*

The United Nations uses the basic criterion of size of economy in defining a developing country. Under this broad heading, various subcriteria are used to define the size of an economy, usually including population and physical area. However, there is no generally acknowledged measure of 'smallness', and the criteria would depend on the purpose of the definition.[34] Since population levels determine many of the basic characteristics of a national economy, this would seem to be the most significant criterion. Under this definition, the size of the economy is directly proportionate to population level and per capita income.

In its fifth programming cycle (1992–1996) the United Nations applied priority economic treatment to 'least developed countries' using the following methodology of distribution:

> Countries with gross national product per capita of $750 or less, to receive 87 per cent of indicative planning figure resources, keeping the weight co-efficients for gross national product per capita and population in the fifth cycle unchanged from those used in the previous cycle.[35]

The United Nations Governing Council also decided to award 7 qualifier points to countries judged to be the least developed among the developing countries, 1 qualifier point to landlocked developing countries, and 1 qualifier point to developing countries which had gained independence since 1985.[36]

### *Some Paradigm Systems of Preferences*

The 1994 ICAO Conference was influenced by the paradigm of the General System of Preferences (GSP) used by the United Nations Conference on Trade and Development (UNCTAD) in its considerations of preferential measures in air transport for developing countries.[37] According to the UNCTAD GSP, different methodologies were used by 27 developed countries (including the members of the European Union, which operate a single methodology) to limit or even eliminate the application of Most Favoured Nation tariffs to certain products imported from developing countries. Arguably, the most relevant analogies for air transport regulation from the GSP paradigm are the ability of countries to 'self-election', whereby they can opt to be a beneficiary under the GSP as a developing country, even though there are no perceived criteria to consider them as such, and the more beneficial treatment accorded to least developed countries in the various GSP schemes.

At the 22nd Session of the Special Committee on Preferences of UNCTAD, held in Geneva on 23–27 October 1995, the Committee agreed that the GSP had fulfilled an important role as a multilateral tool for development, enabling beneficiary countries to achieve fuller integration into the world economy while retaining its validity in the modern international trading context.[38] The Committee also took note of the fact that delegates underlined the importance of transparency, stability and predictability of the GSP schemes if they were to attain its objectives.

Preference-receiving countries under the GSP were of the unanimous view that the preference system should be enlarged in scope to encompass trade in services and investment, in line with the extension of the multilateral trading system to such new areas, the process of globalization and liberalization, the evolving importance of the services sectors for developing countries' economies, and the promotion of investment. There was also broad agreement at the Session that special preferential measures for developing countries in all areas of trade needed to be strengthened, and that preference-giving countries should, as far as possible, provide trading access to developing countries free of duties, ceilings and quotas.[39]

Finally, there was general agreement that the GSP was of critical importance to developing countries, and therefore that it would continue to remain an important activity for UNCTAD.[40]

The relevance of the UNCTAD GSP to air transport in the context of the proposed preferential measures for developing countries lies largely in the fact that it offers a transparent, stable and predictable scheme which is sustained and managed by a regulatory body. The direct application of these principles to an ICAO-sponsored preferential measures scheme would ensure that the air transport industry and civil aviation in general would operate according to a process under which arbitrary deviation from an equitably applied and monitored preferential system would be impossible.

Other useful reference sources in the development of preferential measures in air transport include some of the provisions of the General Agreement on Trade in Services (GATS), Article IV of which suggests three means of increasing participation by countries in the area of trade in service:

- strengthening the domestic services capacity of States, and their efficiency and competitiveness;
- improving access by States to distribution channels and information networks;
- liberalizing market access in areas of export supply relevant to certain countries.

Within GATS, the measures negotiated between developed and developing countries are non-reciprocal, and lead to increased participation in trade by developing countries, rather than offering financial assistance, and encourage developing countries to use them to their individual advantage in their own situations with regard to market access and provision of particular services. Furthermore, under the GATS umbrella, signatory States can file exemptions from the Most Favoured Nation treatment clause and from conditions which may restrict market access. Although GATS only applies to air transport at present in the areas of aircraft repair and maintenance services, the selling and marketing of air transport services and computer reservation systems, GATS can also serve as an analogy in the field of air transport activities in so far as they relate to commercial competition for the operation of air services.

*The Nature and Purpose of Preferential Measures in Air Transport*

Preferential measures are usually granted on a non-reciprocal basis. They are intended to offer external support to create an operating environment in which carriers of developing countries can compete more effectively. As for their application, the States concerned are expected to agree upon methodology and substance according to particular circumstances, subjectively. As mentioned earlier, preferential measures differ from the 'safety net', in that the former seek to ensure that carriers of developing countries can compete in commercial air transport effectively, while the latter tries to ensure effective and sustained participation by all carriers.

Preferential measures are also proactive and positive, and are adopted to ensure the creation of opportunities for the carriers concerned in a competitive air transport market. Although one might argue that preferential measures already exist in the 'fair and equal opportunity clause' of the bilateral air services agreement, this argument has been met by the proposition that this clause is protective, and therefore negative, whereas preferential measures, in the context they are proposed, create opportunities for increasing participation while exposing carriers of developing countries to the full competitiveness of the the market situation.

It is expected that preferential measures, once applied, would be an additional instrument which ensured increased participation by carriers of developing countries. Other measures of commercial cooperation which are used at present, such as joint services among carriers, code-sharing and blocked seat arrangements, and the exchange of personnel training and management expertise also assist in ensuring increased participation by these carriers.

### *Some Suggested Preferential Measures*

ICAO has suggested some preferential measures for the consideration and possible use of its member States:

- the assymetric liberalization of market access in a bilateral air transport relationship to give an air carrier of a developing country more cities to serve, Fifth Freedom traffic rights[41] on sectors which are otherwise not normally granted, flexibility to operate unilateral services on a given route for a certain period, and the right to serve greater capacity for an agreed period;
- greater flexibility for air carriers of developing countries compared to their counterparts in developed countries in changing capacity between routes in a bilateral agreement situation, code-sharing in markets of interest to them, and changing gauge (aircraft types) without restrictions;
- allowing of trial periods, whereby carriers of developing countries can operate under liberal air service arrangements for an agreed period;
- gradual introduction by developing countries of more liberal market access agreements for longer periods than developed countries' air carriers, (in order to ensure participation by their own carriers);
- liberalizing arrangements rapidly by developing countries' own carriers;
- waiving nationality requirements for ownership of carriers of developing countries;
- allowing carriers of developing countries to use more modern aircraft through liberal leasing agreements;
- preferential treatment with regard to slot allocations at airports;
- more liberal arrangements for carriers of developing countries in terms of ground-handling at airports, conversion of currency at their foreign offices, and employment of foreign personnel with specialized skills.[42]

These proposals are intended to give air carriers of developing countries a 'head start' which would effectively ensure their continued participation in competition with other carriers for the operation of international air services. Furthermore, improved market access and operational flexibility are two benefits which are considered as direct corollaries to the measures proposed.

## Comments

While the 'open skies' policy sounds economically expedient, its implementation would undoubtedly phase out the smaller carriers which are offering competition in air transport and a larger spectrum of air transport to the consumer. Lower fares, different types of services and varied in-flight service profiles are some of the features of the present system. It is desirable to introduce a higher level of competitiveness into the air transport industry, and preferential measures for carriers of developing countries would play a major role in this.

In addition to addressing the preferential measures proposed by ICAO, which would be of immense assistance to carriers of developing countries if implemented, it would be prudent for the international aviation and trading community to consider the larger issue of funding, whereby long-term low-interest loans could be made available to carriers of developing countries through such institutions as the World Bank and the International Monetary Fund. Some consideration could also be given to a balanced distribution of aircraft throughout the world, whereby developing countries could have access to aircraft which have been discarded by their more affluent counterparts through an equitable leasing system.

The exemption of aircraft operated by carriers of developing countries from certain technological standards (as far as possible) which apply to modern aircraft, such as aircraft engine emission standards and noise regulations, could also be examined.[43]

Preferential measures may also be considered on a collective basis, whereby air traffic rights could be used by a carrier of one country on behalf of another carrier representing another country. This would help, particularly if a developing country is unable to launch its own airline or cannot allocate its national carrier a particular route due to economic reasons. This principle could also be extended to cover instances where airlines from developing countries could combine their operations by using their collective air traffic rights. For example, airlines of countries A and B which have been granted rights to operate air services from their countries to countries C and D respectively would be able to operate one joint service to countries C and D in one flight, using their collective traffic rights.

As far as possible, developing countries should be released from the obligation to own and control their air carriers, or to have their carriers substantially owned and controlled by their nationals, to allow those countries which cannot fully finance their carriers to maintain them and provide well-rounded competition in the air transport industry.

## Notes

1 *Convention on International Civil Aviation,* signed Chicago, 7 December 1944, ICAO Doc. 7300/6, 1980.
2 The International Civil Aviation Organization is the specialized agency of the United Nations responsible for matters pertaining to the regulation of international civil aviation. ICAO has a membership of 185 States and serves its governing bodies – the Council and the Assembly – through its Secretariat.
3 See 'US, UK to Restart Open Skies Talks in London', *Air Letter,* 2 December 1996, at 2.
4 The current bilateral air services agreement between the two countries, known as the 'Bermuda II Agreement', permits only two US carriers, American and United, to serve London's Heathrow Airport from a limited number of cities.
5 See 'US–UK Open Skies to Add $108 bn to Economy', *Air Letter,* 14 November 1996, at 3.
6 Ibid.
7 'U.S.–Japan, Fairplay Comes First', *Airlines International,* January/February 1996, at 7.
8 *Aviation Daily,* 23 December 1996, at 473.
9 'No Surprise in Japan's Rejection of Open Skies', *Aviation Daily,* 28 June 1996, at 529.
10 'Delta Calls for Open Skies with Europe', *Air Letter,* 24 May 1996, at 1.
11 'US Hong Kong in MOU: DOT Presses to Liberalize Asian Markets', *Aviation Daily,* 2 October 1995, at 3.
12 'SIA Chief Seeks Open Skies between US, Asia', *Air Letter,* 24 June 1996, at 3.
13 'Singapore Airlines CEO says Singapore, Malaysia Ready for Open Skies', *Aviation Daily,* 6 December 1996, at 377.
14 Ibid.
15 'Asian Airlines Urged to Adopt United Stand', *Air Letter,* 1 November 1995, 1.
16 'U.S., Singapore Agree to End Air Restrictions', *Air Letter,* 27 January 1997, at 3.
17 Maurice Flanagan, 'Open Skies and the Survival of the Fittest', *Aerospace,* August 1996, at 16.
18 Henri Wassenbergh, 'De-regulation of Competition in International Air Transport', *Air & Space Law,* 1996, Vol. XXI, No. 2, at 80.
19 See, for example, the Air Services Agreement signed between the Governments of Sri Lanka and Australia, 12 January 1950, Article V(A). See also, Praveen Singh, 'Some Aspects of Australia's Air Services Agreements – Part One', *Air Law,* 1984, Vol. l, No. IX, 158–9.
20 ICAO Doc. 7300/6, 1980.
21 Chicago Convention, Articles 5–16. See also Shawcross and Beaumont, *Air Law* (4th edn), 1988, Vol. I, London: Butterworths, 1988, at para. 201.
22 Chicago Convention, Article 44(a).
23 Chicago Convention, Article 44(f).
24 Chicago Convention, Article 44(i).
25 See Bin Cheng, *The Law of International Air Transport,* London: Stevens & Sons, 1962, at 412.
26 Ibid., at 429.
27 See B. Grossfeld, 'Language and the Law', *Journal of Air Law & Commerce,* 1985, Vol. 50, 793, at 797–8. See also C.G. Weeramantry, *The Law in Crisis,* Sydney: The Law Book Company, 1976, at 133.
28 See Hiller, 'Language, Law, Sports and Culture: The Transferability or Non-transferability of Words, Life Styles and Attitudes through Law', *Valparaiso University Law Review,* 1963, Vol. 12, at 433, where the author stresses that it is

only in recent times that language has attained prominence as a major component of interest in the interpretation of comparative law.

29 For a detailed discussion of the ICAO World-wide Air Transport Conference, see R.I.R. Abeyratne, *Legal and Regulatory Issues in International Aviation*, New York: Transnational Publishers, 1996, at 29–62.

30 See Vijay Poonoosamy, 'Change in the Air', *ICAO Journal*, July/August 1996, at 35–7.

31 The conference noted that preferential measures would indeed vary with the size and competitiveness of a carrier. For example, ICAO statistics reflect that in 1994, 6 of the first 25 carriers who had the largest number of passenger-kilometres performed were from developing countries. These six carriers would seem not to require preferential measures. See A31-WP/37, EC/6, 11/7/95, at para. 2.4.

32 See A31-WP/127, EC/17/20/9/95, at 2.

33 Ibid.

34 See generally UN Doc. A/49/424, General Assembly, 49th Session, 22 September 1994.

35 Ibid., at 16.

36 Ibid.

37 The conference also considered the system introduced by the Fourth Lomé Convention (Lomé IV) which is an agreement between the member States of the European Union on the one hand and developing States of the African, Caribbean and Pacific Group. The Lomé principles admit of the reduction of tariffs for exports of preference-receiving countries. See ICAO Doc. A31-WP/37, EC/6, at 3.

38 *Report of the Special Committee on Preferences on its 22nd session, 23–27 October 1995*, Geneva: United Nations Conference on Trade and Development, TD/B/42/(2)/4, TD/B/SCP/16, at 34.

39 Id., at 36.

40 Ibid.

41 The right to uplift or discharge passengers, mail and cargo in a country other than the grantor State.

42 See *Study on Preferential Measures for Developing Countries*, ICAO Doc. AT-WP/1789, 22/8/96, at A-7–A-9.

43 For a detailed discussion of regulations on aircraft noise and engine emissions, see R.I.R. Abeyratne, *Legal and Regulatory Issues in International Aviation*, New York: Transnational Publishers, 1996, at 271–313.

# 3 Liberalized Trading in Air Transport and the 'Safety Net'

## Introduction

A recently published treatise[1] on the subject of 'open skies' alleges that the existing restrictive regulatory regime has straitjacketed the world's airline industry in a system of bilateral air treaties which has withstood the neo-liberal free trade winds of the post-war era.[2] The author also claims that the United States and European Union are poised to draw up new 'open skies' policies.[3] While it is certainly true that the winds of liberalization are sweeping both sides of the Atlantic, the exuberance stops at the point where one identifies the protagonists of the trend. A recent study[4] claims that the United States' 'open skies' strategy, failed to attract big players due to the fact that the US Government does not have the support of the carriers, which are reluctant to support their government signing such agreements with small countries whose carriers might end up with greater market access, negating the reciprocity and equality promised by the 'open skies' concept.[5]

A significant development of 'open skies' is the imminent multilateral agreement between the United States and the European Union (which also includes Canada, Mexico and Latin America). Many believe that this is just a precursor to a world-wide 'open skies' regime involving Asia as well.[6] However, Barbara Beyer, President of Avmark, recently cautioned that Asian carriers could be seriously affected if they were to be subjected to 'open skies' agreements in their operations between Asia and the United States.[7] She focused particularly on the adverse impact of such agreements on countries with large domestic populations spread out over a vast geographic area, like Thailand, Indonesia, the Philippines, Malaysia and China. The rationale behind this philosophy is that Asian carriers, however large by their standards, are not comparable in size to US carriers, and therefore would be unable to penetrate US domestic markets to the same extent as their US counterparts would be able to exploit domestic Asian markets. Conversely, however, smaller countries such as Singapore and Brunei with no domestic markets would stand to gain from access to the large US domestic market without having to reciprocate in their territories.

A manifestation of the cautious Asian approach to the 'open skies' concept can be seen in the relationship between Japan and the US in their bilateral air services negotiations. Japan Airlines, the largest Asian carrier, has a fleet of 128 aircraft, almost the same as TWA, but many fewer than Northwest, which has a fleet of 400 aircraft. Japan claims that a totally liberalized market access arrangement between the two countries would inevitably result in overall dominance by alliances formed by US carriers to operate air services into Japan.[8] Be that as it may, the stage is now set for regional 'open skies' arrangements, from European market liberalization,[9] to Central American Open Skies,[10] with the United States vigorously encouraging those who are willing to enter into 'open skies' arrangements from other parts of the globe.

Against this backdrop, the success of 'open skies' seemingly hinges on the delicate balance between the prospect of unlimited market access on the one hand, and protectionism on the other. The primeval fear of losing in open competition and being annihilated in the process has naturally and inevitably pervaded the weaker segments of commercial aviation, which feel they do not have the means to withstand airline alliances and mega-carrier strategies.

A compromise between the two extremes has emerged through the work of the Air Transport Regulation Panel of ICAO, which at its Ninth Meeting in Montreal, 10–14 February 1997 recommended to the ICAO Council that it would be impracticable for States to follow a code of conduct which would define actions of unfair competition in all situations. The Panel was of the view that as a safeguard mechanism, States should agree on basic principles that would constitute unfair competition when two or more States agree to move from a rigid bilateral scheme of market access to a more liberalized regime. These principles involve practices related to airlines charging excessive fares and rates and adding excess capacity or frequency of service on routes, resulting in an adverse economic impact on the other carrier.

The safeguards encapsulated in the competition rules of the World Trade Organization, although not applicable to air transport, offer a good comparison with the ICAO 'safety net', so this chapter will compare the effects of the 'safety net' mechanism proposed by ICAO with the safeguards enshrined in the competition mechanism of WTO, to try to establish whether the ICAO 'safety net' is a timely and efficient measure to counter the liberalization proposed by the 'open skies' philosophy.

## Market Access

'Market access' covers the basic rights[11] of air carriers in to the operation of air transport services with relevant governmental approval and also subsidiary rights, such as product distribution, which are inherent in the basic operating rights, which are considered ancillary rights. Market access rights are usually dependent upon such factors as the aircraft type used and their range, airport congestion factors and capacity considerations in the case of the grant of air traffic rights.

The fundamental difference between the predetermination or control of market access as a result of the Chicago Convention's failure to prescribe identifiable rules of commercial conduct in this area and 'open skies', which is the total liberalization of market access, is succinctly explained by Wassenbergh:

> The regulation of international air transport activities gradually is moving from predetermination of capacity to 'open skies', or, in other words, from aiming at an equitable *share* of the international air transportation market for each State to an equitable *participation* of national air carriers in the international air transportation market.[12]

Wassenbergh elaborates his thesis with the explanation that the negotiatory process for air traffic rights, which started with the 1946 Bermuda I bilateral philosophy requiring an *ex post facto* review of prior determination of available markets, has undergone a process of evolution from requiring a fair and equal opportunity for carriers to operate air services, to a fair and equal opportunity for carriers to *compete* in international air transport operations.[13] The word 'compete' then gave way to the words 'effectively participate' in the evolutionary process. The logical conclusion that one can draw from this process is that, at present, the tussle between controlled market access and 'open skies', is a 'tug of war' between air carriers' right to have fair and equal opportunity to compete for air services, and their right to have fair and equal opportunity to participate effectively in the operation of air services.

If one were to argue for controlled market access on the basis that the equitable solution to the problem is to give carriers the opportunity to compete with one another, a small carrier (with less aircraft) than a competitor on a given route could use its numerical inferiority as a negotiating tool. Also, if a carrier belongs to a State which has a large domestic air traffic market, it could object to a carrier with no domestic market gaining access into its country, on the basis that the sense of equitable competition between the carriers would be absent.

On the other hand, if one were to advocate 'open skies' and fair and equal opportunity to effectively participate in a given market, both carriers would be forced to participate in that market within the market's parameters. In other words, if Country A has a large domestic market, and Country B has none, the carriers of Country A would have to share the domestic traffic potential available in its country with the carriers of Country B, without obtaining reciprocal benefits from Country B. Another good example which reflects the inability of the 'open skies' philosophy to offer the ultimate solution to the air traffic rights debate is where one country offers attractive beyond traffic rights, and the other does not. For instance, if carriers from Country A can operate air services to Country B and to six lucrative points beyond, and the carriers of Country B can operate to only two viable points beyond Country A, it is quite natural that the latter carriers would feel that although they were participating in the market for what it is worth, they are not getting as much benefit from the operation of air services in that market as their competitor.

From a purely conceptual perspective, it is unwise in the current context of rapid growth patterns in the demand for air transport services to dismiss the 'open skies' concept or liberalization of worldwide air transport market purely on the grounds that one carrier will lose and another will gain. The air transport industry can no longer be segmented or protected on the basis of a carrier's competitive edge, or lack thereof. The demand for air transport services involves ancillary services and, above all, the most efficient and cost-effective service to the consumer. The 'divide and rule' policy which might have been feasible decades ago when air transport was a luxury rather than a utility can no longer be applied by governments and their carriers without taking into account the fact that air transport is a global industry requiring global participation.

Of course, this is not to say that a small carrier should be swallowed by a mega-carrier and allowed to perish under the 'open skies' doctrine. Rather, a given market should be looked at as a whole, and the carriers which are able to offer more services and gain more profit in that market in an 'open competition' scenario should be allowed to operate air services as they wish, but under certain arrangements with those carriers which are unable to offer comparable services. It matters not whether these arrangements take the form of alliances, franchises or other agreements. More importantly, such arrangements would justify the 'effective participation' element claimed by the 'open skies' concept, and preclude one carrier from being adversely affected by the operation of air transport services by another. More importantly, the consumer would not be caught in the crossfire of competition if such arrangements equitably served all concerned in the process.

Within the above overall sense of effective participation by airlines, market access should be broadly viewed in the present context as an essential tool of commercial air transport which helps optimize efficient and economical communication and trade relations between nations, while at the same time promoting their growth and development, both nationally and regionally.

## The 'Safety Net'

The 'safety net' was first discussed at an international forum at ICAO's Fourth World-wide Air Transport Conference on International Air Transport Regulation, held in Montreal 23 November–6 December 1994. The 'safety net' for liberalized market access was deemed applicable to all three aspects of rights: route rights, which represent geographic specification of routes as agreed areas of air transport service operations, operational rights, which include various physical factors of operation, such as aircraft types, number of aircraft used and number of carriers on a given route, and traffic rights, which reflect details of payload, such as passengers, cargo and mail, and the points from and to which they are carried.

Broadly, the 'safety net' is a capacity freeze which a State can opt to impose on a carrier in extraordinary circumstances, ranging from a State's carrier experiencing a significant decline in its participation in a market segment to a situation where there is a need for a dispute-settlement mechanism to resolve a blatant imbalance of market share in a given market segment.

It was proposed that the 'safety net' would apply to all scheduled and non-scheduled carriers serving the market segment in question, and be applicable for a sustained period of time, continually being monitored to assess its efficacy, and amended as required. The underlying thrust of the 'safety net' was that above and beyond its role as a monitor and tool of sanction, it was a tool for correction of an imbalance in market access.

The 'safety net' is based on the fundamental premise that untrammelled market access for carriers without a mechanism which ensures equitable participation could lead to abuse and result in reduced participation by the less dominant carrier in a given market segment. The 'safety net' therefore serves to maintain a balance in the market. It is essentially an *ex post facto* measure, and is intended to apply retrospectively to a given situation, so it cannot be introduced *a priori* or as a precautionary measure.

Unlike other predetermined commercial arrangements such as pool agreements, which take effect automatically on the occurrence of certain events, the 'safety net' has to be brought into action by the party concerned. Usually, the mechanism which enforces a capacity freeze under the purview of the 'safety net' can be used only in the case of Third and Fourth Freedom traffic – end-to-end traffic between the States concerned. It does not apply *ipso facto* to inequalities generated by the operation of air services on the Fifth Freedom basis, or intermediate and beyond-point markets. However, the proposal considered at the ICAO Conference did not rule out the operation of the 'safety net' to Fifth Freedom operations in instances where an overwhelming imbalance was seen to act to the detriment of one carrier as a result of another's Fifth Freedom carriage of passengers, cargo and mail in a given market segment.

The basic criterion used for determining an imbalance in market access in the context of the 'safety net' is capacity, although in certain instances the application of the 'safety net' and its attendant capacity freeze can also be activated on the uplift and discharge figures of passengers, mail and cargo. The process admittedly becomes more complicated when Fifth Freedom operations are involved, but this does not deter the expectations of applicability of the 'safety net'. This issue becomes particularly sensitive with the involvement of third States. To alleviate this problem, it is often helpful that the 'safety net' applies not as a continuing sanction against an imbalance in the market, but rather as a temporary capacity freezer until the market regains its balance between the parties concerned.

The 'safety net' has been proposed to ensure carrier survival and equitable participation in a market segment. Therefore, it buttresses liberalized market access, and serves as a tool of macro-management, to be used only as a temporary measure to correct a temporary irregularity in the market. The existence of the 'safety net' could act as a 'guarantor', encouraging airline alliances and co-operation involving code-sharing and computer reservation systems.

## Follow-up Action

The ICAO Conference of 1994 generally acknowledged that market access was the pre-eminent consideration in the regulatory framework of air transport, and endorsed the view that States should ensure meaningful and sustained participation by their carriers within the parameters of the Chicago Convention. The conference suggested that market access should be viewed in the context of physical and environmental factors which may act as deterrents to participation.

The conference inevitably agreed in general that although the winds of change were blowing towards liberalization, it would be unrealistic to expect unrestricted market access on a global scale. Therefore, it was imperative to determine how the regulatory framework of air transport could be liberalized within a framework of safeguards that would ensure participation and fair competition. In this context, many delegates acknowledged the need for the introduction of a 'safety net', but were not entirely convinced of the efficacy of the narrow scope of a capacity freeze. In view of the desirability of liberalizing market access in the long term, the conference concluded that, in the long run, the underlying purpose of any future market access should be to optimize efficient and economical trade and communication links between States, and therefore any 'safety net' or safeguards for full market access must recognize the strategic interests of States to participate in international air transport. The conference viewed the 'safety net' mechanism as a good starting point for future work in ensuring fair competition.[14]

In following up the view of the ICAO Conference, the ICAO Air Transport Regulation Panel, at its Eighth Meeting in March 1996, recommended to the ICAO Council that a more meaningful enlargement of the scope of the 'safety net' was necessary, and suggested that a list of participation measures be formulated to cover a greater number of practical situations, to safeguard against an imbalance in market access.[15]

At its Ninth Meeting, held in Montreal, 10–14 February 1997, the Panel reaffirmed the conclusion of its Eighth Meeting that the incremental capacity and tariff variation measures were more suited to participation measures, and should be included in the safeguards. The Panel found a number of problems with constructing both the average cost line and the Discount Fare Index (DFI). It further reported that obtaining the correct cost data was difficult, and allocation of costs to particular city-pairs involved arbitrary decisions. There was a plethora of discount fares and conditions in the market, and modern yield management techniques and marginal pricing meant some seats on a flight could be sold below cost while still covering the overall cost by means of higher-priced fares; the measure also failed to take account of related incentives and inducements, such as frequent flyer bonus programmes. The Panel therefore concluded that, in view of the difficulties involved in its construction and implementation, neither the average cost line nor a DFI merited further development as a quantitative guideline to signal unfair competition.[16] The Panel recommended that States which wished to move towards liberalization of air services in their bilateral and multilateral relationships should consider reaching mutual agreements on the kinds of competitive practice by a carrier or carriers which would be regarded as unfair, using some or all of the following as signals for concern:

- if carriers charge fares and rates on routes at levels which are, in aggregate, too low to cover the costs of providing the services to which they relate;
- if carriers add excessive capacity or frequency of service;
- if the practices in question are sustained rather than temporary;
- if the practices have a serious economic effect on, or cause significant economic damage to, another carrier;
- if the practices reflect an apparent intent, or have the probable effect, of crippling, excluding or driving another carrier from the market;
- if a carrier's behaviour indicates an abuse of its dominant position on a route.[17]

This recommendation and others were relayed by the ICAO Secretary General in a State Letter[18] in June 1997 for States to consider in applying the recommendations in bilateral and multilateral air service arrangements and agreements.

## The Paradigm of WTO Competition Rules

The World Trade Organization, which is not an agency of the United Nations, may reach an understanding with ICAO to address the issue of air traffic rights at an appropriate time in the future.[19] It is therefore relevant to examine the competition rules of WTO.

The genesis of competition law in trade, and therefore of the WTO rules on competition, may well lie in the United Nations Conference on Trade and Employment, held in Havana in November 1947. This conference laid the ground for the International Trade Organization (ITO), the charter of which had two chapters relating to competition. Chapter III of the Charter of the International Trade Organization provided that no Member shall impose unreasonable or unjustifiable impediments that would preclude other members from obtaining, on equitable terms, facilities for economic development. Chapter V, which provided for the elimination of restrictive business practices, requires that each Member will take appropriate measures, individually or through collective involvement, to prevent business practices from affecting international trade thereby leading to restrained competition, limited access to markets or fostered monopolistic practices.[20] The ITO competition rules were embellished with controls over price-fixing and other forms of anti-competitive practices endemic to private enterprises. However, the functioning of ITO never attained fruition and these provisions remained academic. A second attempt was made by the United Nations Economic and Social Council (ECOSOC)[21] and this effort too was destined for failure. The third attempt, made by GATT in 1959, also failed to elicit a concrete proposal. Later, the Organization for Economic Cooperation and Development (OECD) established a system of exchange of information and a procedure for consultation of competition rules among enforcement authorities.

WTO was established on 1 January 1995, and will administer the new global trade rules agreed in the Uruguay Round which came into effect on the same day. These rules, which are the result of seven years of negotiations among member States of GATT, establish the rule of law in international trade – estimated at $5 trillion in 1995. The WTO involvement in world trade is estimated to raise the fiscal proportions of trade to $500 billion by the year 2005.[22] WTO has a membership of more than 150 States, and is far wider in scope than its predecessor, encompassing trade in services, the protection of intellectual property and investment. Unlike GATT – which was a provisional treaty serviced by an *ad hoc* secretariat, WTO is a fully-fledged international organization in its own right, and administers a unified package of agreements to which all member States are committed, serving as an effective watchdog over international trade and as a management consultant. Its economists are required to keep a close watch on the global economy, and provide studies on the main trade issues.

WTO considers that four fundamental factors are shaping the world economy:

1 the broader integration of the world economy;
2 widely divergent trends in developed and developing countries;
3 the spread of market-oriented reforms;
4 the end of the Cold War.[23]

On the subject of market-oriented reforms, WTO believes:

> If there are no rules in trade then the resulting anarchy will inevitably lead to conflict. International norms not only ensure freedom for economic agents to operate in their commercial interest across national frontiers. They also enhance the freedom of governments in their trade policy interventions, by defining the scope of actions permissible within the confines of international law. The behaviour of all governments becomes more predictable when all accept the rules of the game.[24]

Obviously, WTO feels that a coherent set of rules followed in conformity with the accepted norms of international law should govern competition. This does not necessarily mean that WTO is against free trade, it merely means that free trade has to be conducted according to accepted universal norms, and these norms have been explicitly laid out in the WTO Agreement. The trade-in-services portion of the agreement carries specific competition rules. One of the seminal principles of the agreement, enshrined in Article XVII, requires each member State to accord immediately and unconditionally to services and service suppliers of any other member treatment no less favourable than that it accords to like services and service suppliers of any other country.[25] Called the Most Favoured Nations treatment (MFN) clause, this provision *in limine* establishes common ground between trading partners, and creates certain parameters of activity for partners to follow. The MFN clause is the cornerstone of WTO's principles, and acts as the foundation for other WTO competition rules, in particular the elimination of all discrimination from the applicability of the agreement, as reflected in Article V, achieving the dual goal of eliminating existing discriminatory measures and prohibiting new or more discriminatory measures and provisions covering market access under Article XVI.

Transparency is another important concept in WTO's rules, so each member is required to publish promptly and, except in emergency situations, at the latest by the time of their entry into force, all relevant measures of general application which pertain to or affect the operation of the agreement.[26] There is also a requirement to publish international agreements pertaining to or affecting trade in services to which a member is a signatory.[27]

It is claimed that since the primary purpose of the WTO system is to promote trade among its members as liberally and fairly as possible while retaining the essence of non-discrimination in trade practices, the WTO system should guarantee a fair and equitable opportunity for market access by Members' enterprises to the national markets of other members. This is achieved mainly through the removal of governmental barriers as far as possible, and the convergence of national regulatory regimes such as those which relate to intellectual property rights.

One of the most serious challenges faced by WTO in this regard stems from claims by some States of 'unfair trade' by others, where the claimant States feel victimized by private business practices of other States' enterprises, such as anti-dumping, where the exporter is faced with the situation in which imports to its country are precluded by that country, with a view to compelling the consumption of the exporter's goods within the country of production. This practice often leads to price-hiking and protectionism within a market. The WTO rules therefore strive for fair and equal opportunity in competition, in the same way as the bilateral air services agreement.

One of the major considerations of WTO is the perceived incompatibility between countries' business practices and the global enforcement of uniform competition rules. There is an obvious link between business systems and corporate behaviour on the one hand, and competition rules (or the lack thereof) on the other. There is also probably a functional relationship between them, in that the competition rules partly reflect existing business systems and corporate behaviour (a regulatory system functions well only if it is fundamentally accepted). Also, business systems and corporate behaviour often adjust to, and take advantage of, the possibilities opened up by competition rules.

The disparities between what is permitted in one State but prohibited in another may constitute an impediment for enterprises which seek entry into another State's market. Some examples are cited below.

In the European Union, where governmental barriers such as tariffs and import restrictions have been removed, competition policy measures play a vital role in ensuring that the common market operates without hindrance by private restrictive business practices. In the EU, the role of competition policy has increased dramatically with the progressive integration of the common market.

In the Structural Impediment Initiative (SII) negotiated between the United States and Japan during 1989–1990, business customs and corporate behaviour were the major issues. The US Government claimed that restrictive business customs and corporate behaviour were the major impediments which restricted effective market access to the Japanese market by foreign enterprises. In accordance with the SII, both governments have agreed that stricter competition rules in Japan would increase access to the Japanese market for foreign enterprises by removing private restrictive business practices. A number of reforms of the Japanese Anti-monopoly Law resulted from this agreement, including an increase in the administrative surcharge, and criminal fines imposed on enterprises if they engage in cartels.[28] However, this functional relationship between competition rules, business systems and corporate behaviour – rooted as they are in cultural, economic and political traditions – may often limit what can be achieved by partial harmonization of competition rules. Differences in business systems and corporate behaviour are generally wide-ranging and complex, and the application of competition rules may fail to bridge the gap between the two elements. This notwithstanding, a vigorous enforcement of competition rules in trading nations may still be able to play a useful role in preparing common rules which could be made applicable to trading nations. The adoption of common rules of conduct for enterprises may well reduce undue imbalances in different business systems, and could pave the way for enterprises to compete for roles in markets of trading States outside their own marketplace.

WTO could also take into consideration the fact that as the globalization of national economies is achieved by removing governmental barriers to trade such as tariffs and import restrictions, new trade issues may arise, such as the possible incompatibility between different regulatory/business systems among trading States. Differences in domestic regulatory systems and in business customs and behaviours often emerge as barriers to transnational business activities. These differences may take the form of inconsistencies between technical standards, taxation, environmental protection measures, labour standards and other barriers which hamper enterprises seeking to engage in transboundary trade. Such differences obviously create disparity among the States concerned.

Extraterritoriality is one concept which could affect more than one jurisdiction in the application of domestic trade policy. The United States, the European Union and Germany are proponents of extraterritoriality, where competition rules are applied to the commercial conduct of foreign enterprises which trade in countries whose domestic markets are unaffected by such trade. In the seminal *Alcoa* case[29] of 1945, the US courts established the 'effects' doctrine, whereby commercial conduct carried out overseas but intended or calculated to affect the United States would be subject to US anti-trust laws. This doctrine has been followed by the courts in the United States with unfailing consistency, culminating in recent guidelines on international commercial operations adopted by the US Justice Department.[30] These guidelines contain principles that give the United States a wide scope of extraterritorial jurisdiction in respect of anti-competitive practices which foreign enterprises follow in countries outside the United States, provided such activities adversely affect the US market in that particular commercial activity. One of the most compelling features of this legislation is its emphasis on 'market access' for US businesses in foreign countries. A number of hypothetical examples incorporated in these guidelines reflect that the Department of Justice would challenge the conduct of foreign enterprises in foreign countries if such enterprises sought to hinder US enterprises from using opportunities of exportation of goods to a foreign country or investing in a foreign country.

In the famous *Woodpulp* case[31] the Court of Justice of the European Communities decided that EC competition rules apply to agreements of foreign enterprises which were entered into outside the European Community, as long as they were implemented within the common market.

One cannot deny that in this era of global economy, some degree of extraterritoriality in the enforcement of national competition rules is inevitable. A State would therefore be seen as being justified in applying its competition rules to the conduct of foreign enterprises abroad when such conduct affects its economy adversely, particularly where the State in which such conduct occurs has no competition rules or has no intention to prohibit such conduct. This phenomenon is easily reflected by transnational business entities which may engage in restrictive business practices in a 'twilight zone' where no State can fully exercise jurisdiction, and yet the harmful effects of such restrictive business practices may be felt in one or more States. To say that there should be no extraterritoriality of any kind in the application of competition rules would mean that such transnational entities could engage in anti-competitive conduct with impunity.

However, extraterritorial application of competition rules is a costly business, both for the enforcement agency and for the foreign defendants, and is often a second-best solution to the problem of transnational anti-competitive conduct. An extraterritorial application of competition rules is often not as effective as it would be if applied domestically. A State which attempts to apply its anti-competitive laws to a defendant enterprise located abroad could always face difficulties of enforcement and considerations of forum and jurisdiction. There may also be legislation in a foreign State which effectively precludes extraterritoriality.

The *Watchmakers of Switzerland* case[32] of 1955 exemplifies the essential commercial law principle of the United States, that applicability of anti-trust laws on foreign enterprises may often entail conflict with the legislation of other States. The court in this case held that a watch repair enterprise, conducted in the United States by two Swiss corporations, could be subjected to the domestic laws of the United States. The court further held that in order for a foreign corporation to be present within the jurisdiction of a court for purpose of service of process, there must be proof of continuous local activities and a demonstration that under all circumstances of the case the forum is not unfairly inconvenient. Even though the two Swiss entities had no property in the United States and did not carry out their activities directly (the business activities of the Swiss corporations were carried out by an US corporation in the United States), since the Swiss corporations determined the prices and terms of the business enterprise, the court further held that the Swiss corporations could be subjected to anti-trust statutes and tariff laws of the United States.[33]

In the watershed case of *Laker Airways Limited* v. *SABENA Belgian World Airlines*'[34] it was held that territorially based jurisdiction allows states in the United States to regulate the conduct or status of individuals or property physically situated within their territory, even if the effects of that conduct are felt outside their territory, and conduct outside a territory which is calculated to have a substantial effect on that territory may also be similarly regulated. It was also held that a state has jurisdiction to prescribe law governing conduct of its nationals, whether such conduct takes place inside or outside the territory of that state. Accordingly, the plaintiff – Laker Airways Ltd, a British corporation seeking remedy in the United States – whose activities in question took place in countries other than the United States, was deemed to be subject to US anti-trust legislation, on the basis that such activities gravely impaired US interests.[35] In deciding upon the contentious question of whether the law of the United Kingdom should apply to the plaintiff, the court compared the diametrically opposed anti-trust legislation of the United Kingdom and the United States, and held:

> We find no indication in either the statutory scheme or prior judicial precedent that jurisdiction (by the United States) should not be exercised. Legitimate United States interests in protecting consumers, providing for vindicating creditors' rights, and regulating economic consequences of those doing substantial business in our country are all advanced under the congressionally prescribed scheme. These are more than sufficient jurisdictional contacts under *United States* v. *Aluminium Co. of America*[36] and subsequent case law to support the exercise of prescriptive jurisdiction in this case.[37]

In the United States, the scope of anti-trust legislation and protection thereby extends to those persons who are either directly or indirectly affected adversely by anti-trust violations by third parties. The adverse effect on the plaintiff must be one that the laws were written to guard against. An example of this principle can be seen in the *Uranium antitrust litigation* of 1979,[38] where a business entity which indulged in a 'tying arrangement' to sell its product was considered a violation of anti-trust legislation.[39] The tie-in resulted in a drop in demand for the product concerned, giving way to a drop in prices, and adversely affecting competitors.

The role of WTO in extraterritoriality becomes significant when one considers the eventuality where the extraterritorial application of competition rules becomes too costly or burdensome on States concerned. WTO offers its own dispute-settlement process, and a framework within which members may seek positive comity and a certain convergence or harmonization of competition rules. There have been several proposals for convergence, the most practical and well thought out of which is the Draft International Antitrust Code (DIAC) proposed by a group of competition law scholars, the Munich Group. The DIAC proposes that there should be a comprehensive international anti-trust code covering the major areas of competition law, such as horizontal agreements, vertical agreements, mergers and acquisitions, and the relationship between competition law and industrial policies. It also recommends the establishment of an international anti-trust agency to share responsibility for enforcing international competition rules with national governments.

Ideas expressed in the DIAC are similar to Chapter V of the WTO Charter, giving the impression that the DIAC may well have been drafted along the lines of the schemes of international anti-trust enforcement contemplated by the WTO Charter. The DIAC remains the most ambitious of the proposals made in recent years.

Another attempt at international anti-trust regulation was made by a task force established by the American Bar Association which issued a report[40] advocating an agreement among States with regard to some basic principles on unlawfulness of cartels and unification of filing requirements under the merger laws of various States. The report contains a modest recommendation seeking partial harmonization through an agreement among States on basic principles and does not seek the establishment of a comprehensive international authority to enforce international rules.

Professor Eleanor Fox of New York University Law School has developed the idea of the DIAC further, proposing a scheme in which States would agree on 'a few fundamental world-linking principles' of competition policy, such as prohibition of cartels and positive comity.[41] Fox's proposal basically requires each State to achieve convergence of competition rules while adopting fundamental principles established in an international agreement.

The advantage of the DIAC approach to establishing an international code is that the rules and obligations of member States would be plain, and member States would have a clear goal. A similar approach has been made within the framework of the WTO, in the area of intellectual property. In the Agreement on Trade-related Intellectual Property Rights (TRIPs), principles with regard to the minimum protection of intellectual property rights and the enforcement of the rights under intellectual property laws are clearly laid out and Members are obliged to incorporate these principles in their domestic legislation, allowing for a grace period in the case of developing countries. In this respect, the DIAC approach has a precedent in the WTO system.

The disadvantage of a comprehensive international code approach may be that it lacks flexibility. It is often true that when comprehensive principles are already declared, member States have no choice but to accept them, and there may well be justification to consider principles other than those declared in the code which may be more feasible. There could even be the possibility of applying a different combination of such principles.

As mentioned earlier, TRIPs is an attempt to accomplish convergence of intellectual property laws of members. If TRIPs proves to be successful, then an international code approach may serve as a model for international competition laws. Since TRIPs was formally initiated only at the beginning of 1995, it is premature to predict the prospect of domestic implementation of such a scheme by members at present.

Yet another approach is the 'instalment' or 'evolutionary' approach, for which there is an important precedent in WTO. This precedent, which is adopted in GATS, provides for a general scheme for future negotiations on the liberalization of trade in services within the general principles of the Most Favoured Nation treatment and transparency clauses. At present, the liberalization of trade in services has been left to future negotiations, and GATS only provides for a scheme of negotiation, largely due to the fact that trade in services is a complex field involving complicated and diverse issues. However, it is encouraging that the GATS scheme could be drawn on by members if the need arises in the future.

As to the question whether the GATS negotiating scheme should be adopted with regard to international competition policy, the main consideration should be that if this is ever considered, it should coincide with consideration of a scheme within the WTO for negotiating international anti-trust principles. Negotiations may be on a total harmonization or a partial harmonization basis. Such an approach would have the advantage of the possible introduction by members of a variety of international competition agreements out of which they could select a suitable one. Also, if this approach is adopted, it would be important that members had a firm, declared commitment to promote competition law and policy, both internationally and domestically. As in GATS, it may also be necessary to establish a schedule within which negotiations should be carried out.

A declaration of the fundamental principles of competition would also be necessary. This declaration should contain analogous provisions to Most Favoured Nation treatment, national treatment and transparency. Consideration should also be given to prohibition in principle of cartels, resale price maintenance, boycotts and other measures. One should, at the same time, be cautious that given a wide variety of principles that are followed by members with regard to other areas such as mergers and acquisitions, vertical non-price restraint and predatory pricing, it may be feasible merely to declare general and abstract principles which require members to promote competition policy in such areas.

Although WTO is not the only forum in which a scheme of convergence of competition laws can be accommodated (the OECD, for example, would also be an appropriate forum, as would UNCTAD, whose work has demonstrated that it could accommodate this issue), there is a compelling reason for such a scheme to be considered under the WTO umbrella, due to the WTO's large membership. Among the more than 125 States which participated in the Uruguay Round leading to the establishment of the WTO Agreement, not all of them have competition laws, and many of them are still not ready for them. When an international competition code is drafted, it is logical to expect a certain degree of universality in its principles, and this could be accomplished on a wider scale given the WTO's membership.

Professor Petersmann has recommended[42] that an international competition code may be accommodated as an agreement of Annex 4 of the WTO Agreement, which contains optional agreements. Petersmann examines the idea of a smaller number of nations entering into such an agreement initially, such as the United States, Japan and members of the European Union, with Canada and Australia joining in. A grace period for developing States to join the agreement has also been addressed. He believes that, at least in the initial stage, an international competition code among a smaller number of members may work more effectively. According to Petersmann, such an agreement may address market access issues effectively.

Generally, it is felt that the inclusion of an international competition code in the WTO Agreement would have the advantage that co-ordination between competition policy and other policies embodied in WTO agreements such as TRIPs, the Safeguard Agreement and the Antidumping Agreement would be accomplished more easily than if a competition code was established separately from the WTO. Another envisaged advantage is that the dispute-settlement process incorporated in Annex 2 of the WTO Agreement could be used.

## Comments

Perhaps the only similarity between the competition rules of the air services agreement and the WTO competition rules is the insistence by both systems on the requirement of fair and equal opportunity. The current bilateral structure of the air services negotiations will remain in force as long as States consider subjectively the potential of air traffic that their carriers would have over others, by excluding others from given market segments. States can do this not only because of Article 6 of the Chicago Convention, but also by virtue of the underlying principle of sovereignty which legally entitles a State to prohibit a carrier from flying into or out of its territory without that State's permission. As the preceding discussion has revealed, the protectionist attitude that pervades commercial air transport is not limited to struggling carriers from developing nations, but also applies to mega-carriers which 'protect' what they believe to be a legitimate share of their market. Against this backdrop, the term 'market access' can only be used together with the word 'reciprocity'. The status quo in commercial aviation is therefore by no means consistent with the competition principles advocated by the WTO.

If the concept of market access for commercial aviation is to be consonant with the WTO competition rules, the first step the aviation community would have to take is to change its overall philosophy and consider all international air traffic as international property, rather than national property. This calls for a radical change in international policy on the subject of air traffic rights, where individual States would be considered as having an overall duty towards their citizens, and whereby citizens would be considered units of an international community of nations, rather than units of a particular State. In other words, States would represent citizens as nationals in an international society. The international traffic market would then be taken as a whole, and nations would adapt themselves to an extranational approach in sharing international air traffic. Once the extranational philosophy was in place, it would not be difficult to consider extraterritoriality in competition in a manner compatible with WTO competition rules, particularly in the context of the latter's emphasis on uniformity. The principles of transparency, Most Favoured Nation treatment and dispute-resolution could then all fall into place.

Although the above proposal may sound logical and workable, it cannot be denied that States have jealously guarded their historical rights to air traffic over the past fifty-one years, and would therefore be reluctant to embrace a multilateral approach and enter into open competition.

The most incontrovertible conclusion that one can arrive at on this issue is that the world is not ready for unlimited market access on a global scale. It is even doubtful whether a successful regional 'open skies' system could be viable at present between the regions of the world. Given this fact, one has inevitably to turn to safeguards to ensure balanced market access and participation by all carriers concerned.

Although global 'open skies' are not a possibility, this should not deter those who wish to liberalize market access bilaterally or plurilaterally. This principle, taken one more step forward, should encourage the timid and the less fortunate to enter into more liberalized arrangements with those who are capable of reaching the available market, provided the participation of the former category is ensured through suitable safeguards and mutually beneficial financial arrangements with the latter.

## Notes

1 Brian F. Havel, *In Search of Open Skies*, Deventer: Kluwer, 1997.
2 Id., at 1.
3 Id., at 2.
4 Joan M. Feldman, 'It's Still a Bilateral World', *Air Transport World*, 1997, No. 8, at 35.
5 Ibid.
6 'U.S. Anticipate Open-Skies Treaties between Asian Economies', *Aviation Daily*, 16 September 1997, at 475.
7 'Asia Warned over Open Skies Pact with U.S.', *Air Letter*, 30 September 1997, Vol. 13, No. 838, at 2.
8 'Japan Says U.S. Holds up Aviation Deal, *Air Letter*, 6 August 1997, Vol. 13, No. 800, at 1.
9 See 'European Market Liberalization Moves to Centre Stage', *Aviation Daily*, 8 January 1997, at 4.
10 'Honduras, El Salvador, Guatemala, Join Panama in Open Skies', *Aviation Daily*, 30 April 1997, at 185.
11 A basic market access right is defined as 'a conditional or limited right or privilege (usually set out in an international agreement) granted by one State to another State for use by an air carrier or carriers designated by that other State and may consist of agreed: geographic specifications of routes the air service may take; physical specifications regarding designation of an air carrier or carriers and how a designated carrier may employ aircraft; and physical and/or geographic specifications of what kind of traffic may be carried. Such rights in total determine the access of market access granted.' See *Manual on the Regulation of International Air Transport*, 1996, Doc. 9626 (1st edn), Montreal: ICAO, at 4.1–2.
12 Henri Wassenbergh, 'De-regulation of Competition in International Air Transport', *Air & Space Law*, 1996, Vol. XXI, No. 2, at 80.
13 Ibid.
14 *Report of the World-wide Air Transport Conference on International Air Transport Regulation, Present and Future, Montreal, 23 November–6 December 1994*, Doc. 9644, AT Conf/4, at 20.
15 See *Report of the Eighth Meeting of the Air Transport Regulation Panel, Montreal, 18–22 March 1996*, ATRP/8, at p. 6, para. 16.
16 See *Report of the Air Transport Regulation Panel, Ninth Meeting, Montreal, 10–14 February 1997*, ATRP/9.
17 Id., Recommendation ATRP/9-1, at 5.
18 SP 38/1-97/58, 27 June 1997.
19 See ICAO Assembly Working Paper A31-WP/224, P/57, 2/10/95, at 36.1:17.
20 For a detailed discussion of the ITO, see Robert R. Wilson, 'Proposed ITO Charter', *American Journal of International Law*, October 1947, Vol. 41, No. 4, 879, at 881 and 882.
21 UN Economic and Social Council, Official Records, 134th Session, 546th meeting, 5/SR.546, 11 September 1951. See also *Report of the Ad Hoc Committee on Restrictive Business Practices*, E/2380, 30 March 1953.
22 *Focus Newsletter*, Geneva: WTO, January/February 1995, at 2.
23 See speech of Peter D. Sutherland, Director General of WTO, World Trade Organization Press Release, PRESS/1, 95-0156, 27 January 1995, at 1.
24 Id., at p.5.
25 General Agreements on Tariffs and Trade, Multilateral Trade Negotiations Final Act Embodying the Results of the Uruguay Round of Trade Negotiations,

Marrakesh, 15 April 1994, *ILM*, 1994, Vol. 33, No. 1,125, Annex 1B, Part II, Article II.
26 Id., Article III.
27 Ibid.
28 See Matsushita, 'The Structural Impediments Initiative: An Example of Bilateral Trade Negotiation', *Michigan Journal of International Law*, Winter 1991, Vol. 12, No. 2, at 436–49.
29 *United States* v. *Aluminium Company of America* 148 F 2d 416 (2nd Cir. 1945).
30 See BNA, *Antitrust and Trade Regulation Report*, 20 October 1994, Vol. 67, No. 1,685, at 488 *et seq*.
31 *Ahalstrom Osakeyhtio* v. *Commission* (1988) ECR 5,193.
32 *United States* v. *The Watchmakers of Switzerland Information Center, Inc. et al.* 133 F Supp. 40.
33 Id., at 41.
34 731 F 2d 909 (1984).
35 Id., at 910.
36 148 F 2d 416 (2nd Cir. 1945).
37 731 F 2d 909 (1984) 945–6.
38 *In re Uranium Antitrust Litigation, Westinghouse Electric Corporation* v. *Rio Algom Ltd et al.*
39 A tying arrangement is the sale of one item (the tying product) only on condition that the buyer would take the second item (the tied product) from the same source. Such arrangements are *per se* unreasonable and violative of antitrust laws if the tie-in involves two distinct products, and the party has sufficient economic power in the tying market to impose significant restraints in the tied product market.
40 Washington: American Bar Association, 1976.
41 See generally Eleanor Fox, 'Antitrust, Trade and the 21st Century: Rounding the Circle', *Record of the Association of the Bar of the City of New York*, 1998, Vol. 1, at 535–88.
42 Petersmann, 'Proposals for Negotiating International Competition Rules in the GATT–WTO World Trade and Legal System', *Aussenwirtschaft*, 1994, Vol. 49, No. II/III, at 231–77.

# 4 Distribution of Computer Reservation Systems

## Introduction

The Internet is the product of the interconnection of computers and computer networks worldwide,[1] within which exists 'cyberspace' – a global medium of communication which links people, corporations, institutions and governments throughout the world.[2]

Cyberspace has attracted numerous illegal acts by its very nature, being intangible and elusive. Copyright infringement is by far the most prolific illegal activity in cyberspace, causing the loss of tens of billions of dollars' worth of revenue.[3] This prolific increase in copyright infringement on the Internet may be attributable to the ease with which one can copy work between computers.

Courts in common law jurisdictions are generally of the view that the copying of a work into a computer's random access memory (RAM), which takes place automatically when the work is transmitted from another computer, could *ipso facto* infringe the copyright owner's rights. *A fortiori*, a third party who accesses such information without permission, even though they might not know that the information had been decoded by a person other than the owner of the information, would also be guilty of the copyright infringement.

Against this backdrop, which offers cyber-offenders a great deal of room for manoeuvre, the airline's computer reservation system (CRS) remains vulnerable to copyright infringement. This chapter will examine the legal implications of copyright infringement relating to the CRS, and the liability of the offender. There will also be an initial discussion on the evolution of CRSs, in the airline industry and the regulatory regime which applies to CRSs.

## Computer Reservation Systems in Air Transport

On 25 June 1996, the Council of the International Civil Aviation Organization (ICAO)[4] adopted a revised Code of Conduct for the Regulation and Operation of Computer Reservation Systems. The revised Code replaced the version the ICAO Council adopted in 1991,[5] and took effect from 1 November 1996.

The revised Code addresses current market practices and recommendations made about CRSs at ICAO's World-wide Air Transport Conference held in 1994[6] that it should:

1 take into account developments in national and regional regulation, as well as technological and commercial development since the adoption of the previous Code in 1991;
2 reflect transparency, accessibility and non-discriminatory application;
3 include elements which give particular attention to booking data and display criteria;
4 maintain particular focus on the participation of developing countries, and address the retention of Article 10 of the present Code (Safeguards for Developing Countries);
5 seek compatibility with the General Agreement on Trade in Services, which also covers computer reservation systems.

The revision of the Code was also encouraged by ICAO Assembly Resolution A31-13 of the 31st Session of the ICAO Assembly in Montreal, 1995, which recognizes, *inter alia,* that computer reservation systems provide substantial benefit to both the air transport industry and to air transport users, and are also powerful marketing tools which play an important role in the distribution of market access. The Resolution requested the ICAO Council to review the form and content of the ICAO CRS Code of Conduct of 1991, and urged States to co-operate at bilateral, regional and inter-regional levels to implement the Code.

The main revisions contained in the revised Code of 1996 relate to the extension of its application to non-scheduled air services (such as charter services) and information systems such as the Internet. The Code also further strengthens the protection of privacy of personal data, ensures that passengers are informed of code-shared and non-scheduled flights, establishes more criteria for financial mechanisms relating to the charging of fees for services rendered, and prescribes more specific ways in which flight details can be displayed.

The revised Code does not require formal notification by States of its ratification or adherence, but ICAO has requested that each State advise ICAO if it decides to adhere to the principles laid out in the Code.

One of the main thrusts of the ICAO Code is applied through Article 3, which extends its scope of application to computer information systems which provide displays of schedules, space availability and tariffs of air carriers, without the capability of making reservations. Therefore, in general terms, although the Code is designed to regulate the distribution of international passenger air service products through CRSs, it is deemed to apply to computer systems such as the Internet in the area of computer information systems. Of course, the Code essentially and exclusively applies to computer reservation systems (systems of more than one airline), thus effectively precluding its applicability to the instance of a Web site of an airline accessed through the Internet, which displays only that airline's flight schedule details.

Article 3 brings to bear the significance of legal implications that may follow the use of the Internet for tracking airline schedules and flight information. The legal consequences of transborder data flows and the competition that would follow the possibility of non-airline private companies and organizations placing airline schedules in their own Web sites pose real challenges to legal reasoning. This chapter will address these issues in the light of international regulation of computer reservation systems.

## Regulatory Implications

### *The ICAO Code*

The 1996 ICAO Code of Conduct on CRSs has the support of a Council Resolution which highlights the fact that the Code is the result of comments by States at the 1994 ICAO World-wide Air Transport Conference, and urges all Contracting States to follow the Code, and notify the Secretary General when they decide to do so.[7]

The Code is based on three basic principles: transparency, accessibility and non-discrimination, with the aim of promoting and enforcing fair competition among airlines. Wherever possible, therefore, the Code adopts a common approach to encompass and accommodate the general thrust of national legislation and regulations, while assisting developing countries which may not have the infrastructure to strictly conform to all the provisions of the Code.

Article 4 of the Code requires States to ensure compliance of the provisions of the Code by air carriers, subscribers and system vendors. It is interesting to note that the Code is wide in application, defining a system vendor as any entity which operates or markets a CRS, bringing into its scope entities other than airlines which may market CRSs. These system vendors are allowed by the Code to provide CRS services in the territories in which they conduct business , on a non-discriminatory basis and consistent with any bilateral or multilateral agreements or arrangements to which relevant States are parties. The Code also requires States to treat all system vendors impartially with regard to their CRS activities in their territories. One of the ways in which this impartiality is achieved by the Code is by prescribing the free flow of information within the national boundaries of States.

A system vendor is required by the Code to permit any air carrier which is prepared to pay the vendor's fees to participate in the CRS system run by the system vendor. Article 5 of the Code – which contains this requirement – clearly precludes any possibility of a system vendor selecting its own airlines for its reservation system. The provision further prohibits a system vendor from imposing conditions on airlines so that the system vendor can only use a certain proportion of the airlines' activities in the CRS or use aspects on the system which are not directly related to the process of distributing a carrier's air transport products through the CRS. The system vendor cannot disseminate among participating carriers in the CRS services it offers, nor can it charge fees which are discriminatory. It cannot structure the CRS in a manner which leaves small air carriers at a disadvantage, nor unreasonably structure it so as not to relate to the service provided. Article 5 further requires the system vendor, *inter alia,* not to manipulate the information provided by carriers in any way that would result in information being displayed inaccurately or with discrimination.

Article 6 of the Code effectively precludes a system vendor from discriminating among subscribers, and, *inter alia,* from linking any commercial arrangements applying to the sale of air transport services of any carrier to the manner or form in which a subscriber may attempt to select air services through the system vendor's CRS. Article 7 strengthens this requirement by prescribing that the system vendor must make available a principal display or displays of airline schedules with consistency in terms of the schedules of all participating air carriers and all city-pair markets. Moreover, the system vendor cannot be influenced, directly or indirectly, by the type or identity of the carrier or airport when it places information on its CRS.

Article 7 also prescribes government criteria for the inclusion of information on CRSs. These include the types of flights a principal display should include, and their order (non-stop flights to be reflected first, followed by other direct flights not involving change of aircraft, etc.).

An air carrier which provides information to the system vendor must ensure that the information provided is accurate and does not misrepresent services. Article 8 which stipulates this also ensures that air carriers cannot unreasonably refuse to participate in CRSs available in their jurisdictions, nor refuse to provide information on schedules or tariffs to a system vendor when such information is vital to a subscriber. The air carrier cannot restrict the system vendor to using a particular CRS for sales of services of the carrier, particularly in instances where the carrier has a financial interest in the CRS concerned, or when such restrictions would adversely affect the CRS transaction between the system vendor and the air carrier concerned by unfairly favouring the CRS.

According to Article 10 of the Code, a subscriber or travel agent who passes on information contained in CRSs to a user has to abide by Article 7 of the Code. Furthermore, Article 10 provides that a subscriber may not manipulate information given by the CRS in order to misrepresent information to the air transport services user, nor make fictitious and invalid reservations through a CRS. The subscriber is also required, *inter alia,* to be responsible for the accuracy of the information they enter into the CRS.

Article 11 of the ICAO Code sets stringent standards for personal data privacy calling for States to take appropriate steps to ensure that all concerned with CRS operations safeguard the privacy of personal data, and do not release such data without the consent of the passenger concerned.

In the context of the above discussion, it is incontrovertible that the ICAO CRS Code also applies to any entity which provides information of two or more air carriers on the Internet, ensuring that the entity which provides such information does so within certain parameters which would not contravene transparency, accessibility and non-discrimination. The Code also implicitly permits an entity other than an airline to be a system vendor and provides CRS services to users, but does not address issues of competition which may ensue between the airlines which provide such services and other commercial entities whose principal business is not related to the provision of commercial air services, but which provide CRSs through the Internet.

Another issue which the ICAO CRS Code does not address – and indeed one which is not within the scope or mandate of the Code – is the question of transborder data flows and rights and liabilities of the service provider or systems vendor and service user in relation to access to information across national boundaries. This issue is largely one of private international law, and should be addressed outside the purview of the international regulatory regime now applicable to CRSs.

## Other CRS Codes

In October 1993, the Ministers of the European Commission adopted a CRS Code developed by the European Civil Aviation Conference (ECAC) for application to the European States which are members of ECAC. The ECAC CRS Code, which is generally not incompatible with the ICAO Code introduced later (and which, unlike the ECAC Code, is deemed to apply world-wide), does not rigidly restrict itself to intra-European application except in the context of CRSs and the sale or marketing of the air transport product within ECAC member States. Article 1 of the Code provides, *inter alia,* that system vendors need not necessarily be of European nationality. While Article 3 of the ECAC Code prohibits a system vendor from attaching any unreasonable conditions of contract to a participating carrier, the Code also explicitly provides in the same Article that a participating carrier need not be restricted to one CRS system, for displaying its flight schedules.

The ECAC Code of 1993 – which entered into force on 1 August 1994 – replaced an existing Code which had entered into force on 1 August 1989. It identifies a system vendor as any entity and its affiliates which is or are responsible for the operation or marketing of CRS, and provides in Article 5 that displays generated by a system vendor must be clear, non-discriminatory, and must not show inaccurate or misleading information as a result of the system vendor's or any other person's negligence. The provision also requires the system vendor to provide a principal display or displays for each individual transaction through its CRS, and specifies that a consumer shall have the right to have, on request, a principal display limited to scheduled or non-scheduled services.

The US CRS Rules, which were issued on 15 September 1992, are somewhat different in content from both the ICAO and ECAC CRS rules. First, the US rules provide for the operation of a computer reservation system comprising information on schedules, fares, and so on, offered by only one carrier or its affiliates in the United States. The US Code recognizes a system owner (rather than a system vendor), which is a carrier that holds 5 per cent or more of the equity of a system, that has one or more affiliates which hold such an equity interest, or that together with affiliates holds such an interest.

Therefore, the US Code, *in limine,* rules out the involvement of entities other than airlines in the provision of CRS services within the United States. Furthermore, the Code allows one carrier to operate a CRS service within the country. The overall principles of the Code are not incompatible with those of the ICAO and ECAC Codes, however, since the Code provides for fair and equal display of information without discrimination.

Part 255.9 of the US Code (Carrier-owned Computer Reservation Systems) allows the use of third-party computer hardware or software in conjunction with CRSs, except in instances where such use would adversely affect the integrity of the CRS system. Furthermore, the same provision adds that no system may prohibit the use of a CRS terminal to access directly any other system or database by the system. It also calls for a system to make available to developers of third-party hardware and software the non-proprietary system architecture specifications and other non-proprietary technical information needed to enable such developers to create products which would be compatible with the system.

The above provision seemingly leaves it open for entities other than airlines to offer CRS details of airline flight schedules through the owner airlines concerned. Of course, for these entities to make available to subscribers the facility of booking a seat on an airline, there must be agreement between the airline and the entity concerned, but the entity may find it easier to merely offer information of airline flight schedules on a composite CRS without giving the user the ability to pre-book.

The General Agreement on Trade in Services and Related Instruments (GATS) of the General Agreement on Tariffs and Trade (GATT), which now falls under the purview of the World Trade Organization, also encompasses computer reservation systems of air carriers.[8] The GATS Annex on Air Transport Services includes CRS within GATS, and defines CRSs as 'services provided by computerized systems that contain information about air carriers' schedules, availability, fares and fare rules, through which reservations can be made or tickets may be issued'. This definition also does not necessarily exclude any computerized system offering details of flight information and fares of airlines, thereby leaving room for any entity other than owner airlines to participate in CRSs over the Internet.

The cornerstone of GATS – the Most Favoured Nation treatment clause – applies to CRSs under GATS by virtue of Article II of the Agreement, which provides that each member State shall accord immediately and unconditionally to services and service suppliers of any other member State treatment no less favourable than that it accords to like services and service suppliers of any other country. Although this principle establishes a cohesive system of commercial unity and equity among WTO member States, the Most Favoured Nation principle is not sacrosanct, and can be obviated by an exemption filed under the Annex on Article II Exemptions. In practicality, therefore, while Most Favoured Nation treatment ensures that all WTO member States are treated on the same basis (or no worse than the member which gets the best deal) in terms of the exchange of information under CRSs, this treatment can be withdrawn from another by any member State by filing an exemption under the Agreement itself. Such exemptions are reviewed by the Council for Trade in Services when they exceed five years, and no exemption is expected under the Annex to exceed a period of ten years.

Article XIV of the GATS Agreement provides exceptions to the practices enshrined in the Agreement by providing that a member State may invoke the necessity to take measures on the grounds, *inter alia*, of public order or public morality, and to protect human, animal and plant life or health.

The GATS Agreement has incorporated some positive measures which are calculated to assist trade in relation to CRSs. Article IV encourages and assists the participation of developing countries by requiring the improvement of their access to distribution channels and information networks. The provision also calls for the strengthening of domestic services in developing countries, and provides for the liberalization of market access in sectors and modes of supply of export interest.

There are also other provisions in the GATS Agreement which establish general principles which may apply to the provision of CRS by entities other than air carriers. The principles of transparency which are enshrined in Article III call upon member States to provide information and publish, where necessary, the details of implementation of the Agreement. Article III *bis* precludes member States from requiring of other member States confidential information which, when disclosed, would hinder or impede law enforcement or otherwise be contrary to public interest. The provision also applies the requirement of confidentiality to preserve the commercial interests of parties, whether public or private.

### *Comments*

Twenty years ago, the commercial interests involved in the distribution of the airline product were autonomous and neutral. The travel agent around the corner would provide information on the best connection and fare. The agent frequently obtained this information by thumbing through a compendium of schedules provided neutrally by airlines and edited by a publishing house. After the best connection was identified, the agent used the ticket stock of the airline concerned (provided by the airline) and wrote a ticket for the passenger.

Today, this same process is accomplished by displaying the best connection on a computer screen and entering the necessary codes to make or confirm a reservation. Most airlines own the CRSs which operate in these agents' offices, and earn on average 40 per cent of the gross income on the provision of such automation facilities to the agent.

The automation revolution of the 1990s has led organizations to realize the vast earning potential of diversifying their information networks to commercial activities other than their principal businesses. It is not unrealistic, therefore, to expect some of these large commercial entities to seek to include airline products, which are so dependent on information. As a result, some airlines have shown apprehension at losing control over the distribution of their product.

## Legal Implications

The initial issue which emerges when the display of CRSs on the Internet is considered is the fact that a CRS system would be legally considered 'computer software' which is developed for a specific project and 'sold' as a packaged software to commercial entities operating their Web site on the Internet. Strictly speaking, the word 'sold' cannot be used in this context, since, legally, software is considered a species of intellectual property which would be protected by the law of copyright. Therefore, the operator or owners of CRS system software would license the right of another entity to use the computer program in question.

Fundamentally, one has to determine who has what legal right to use the information contained in a CRS accessed over the Internet. The starting point is when the initial database of the CRS owner connects to telecommunications distribution networks, which then deposit the information on the Internet after transgressing national borders with no delay and no need for physical conveyance to achieve the transfer. These information transfers cannot be placed in the control of a single nation, and bring to bear the inherent difficulties posed by the notion of 'tangibility'. This notion articulates the necessity for the application of copyright laws to a *tangible* medium of expression. Although in the incipient stage of copyright law enforcement, the notion of 'tangibility' was not applied to information existing in databases in electronic form, Section 102(a) of the US Copyright Act of 1976 provided the basis for electronic information to be considered tangible by stipulating that any original works of authorship, if they are in a medium of expression from which they can be perceived, reproduced or otherwise communicated, either directly or with the aid of a machine or device, can be treated as tangible information for the purpose of copyright laws.

The seminal US case of *Leon* v. *Pacific Telephone and Telegraph Co.*[9] established the principle of copyright infringement even in the instance where a person uses an original work of authorship to rearrange the contents of that work. The *Leon* decision is a relevant source for the area of copyright and CRSs, since it concerned the conversion of an alphabetical telephone directory into a numerical telephone directory, where the defendant rearranged the original information compiled by the plaintiff into a directory which ran in numerical succession of telephone numbers.

Although the *Leon* decision influenced subsequent decisions[10] that copyright laws should protect the labours of the initial author, not the substance of information in particular, the case of *Triangle Publications* v. *Sports Eye Inc.*[11] reflects the fact that copyright laws do not exclude the protection of organizations. In this instance, the court held that copyright extended to the method or form of expressing the data.[12]

The 1977 case of *New York Times Co.* v. *Roxbury Data Interface*[13] introduced a new dimension when the court held that protection could be afforded to rearranging or recompiling information, based on the 'doctrine of fair use'. Under the doctrine, the court held that the defendant's copying of entries from the *New York Times Index* for its own index was not a copyright infringement. The court based its reasoning on the fact that the defendant had made 'slight' use of the plaintiff's index in building his own, and as such, the defendant's act constituted 'fair use' of the plaintiff's index.

Other intellectual property rights protection which may affect the use of CRSs in the Internet can be derived from patent law, the laws relating to trade secrets and the laws of unfair competition. Of these, perhaps the most relevant to CRSs are the legal principles related to unfair competition,[14] which are intended to protect the fruits of one's labour from being misappropriated by another. Principles of unfair competition are usually contained in national laws, and are therefore applied on a common law basis.

The second consideration in the area of CRSs and their use over the Internet relates to transborder data flow and proprietary rights in information. In other words, who is the owner of a CRS which is displayed over the Internet? Is information on airline schedules provided at the international level an intellectual asset which belongs to the whole of humanity, and is it an international service provided to the world at large, and therefore a marketing tool? The obvious answer to this seems to lie in the fact that transborder data flow will have no value if there is no market value for the information provided. Consequently, a CRS system which appears on the Internet would obviously aim to accomplish airline reservations, and would therefore be a marketing tool. It could therefore be categorized as an international service and an asset which broadly belongs to the intellectual community.[15] However, one has to draw a line against piracy of information by unscrupulous entities, so new rules have been considered necessary, particularly when the authors of a system are in various locations, contributing information to a composite 'work product'.

In the event that an author's work is unjustly taken by an entity and displayed on the Internet, which is consequently accessed by the world at large, questions such as 'When or at what point is liability incurred by the entity?' and 'When is a contract concluded – at the point when the airline reservation is made across the boundaries of a State or country in which the CRS was put into the Internet, or at the input of information state?' become relevant. In 1980, two US professors addressed these questions and concluded:

> First, liability is incurred neither at input nor output, but within the computer network. Second, what protects the author or publisher is physical control of the text for there is no count of its reproduction once it is out of his hands. Third, a billing system operated by the network is necessary if fee collection is to be easy. Without that there is too much red tape in making arrangements for occasional access. Fourth, once the publisher's text has been read by someone else, evasion of royalty payments is quite easy because the reader can store the text in his computer and do whatever he wants with it. Computer copying is even easier than photocopying.[16]

These commentators also envisioned difficulty in controlling the display of information obtained through transborder data flows, and recognized that each time a person accesses such information anywhere in the world, the information would be used and would be tantamount to being printed. Their conclusions, which are valid to the area of CRSs on the Internet, were that a proper definition and delineation should be accomplished by the application of types of conduct leading to computer fraud, abuse, negligence and breach of contract. It was their view that mechanisms through which such grievances may be redressed would then logically follow.[17]

## Comments

The above vision is the starting point for the introduction and implementation of a suitable legal regime concerning the use of CRSs on a global basis through the Internet, but this will depend on definitions and delineation of legal principles with regard to such practices as computer fraud and abuse being set in place. First, measures must be taken at national level, where States could follow the broad principles of the ICAO CRS Code, on the basis that ICAO is the acknowledged world regulator of international civil aviation, and has a mandate under Articles 44(a), (d) and (e) of the Chicago Convention. The first provision gives ICAO a mandate to ensure the safe and orderly growth of international civil aviation throughout the world; the second calls upon ICAO to meet the needs of the peoples of the world for safe, regular, efficient and economical air transport, and the third provision requires ICAO to ensure the prevention of economic waste caused by unreasonable competition.

Taking a cue from ICAO's overall mandate, therefore, it is not difficult to conclude that the ICAO CRS Code is the fundamental postulate for States to draft and implement their own laws in order to prevent and punish computer fraud, abuse, negligence and breach of contract in instances such as those emerging from the use of CRSs on the Internet. For instance, States could give teeth to Article 11 of the ICAO Code, which calls for appropriate measures by States to ensure that all parties involved in CRS operations safeguard the privacy of personal data by exercising their authority over air carriers, systems vendors and subscribers to make sure that data on CRSs are protected.

Undoubtedly, the single most important consideration that States have to address when drafting local legislation on the Internet is the nature of the elements involved. The first important issue is that the Internet is not a single, tangible element, but a 'giant network which interconnects innumerable smaller groups of linked computer networks'.[18] This principle must be linked with the very notion of intellectual property, which, as discussed earlier, relates to an original work of authorship which can be perceived, reproduced or otherwise communicated either directly or with the aid of a machine or device. Therefore, intellectual property rights stem from the originality of a document and its position in cyberspace. Legislators should also bear in mind that long before the computer was introduced in commercial scales such as through the Internet, intellectual property law evolved through the common law of torts and legislation. Therefore, it follows that, once a plaintiff successfully establishes a *prima facie* case of intellectual property rights infringement, they would be entitled to damages and compensation for lost income and profits. Also, when one attempts to or actually infringes copyright, the property taken need not necessarily have been protected by a copyright notice. The infringement must be calculated to obtain commercial advantage or financial gain for the person who perpetrates the act.

Perhaps the greatest challenge for both international and national legislators on the complex issues of the effect of cyberspace on intellectual property and the application of principles of the laws of contract to activities in cyberspace (for purposes of establishing jurisdiction) is that cyberspace has no boundaries, and is therefore impervious to national legislation. For instance, would State A be able to legislate, or would a court in that State be able to decide on the contractual rights of a person who makes an airline computer reservation in State A on a CRS which originated in State B? If such a consideration was to be addressed within the same country, matters would be much more simple, as in the case of *US* v. *Thomas*,[19] in which a Tennessee court convicted the plaintiffs, who had operated a bulletin board carrying lewd images from California. Although the plaintiffs' activity was not an offence under the laws of California, it was an offence under Tennessee law. One could conclude from this decision that while this common law principle may be workable on an inter-state basis, it remains to be seen whether, on an international basis, punishment for a computer offence would be enforceable in a jurisdiction if the origin of the offence (such as the input of stolen CRS material) lay elsewhere.

The *Thomas* decision in the United States does not conclusively establish that jurisdictional questions may be resolved only within states of the same country. Since the subject of offences committed in cyberspace or civil liability incurred in activities therein are fundamentally grounded on the laws of tort and contract at common law, it is possible for States to introduce national legislation demarcating jurisdiction to be applicable in such instances.

The above discussion shows that the fundamental approach towards a common law legislative structure to regulate cross-border cyberspace activity can be derived from existing legal principles relating to non-cyberspace activity. Therefore, it would not be difficult for States of common law jurisdictions to enact appropriate legislation, should they choose to do so.

## Notes

1 See *ACLU* v. *Reno* 929 F Supp. 824, at 830 (ED Pa 1996).
2 Id. At 831. The term 'cyberspace' was coined by William Gibson in his 1984 novel *Neuromancer*.
3 See Marc S. Friedman et al., 'Infojacking: Crimes on the Information Superhighway', *NJLJ*, 1995, Vol. 140, 658, at 658.
4 The International Civil Aviation Organization is a specialized agency of the United Nations which is responsible for the regulation of international civil aviation world-wide. ICAO comprises a membership of 185 States.
5 See R.I.R. Abeyratne, *Legal and Regulatory Issues of Computer Reservation Systems and Code Sharing Agreements in Air Transport*, Paris: Editions Frontière, 1995.
6 For a detailed discussion of the conference see R.I.R. Abeyratne, 'The Worldwide Air Transport Conference and Air Traffic Rights – A Commentary', *European Transport Law*, 1995, Vol. XXX, No. 2, 1 at 131–47.
7 Attachment A to State Letter EC 2/28-96/74. The State Letter communicated to Contracting States the 1996 ICAO CRS Code of Conduct and the Council Resolution.
8 Other areas included in the Annex are aircraft repair and maintenance services and the selling and marketing of air transport services.
9 91 F 2d 484 (9th Cir. 1937).
10 *National Business Lits* v. *Dun and Bradstreet Inc.*, 552 F Supp. 89 (ND Ill. 1982), *Dow Jones & Company, Inc.* v. *Board of Trade of the City of Chicago*, 546 F Supp. 113 (SDNY 1982).

11 415 F Supp. 682 (ED Pa 1976).
12 Id., at 685–6.
13 434 F Supp. 217 (DNJ 1977).
14 Patent law relates to mechanical devices and trade secrets relate to formulae or information which gives the author a competitive edge over other competitors. Since the CRS is a 'service' provided by airlines, it may not strictly conform to the definition of 'trade secret'.
15 See Lemoine, 'Transborder Data Flows', *Information Systems Magazine,* Spring 1979, at 30.
16 Pool and Solomon, 'Intellectual Property and Transborder Data Flows', *Stan. Journal of International Law,* 1943, Vol. 16, 114, at 121.
17 Id., at 123, 133 and 137–8.
18 See *ACLU* v. *Reno,* 929 F Supp. 824, at 830 (ED Pa 1996).
19 839 F Supp. 1,552.

# 5 Airline Ticket Auctions on the Internet

## Introduction

Auctions on the Internet are the latest online trend and the trendiest are the airfare auctions held on the World Wide Web. At the time of writing, a round trip ticket from Montreal to Toronto was being auctioned with the starting price at $99.[1] The person seeking to purchase a seat on a flight names the price they would be prepared to pay for an airline ticket, and the airline tries to match the price and sell a seat on its flights with empty seats. The higher one bids, the better the likelihood of securing a seat. The server on the Internet receives a nominal fee if a deal is struck between the person seeking a seat on an airline and the airline which offers one at the price quoted.

The phenomenal growth of activity through the Internet leaves no room for doubt that commercial competition has been profoundly influenced by cyber-contracts. The Internet has not only changed the way the world conducts business, but has also become the most prolific medium of commercial activity, reflected in the fact that by the year 2002, businesses will buy and sell $327 billion worth of goods over the Internet, with the current trend of traffic on the Internet doubling every 100 days.[2]

Cyber-contracts are commonly called 'click-wrap' agreements[3] and are formed over the Internet in their entirety. The essence of a 'click-wrap' agreement is that when offerees visit the Web site of a person who has advertised his goods for sale at a given price and agrees to buy those goods, indicating their assent to be bound by the terms of the offeror or person who offers to sell goods on the Internet, a contract is concluded. There is no paper exchange, nor is there the need for the signature of either parties to the contract.[4]

In the case of airline seat auctions, the position becomes reversed, in that the person who offers becomes the visitor to the Web site. The airline merely posts an initial bidding price for a given sector of travel on its Web site, thus making to the world at large what is called an 'invitation to treat' at contract law, and it is open to anyone to offer to buy the product at a nominated price. Once the offer is made, the airline may accept it, thus becoming the offeree or acceptor.

## Nature of the Contract

Usually, a contract is concluded when, in response to an offer made by an offeror, the offeree indicates acceptance to the offeror. In cases of simultaneous communication of the offer and acceptance made face-to-face by the offeror and offeree, the essentials of a contract are clear. However, when parties are not in close proximity to each other and communicate their dealings over a telecommunications medium, the process may become slightly more complicated, in that it may not always be clear as to what constitutes an offer or an acceptance. In such instances, it largely becomes a matter of interpretation as to whether both the offeror and the offeree had the intent to conclude the contract.

The element of intention to contract and to conclude the process on the part of both the offeror and offeree is initial to the formation of the contract. Courts have insisted that proof of an offer to enter into legal relations upon definite terms must be followed by the production of evidence from which the courts may infer an intention by the offeree to accept that offer. Thus the statements made by the parties in the process of negotiations are of extreme importance in the determination of a concluded contract. The 1840 case of *Hyde* v. *Wrench*[5] offers the seminal principle that a series of communications from either party may impinge on an original offer. In the *Hyde* case, the defendant, on 6 June, offered to sell an estate to the plaintiff for £1,000. On 8 June, in reply, the plaintiff made an offer of £950, which was refused by the defendant on 27 June. However, on 29 June, the plaintiff wrote to the defendant that he was now willing to pay £1,000.

The importance of the *Hyde* decision lies in the fact that the court held that no contract existed. The plaintiff had, by rejecting the offer made on 6 June, precluded himself from reviving the offer later. In other words, once an offer is rejected by the offeree, they cannot go on the basis that the offer would still stand in its original form. When this principle is applied to an auction situation where the airline is offering to consider bids over the Internet from the public, any offer made by a member of the public for a seat on a flight cannot be rejected by the airline and later revived.

Of course, a counter-offer situation is different, where an airline nominates an alternative sum as acceptable. For example, if A offers over the Internet $100 as the price he would pay for a seat from Montreal to Toronto, the airline concerned can counter-offer the seat at $125, thus making itself the offeror. Unlike in the *Hyde* case, here there is no outright rejection of the offer.

In the instance of an auction carried out over the Internet, the primary issue at stake in the determination of a contract is whether the parties intended the contract to be concluded. For instance, if a person offers a certain price to the airline over the Internet and the airline gives them a reference number, the allocation of that number may not necessarily indicate acceptance of the offer by the airline. The 1989 US case of *Corinthian Pharmaceutical Systems Inc.* v. *Lederle Laboratories*[6] is a good analogy. In the *Corinthian* case, a person dealing in medicinal drugs on a wholesale basis ordered a consignment of drugs through a computerized telephone ordering system. The order was placed strategically a day before a price increase was to take effect. The wholesaler ordered through the manufacturer's automated telephone order system and, after the order message was placed by him, he was allocated a 'tracking number' by the manufacturer's computer system. There was absolutely no human interaction in the transaction. Subsequently, when the manufacturer refused to sell the consignment of drugs as ordered by the wholesaler at the pre-increase price as ordered, the court held with the manufacturer's position that the tracking number issued by the manufacturer's computer was not an acceptance of the offer, but merely an acknowledgement of the receipt of the order or offer in contractual law terms. The court concluded that no contract had been concluded, and the wholesaler was denied purchase of the goods at the lower price.

The early case of *Henkle* v. *Pape*[7] brings out another difficulty that might arise from contracts transacted through the Internet. The *Henkle* case, decided in 1870, concerned a transaction carried out through telegraphic messages for the sale of up to fifty rifles. The offeror sent the offeree a telegraphic message offering to buy three rifles, but the message was transcripted to the offeree as 'the' instead of 'three' rifles. Accordingly, the offeree held the offeror liable for the purchase of all fifty rifles. The court held that the offeror could not be held liable for the error of the telegraph clerk who had wrongly deciphered the message, and therefore no contract had been concluded.[8]

The 1870 principle of the *Henkle* decision still holds water in the instance of a contract transacted through the Internet, in that the latter instance, like the *Henkle* case, involves a contract negotiated through electronic means where there is always the risk that messages intending to create contractual obligations may not reach their destination, or even perhaps more ominously, are received by the recipient in a form other than the one sent originally by the sender. In the seminal Canadian case of *Kinghorne* v. *The Montreal Telegraph Co.*[9] decided in 1859, the court subsumed the reasons behind the determination of an electronic contract which may still apply:

> We must look, I think, in the case of each communication, at the papers delivered by the party who sent the message, not at the transcript of the message taken through the wire at the other end of the wire, with all the chances of mistakes in apprehending and noting the signals, and in transcribing for delivery.[10]

Of course, compared to early telegraph systems, which caused numerous problems, the Internet is more reliable, and errors such as those encountered in the *Henkle* and *Kinghorne* cases may not be commonplace. However, there is still the possibility of garbled messages flowing through the Internet, in which circumstances courts would have no hesitation in determining the real intent of the parties to conclude a contract as the preliminary issue.

The above concerns are by no means intended to suggest that contracts through the Internet are questionable in general terms. In fact, current computer-based technologies are more effective than earlier technologies at assisting parties to the contract to conclude their agreement unambiguously. For example, electronic data interchange (EDI) as a commercial medium has evolved in Canada to the extent that the EDI Council of Canada's Model TPA (Trading Partner Agreement) encourages parties to be extremely precise in identifying particular messages as constituting an order (or offer) by introducing a two-phased process: the first using a functional acknowledgement of the offer (such as the tracking number in the *Corinthian* case), and the second using a purchase order acknowledgment.

## Time and Place of Contract

When parties sign a contract simultaneously in a face-to-face setting, there is no doubt as to when and where the contract comes into being. However, it is often not a trivial legal task to determine when and where, when either an offer, or an acceptance, or both, are sent by telegraph, telex, fax, EDI, e-mail or via the Internet, or are communicated by telephone. The uncertainty began even before the advent of the telegraph, with the mail delivery system.

The general contract law principle is that an offer is not considered accepted until the acceptance of the offer is received by the offeror. In England in the nineteenth century, an exception to this rule was developed by judges for offers and acceptances sent by the mail. The so-called 'post box rule' or 'expedition theory' prescribes that where an offer is made in the mail, the contract takes effect immediately at the time acceptance is posted in the mail (rather than when the acceptance is actually received by the offeror) where use of the mail is reasonable in the circumstances or expressly contemplated by the parties. This rule effectively precludes the need to hold the offeree responsible for delays in communications, and places the burden of uncertainly of the waiting period on the offeror: the offeror does not know that it has earlier concluded a binding contract until it receives the offeree's acceptance in the mail, whereas the offeree knows that the contract came into existence the moment they posted its reply letter. Shifting this risk to the offeror, and giving the concomitant assurance to the offeree, was reasonable because of the increased reliability of the Royal Mail in the 1800s, to the point where multiple deliveries a day in larger urban centres were the norm. The expedition theory is a good example of a legal doctrine being firmly grounded in the communication environment and commercial processes of its day.

As the telegraph, telephone and other new communications technology evolved into widespread use, cases established principles as to when and where contracts were concluded. In *Carow Towing*, an early Canadian case, courts held that a contract entered into by telephone should be treated like a letter and should follow the expedition theory, with acceptance occurring at the place the acceptance is spoken, and not where the offeror hears the acceptance.[11] By contrast, in the *Entores* case,[12] a later British decision, Lord Denning concluded that for simultaneous communications like the telephone, the place where the contract is concluded is where the offeror hears the acceptance, and thus, if the line goes dead during the telephone conversation, the onus is upon the offeree to call back the offeror to ensure the words of acceptance had been communicated to the offeror. Subsequent cases in Canada have followed the decision in *Entores* rather than the approach in *Carow Towing*,[13] with the exception of Quebec, where, until recently, the preponderance of case law has followed the principle that telephone contracts arise when and where the offeree speaks their acceptance;[14] since the enactment of the current Civil Code of Quebec in January 1994, Article 1387 explicitly provides that in respect of telephone contracts, acceptance occurs when and where the acceptance is received. It is interesting to note that the *Entores* decision was also followed in two fax cases, one in Nova Scotia[15] and one in New Zealand,[16] where each held that a contract made by fax arises when the offeror receives by fax the acceptance of the offered.

Courts in the *Entores* case also held that telex technology results in instantaneous communications, with the result that acceptance occurs when the message is received by the offeror. This approach was confirmed in a decision by the House of Lords in the *Brinkibon* case.[17]

In this case, the court held that although telex communications should be categorized as simultaneous, in each case the specific constituent elements and factors in the communications system concerned need to be carefully considered:

> The senders and recipients may not be the principals to the contemplated contract. They may be servants or agents with limited authority. The message may not reach, or be intended to reach, the designated recipient immediately; messages may be sent out of office hours, or at night, with the intention, or on the assumption, that they will be read at a later time. There may be some error or default at the recipient's end which prevents receipt at the time contemplated and believed in by the sender. The message may have been sent and/or received through machines operated by third persons. And many other variations may occur. No universal rule can cover all such cases; they must be resolved by reference to the intentions of the parties, by sound business practice and in some cases by a judgment where the risks should lie.[18]

The recognition of the above facts in the *Brinkibon* case raises a number of emerging issues in respect of EDI, e-mail, and Internet communications. Certain EDI transmissions, for example, will fall into the simultaneous communications category. Much of EDI is effected not between the trading principals, however, but by use of intermediaries, so-called value-added networks (VAN) or service providers. An EDI message could be routed through the message sender's VAN, then through the recipient's VAN, and finally to the recipient. Similarly, e-mail messages over the Internet may be routed to electronic mailboxes from which the recipient then has to download them. In such instances, it may be more difficult to conclude that the simultaneous communication rules should apply. Also, it may be difficult to determine when exactly an electronic message arrives at the recipient's location for purposes of being recognized as legally effective. For instance, an early British case held that a letter sent in a sealed envelope is not considered received until it is opened by the addressee personally.[19] Whether such a rule should apply in the case of e-mail or whether an e-mail message should be deemed received when it is available to be viewed by the intended recipient, regardless of the time at which the recipient actually reads the message, is a moot point. Another question is when should a telex or fax be deemed to have arrived at a workplace? In one case,[20] the answer pointed to when the message was received by the recipient's machine (on a Friday after business hours, and not three days later on a Monday morning when the person actually read the telex).

Given these ambiguities, prudent users of electronic commerce should try to avoid having to refer these issues to a judge by providing, in their EDI Trading Partner Agreement or other similar document, precisely what electronic message must be received by which computer (i.e., the recipient's or the recipient's VAN) in order for a contract to arise, thereby bringing clarity to the questions of when and where the electronic contract arose. As to the 'where' question, the parties to the TPA would be well advised to select a governing law in advance, and to make sure the VAN agreements contain the same jurisdiction, so that there is no question which law would apply if it were ever considered necessary to resort to adjudication. This is particularly true for EDI and Internet transactions, where each trading partner's VAN, or Internet service provider, may be in a jurisdiction different from the customer, and therefore the laws of four different jurisdictions may apply if the parties remain silent on the governing law question. In such circumstances, as Lord Denning observed in the *Entores* case concerning two parties in different jurisdictions, the problems arise since the laws of the respective jurisdictions are different. Therefore, predicting a court's probable response is difficult, given that the court will invariably try to seek the most just remedy under the circumstances, but in some cases this is truly a difficult task. An example is the court's commentary in the *Export Packers* case, where the judge recommended that the various rules developed by the law over the years, such as the simultaneous communication rule in the *Entores* case, should not be applied in a rigid fashion:

> When the common law rules relating to offer and acceptance were under development the telephone did not exist. At that time agreements were made by two or more persons getting together and reaching a common understanding. As the postal system came into being elaborate rules were made by the courts covering the mechanics of reaching a bargain by mail. Today a person ordinarily resident in British Columbia may telephone from Japan where he is on a business trip to a person ordinarily resident in Ontario but who is also then visiting Italy. They may agree to the same kind of contract which is the subject-matter of this writ. It does not necessarily follow the place where the contract was made was Japan and that Japanese law governs its interpretation. Alternatively, it would be hard to argue the place where the contract was made was Italy and the law of that country ought to apply to its interpretation.[21]

This dictum clearly confirms the benefit accrued to users of electronic commerce in crafting their own rules for dealing with issues of formation of contract. Making commercial relationships more secure and predictable through contract, can be a costly and time-consuming exercise, however. Therefore, this may be an area for law reform. In the United States, the National Conference of Commissioners of

Uniform State Law are already working towards establishing new rules under the Uniform Commercial Code that would take the view that Internet communications are instantaneous in nature, and that a contract therefore comes into existence when the sender of the offer receives an electronic message signifying acceptance. However, this does not answer the question as to when the acceptance is effective if the offeror was not present before the computer – in other words, does receipt require a human intervention and acknowledgement. In determining this question, the following should be observed:

- the purpose and function of the rule;
- who would be prejudiced by a particular holding;
- the reasonable expectations of the parties;
- on whom is it reasonable to place a burden for helping to 'fix' the system if indeed it needs it.

## Issues of Jurisdiction

Perhaps the single most important issue in cyber-contracts is that which pertains to jurisdiction. Given the World Wide Web and its global application, the most compelling question in this regard would pertain to the transboundary applicability of an Internet contract. In this regard, the most convenient analogy comes from the two jurisdictions of Canada and the United States. Would an offeror in Canada, who offers $500 over the Internet for a round trip between Toronto and Miami, be able to enforce an auction agreement against a US airline at its home base in Florida? In a case decided in 1952[22] in Canada, where the plaintiff brought a case to the Ontario High Court against a US radio station which was allegedly broadcasting libellous statements which could be heard over the air waves in Canada from across the border, the defendant radio station brought up a motion of dismissal, alleging that the Ontario Court in Canada had no jurisdiction to hear a case against a party to the action which was an enterprise based in the United States. The court disagreed, and held:

> A person may utter all the defamatory words he wishes without incurring any civil liability unless they are heard and understood by a third person. I think it a 'startling proposition' to say that one may, while standing south of the border or cruising in an aeroplane south of the border, through the medium of modern sound amplification, utter defamatory matter which is heard in a Province in Canada north of the border, and not be said to have published a slander in the Province in which it is heard and understood. I cannot see what difference it makes whether the person is made to understand by means of

> the written word, sound-waves or ether-waves in so far as the matter of proof of publication is concerned. The tort consists in making a third person understand actionable defamatory matter.[23]

In the more recent case of *Pindling* v. *National Broadcasting Corporation*[24] in respect of a US television broadcast received in Canada, the Ontario High Court held that the Prime Minister of the Bahamas was entitled to bring the case to Canada, instead of the United States. The *Pindling* decision illustrates well the principle of 'forum shopping' which can be culled from the television context and be held applicable to the analogous situation of a contract transacted over the Internet.

The above principle may be derogated only in an instance where the court seized of the case could invoke the principle of 'forum non convenience', which allows the transfer of a suit from an originally filed jurisdiction to some other jurisdiction which is better placed to hear the case concerned. In the 1996 case of *National Bank of Canada* v. *Clifford Chance*,[25] the Canadian courts, which were charged with hearing a case where a Toronto based firm had contracted with a law firm in the United Kingdom, transferred the case to the United Kingdom although the contract was concluded in Toronto, on the grounds that the contract concerned a UK-based project and the legal advice obtained had been UK law given by lawyers in the United Kingdom. Based on the *Clifford Chance* principle, it would not be unusual for a common law court to determine that in an auction for an airline seat, where the offer emanates from, say, Canada over the Internet for a seat leaving the United Kingdom on a UK-based carrier, the applicable jurisdiction would lie with the courts in the United Kingdom, although the contract itself may have been concluded in Canada.

There is a dichotomy in the judicial thinking with regard to cases involving contracts concluded over the Internet. On the one hand, courts are refusing to bring persons into a jurisdiction purely because they contracted with a business entity which is based in that jurisdiction. This approach is illustrated by the 1994 US decision in the case of *Pres-Kap, Inc.* v. *System One, Direct Access Inc.*,[26] where the court refused to grant jurisdiction to Florida, where a resident in New York had used a Florida-based online network information service merely to gain access to a database. Similarly, the court in the famous 1997 *SunAmerica* case[27] refused to find jurisdiction in a trademark case solely on the basis of the defendant's operation of a general access Web site:

> Plaintiffs ask this Court to hold that any defendant who advertises nationally or on the Internet is subject to its jurisdiction. It cannot plausibly be argued that any defendant who advertises nationally could expect to be hailed into Court in *any* state, for a cause of action that does not relate to the advertisements. Such general advertising is

> not the type of 'purposeful activity related to the forum that would make the exercise of jurisdiction fair, just or reasonable.'[28]

Similarly, in the 1997 case of *Hearst Corporation* v. *Goldberger*,[29] where the defendant operated a passive general-access Web site, the courts were of the view that to open world-wide jurisdiction merely because the Internet offered world-wide access would be iniquitous:

> Where, as here, the defendant has not contracted to sell or actually sold any goods or services to New Yorkers, a finding of personal jurisdiction in New York based on an Internet website would mean that there would be nationwide (indeed, worldwide) personal jurisdiction over anyone and everyone who establishes an Internet website. Such nationwide jurisdiction is not consistent with traditional personal jurisdiction case law nor acceptable to the Court as a matter of policy.[30]

The *Hearst Corporation* decision seems to have followed the observation of a case[31] decided one year earlier, where the court held:

> Because the Web enables easy worldwide access, allowing computer interaction via the Web to supply sufficient contacts to establish jurisdiction would eviscerate the personal jurisdiction requirement as it currently exists; the Court is not willing to take this step. Thus, the fact that Fallon has a Web site used by Californians cannot establish jurisdiction by itself.[32]

The second line of judicial thinking is the converse to the above approach, where courts have imputed to the non-resident defendant responsibility for complexities brought about the Internet in its universal applicability. Therefore, in *Compuserv Incorporated* v. *Patterson*,[33] the courts held a Texas-based computer programmer legally responsible for his Ohio-based computer network online service, and found him to be under Ohio law. Although the defendant had never visited Ohio, he was nevertheless found to be subject to Ohio law on the basis that an electronic contract had been concluded in Ohio, where the defendant was distributing his product.

The principle of universal application of jurisdiction has been invoked in other instances, where courts have accepted jurisdiction on the basis of sales made to customers through the defendant's Web site,[34] or based on soliciting donations,[35] or based on subscribers signed up by the defendant for services delivered over the Internet,[36] or for having follow-on contacts, negotiations and other dealings in addition to, and often as a result of, the initial Internet-based communication.[37] The common thread which runs through the fabric of judicial thinking in this regard is that parties who avail themselves of technology in order to do business in a distant place should not then be able to escape that place's legal jurisdiction. These cases are all-embracing, from contract breach claims to tort, including trade libel; in several cases, courts have even found jurisdiction in trademark infringement matters merely on the basis of a defendant's general access Web site,[38] or linking to a national ATM network through a telephone line indirectly through an independent data processor in a third state.[39]

An overall evaluation of the US civil cases discussed above reflects that while the general trend is for courts to assert jurisdiction over non-residents based on their Internet activities, there are still a few situations where some courts may not apply jurisdiction.

Although the choice of forum may extend universally, it does not necessarily mean that enforcement from a judgment would automatically follow. In the case of *Bachchan* v. *India Abroad Publications Incorporated*,[40] the plaintiff, who was a national of India who had won the right to have his case heard in the United Kingdom, was unable to enforce judgment in New York. The New York courts held that the UK law applicable to the case did not accord with US law, and therefore the decision could not be recognized as enforceable in the United States.

## Comments

Operators of Web sites must exercise caution in order to avoid being hauled into any jurisdiction in the event of adjudication and airlines which auction their seats over the Internet are no exception. The first thing airlines must address is the need to establish with their possible clients over the Internet an explicit agreement prescribing applicable or governing law with regard to the agreement, and an agreed jurisdiction in case of dispute. The airlines must also set out, as a condition, the types of person it will not enter into contract with (such as persons whose geographic location may not offer the airline benefit from the contract).

Airlines which advertise their seats for auction on the Internet should have well thought out, well-drafted conditions of contract which offerors must be required to read carefully and mouse-click to indicate that they agree with them before they make their offers.

## Notes

1 See 'Online Airline Ticket Auctions Have Yet to Take Off', *The Gazette*, Montreal, 8 August 1988, at 16.
2 See International Counselor, *Electronic Commerce: An International Overview*: <http://www.intcounselor.com/eleccomm.html>.

3 Click-wrap agreements derive their name from shrink-wrap agreements, under which most software is sold today. It is a well established fact that in common law jurisdictions, click-wrap agreements are enforceable contracts. See *Hotmail Corporation* v. *Van Money Pie, Inc. et al.*, C98-20064 (ND Cal. 20 April 1998), where the US District Court for the Northern District of California agreed that once an offeror clicks on the button 'I agree' (denoting that they accept all conditions of the offeree), a valid and effectual contract is concluded.
4 For more information, see Martin H. Samson, 'Click-wrap Agreement Held Enforceable', *New York Law Journal*, 30 June 1998, reported on: <http://www.ljx.com/Internet/0630 click.html>.
5 (1840) 3 Beav. 334.
6 724 F Supp. 605 (SD Ind. 1989).
7 (1870) 23 LT 419.
8 See also, *Harper* v. *Western Union Telegraph Co.*, 130 SE 119 (SC 1925), *Postal Tel. Cable Co.* v. *Schaefer*, 62 SW 1,119 (Ky App. 1901).
9 (1859) 18 VCQBR 60.
10 Id., at 64.
11 *Carow Towing Co .* v. *The 'Ed. McWilliams'* (1919) 46 DLR 506 (Ex. Ct).
12 *Entores, Ltd* v. *Miles Far East Corporation* [1955] 2 All ER 493 (CA).
13 See, for example, *McDonald & Sons Ltd* v. *Export Packers Co. Ltd* (1979) 95 DLR (3d) 174 (BCSC). See also *Re Viscount Supply Co. Ltd* (1963) 40 DLR (2d) 501 (Ont. SC) and *National Bank of Canada* v. *Clifford Chance* (1996) 30 OR (3d) 746 (Gen. Div.).
14 *Rosenthal & Rosenthal Inc.* v. *Bonavista Fabrics Ltd* [1984] CA 52 (Que. CA).
15 *Balcom (Joan) Sales Inc.* v. *Poirier* (1991), 288 APR 377 (NS Co. Ct).
16 *Gunac Hawkes Bay (1986) Ltd* v. *Palmer* [1991] 3 NZLR 297 (H. Ct).
17 *Brinkibon Ltd* v. *Stahag Stahl and Stahlwarenhandelsgesellschaft mbH* [1982] 1 All ER 293 (HL).
18 Ibid., at 296.
19 *Arrowsmith* v. *Ingle* (1810) 3 Taunt. 234.
20 The *Pendrecht*, [1980] 2 *Lloyd's Report* 56 (QB).
21 *McDonald and Sons Ltd* v. *Export Packers Co. Ltd* (1979), 95 DLR 3dl 174 (BCSC), at 180.
22 *Jenner* v. *Sun Oil Co. Ltd* (1952) 16 CPR 87 (Ont. HCJ).
23 Ibid., at 98–9.
24 (1984) 49 OR (Ed) 58 (HCJ).
25 (1996) 30 OR (3d) 746 (Gen. Div.)
26 636 So. 2d 1351 (Fla App. 1994).
27 *IDS Life Insurance Co.* v. *SunAmerica, Inc.*, 958 F Supp. 1258 (ND Ill. 1997), aff'd in part, vacated in part, 1998 WL 51350 (7th Cir.) (Westlaw).
28 Ibid., at 268.
29 1997 WL 97097 (SDNY) (Westlaw).
30 Ibid., para. 1. For a similar result, see *Cybersell, Inc.* v. *Cybersell, Inc.*, 44 USPQ 2d 1928 (9th Cir. 1997) and *Blackburn* v. *Walker Oriental Rug Galleries*, No. 97-5704 (ED Pa 7 April 1998), reported in *Computer & Online Industry Litigation Reporter*, 21 April 1998, at 4.
31 *McDonough* v. *Fallon McElligott, Inc.*, 40 USPQ 2d 1,826 (SD Cal. 1996).
32 Ibid., at 1,828.
33 89 F 3d 1,257 (6th Cir. 1996).
34 *Digital Equipment Corporation* v. *AltaVista Technology, Inc.*, 960 F Supp. 456 (D Mass. 1997). See also *Cody* v. *Ward* 954 F Supp. 43 (D Conn. 1997), where a court took jurisdiction based on telephone and e-mail communications that consummated a business relationship begun over Prodigy's *Money Talk* discussion forum for financial matters. In partially justifying this decision, the court noted

that the use of fax technology, and even live telephone conferences, can greatly reduce the burden of litigating out-of-state.

35 *Heroes, Inc.* v. *Heroes Foundation*, 958 F Supp. 1 (DDC 1996).

36 *Zippo Manufacturing Company* v. *Zippo Dot Com, Inc.*, 952 F Supp. 1,119 (WD Pa 1997).

37 *Resuscitation Technologies, Inc.* v. *Continental Health Care Corp.* (1997) WL 148567 (SD Ind.) (Westlaw). The court in this case was not concerned that the defendants had never visited the forum State in person, and concluded at para. 5: 'Neither is the matter disposed of by the fact that no defendant ever set foot in Indiana. The "footfalls" were not physical, they were electronic. They were, nonetheless, footfalls. The level of Internet activity in this case was significant.' See also *EDIAS Software International, L.L.C.* v. *BASIS International Ltd*, 947 F Supp. 413 (D Ariz. 1996). In this case the court summed up the essence of many of the Internet jurisdiction cases by stating at 420: 'BASIS [the defendant] should not be permitted to take advantage of modern technology through an Internet Web page and forum and simultaneously escape traditional notions of jurisdiction.' See also *Gary Scott International, Inc.* v. *Baroudi*, 981 F Supp. 714 (D Mass. 1997).

38 *Panavision International, L.P.* v. *Toeppen*, 938 F Supp. 616 (CD Cal. 1996); *Maritz, Inc.* v. *CyberGold, Inc.*, 947 F Supp. 1,328 (ED Mo. 1996); *Inset Systems, Inc.* v. *Instruction Set, Inc.*, 937 F Supp. 161 (D Conn. 1996). In the latter case, the court observed at 165: 'In the present case, Instruction has directed its advertising activities via the Internet and its toll-free number toward not only the state of Connecticut, but to all States. The Internet as well as toll-free numbers are designed to communicate with people and their businesses in every state. Advertisement on the Internet can reach as many as 10,000 Internet users within Connecticut alone. Further, once posted on the Internet, unlike television and radio advertising, the advertisement is available continuously to any Internet user. ISI has therefore, purposefully availed itself of the privilege of doing business within Connecticut.'

39 *Plus System, Inc.* v. *New England Network, Inc.*, 804 F Supp. 111 (D Colo. 1992).

40 585 NYS 2d 661 (Supp. 1992).

# 6 Outsourcing and the Virtual Airline

## Introduction

A significant consequence of the recession during the early 1990s has been a growing reliance by airlines on outsourcing their business requirements. Heavy financial losses and lack of capital have added to today's airlines' problem of lack of traditional bank funding. In recent times, a large number of airlines have looked elsewhere for much needed resources, such as aircraft, personnel, engineering and maintenance and ground services, in order to cut down on regular remuneration packages which may need to be given to local employees, thereby conserving vital capital for their financial sustenance.

One of the key areas in which airlines have sought outsourcing is aircraft leasing. In 1996, there were 34 major leasing companies which owned 1,760 jet aircraft. At the end of 1995, there were 36 major leasing companies owning 1,740 jet aircraft, compared with 1,812 commercial jets owned by the same number of companies in the previous year.[1] Airlines, like other business enterprises, are adopting the financial strategy of conserving scarce capital resources to meet the growth in world trade, which in 1996 alone increased by 6 per cent.[2] In 1996, world Gross Domestic Product (GDP) grew by approximately 3.8 per cent in real terms, following growth of 3.1 per cent in 1995.[3] In civil aviation terms, the growth in trade can be judged from the fact that in 1996, the total scheduled air traffic carried by the 720 airlines of ICAO member States amounted to a total of about 1,380 million passengers and some 23 million tonnes of freight. Of this, North American airlines carried 37 per cent of traffic, carriers in the Asia-Pacific region carried 27 per cent, and European carriers carried 26 per cent. Latin American, Middle East and African air carriers carried 5, 3 and 2 per cent respectively.[14]

The rapid growth in demand for air transport services and the huge cost involved in providing them have led to the concept of the 'virtual' airline – an airline which operates with leased aircraft for the most part, and contracts out, *inter alia,* its engineering services and ground handling services, leaving a few areas of core management to be handled by the airline itself.

One of the key objectives of the virtual airline is to achieve the much coveted 'lean and mean' status as a business venture. This modern trend has its genesis both in the recession of the early part of the 1990s and the winds of regulatory liberalization which swept the world of commercial aviation, bringing in increased competition among air carriers. The aim of the quintessential carrier of the 1990s was therefore to cut costs and improve efficiency. The reduction of unit costs is inextricably linked with the health of an airline's fleet and average aircraft size, average sector distance operated upon, and overall carriage of passenger, mail and cargo. These factors are keyed in to passenger and cargo load factors and yield management, which are in turn determined by revenue obtained per revenue passenger and tonne-kilometre.

These results can be often achieved more easily by outsourcing, particularly where airlines do not have the infrastructure to provide on-site personnel and space for such services as engineering, maintenance and ground handling services. By doing this, airlines may gain a competitive edge, but safety considerations may be jeopardized, particularly if the airlines concerned and their States do not insist on safety standards prescribed internationally at the point of contracting out, and, *a fortiori,* do not ascertain whether safety standards have been followed in the maintenance of their aircraft and ground services by third parties.

This chapter will examine some of the legal implications of outsourcing in the airline industry.

## Aircraft Leasing

The first major consideration in outsourcing is the leasing of aircraft by an airline. The registration of the airline is the paramount legal consideration when an airline uses leased aircraft, since the basic postulate of law which currently applies to the legal identity of aircraft lies in Article 17 of the Chicago Convention,[15] which states that aircraft have the nationality of the State in which they are registered. The Convention further provides that an aircraft cannot be validly registered in more than one State, but its registration may be changed from one State to another.[6] With regard to the registration or transfer of registration of aircraft, the Convention provides that this has to accord with the applicable national laws and regulations of the States concerned.[7]

The most fundamental characteristic of an aircraft at international law is its nationality. Both the Paris Convention of 1919[8] and the

Chicago Convention provide that the nationality of an aircraft is governed by the State in which such aircraft is registered. The Tokyo Convention on Offences Committed on Board Aircraft (1963)[9] provides that the State of registration has jurisdiction over offences and acts committed on board.[10] Therefore, it is reasonable to conclude that the national status of an aircraft would depend on the fact of its registration and to this extent is not dissimilar with the maritime law concept of nationality of ships. The most explicit pronouncement on nationality of vessels was given by the International Court of Justice in the famous *Nottebohm* case,[11] where the court held:

> The character thus recognized on the international level as pertaining to nationality is in no way inconsistent with the fact that international law leaves it to each State to lay down the rules governing the grant of its own nationality. The reason for this is that the diversity of demographic conditions has thus far made it impossible for any general agreement to be reached on the rules relating to nationality, although the latter by its very nature affects international relations. It has been considered that the best way of making such rules accord with the varying demographic conditions in different countries is to leave the fixing of such rules to the competence of each State. On the other hand, a State cannot claim that the rules it has thus laid down are entitled to recognition by another State unless it has acted in conformity with this general aim of making the legal bond of nationality accord with the individual's genuine connection with the State which assumes the defence of its citizens by means of protection as against other states.
>
> ... According to the practice of states, to arbitral and judicial decisions and to the opinions of writers, nationality is a legal bond having as its basis a social fact of attachment, a genuine connection of existence, interests and sentiments, together with the existence of reciprocal rights and duties. It may be said to constitute the juridical expression of the fact that the individual upon whom it is conferred, either directly by the law or as the result of an act of the authorities, is in fact more closely connected with the population of the State conferring nationality than with that of any other State. Conferred by a State, it only entitles that state to exercise protection vis-à-vis another State, if it constitutes a translation into juridical terms of the individual's connection with the State which has made him its national.[12]

In the case of aircraft, the concept of registration and nationality has evolved with changing conditions of civil aeronautical activities relating to the development of airline contracts concerning the use of aircraft which brought in fiscal advantages to airlines. Specific contracts, such as leases, charters and interchange of aircraft are now helping air carriers avoid the need to find money to buy new aircraft. More carriers are now entering into short-term lease agreements to keep their operations afloat, and such 'dry' or 'wet' lease agreements[13] necessitate a closer look at the requirements of registration and nationality as dictated to by the Chicago Convention.

In order to accord with commercial exigencies relating to leases and charters in the air transport industry, ICAO has introduced Article 83 *bis* to the Chicago Convention, which provides that when an aircraft registered in a contracting State is operated pursuant to a contract for the lease, charter or interchange of the aircraft by an operator which has its principal place of business, or if it has no such place of business, its principal residence in another State, the State of registry of the aircraft concerned may, by agreement with such a State, transfer all or part of its duties as State of registry to such other State.[14] Technically, this means that a State may lease aircraft registered in another State and, by mutual agreement, take over responsibilities of the State of registration in respect of that aircraft. Under these circumstances, it may be reasonable to assume that if an aircraft leased by a State performs functions of a military nature for the lessee State, such a State could be considered the State of registration if an agreement to that effect had been put into effect between the lessor and lessee.

Article 83 *bis* of the Convention was opportune, in that it was adopted at a time when trade barriers were rapidly being dismantled and many industries were being globalized. Instances of as many as nine multinational partners in one industry are not uncommon in today's commercial world. In particular, commercial trends in the United States and United Kingdom show new, emergent large airlines with the participation of more than one nationality.

Although the current bilateral regulatory structure calls for substantial ownership and effective control of airlines by nationals or companies of a designating State – which essentially means that for Country A to designate its airline to operate commercial flights, the airline must be substantially owned and effectively controlled by nationals or companies of Country A – this requirement is increasingly becoming impracticable to fulfil in various instances. In recognition of one such circumstance at its 24th Session the ICAO Assembly adopted Resolution A24-12, which recognized the political reality of regional groupings of States into composite economic entities, forming a community of interest. The Assembly recognized that such a community of interest, when applicable to groups of developing States, would require their airlines to be identified on a common basis with regard to their substantial ownership and effective control in the context of bilateral regulation of air traffic rights. Therefore, the ICAO Assembly urged contracting States to allow an airline substantially owned and effectively controlled by one or more developing State of States (or its or their nationals) belonging to a regional economic grouping to exercise the route rights and other air transport rights of any developing State or States within the same grouping under mutually acceptable terms.

There are other instances, such as when airlines have multinational ownership (such as Gulf Air, Air Afrique, SAS and LIAT), have their ownership registered in one country but are accepted as airlines of another (such as Britannia and Monarch, owned in Canada and Switzerland respectively, but which operate air services as designated carriers of the United Kingdom), and are owned by legal persons whose businesses are not domiciled in the country in which the carrier has its place of business (such as Cathay Pacific Airlines).

The 'Third Package' of the European Union, which allows for airlines within the EU to be owned by nationals or companies of any member State, gives further credence to the compelling need to consider the element of designation of airlines outside the purview of the philosophy of 'substantial ownership and effective control' required by the current bilateral regulatory regime.

In view of the above developments, the dictates of aircraft financing require financiers to be aware of the multitude of possibilities of litigation for ownership and control of aircraft financed by them, and also the legal implications of aircraft leasing in the modern context. Donald Bunker states:

> The concept of registration has now developed such that financiers of commercial aircraft for use internationally must be well aware of the effect that the country of registration could have on their rights. The relatively liquid world market in used aircraft makes aircraft financing quite attractive to many investors. However, most prudent financiers like to be assured of being able to obtain possession of their equipment, free and clear of a defaulting debtor's rights and deregistered by the operator's country so that an efficient realization of their security could be achieved.[15]

From the point of view of the airline which leases aircraft and sustains damage to the aircraft and to its passengers, the legal relationship between lessor and lessee of property would apply in common law jurisdictions. The lessor of the aircraft would usually be covered by its own insurance or by an indemnification agreement between the lessor and lessee. In a typical financial lease agreement of aircraft, the position of the lessor could be that of a lender at common law, and to that extent it would be protected from the mere presumption *ipso facto* that it is liable by virtue of its ownership of the aircraft. However, this is not strictly an inflexible rule, and different jurisdictions may impose strict liability in certain situations.[16] There is also the possibility that rules of negligence may apply in certain jurisdictions where an injured party – the lessee – may seek redress from the lessor of the aircraft. Such claims are often prompted by the favourable financial circumstances of lessors.

The protection of the lessee in instances of damage is usually assured by the liability insurance obtained by the lessee. The lessee could also qualify the indemnity agreement signed with the lessor such that the lessee's liability would be valid and effectual only in instances when the lessor is not negligent or in default of the agreement. The lessee would therefore be protected against such acts as arbitrary seizure of property by the lessor. Other legal measures available to the lessee are its capacity and legal right to insert a clause in the lease agreement that the leased property is accepted by the lessee on condition of warranty as to the quality of the property, and its ability to obtain warranty direct from the manufacturer.

## Outsourcing of Services

A virtual airline may often contract out substantial services required to carry out its commercial obligations, including engineering and maintenance services, ground handling services and reservations systems. In all these instances, the airline would be directly liable for any damage caused to its clients, who retain privity of contract directly with the airline concerned. However, under the same privity doctrine, a third party (be it an airline passenger, consignor or bystander) who is affected by a lapse of services rendered may sue the service provider. For instance, if Airline A contracts out engineering services to Company B and a person is injured as a result of defective work by Company B even after Airline A sells or leases out the aircraft concerned to Airline C, the injured person (who could be a passenger of Airline C) may sue Company B for services rendered during its contract with Airline A.

The above principle of extended privity of contract is based on the use with which the property in question is associated, and the services rendered by the defendant. In the 1949 case of *Smith and Snipes Hall Farm, Ltd* v. *River Douglas Catchment Board,*[17] the Court of Appeal successfully applied the doctrine of extended privity to an instance where a previous landowner who had owned a property and had effected improvements on it had been sued by a person who had bought the property from the subsequent landowner. The court held that the landowner who effected the improvements had done so on the implied legal premise that the improvements were carried out for the benefit of anyone to whom the land might be transferred subsequently or anyone who would use the land. This seminal decision may be applied by analogy at common law to a person who is injured or suffers other damage as a result of engineering services which had been contracted out by an airline which was entrusted with the aircraft in which the plaintiff suffered the damage or injury.

In essence the doctrine of privity of contract means two things:

1 a party to a contract has a right of action;
2 a non-party to a contract does not have an action.

Therefore, extended privity means that any person who suffers or incurs loss as a consequence of a contract formed between others is privy to the said contract.

As for outsourcing services such as ground handling and computer reservation systems, these would fall under the principles of the law of agency, where the airline concerned would be the principal, and the service provider would be the agent. Such agency relationships may arise by express agreement between the airline and the service provider. The agreement cannot be held valid if consent of both parties is not evident and such consent is not manifested in writing.[18]

The service agreement adopts the usual practice of recognizing that the agent is authorized by the principal (the airline) to provide a service to prospective passengers and consignees. In the final analysis, therefore, the initial contract between the principal and agent enables the agent to enter into another contract, this time with the client of the airline. Privity of contract is maintained between the client and the airline through the nexus of the agent. The airline, as the principal, is generally responsible for the acts of its agents in the provision of the service concerned. The question is whether the airline would always be responsible for the acts of its agents.

The principal gives its agent authority to act in two different ways: actual authority and apparent authority. Actual authority is a legal relationship between principal and agent created consensually by agreement to which the only parties are principal and agent.[19] Apparent authority, which is usually not applicable in the instance of outsourcing, is founded on the appearance given by an ostensible agent that it is conducting the business of the airline.

Apparent authority is imputed to the agent on the basis that the airline should not allow a person to sell its name, and should not indicate in the slightest manner that a person can sell on behalf of the airline. If this happens, the airline is clearly liable for such a person's act, even though the airline did not expressly or orally give a mandate to the person to act as its agent. The airline in this instance has the onerous task of proving that the person had no basis to act as its agent, and that it took all precautions against such contingency, or that it could not take such precautions.

The uncertainty which enveloped the terms 'actual' and 'ostensible' authority was finally settled in 1971 in the case of *Burt* v. *Claude*

*Cousins & Co. (CA)*,[20] where actual authority, whether express or implied, was identified as authority which the principal was aware of, whereas ostensible authority was a mere representation by a person purporting to be an agent.[21] However, the fact remains that in the area of general sales agency, the principal is *prima facie* liable for both actual and ostensible authority, unless in the latter the airline proves that the person purporting to be the agent did not have any justification for thinking so.

Although the service provider in international aviation cannot strictly be classified as an independent contractor in terms of tortious liability, it is arguable that it is one in the face of provision of ground handling and reservation services. It is its own master, and the airline does not supervise it *stricto sensu*, although it is supervised or observed with regard to its potential from time to time. However, the distinct laws of agency classify it as an agent, which makes the airline generally liable for the agent's acts. Assuming it is an independent contractor, the airline is liable for its acts, on the basis that the airline made an error in judgement in appointing it.

Although the general principle of contract law maintains that the principle is *prima facie* liable for the acts of the agent, the principal may repudiate liability in several specific circumstances. If the agent acts without authority or exceeds its authority, as in the case where the agent makes a reservation without ascertaining whether such a reservation is possible, the principal can set aside the transaction and consider itself immune from an action by a passenger who does not obtain a seat in a flight due to the agent's failure to adhere to established procedure. An agent which endeavours to provide a service has to answer for any lapse by which a passenger suffers. Not only is the agent liable to answer to its principal, but the principal may also totally repudiate the claim of the passenger.

An agent acts at law in a fiduciary capacity, and is therefore expected to exercise a reasonable quantum of diligence whilst still acting on behalf of its principal. Not only does the agent have to carry out the instructions of the principal airline as per the conditions of contract, it is also expected not to prejudice its principal by contracting with passengers to its exclusive benefit, to the detriment of the airline. If the agent disregards standard procedure and negligently or wilfully provides the service it is expected to provide, it does not comply with what is required of it in the written agreement signed with its principal. The latter may, in such instances, have immediate recourse to the law to indemnify itself from liability. In this context, the airline may sue the agent for damages and successfully recover them if:

- the agent exceeds its authority;

- the agent is guilty of breach of warranty of authority;
- the agent has acted to obtain secret profits for it (this includes acts carried out by the agent to prejudice the principal's interests and gain an undue advantage for it);
- the agent has accepted a bribe in the carrying out of its business;
- the agent has failed to carry out its instructions as per the letter of the contract;
- the agent has been negligent in the exercise of care and skill;
- the agent has delegated authority without prior sanction from its principal.

Early law accepted the proposition that the agent of a foreign principal was presumed to contract personally unless a contractual document specified otherwise.[22] This legal principle was exclusive to the instance of a foreign principal and a local agent, as in the instance of a general sales agency agreement. The argument adduced in favour of this attitude was that once the foreign principal grants an agent who is in an overseas location actual authority, the agent trades on its own without being in any way related to the principal in the execution of the transaction. However, in the 1968 decision of *Teheran-Europe Co. Ltd* v. *S.T. Belton (Tractors) Ltd*,[23] this approach was totally rejected by the British Court of Appeal. In this case, the plaintiffs, a Persian company whose principal place of business was in Teheran, were in the practice of buying British machinery from England through an English agent. In one such transaction, the agent procured machinery from England for the principal company, but the principal company found they did not meet contractual standards on delivery. The principal company sued the British company for breach of contract. The defendants denied the claim on the basis that the principal company was undisclosed by the local agent, and in any event, the local agent had independent and exclusive privity of contract. The Court of Appeal rejected this contention, and held that the undisclosed principal had never lost its status as principal, and that a foreign principal could sue and be sued for an act involving its agent and a third party. Diplock LJ, on the subject of actual authority, which in this instance the agent exercised, stated:

> When an agent has such actual authority and enters into a contract with another party intending to do so on behalf of his principal, it matters not whether he discloses to the other party the identity of his principal, or even that he is contracting on behalf of a principal at all, if the other party is willing or leads the agent to believe that he is willing to treat as a party to the contract anyone on whose behalf the agent may have been authorized to contract.[24]

The principal airline may terminate the agency agreement in other instances, such as by express revocation, either under the terms of a contractual agreement or in instances where its agent is guilty of an offence which precludes it from performing its functions, becoming bankrupt or mentally disordered, by the stipulated passage of time in the agreement whereby the agent becomes *functus officio*, and by the execution of a power of attorney, whereby the principal transfers the agent's functions to another. However, the mere termination of the agency will not necessarily preclude the principal's responsibility, unless the principal issues proper notice of revocation to third parties who may rely on the agent's authority. If the principal fails to give such notice, a third party may presume the agent's apparent authority and transact with the agent. In *Scarf* v. *Jardine*,[25] Lord Blackburn, citing a previous decision,[26] stated:

> There is a duty upon that person who has given that authority if he revokes it, to take care that notice of that revocation is given to those who might otherwise act on the supposition that it otherwise continued.[27]

Outsourcing of services therefore brings to bear legal implications for the virtual airline, which may address established tort law principles of strict liability and contract law principles of agency. The principal concern of the airline in these circumstances should be to focus on the indemnity provisions of the outsourcing contract. For example, there should be special mention in the agency agreement of the agent's liability for not following established procedures in civil aviation. Examples of prudent airline procedure in ground handling services would be proper examination of a passenger's travel documents and reservation status. In the instance of contracting out engineering services, the virtual airline may need to align the indemnity provisions of the agreement to ensure that the services provided meet with accepted universal standards of aircraft engineering.

## Comments

On the issue of outsourcing, the virtual airline has to contend with the parties concerned regarding the legal problems which may emerge as a result. The more complicated issue of the safety aspect of outsourcing, which involves several other entities, such as the States and international community, including ICAO, is dealt with in Chapter 10. Over the years, ICAO has played a seminal and alert role in monitoring safety in civil aviation, and has diligently endeavoured to enhance ICAO SARPs and obtain compliance with these provisions.

## Notes

1 *The World of Civil Aviation – 1995–1998*, ICAO Circular 265-AT/109, Montreal: ICAO, 1995, at 33.
2 *Annual Report of the Council*, Montreal: ICAO, 1996, at 1.
3 Ibid.
4 Id., at 3.
5 *Convention on International Civil Aviation*, signed Chicago, 7 December 1944. See 15 UNTS 295, ICAO Doc. 7300 (6th edn), 1980.
6 Id., Article 18.
7 Id., Article 19.
8 *Convention for the Regulation of Aerial Navigation*, signed Paris, 1919, Articles 5–10.
9 *Convention on Offences and Certain Other Acts Committed on Board Aircraft*, signed Tokyo, 14 September 1963. See ICAO Doc. 8364.
10 Id., Article 3.
11 *ICJ Reports* (1955), at 1.
12 Ibid., at 3.
13 A 'dry' lease is where an aircraft is leased by a lessor to a lessee without a crew; a 'wet' lease is where an aircraft is leased together with the lessor's crew.
14 In 1993, 76 States had ratified Article 83 *bis*. The provision needs to be ratified by 98 States for it to come into effect. See *Annals of Air & Space Law*, Vol. XVIII, Part II, 1993, at 155.
15 Donald H. Bunker, *The Law of Aerospace Finance in Canada*, McGill University, 1988, at 157.
16 Id., at 288.
17 1949 2 KB 500; also 1949 2 All ER 179.
18 See *Heard* v. *Pilley* (1869) 4 Ch. App. 548, per Lord Cranworth.
19 See G.H. Treitel, *The Laws of Contract* (5th edn), London: Butterworth, 1975, at 535. See also *Heard* v. *Pilley*, 4 Ch. App. 548, at 548.
20 (1971) 2 QB 426.
21 Id., at 454, per Megaw LJ.
22 Bowstead, *The Law of Agency* (14th edn), London: The Law Book Company, 1976, at 233–44.
23 (1968) 2 QB 545.
24 Ibid., at 555.
25 (1882) 7 App. Cas. 345.
26 *Freeman* v. *Cooke* 2 Ex. 654.
27 *Scarf* v. *Jardine* (1932) 8 App Cas. 357, at 425.

# 7 Franchising in the Airline Industry

## Introduction

One of the more recent marketing initiatives to emerge in the airline industry is franchising. In its contemporary form, franchising has permeated a wide spectrum of businesses, introducing a sophisticated business relationship between two parties, thereby creating a contractual relationship. The franchisor, which develops a unique and individual way of conducting business, permits the franchisee to make use of the franchisor's trade name and methods in the franchisee's business, subject to controls imposed by the franchisor.

The application of the principles of franchising fits in well with the modern exigencies of airline business, where the brand image developed and projected by a highly successful airline has become of increasing importance to passengers, thus making an airline's logo a marketable quantity. Some major airlines have indeed capitalized on this commercial possibility by developing much-vaunted and attractive consumer-based brand personalities, and using them as marketing tools to attract potential franchisees.

A fundamental advantage offered by franchising is that it allows airlines to extend their brand to routes which would otherwise be commercially unviable without operating air services to such routes themselves, avoiding the risk of capital investment.

A notable example of franchising in the European airline business is British Airways, which had six franchising agreements in the year ending March 1996.[1] In 1996, the six franchisees, most of which operated under the name British Airways Express, with the exception of two which operated under the name British Airways, carried 3.4 million passengers to 80 destinations. The franchisees paid British Airways a fixed fee for the services they were obliged to use – such as reservations systems – and a fixed royalty for the use of the brand of the airline.[2] The franchisees could also offer their passengers Air Miles on British Airways' frequent flyer scheme.

Extending its franchising agreements to international operations outside Europe, British Airways has also signed an agreement with Comair of South Africa, which has been obliged under the franchise provisions to repaint its fleet in British airways livery, outfit its cabin and customer service staff in British Airways uniforms, and offer a typical British Airways in-flight service on Comair's franchised flights.[3]

The other large British carrier, Virgin Atlantic, has also been reported to be considering extending its short-haul franchise operations to longer routes. In 1994, Virgin Atlantic was operating two extremely profitable franchised flights between London and Athens, and London and Dublin, where the two routes were operated by independent carriers which used the Virgin brand name and livery on their aircraft.[4]

Another significant example of franchising agreements in the airline business is the one signed by Air France and BritAir, whereby BritAir placed its entire staff and 23 aircraft under the Air France brand name, in exchange for Air France[5] granting a dozen of its routes to BritAir, which operated 150 daily flights on these routes. Encouraged by the commercial efficacy and profitability of this agreement, Air France has been seeking additional franchising agreements with smaller airlines in order to maximize the passenger flow into its hub at Roissy Charles de Gaulle Airport in Paris.[6]

In October 1996, Lufthansa entered into a unique franchising agreement with Augsburg Airways, forming a partnership named Team Lufthansa, whereby Augsburg Airways operated, at its own cost, three German domestic routes with Lufthansa flight numbers and under quality control by Lufthansa.[7]

One of the compelling reasons for franchising's emergence as a marketing tool in the airline industry, particularly in Europe, is the European air travel market's polarization between scheduled flights and unscheduled charter carriers. The number of European charter carriers has grown prolifically in the last two decades, as part of a backlash against increasingly high scheduled fares. In 1996, it was reported that, in the United Kingdom alone, 14 million passengers used charter flights on their vacation.[8] The growing disparity between the fares of scheduled carriers and the low package fares offered by charter carriers have allowed European franchisees to compete for both scheduled and unscheduled routes, offering the traveling public a comparatively low fare for a customized flight under the brand name of a large carrier.

The major concern caused by franchising is that major airlines use the services of smaller airlines to carry out franchise services by using a mix of franchise/code sharing agreements in order to avoid having to operate on revenue-losing routes themselves, while retaining their presence on these routes through the franchisees' operations. The European Union has claimed that by using franchising agreements like this, major airlines have retained both their unprofitable routes and the valuable slots that go with them.[9]

This chapter will examine the nature of the franchising contract, and assess its legal implications for the airline industry.

## The Nature of Franchising

Franchising, which has frequently been described as 'one of the greatest inventions of western capitalism'[10] and the 'dominating force in the distribution of goods and services',[11] is perhaps best described as the only form of business organization which, by its very nature, creates business units, providing new entrepreneurs, new jobs, new services and new export opportunities.[12] The symbiotic relationship forged between the franchisor and the franchisee can form a mutually convenient commercial arrangement between the parties:

> Franchising has provided the means for merging the seemingly conflicting interests of existing businesses with those of aspiring entrepreneurs in a single process that promotes business expansion, entrepreneurial opportunity and shared cost and risk.[13]

Be that as it may, one of the most serious shortcomings of the commercial relationship established by the franchise contract is the oft-experienced imbalance in power between the franchisor and the franchisee in favour of the former, and the lack of information exchange between the parties to the contract. These factors have given rise to the suggestion that the traditional freedom of contract principles which obtain at common law be modified to accommodate the franchise phenomenon. This call for modification of contract law principles to accord with the synergic relationship created by a franchise agreement is primarily based on the concern that the time and money invested by a franchisee in the promotion of the franchisor's trade name and trade marks can be jeopardized, and even forfeited, by the arbitrary action of the franchisor.[14]

In the context of franchise agreements between airlines, the personality of the franchisor, which lends its goodwill to the franchisee, plays a key role. The traditional view that goodwill is retained by, and belongs to, the franchisor also applies in the commercial aviation context, where the franchisee simply acquires a right to participate in a business system for a term and in a manner prescribed by the franchise agreement. The franchisee usually does not retain a right to assign the franchise to a third party, have the agreement reviewed on termination, or demand compensation upon non-renewal of the contract. However, there have been instances, particularly in the United States, where courts have been favourable towards protecting a franchisee's investment from forfeiture through the arbitrary and capricious action of a franchisor.[15]

The observation of Lord McNaughten in 1901 about goodwill – that it is a thing very easy to describe, but very difficult to define[16] – still applies today in the field of airline franchise. The goodwill which is traded in a franchise agreement is essentially the benefit and advantage derived from the use of a good name, reputation and connections of a business. Goodwill or personality of an airline is the one attractive force that brings in customers. In the same case, Lord Lindley added that goodwill includes:

> Whatever adds value to a business by reason of situation, name and reputation, connection, introduction to old customers and agreed absence of competition, or any of these things, and there may be others which do not occur to me.[17]

One of the salient features of a franchise agreement is that goodwill or personality, which is the pivotal ingredient and the main attraction which draws in money to the franchisor, does not act to the benefit of the franchisee at the termination or non-renewal of a franchise agreement. In other words, the franchisee airline cannot claim compensation from the franchisor for goodwill accrued to the latter during the period of the franchise agreement due to the operation of services by the franchisee. This traditional view was confirmed in the 1989 Australian case of *Kanoa Ply Ltd* v. *BP Oil Distribution Ltd*[18] where the Court held that an oil company franchisee had no right of compensation for goodwill lost when a service station lease and dealer trading agreement were not renewed. It was the court's view that on expiry of the statutory tenure there was no further obligation to renew the contract and no requirement to pay compensation in respect of goodwill acquired by the oil company through non-renewal of the franchise agreement. Lockhart, Wilcox and Grammon JJ held:

> Under the general law, in the absence of any special covenant and any other applicable statute, upon the tenancy of the appellant coming to an end, the benefit of any goodwill of the character described above would ensure to the benefit of the first respondent as lessor ... Where a franchisor elects to grant a new lease the franchisee has the benefit of continued exploitation of the goodwill of the site ... But where a franchisor elects not to grant a new lease, the franchisee is turned from the site without compensation for any goodwill which it may have developed during its period of occupancy. A franchisee, such as

> the appellant, may regard this result as harsh, the harshness being exacerbated if it should be the case – we do not know whether it is so – that franchisors are more likely to decide themselves to operate sites to which substantial goodwill attaches. But if this result is harsh, it is a product of the circumstances that the law does not require the franchisor who elects not to renew to pay any compensation to the franchisee.[19]

It therefore follows that if the franchisee wishes to seek compensation for its investments of money and services which enhance the goodwill of the franchisor after the termination of the contract, such must be stipulated in the contract document itself and compensation sought explicitly in the contract. This principle also applies to assignment, since usually the franchisee is not allowed to assign or sell the business while it is subject to the franchise contract. Therefore the franchise contract usually includes a term or provision regarding assignment, allowing for such but calling for the franchisor's consent before the fact.

The stark finding in the *Kanoa* case that a franchisee has no entitlement to goodwill at the end of the franchise term may be open to criticism in the context of airline franchising contracts. Although, admittedly, the initial goodwill of the franchise business obviously reflects the investment of the franchisor, the investments and entrepreneurial activities of the franchisee – particularly in the context of the airline industry, where the franchisee would obviously be rigorously contributing to the franchise business through systems promotions and advertising which would clearly enhance the goodwill accruing to the franchise system – should not be so readily dismissed. It would be reasonable to expect a court of common law jurisdiction to take cognizance of the particular marketing and commercial exigencies of the airline business in recognizing the enhanced goodwill that a franchisee would obtain in an airline franchise situation. The particular characteristics of the relationship in question would, of course, be the primary consideration in such a determination.

## The Franchise Agreement

A franchise agreement is usually a contract entered into between the franchisor and the franchisee in which the relationship between the parties is described at length and in detail. The agreement would, *inter alia,* cite parties to the agreement, their names, business addresses and other details as relevant; the business structure being licensed to the franchisee, including the business name, trade works, appearances and trade secrets; the duration of the franchise and any renewals or options to renew the franchise at the end of the term; the fee or fees payable by the franchisee to the franchisor; the territorial limits of the franchise; training requirements of the franchisee's staff; the obligations of the franchisee to abide by the franchisor's business structure; the obligations (if any) of the franchisor to modify the business structure and standards of the request of the franchisor, and other obligations of the franchisee which are essentially required for the successful running of the business as though it were run by the franchisor.

The last category of service obligations of the franchisee are most onerous, in that they may stipulate that the franchisee must buy the franchisor's products, and may oblige it to cease selling particular products. In addition, most franchise agreements require the franchisee to purchase products or services from suppliers which are approved by the franchisor and at prices which are not at the sole discretion of the franchisee. Another burdensome obligation relates to the manner and scope in which advertising and promotions of the franchised product are carried out. In addition, the franchisee is frequently required to maintain financial records as required by the franchisor, and take out insurance policies as required by and stipulated in the agreement itself. However, the most significant characteristic of the franchise agreement remains the usual provision relating to the termination of the agreement, which gives the franchisor discretion and flexibility in certain circumstances, as predetermined in the contract.

The above provisions, and any others depending on the nature of the agreement, are usually couched in terms which license the franchisee to use the business format or structure of the franchisor. The fundamental difference between franchise relationships and those formed by contracts of agency and partnership are that the franchisor and franchisee remain totally independent of each other, and one cannot be liable for the act of another unless specified by contractual agreement by the parties that an agency relationship exists between them or such a relationship can be deduced by their subsequent conduct. Therefore, once a franchise agreement is put in place between the franchisor and franchisee, they usually remain independently liable for their actions.

Prior to the formation of the contract, the franchisor is usually expected, and often required, to disclose to the franchisee an estimate of its earning possibilities under the franchise agreement. The franchisor also advises the franchisee of the burdens and expenditure which are likely to confront it.

Although, in principle, common law considers the franchisor and franchisee as separate entities which are responsible individually for their actions, courts in the United States have measured the extent of control exercised by a franchisor over a franchisee, and have identified a number of contractual powers that may indicate actual authority of a franchisor over a franchisee. Often, this leaves the franchisor in a quandary between exercising control to protect its business name, while at the same time avoiding excessive control in order to obviate claims of vicarious liability from aggrieved plaintiffs.[20] Some of the areas in which actual authority of the franchisor over the franchisee have been considered are accounting, where the franchisor imposes certain accounting procedures on the franchisee,[21] and in the control of the franchisee's staff, who may, by agreement between the parties, come within the purview of the franchisor.[22]

Courts in the United States have also considered, in certain instances, whether a franchisee represented to the outside world that it had the apparent authority of its franchisor to act on behalf of the franchisor. One of the most common instances where apparent authority can be deduced by the conduct of the franchisee may occur in the field of advertising in the name of the franchisor.[23] Courts have also considered imputing authority to the franchisee in instances where it represents only the name of the franchisor in letterheads used for the conduct of the franchised business.[24]

The relationship between the franchisor and the franchisee upon termination of a contract and the subject of renewal would essentially depend on the terms of the contract itself. Courts would also consider the conduct of the franchisor in other franchise arrangements, and the conduct of the franchisee in the performance of the contract. The airline franchise contract would accordingly be interpreted based on its provisions and on the conduct of the parties. A franchisor airline which holds many separate franchise contracts with franchisees would be judged on its treatment of the majority of the franchisees, and the courts would accordingly assume that this treatment reflected the general policy of the franchisor.

The 1975 consideration of the franchise chain McDonald's serves well as an analogy, in that the US courts took into account the fact that McDonald's had renewed 93 per cent of its franchise agreements for 20 years, and therefore concluded that the 7 per cent of franchisees whose agreements had not been renewed by McDonald's would have presumably given cause for the non-renewal.[25]

## Comments

The franchising agreement in the airline industry generates a symbiotic relationship between the parties where, for a licence fee, one party (the franchisor) allows the other (the franchisee) to operate on routes which do not generate income for the franchisor. The main purpose of this type of agreement is to co-ordinate economic activities between legally independent entities within a legal framework. The franchise agreement therefore represents the adaptation of the business world to the need to supply goods and services to the consumer more efficiently. The franchise agreement remains, in this sense, a rational compromise between the principles of the classical laws of contract and the principles of corporate organization. The critical interdependence of the parties and their relational intensity, and the marked one-sidedness which grants dominance to the franchisor form a cohesive symbiosis which is only characterized by the substantial benefits both the franchisor and the franchisee usually gain from their relationship. Airline franchise agreements in particular personify the inherent benefits of the franchise concept, by enabling the franchisor to exploit its superior product knowledge and goodwill or personality without risking its own capital, whilst at the same time enabling a franchisee without any substantial experience to have access to the franchisor's business methods and reputation.

The disadvantage of this immensely prolific commercial phenomenon is that there must be a compromise between the expansion of corporate organization and the possible exclusion of small businesses which franchising is calculated to bring about. When applied to smaller carriers, particularly of the developing nations, franchising of the airline product between larger carriers and smaller carriers of the developed world may have this effect, particularly with regard to their Fifth Freedom flights.

The overall issue of imbalance in competition in the aeropolitical world was addressed by an initiative of the International Civil Aviation Organization in 1944, which has developed into an in-depth consideration of preferential measures for carriers of developing nations (see Chapter 2).

In the ultimate analysis, it is not contended that franchising in the airline industry should be totally obviated. Rather, the practice should be viewed as a non-exclusionary marketing tool, which is applied by States and their carriers while giving due consideration to the commercial disadvantages that some instances of franchising may impose on smaller carriers of the developing world. The role of the law would play a critical role in this regard, where States could give serious consideration to implementing ICAO initiatives on preferential measures through their respective legislatures.

## Notes

1 These agreements were with City Flyer Express, Maersk Air, Brymon Airways, Loganair, Manx Airlines Europe and GB Airways. See 'Keeping Up Appearances', *Airline Business*, October 1996, at 38.

2 Ibid.

3 'British Airways Signs up Comair of South Africa as Franchise Partner', *Aviation Daily*, 13 June 1996, at 434.

4 'Virgin Long-haul Franchise Talks', *Travel Weekly*, 2 March 1994, at 4.

5 'Air France Takes over Regional Airline under Franchise Deal', *Aviation Daily*, 29 April 1997, at 179.

6 See 'Air France Chairman Seeks More Franchises', *Air Letter*, 17 January 1997, No. 13,661, at 2.

7 'Lufthansa Announces First Franchise Partner', *Air Letter*, 3 October 1996, No. 13,591, at 1. See also 'Lufthansa Signs Augsburg Airways as Franchisee', *Aviation Daily*, 3 October 1996, at 19.

8 'Never the Twain', *Air Transport World*, October 1996, at 67.

9 'EC Concerned that Franchising in Blocking New Entrants', *World Airline News*, 17 April 1995, at 6.

10 US House of Representatives Committee on Small Business, *Franchising in the U.S. Economy: Prospects and Problems*, Washington, DC: US Government Printing Office, 1990, at 1.

11 Ibid.

12 See *Franchising in the Economy, 1983–1985*, Washington DC: US Department of Commerce, 1985, at vi.

13 US House of Representatives Committee on Small Business, op. cit., at 12.

14 See Rau, 'Implied Obligations in Franchising: Beyond Terminations 1992', *The Business Lawyer*, Vol. 47, at 1,053.

15 See *Shell Oil Co.* v. *Merinello* 63 NJ 402, also 307 A 2d 598 (1973). See also Pitegoff, 'Franchise Relationship Laws: A Minefield for Franchising', *The Business Lawyer*, No. 45, 1989, at 289.

16 *Inland Revenue Commissioners* v. *Muller and Co.'s Margarine Ltd.* (1901) AC 217, at 223.

17 Id., at 235.

18 (1989) 91 ALR 251.

19 Id., at 257–8.

20 Franchisors must carefully consider and balance the degree to which controls will be exercised over franchisees. See, for example, *Diaz* v. *GIMAC Marina, Inc. Bus. Fran. Guide* (CCH), para. 7,916 (NY Sup. Ct 1983); *Meyers* v. *Coca-Cola Co. Bus. Fran. Guide* (CCH), para. 8,004 (Pa Commw. 1983); *Singleton* v. *International Dairy Queen, Inc.*, 332 A 2d 160, at 162–3 (Del. 1975); *Nichols* v. *Arthur Murray, Inc.*, 248 Cal. App. 2d 610, 56 Cal. Rptr 728, 732 (1967); *Porter* v. *Arthur Murray, Inc.* 249 Cal. App. 2d 410, 57 Cal. Rptr 554, 560 (1967). See generally Annotation, *Vicarious Liability of Private Franchisor*, 81 ALR 3d 764 (1977).

21 See *Drexel* v. *Union Prescription Centers, Inc.*, 582 F 2d 781, 787 n 3 (3rd Cir. 1978) (retention of right to audit books a factor suggesting control); *Murphy* v. *Holiday Inns, Inc.*, 219 SE 2d 874, 878 (Va. 1975) (inability to control franchisee's business expenses a factor suggesting lack of control); *Beck* v. *Arthur Murray*, 245 Cal. App. 2d 976, 54 Cal. Rptr 328, 329 (1966). Other cases have suggested that required reporting procedures are indicative of control over daily operations. See, for example, *Billops* v. *Magness Construction Co.*, 391 A 2d 196, 198 (Del. 1978); *Aweida* v. *Kientz*, 536 P 2d 1,138, 1,140 (Colo. Ct App. 1975) (daily sales reports); *Weil* v. *Arthur Murray, Inc.*, 324 NYS 2d 381, 387 (Sup. Ct 1971) (weekly sales reports).

22 One court has stressed the absence of control over the performance of the franchisee's employees, and the absence of the franchisor's ability to hire and fire, as evidence that it 'did not retain any day-to-day supervisory control'. *Coty* v. *US Slicing Machine Co.*, 373 NE 2d 1,371, 1,375 (Ill. App. Ct 1978); see also *Chevron USA, Inc.* v. *Lesch, Bus. Fran. Guide* (CCH), para. 9,583 (Md 1990); *Cobbs* v. *Popeyes, Inc.*, 373 SE 2d 233 (Ga Ct App. 1988); *Slates* v. *International House of Pancakes, Inc.*, 413 NE 2d 427, 464 (Ill. App. Ct 1980); *Nichols* v. *Arthur Murray, Inc.*, 248 Cal. App. 2d 610, 56 Cal. Rptr 728, 730 (1967). Other courts have viewed employee controls as tending to show day-to-day control. See *Porter* v. *Arthur Murray, Inc.*, 249 Cal. App. 2d 410, 57 Cal. Rptr 554, 558 (1967) (ability to hire and fire); *Drexel* v. *Union Prescription Centers, Inc.*, 582 F 2d 781, 788 (3rd Cir. 1978) (ability to supervise employee actions); *Weil* v. *Arthur Murray, Inc.*, 67 Misc. 2d 417, 324 NYS 2d 381, 387 (1971). Cf. *Evans* v. *McDonald's Corp., Bus. Fran. Guide* (CCH), para. 9,869 (10th Cir. 1991) (lack of control over franchisee's labour practices doomed labour law claim by employee of franchisee against franchisor).

23 See *Crinkley* v. *Holiday Inns, Bus. Fran. Guide* (CCH), para. 9,096 (4th Cir. 1988); *Flanagan* v. *Beagles, Bus. Fran. Guide* (CCH), para. 9,265 (Tenn. Ct App. 1988) (dealer's right to use manufacturer's trade marks in brochures and advertising, discretion to extend or withhold warranty, letter to customer raised jury question on issue of apparent authority); *Burkland* v. *Elec Realty Associates*, 740 P 2d 1,142 (Mont. 1987); *McDonald* v. *Century 21 Real Estate Corp.*, 331 NW 2d 606 (Wis. Ct App. 1983); *Billops* v. *Magness Construction Co.*, 391 A 2d 196, 198 (Del. 1978); *Johnston* v. *Am Oil Co.*, 215 NW 2d 719, 721 (Mich. Ct App. 1974); but see *Ortega* v. *General Motors Corp., Bus. Fran. Guide* (CCH), para. 7,593 (Fla Dist. Ct App. 1980) (mere fact that dealer displayed manufacturer's trade marks and signs did not constitute apparent agency). Cf. *NBA Properties, Inc.* v. *Gold, Bus. Fran. Guide* (CCH), para. 9,558 (1st Cir. 1990) (franchisor not liable for trade mark infringement committed by a franchisee that knowingly violated an injunction against such acts).

24 See *Vowels* v. *Arthur Murray Studios, Inc.*, 163 NW 3d 35, 37 (Mich. Ct App. 1968); *Beck* v. *Arthur Murray, Inc.*, 245 Cal. App. 2d 976, 54 Cal. Rptr 328, 330 (1966).

25 M. Love, *McDonald's: Behind the Arches*, New York: Bantam Books, 1986, at 407.

# 8 The Aerospace Plane and its Implications for Commercial Air Traffic Rights

## Introduction

With the successful launch of the Space Shuttle *Columbia* on 12 April 1981, the world entered a new age of space exploitation, leaving behind the period of space exploration which seemingly started in 1957 with the launch of the Russian *Sputnik*. Understandably, the world was elated at the phenomenon of the space shuttle, to the extent that a space technologist at NASA predicted:

> I am convinced that by 1990 people will be going on the shuttle routinely – as an aircraft ... [1]

Of course, this has not yet happened. One must concede, however, that the expert's prophecy was at least partially correct, in that by 1990 we were actively involved with the concept of the aerospace plane, of which the space shuttle was a precursor.

The space shuttle was initially described as a space-faring cargo ship, and corresponded to the generally accepted definitions of a spacecraft: a rocket-propelled vehicle designed to move in earth orbit or outer space. The space shuttle also had characteristics of an aircraft, in that it had the capacity to re-enter the atmosphere and land like an aircraft. The space shuttle therefore created problems of jurisdiction for space law, with questions such as: 'What legal regime should govern the operation of the space shuttle?' and 'At what point would the space shuttle be considered an aircraft, if at all?'. This dilemma was succinctly identified by two commentators in 1982:

> A quarter century ago, in the early period of space activity, there appeared to be a straightforward distinction between 'aircraft' and 'spacecraft' in terms of the means by which the two types of vehicles were supported in space. 'Aircraft' were deemed to 'fly', being supported aerodynamically on wings, whereas 'spacecraft' were maintained in orbit due to their momentum by the grace of 'orbital mechanics' ... Various forms of 'near earth surface' vehicles are now possible which support themselves above ground without resort to aerodynamic means. These range from magnetic levitation vehicles, through VTOL vehicles relying on the reaction thrust of jet or rocket engines, to one-man jet or rocket propulsion gear. More significantly the clearly successful 'shuttle' hybrid vehicle is an early precursor of what may likely develop into the dominant form of 'near-space vehicle'. Clearly the seemingly obvious distinction has disappeared and will likely be considered merely an anachronism in the future.[2]

In the face of this dilemma, another emergent issue posed an additional dimension to the problem. As Professor Bockstiegel aptly identified in 1983:

> [Space law] ... is the newest main field of international law ... and it depends more than most other fields on probable and fast technical progress ...[3] It is obvious that the application of space technology will lead to the growing commercialization of space activities, since such service – at least in the long run – can only be maintained and expanded, if it is self financing ...[4]

Since the existing treaties and other rules of space law have mainly been formulated against this background and with the intention of exploratory space activities, new regulatory attempts will have to take into account as far as possible, the economic and technical environment of the commercialization of space activities if real progress in the development and formulation of space law is to be made.

This chapter will examine the effect the aerospace plane will have on the already contentious issue of air traffic rights, given the highly commercial trends within the air transport industry in modern times, particularly in the face of modern commercial tools such as alliances between mega-carriers and code-sharing agreements. Although, admittedly, the aerospace plane will not become an operational reality until at least the early part of the 21st century, its advent nevertheless promises to introduce some radical challenges to the present structure of air services agreements.

## The Aerospace Plane

An aerospace plane is a hypersonic, single-stage, orbiting reusable vehicle that takes off and lands horizontally on a conventional runway.[5] This is a broad definition, but it serves to cover various technical configurations and models of aerospace planes.

The aerospace plane will be constructed using aeronautical and space technologies, and would be able – and indeed required – to fly both in the atmosphere and outer space. In these circumstances, the fundamental issue at hand is the application of appropriate laws to the aerospace plane's activities.

At an open forum discussion held on 6 April 1989 during the Annual Meeting of the American Society of International Law in Chicago,[6] the legal and policy issues of the aerospace plane were brought into focus, and on the subject of delimitation of applicable laws, a view was expressed by academics of McGill University's Institute of Air and Space Law that the activities of the aerospace plane as a space-traversing device used for point-to-point earth transportation could be governed by air law. They felt that should the principle of air law apply, it was necessary for bilateral agreements to be signed between States prior to an international flight by the aerospace plane. Professor Christol, on the other hand, believed that enormous benefit can be derived through the application of either the air or the space law regime,[7] leading some to believe that the dilemma would best be left unresolved for the present, since it is premature to speak of an autonomous law for aerospace planes.

Vereschetin adopted a logical approach when he observed:

> As to 'ordinary' space planes, if their *raison d'être* is the delivery of cargo or persons to and from space, they should be treated, in principle, from the very beginning until the end of their mission as 'space objects' within the meaning given to this term in space law. Conversely, if any are destined for Earth-to-Earth transportation and, if during their operation they only traverse the fringes of outer space, these vehicles should be legally treated as aircraft.[8]

Tanja Masson-Zwaan agreed, saying:

> After all, the transit through near space which is involved is *incidental* to the main transit which takes place within the airspace. Generally, the aerospace plane will be subject to the sovereignty of the State whose airspace it is in. It must comply with the rules set by ICAO and, if applicable, the tariff regulations set out by IATA ...[9]

Speaking from a purely commercial point of view, it follows logically that an aerospace plane which transports persons and goods between States should be considered an aircraft, even if it traverses through space at a certain point in its flight. However, the two commentators' views above are not clear enough to arrive at an acceptable conclusion. For instance, what does the first commentator mean when he uses the term 'fringes of outer space'? Legally speaking, outer space is outer space, and any operation of a flight by a vehicle of any description over and beyond the atmosphere would bring such activity within the purview of the outer space treaties. The second commentator makes it even more confusing when she observes that the aerospace plane will be subject to the sovereignty of the State whose airspace it is in. This is an incontrovertible fact which need not be stated, since any object within the airspace of a territorial State would indeed be subject to that State's sovereignty.

Gorove addresses a compromise which would set the upward limit of national sovereignty at a specific height anywhere between the area where satellites can orbit the earth and where aircraft can fly, and at the same time not require special permission from the underlying State to traverse space above this height on the way to and from outer space, or alternatively, to give space-faring nations the right of innocent passage through this area while ascending or descending from outer space. The problem with innocent passage, as Gorove validly points out, is that disputes can arise out of the interpretation of what constitutes innocent passage, and also from the determination as to whose interpretation will prevail.[10] Another problem that would have to be addressed if the limit of national sovereignty is extended in this manner would concern the provision of air navigation services while the aerospace plane is in outer space above a particular State which is not equipped to provide that service.

As the following discussion will demonstrate, there is absolutely no difficulty from a commercial standpoint in applying exclusively the principles of air law to the operations of an aerospace plane which carries passengers and goods from one State to another, traversing outer space in the process. However, the commercial implications of this application are quite considerable, and would bring to bear the need to address its effect on current commercial practices with regard to air traffic rights.

## The Aerospace Plane and Air Traffic Rights

The issue of air traffic rights is addressed in the Chicago Convention of 1944,[11] which provides that where non-scheduled air services are concerned, contracting states agree that aircraft of a State may make flights into or transit non-stop across the territory of other States without obtaining permission from the State flown over.[12] However, scheduled air services can be operated only with the special permission or authorization of the grantor State,[13] requiring a bilateral air services agreement between the two States concerned, or a multilateral air services agreement between States concerned. This has led to a sustained system of negotiations between States for rights of their aircraft to operate commercial scheduled flights into other States.[14]

Of the many considerations addressed at negotiations between States regarding air traffic rights of their carriers, perhaps the most contentious, and indeed important from a commercial point of view, is the insistence that there should be fair and equal opportunity for the airlines of each State to operate air services between the territories of those States. At the time of writing, six US carriers had protested to President Clinton, calling for the suspension of the 'open skies' negotiations between the United States and the United Kingdom, which, if successful, would grant carriers of both States unlimited access to each other's territories in the operation of flights. The carriers alleged that the alliance between British Airways and American Airlines would act to those six carriers' detriment if there was an 'open skies' policy.[15] At the same time, the United States also received notice of rejection from the Japanese authorities of its proposal for an 'open skies' agreement with Japan. Comments of disappointment from the United States more than adequately subsume interests at stake in current air traffic rights negotiations:

> Japan's proposal makes explicit their real intent, which is to offer the U.S. some tightly regulated opportunities to serve Japan from smaller U.S. markets in return for the U.S. surrendering control of the Asian market to Japan's high cost carriers. Japanese negotiators seem more intent on protecting intra-Asian air service markets for Japanese carriers by blocking out U.S. carrier competitors than they are in opening the U.S./Japan aviation market.[16]

Japan responded with the view that, while under the current bilateral air services agreement between the two countries, US carriers have unlimited rights to fly beyond Japan, Japan Airlines – which was the only Japanese airline at the time the agreement was signed – has nothing.[17] By this statement, Japan has brought into focus the fair and equal opportunity principle.

On the other hand, Singapore Airlines has been requesting the air transport industry to consider the 'open skies' concept favourably, calling for 'open skies' between the United States and Asia, to match transatlantic agreements.[18] Similarly, Delta Airlines has made a strong plea for 'open skies' between the United States and Europe, entreating the European Union to heed the liberal approach taken by both US and European carriers towards the path of 'open skies'.[19] Maurice

Flanagan, Group Managing Director of Emirates, the carrier of Dubai, claims that there is one place world-wide where 'open skies' are granted unconditionally to all carriers – Dubai – and adds that the current international aeropolitical environment indulges and excuses overprotectiveness.[20] There is very little doubt that this overprotectiveness stems from a perceived difference between stronger and weaker air carriers, where the weaker carriers jealously invoke the 'fair and equal opportunity' clause to seemingly protect what they identify as their 'market share'.

The question arises as to whether there is such a thing as 'market share' in the modern context of alliances, code-sharing agreements and 'block-seat' arrangements. Professor Wassenbergh offers a solution:

> Open skies means free access to foreign air traffic markets. But how to use such free access? Not all air carriers may be able nor be located in a place enabling them to successfully compete. The only way we see for the weaker national air carriers to survive and maintain their effective participation in the international air traffic market is by cross border co-operation with a stronger air carrier.[21]

Wassenbergh concludes that the objective must be to provide the world with an optimum air transportation network, operated with a minimum of harm to the environment, and with an option for every State to participate in the provision of the system, or alternatively in the benefits of operating the system.[22] This is a noble objective, but is still far from being achieved through a workable formula. If, as Wassenbergh correctly states elsewhere, the future of international aviation lies in a group of air carriers that serve whole world regions, bonded together by commercial trade agreements, and region-dominating carriers which will replace the national flag-carriers that have ruled international skies since the First World War,[23] the aerospace plane, once introduced to the market on a regular, commercially operational basis, would further erode the fast-disappearing 'fair and equal opportunity' principle.

The aerospace plane, which would drastically reduce flying time between such city-pairs as Los Angeles on the one hand and Tokyo and Sydney on the other, would inevitably create hubs whereby regional carriers would converge with passengers (and cargo, to a lesser extent) destined for carriage in the aerospace plane. In the long run this may lead to passengers of conventional aircraft being 'siphoned off' to the aerospace plane. For example, hypothetically, a passenger embarking in Bombay for Tokyo may find that he would save time by travelling to an intermediate point and connecting with the aerospace plane from a point such as Singapore, and such an alternative may deprive airlines which do not use the aerospace plane in their fleet but operate air services between Bombay and Tokyo of that passenger's custom. The use of hubs from which the aerospace plane flies would therefore be greater, and there would be more scope for larger and more prolific alliances between carriers to pool their resources in maximizing the carrier of passenger traffic. The scenario adds to the thrust of Wassenbergh's vision of greater emphasis being placed on alliances in the future.

It is incontrovertible that, at least at the introductory stages of the aerospace plane, it would operate on a Third and Fourth Freedom basis: from point to point, without Fifth Freedom traffic being embarked or disembarked on the way, such as is the case now. Take, for instance, the earlier example of traffic between Los Angeles and Sydney (Australia), where a journey which takes at least 18 hours by a B747 aircraft would be accomplished by the aerospace plane in four hours on a direct flight. If the aerospace plane becomes large enough one day to carry more than 300 passengers in each flight, it would be analogous to a present-day A310, MD11 or even B747 aircraft. Assuming the Americas, Europe and some States in Asia would use the aerospace plane to start with, there would be a Third and Fourth-Freedom traffic rights regime under which air services negotiations would be restricted to the States which use the aerospace plane. The frequency of operations negotiated for would entirely depend on how successfully States attracted traffic to their aerospace planes.

## Commercial Aspects

The aerospace plane is really the third stage of accelerated air transport, the first being the Anglo-French Concorde supersonic aircraft. At the time of writing, the second stage – a supersonic successor to Concorde – was being considered, to form a closer link between subsonic air transport and the aerospace plane.

The Concorde is the only aircraft at present capable of covering 6,000 kilometres in three hours with 100 passengers on board without in-flight refuelling, but the ageing Concorde's range is limited by its fuel-thirsty engines, and is unable to cope with the growing demand for long-range flights, such as the 10,000 kilometre run between Los Angeles and Tokyo.

Concorde's successor will therefore need to cover a range of at least 10,000 kilometres in supersonic cruise mode (possibly even 12,000 kilometres), while carrying 250–300 passengers in a three-class configuration. As for fares, they would have to be comparable with existing first class fares, or at least business class fares. It would be logical to assume that the aerospace plane, to compete with the future Concorde, would have to offer comparable services and fares and it would have to match the Concorde in capacity, which would mean that fuel-efficiency would indeed be a key consideration in its design.

Assuming that the aerospace plane can offer comparable features to the Concorde, with the added advantage of speed, at first it would presumably be operated by airlines of a few developed States, leading to a hub-and-spoke air transport service. One could therefore envisage a proliferation of feeder services carrying passengers to the hub where the aerospace plane operates. In the face of the present trend towards liberalization of air transport services, at least in the context of the aerospace plane, the need for predetermination of capacity on the Bermuda I model of 1946 could be resuscitated,[24] in order to curtail the number of feeder services operated into a hub.

Practically, such a situation, where Third and Fourth Freedom air traffic rights are once again given prominence under the Bermuda I umbrella, would give rise to a dichotomy. On the one hand, when States negotiate bilaterally for air traffic rights in relation to Third and Fourth Freedom traffic, the airline of the State which has the hub for the aerospace plane may wish to carry as much feeder traffic on its own services. This tug of war for a share of Third and Fourth Freedom feeder traffic may result in a back-to-basics approach, where fair and equal opportunity under Bermuda I is considered to relate to sharing air traffic between carriers, not necessarily to competition between carriers. Under such a commercial environment of rigid negotiation, carriers may return to insisting on fair and equal opportunity to compete. In any event, the aerospace plane will inevitably introduce a generic commercial regime that will need careful commercial strategy on the part of both large and small carriers.

In their consideration of Third and Fourth Freedom (feeder) traffic, States might find relevant the concept of the 'safety net' which emerged from ICAO's Fourth Air Transport Conference held in November–December 1994[25] and which has already been discussed. The 'safety net' is designed to provide an integrated, interrelated package of provisions that would enable States, compatible with global trends and regulatory practices in other areas of economic relations, to move towards a more open, competitive air transport sector. Under the 'safety net', which would apply to all carriers alike – irrespective of their commercial advantages – each party grants unrestricted basic market access rights to each other party for use by their air carriers for services touching the territories of both parties (without cabotage rights). Seventh Freedom carriage (services touching the territory of the granting party but not that of the designating party) and cabotage rights would be optional.

The 'safety net' also gives each party the right to impose a capacity freeze. Such a freeze would be implemented only in instances where a rapid and significant decline occurred in a party's participation in a country-pair market. It is not an automatic mechanism which comes into play immediately when a market share goes below a certain amount, but requires the affected party to assess whether or not to initiate the capacity freeze when, for example, the capacity offered by its carriers falls below 50 per cent of that offered by the carriers of the other party. Incontrovertibly, therefore, invoking the 'safety net' is based on flights offered in the country-pair market by Third and Fourth Freedom operations. The 'safety net' is being studied further by ICAO's Air Transport Regulation Panel, which is continuing to hold sessions.

Another mechanism to emerge from the ICAO World-wide Air Transport Conference of 1994 which may interest States in the context of feeder traffic in relation to the aerospace plane is 'preferential measures in the economic regulation of international air transport to ensure the effective participation of developing countries in such transport'. This has been discussed at length earlier. Consideration of these preferential measures emerged as a result of the recognition by the Conference that a liberalized regulatory regime would have credibility only if it were based on existing realities and provided for sustained participation by all States, including developing ones. In this context, one of the compelling realities which needs to be addressed is the disparity in the economic development and the competitive situations between the air carriers of many developing countries and those of most developed countries. In recognition that these disparities, which may affect the size and competitiveness of air carriers between and among States, could limit the real and effective participation of developing countries in air transport, it was felt that some practical supportive measures in the form of preferences were necessary.

Preferential measures, which are quite separate and distinct from the safeguards of the 'safety net', have three basic characteristics:

1 they are usually granted on a non-reciprocal basis, and the State granting the preference should not expect reciprocal treatment from the beneficiary State;
2 they are granted to air carriers of developing countries where the disparities in size and competitiveness are such as to warrant special treatment;
3 they offer external support, and are designed to create an operative environment which would enable airlines of a developing country to improve their ability to compete in the air transport market.

Above all, these measures are subject to bilateral or multilateral agreement between the States concerned.

The 'safety net' and preferential measures would warrant closer scrutiny if a hub-and-spoke system developed for the aerospace plane. One is encouraged by the fact that the 'safety net' mechanism will be further developed by ICAO Air Transport Regulation Panel, and could well prove to be an effective tool for the attainment of commercial harmony between carriers when they are faced with more efficient and faster aircraft, such as the aerospace plane, in future.

## Code-sharing Agreements

The advent of the aerospace plane will also increase the pressure on airlines to enter into code-sharing agreements with each other.

Code-sharing between two airlines means that two different airlines effectively pose as one, sharing or rotating aircraft crew and responsibility.[26] It has been called a little more than a glorified interline agreement, whereby one airline operates a flight, but both its and another carrier's codes are used.[27] Thus, for example, a passenger who contracts with airline A to travel from Canada to Australia may find themself in the same aircraft with a passenger who contracted with airline B for the same journey.

The US Department of Transportation (DoT) uses a somewhat technical definition for code-sharing, referring to it as

> ... a common airline industry marketing practice where, by mutual agreement between cooperating carriers, at least one of the airline designator codes used on a flight is different from that of the airline operating the flight.[28]

The DoT then classifies code-sharing into two types: typical international airline operations, where two or more airlines each use their own designator codes on the same aircraft operation, and domestic code-shared flights, where the code on the passenger's ticket is not that of the operator of the flight, but where the operator does not offer the service in its own name. The DoT goes on to bifurcate international code-sharing, where, in the first category, only one segment of the journey – which usually involves a connection – operates under two different codes, one used by an airline for its local traffic, and the other used by its partner for the entire journey, whereas in the second, the entire journey is advertised and displayed under the codes of the two airlines, which share the flight concerned.[29]

The marketing benefits of code-sharing have been identified as the ability of airlines to co-ordinate schedules, transfer baggage easily, conduct common marketing activities, use through-fares, share check-ins, share airport lounges, share frequent flyer programmes and agree upon exactly which airline is legally responsible for the passenger's whole journey by air. American Airlines, one of the early proponents and participants in the code-sharing concept, adds safeguarding traffic rights to this list, since it claims that a stronger carrier in the market could be forced to code-share with a weaker national carrier, thus spreading commercial benefits on a given route equitably among two carriers.

One of the most scathing attacks on code-sharing is that it seeks to create the illusion that inter-line connections between code-sharing partners are equivalent to on-line connections, which is not so. It is claimed that this alleged illusion is successful because passengers prefer on-line to inter-line connections by a ratio of approximately four to one. Robert Crandall, Chairman of American Airlines, is of the view that allowing foreign carriers to deceive consumers that a domestic code-shared service is really an extension of an international service of a foreign carrier effectively precludes genuine carriers from building strong, dependable on-line services.[30] Crandall also believes that code-sharing is an anti-consumer marketing activity, in that it causes multiple listings of the same flights in computer reservations systems and printed multi-airline schedules, thus debasing the quality of the information available to consumers.[31]

Code-sharing really gathered momentum with the introduction of computer reservations systems. Major US airlines found it attractive to engage in code-sharing in relation to CRSs, as this gave them more exposure on the CRS screen. Although code-shared flights may not yet be indentified as such, they do now appear in CRSs as on-line connections, and are thus given priority over inter-line connections, giving them a higher profile, so that they are more likely to be booked by a travel agent.[32] Including code-shared flights, which appear as 'connections with aircraft change', means that they can appear at least four times on the same screen. Some countries therefore view code-sharing agreements as effective marketing tools, and dissociate the concept entirely from the issue of traffic rights.

In January 1995, US Secretary of State for Transportation Fedrico Pena announced the International Aviation Policy Statement of the United States, which primarily endorsed code-sharing as a cost-effective way for carriers to enter new markets and expand their systems.[33] Earlier, in December 1994, the US DoT had released the report on international code-sharing which it had commissioned from Gellman Research Associates.[34] Secretary of State Fedrico Pena referred to the study as follows:

> This study fully supports the department's international aviation policy statement. It demonstrates that the movement towards globalization and transnational alliances through code sharing and liberalized bilat-

eral arrangements delivers benefits not only for United States consumers but for the United States airline industry as well.[35]

One of the issues that emerged from the study was that the critical factor in code-sharing is not whether it is good or bad, but whether it has certain undesirable effects that need to be addressed by policy makers. Based on an econometric consumer choice model that compared certain code-sharing agreements with non-code shared flights, the study concluded that the negative impact on consumers as a result of potential deception is inconsequential, as any impact of such misleading practices would be cushioned by existing DoT safety nets. The GRA study's findings were also consistent with the overall DoT perception that all international traffic will ultimately be restructured into long-haul services linking intercontinental hubs, with intraregional spokes feeding traffic, leading to the proliferation of airlines and the expansion of code-sharing.[36]

The study concluded that benefits to consumers, estimated at $37.4 million, were minuscule compared to the approximately $10 billion that passengers spend each year on transatlantic tickets. Even if one were to assume, as the study suggests, that the figure should be doubled, a gain of around $75 million is still comparatively inconsequential. Another conclusion was that the consumer benefits of code-sharing were difficult to quantify in fiscal terms, but could be measured in terms of higher convenience, higher quality of airline service, and time savings generated through the faster flight times offered by code-shared flights.

## Features of Code-sharing

Code-sharing means that the flight code for one airline is used on one or more flights operated by another airline. One of the commonest uses of the term is to signify that two airlines have concluded an arrangement according to which two or more connecting flights are offered under a common designator code and flight number or those of both airlines, although individual segments are only operated with aircraft of one airline.

Code-sharing arrangements can form part of larger co-operation arrangements between the parties, including provisions on such issues as, for example, revenue or profit-sharing, capacity allocation (block-spacing), co-ordination of schedules, baggage handling and usage of nearby gates at the same airport, or the same airport in an airport system.

While code-sharing was initially mainly carried out between carriers in bilateral traffic, so-called 'third-country' code-sharing is becoming more and more important. This refers to arrangements between carriers of which at least one carrier does not have the nationality of either of the two countries touched by the service which is the subject of the arrangement.

Some aeronautical authorities world-wide consider that such code-sharing arrangements require an authorization. Some consider it as a normal co-operation (or marketing) arrangement between airlines, requiring no approval at all.

Code-sharing has considerable advantages for the two partners of such an arrangement. One of the main advantages is the more efficient and effective use of expensive aircraft. By concluding code-sharing arrangements an airline, at the same time, is able to reduce the operations of its own aircraft and to offer more flight connections under the airline's own designator code and own flight number. In addition to this, the economic risk of operating a route is reduced, and handling and air navigation fees are reduced. As a result of a code-sharing arrangement, an airline might also find it worthwhile to fly to points it had not previously served.

A further potential advantage for the code-sharing partners is the favoured treatment their connections enjoy in some computer reservation systems. Many systems outside the European Union and the ECAC area show code-sharing connections as on-line connections, ranking them higher than other inter-line connections, so code-sharing connections tend to be booked first. This can create considerable competitive advantages for the code-sharing partners compared to those competitors who have to show the same connections with a non-code-sharing partner as regular inter-line connections. Code-sharing arrangements can also lead to a situation where the many possible combinations of the codes of the partners will lead to excessive exposure on CRS displays, thereby forcing competitors off the initial screens, but the European CRS rules limit these possibilities. Code-sharing can also provide considerable marketing advantages for the partners of such an arrangement. Code-sharing arrangements involving a bigger and a smaller carrier which was hitherto only active in national air traffic can enable the smaller carrier to participate in international air traffic beyond the national framework and, in principle, this is likely to be good for competition.

It is possible that carriers participating in such a code-sharing arrangement might agree not to start up any new services or terminate any existing ones on the route in question and they might even refrain from competing with any connecting services each operated. This means that code-sharing arrangements, in extreme cases, might lead to a restriction of competition, but such an effect is more likely where code-sharing arrangements form part of larger co-operation arrangements between the parties, or where code-sharing covers less busy routes.

The increase in the number of air services offered under the designator code of each code-sharing partner benefits the passenger because, as a rule, the code-sharing partners co-ordinate their flight schedules so that connecting destinations which otherwise could only be reached after considerable delays can now, despite a change of airline, be reached after only a short interim stop.

When a passenger books a flight, it can be difficult to tell whether they will have to change aircraft and, above all, airline *en route*, so a passenger may be carried without prior notice by an aircraft of a different carrier. Such problems arise only in the passenger has been misled during the booking process, however, and this is less likely in Europe, where the CRSs are obliged to show the identity of the air carrier actually operating the flight. Furthermore, a condition can be placed on carriers via their operating permits to the effect that they must ensure that passengers are informed of the identity of the carrier performing a particular service.

At best, code-sharing arrangements lead to a situation where the carriers involved can reduce the use of their own aircraft on certain routes, leading to a reduction in fuel consumption, and therefore lower air pollution, as long as the aircraft freed in this way are not used to provide additional flight connections. It could also mean that airport slots could be freed for other flight connections. In addition, routes that had been served by both partners with their own aircraft from and to the same airport which might have had to be discontinued because of low load factors could still be served by one code-shared flight. A further advantage could be that airports that at the moment only have few connections to international destinations will be able to attract international air traffic, benefiting airports as well as passengers. On the other hand, code-sharing might also lead to a situation where one partner only serves a few central gateways in the territory of the other partner with its own aircraft, and the other partner operates the national feeder services. This could result in fewer airports handling traffic and, more specifically, fewer movements as segments of long-haul operations. As international passengers would still pass through the airport concerned, this could lead to a decline in the number of flights.

The regulatory treatment of code-sharing arrangements may be characterized by two different approaches.

On the one hand, code-sharing is seen primarily as a mere marketing tool which does not require any prior authorization from the competent authorities (unless required explicitly in any applicable bilateral or multilateral arrangement). This view is essentially based on the argument that code-sharing does not imply any additional operations or any increase in capacity, but merely improves the marketing possibilities of existing services.

On the other hand, code-sharing is seen as an (at least indirect) form of market access for a code-sharing carrier which requires prior authorization on the basis of underlying traffic rights and/or special code-sharing rights. In support of this position, it is usually argued that the code-sharing carrier offers the service as if it were its own, and thus may circumvent agreed frequency and capacity restrictions.

Since States enjoy sovereignty over their airspace the States involved would seem to be able to regulate the matter as they wish.

The code-sharing agreements concluded between US and European carriers for routes between the USA and Europe, as well as the exchanges of views among the governments of the ECAC States, have presented the question of whether code-sharing can be seen separately from the traffic rights and frequency or capacity framework. In other words, on the basis of such co-operation arrangements, can services be operated to points for which no traffic rights exist, or for which code-sharing services have not been expressly agreed between the States concerned?

In the light of the above discussion, the following issues may be identified as being worthy of consideration:

- the impact of code-sharing arrangements on bilaterally agreed frequency and capacity restrictions;
- restrictions that mean a carrier can show its designator code and its flight number on a segment to be operated by its code-sharing partner only if the carrier has obtained traffic rights for that segment but does not operate on it;
- whether code-sharing under agreements between governments should be treated as traffic rights, or whether they should be regarded as commercial arrangements that require no official approval;
- the need for regulations covering competition aspects of code-sharing;
- the usefulness of agreeing on regulations for third-country code-sharing on routes via intermediate points, or code-sharing between carriers of one party and those of a third State;
- the relevance of principles of reciprocity, such as that a third country whose airline concludes a code-sharing arrangement with an airline from one of the two contracting States which concerns services from points in the territory of the other contracting State should grant similar code-sharing rights to the airlines of the other contracting State.

Owing to increasing interest in code-sharing among airlines, a global network of co-operating airlines may develop very quickly. Not all States agree how code-sharing should be dealt with, though few doubt its importance.

## Comments

In commercial terms, the aerospace plane will be one more feature in the air transort industry which will call for the world to move from total restraint of competition to a more rational approach. Of course, as Wassenbergh observes, governments must closely control the activities of the air carriers in the markets they serve, but contrived notions of predetermined capacity should not be a factor in the commercial assessment of the aerospace plane's potential. Rather, the focus should be on commercial co-operation between air carriers.

## Notes

1 See *National Geographic,* March 1981, at 317.
2 S. Mishra and T. Pavlasisk, 'On the Lack of Physical Bases for Defining a Boundary between Air Space and Outer Space', *Annals of Air & Space Law,* 1982, Vol. VII, 399, at 409.
3 Karl-Heinz Böckstiegel, 'Prospects of Future Development in the Law of Outerspace', *Annals of Air & Space Law,* 1983, Vol. VIII, at 305.
4 Id., at 314.
5 Razanowski, Moleff and Smith, *The U.S. National Aero-space Plane: A Comparison with Aero-space Programs in Other Countries, and Future U.S. Options,* CRS-3, Washington, DC: Congressional Research Service, Library of Congress, 1989.
6 Among the issues discussed at this conference were the application of law, the status of passengers as 'astronauts', registration and liability. See *Journal of Space Law,* 1989, Vol. 17, No. 1, at 73–4.
7 Christol, 'The Aerospace Plane: Its Legal and Political Future', *Space Policy,* 1993, No. 9, at 35.
8 V.S. Vereschetin, 'Next Steps in International Space Law', in Nandasiri Jasentuliyana (ed.), *Perspectives on International Law,* Deventer: Kluwer, 1995, at 463–70.
9 Tanja L. Masson-Zwaan, 'The Aerospace Plane: An Object at the Cross-roads between Air and Space Law', *Air and Space Law De Lege Ferenda: Essays in Honour of Henri A. Wassenbergh,* Martinus Nijhoff, 1992, 247, at 257–8.
10 Stephen Gorove, 'Legal and Policy Issues of the Aerospace Plane', *Journal of Space Law,* 1988, Vol. 16, No. 2, 147, at 150.
11 *Convention on International Civil Aviation,* ICAO Doc. 7300/6 (6th edn), 1980.
12 Id., Article 5.
13 Id., Article 6.
14 For a detailed discussion on the current global situation of air traffic rights see R.I.R. Abeyratne, 'The Air Traffic Rights Debate: A Legal Study', *Annals of Air & Space Law,* 1993, Vol. XVIII, No. 1, at 3; R.I.R. Abeyratne, 'The Worldwide Air

Transport Conference and Air Traffic Rights: A Commentary', *European Transport Law*, 1995, Vol. XXX, No. 2, at 131–47.

15 'U.S. Airlines Urge Halt to U.K. Open Sky Talks', *Air Letter*, 25 July 1996, at 3. See also 'Fly America Equals U.S. Protectionism?', *Avmark Aviation Economist*, April/May 1996, at 3–6.

16 'No Surprises in Japan's Rejection of Open Skies', *Aviation Daily*, 28 June 1996, at 529.

17 'U.S.–Japan: Fair Play Comes First', *Airlines International*, January/February 1996, at 7.

18 'SIA Chief Seeks Open Skies between U.S. and Asia', *Air Letter*, 24 June 1996, at 3.

19 'Delta Calls for Open Skies with Europe', *Air Letter*, 24 May 1996, at 1.

20 Maurice Flanagan, 'Open Skies and the Survival of the Fittest', *Aerospace*, August 1996, at 16.

21 Henri Wassenbergh, 'De-regulation of Competition in International Air Transport', *Air & Space Law*, 1996, Vol. XXI, No. 2, 80, at 83.

22 Id., at 89.

23 'New Economic Forces Reshape Global Aviation', *Aviation Daily*, 20 November 1995, at 283.

24 For a discussion on predetermination of capacity and its commercial implications, see Wassenbergh, op. cit., at 80–9.

25 For a detailed discussion and analysis of the conference, see Abeyratne, 'The World-wide Air Transport Conference and Air Traffic Rights', op. cit., at 131–47. See also R.I.R. Abeyratne, 'The Air Traffic Rights Debate: Where Does Everyone Stand?', *Lloyd's Aviation Law*, 1 September 1995, Vol. 14, No. 17, at 1–6. A commentory on the Conference is also contained in B.D.K. Henaku, 'ICAO: Fourth Air Transport Conference', *Zeitschrift für Luft- und Weltraumrecht*, September 1994, at 247–56.

26 'Code Sharing: If It's Tuesday, This Must be Aeroflot', *Airways*, January/February 1995, at 19. See also 'Is Airline's Gain Consumer's Loss?', *Avmark Aviation Economist*, October 1994, Vol. II, No. 8, at 13.

27 'Coded Warnings', *Airline Business*, January 1995, at 26.

28 *Avmark Aviation Economist*, October 1994, Vol. II, No. 8, at 16.

29 Ibid.

30 See Robert Crandall, 'Chicago's Legacy: Barriers to Multilateral Liberalization', *Viewpoint*, 1996, Vol. 2, No. 1, 6, at 12. Crandall cites the example of the British Airways–USAir code-sharing agreement which allegedly allows British Airways access to nearly six times as many world city-pair markets as are available to American Airlines. He further claims that since British Airways now has the ability to gather passengers from almost anywhere in the United States and fly them across the Atlantic, and since it has created pseudo-hubs in the United States to connect with its real hub at London Heathrow, neither the British Government not British Airways would have any incentive to let American Airlines or any other US carrier compete with British Airways for any substantial portion of the traffic flowing across Heathrow from countries around the world to and from the United States.

31 Ibid.

32 See Jan Ernest C. de Groot, 'Code Sharing – U.S. Policies and Lessons for Europe', *Air & Space Law*, 1994, Vol. XIX, No. 2, 62, at 64.

33 'Coded Warnings', *Airline Business*, January 1995, at 26.

34 The objectives of the study were: to develop a methodology to assess the effects of code-sharing on the level and distribution of traffic among carriers, with the capability to measure the effect of future code-sharing agreements; to examine the effects of code-sharing on the costs and profitability of airlines; to

assess the effects of code-sharing on consumers of airline services, and to project the future use and impact of code-sharing over the next twenty years.

35 'GRA Report Sanctifies DoT Policy', *Avmark Aviation Economist*, December 1994, at 2.

36 Ibid.

# 9 The Automated Screening of Passengers and the Smart Card

## Introduction

One of the most exciting developments in air transport in recent times is the development of the 'smart card' – a plastic card resembling a credit card – which will enable air travellers to be cleared through airport customs and immigration control automatically. Once it is introduced effectively and efficiently on a large scale, automatic screening of travellers is expected to offer a major breakthrough in the facilitation of air transport.

The smart card is prepared using a biometric measuring device which scans and stores data on certain physical characteristics of a person on the 'smart card', which can then be used as a travel document, to verify that the holder of the card is the true owner by checking the biometric data against a central database.

The preferred, and perhaps easiest, method of doing this is to scan a person's hand and store biometric information on the card so it can be checked at control points. The identification process and subsequent clearance of passengers only takes seconds, simply requiring them to place their hand on a scanner while swiping or feeding the card through a reader.

Some automated passenger screening systems are already in use, notably the INSPASS system in the United States. Australia, Canada, the United Kingdom, the Netherlands and Germany are also considering introducing the smart card, and it has been envisaged that world-wide use of automated screening of travellers would speed up the admission process, guarantee greater security, use immigration and customs resources more effectively and efficiently, avoid unnecessary expenditure involving inadmissible passengers, and, most importantly, alleviate the airport congestion problems which will result from increased passenger traffic at airports in the future.

However efficient the automated screening of air travellers is, it is incontrovertible that such a process has legal implications. The screening process to identify travellers would require their consent. A more serious implication would be the legalities involved if a technical flaw in the system barred a genuine passenger from entering a country. In such an instance, the legal validity of the data on the passenger, their admissibility in court, and the liability of the authorities concerned become relevant.

This chapter will examine some of the areas of law which have emerged in common law jurisdictions on the subject of electronic data interchange and legal liability which may apply by analog to passengers who are categorized as inadmissible by the automatic screening process.

## Regulatory Provisions

Regulatory provisions pertaining to the custody and care of passengers are contained in Section E of Chapter 3 of Annex 9 to the Chicago Convention,[1] which provides *in limine* that the public authorities concerned shall, without unreasonable delay, accept passengers and crew for examination as to their admissibility into the State.[2] There is also a provision calling for co-operation between contracting States and operators in establishing the validity of travel documents.[3] Furthermore, each contracting State is empowered to seize fraudulent, falsified or counterfeit travel documents of inadmissible persons. The same provision requires State authorities which discover the inadmissible passenger to provide a photocopy of the forged travel document together with a covering letter to the airline which carried the inadmissible passenger to that country.[4] The operator is responsible for transporting the passenger back to their point of departure.[5]

If smart cards are used as travel documents, it may not be possible for the authorities concerned to comply with the above provision of Annex 9. Instead, they would have to provide the operator with details of computer records and other documentation as evidence of the fraud or irregular conduct of the inadmissible passenger. The difficulty posed by this eventuality would be that if a disgruntled or aggrieved inadmissible passenger decided to seek adjudication in the courts, either against the authorities concerned or against the operator, or both, the courts would have to consider the validity and admissibility of the computer data presented as evidence in support of the claim.

This anomaly is compounded by the fact that Standard 3.41 of Annex 9, which requires the removing State to issue a covering letter together with the photocopy of the fraudulent document, has a Note which directs the reader to a suggested format for the covering letter. The covering letter, which appears in Appendix 9 to the Annex, is addressed to the appropriate authority at the original point of embarkation of the passenger, to which they are to be returned by the operator. The letter states that the fraudulent travel document, which will be required as evidence in the inadmissible passenger's prosecution in the removing State, has been impounded. The photocopy is presumably to be issued as an interim measure, until the original is returned after legal proceedings. The problem is, if a passenger found to be inadmissible through automated screening elects to take legal action against the operator in the State which issued the smart card, seeking redress for the automation irregularity which led to denial of access, they would be left only with a photocopy of the smart card to present as evidence before the Court. Therefore, in order to comply with Appendix 9 to the Annex in a meaningful way, the removing State may have to produce electronic data evidence to show why the passenger was refused entry.

## Legal Issues

The obligation on a removing State to produce computer evidence to support an inadmissible passenger's deportation is judicially supported in the analogous decision of *American Banker Insurance Co.* v. *Caruth*,[6] where the court held that a party's failure to produce computer documents can result in the court ruling in their opponent's favour. In this instance, the Texas Court of Appeal awarded judgment against a complainant which failed to produce relevant computer files within the time limit set by the court. The principle that the State is obliged to produce files containing electronically stored data is contained in the 1979 judgment of *Ball* v. *State of New York*,[7] where Moriarty J held that if a claimant demanded the retrieval of computer information pertaining to their case, a state was legally obliged to produce that information to court. That principle was endorsed by the 1993 decision of *First Technology Safety Systems Inc.* v. *Depinet*,[8] where it was held that a trial court has judicial discretion to grant an *ex parte* seizure order to preserve electronic evidence or to promote the interests of justice.

The information provided must be reasonably decipherable and usable. Above all, the person requesting the information as evidence should be able to access the data. In *Greyhound Computer Corp., Inc.* v. *IBM*,[9] where the defendant provided computer data which was unreadable by the plaintiff, the court ordered the defendant to assist the plaintiff in accessing the information by supplying materials and personnel.

Judicial support and the topical relevance of the requirement in Appendix 9 to Annex 9 and its applicability to smart cards is reflected in the 1995 decision of *National Union Electric Corporation* v. *Matsushita Electric Industries,*[10] where the Court held:

> ... we now live in a society where much of the data which our society desires is stored in computer discs. This process will escalate in years to come; we suspect that by the year 2000 virtually all data will be stored in some form of computer memory.[11]

The court further held that information stored in electronic form would be easier to search and manipulate and, in this particular instance, requested the parties to litigation to provide electronic copies of evidence, even though the information was already available on paper. Therefore, by applying the *Matsushita* decision to Annex 9, one could validly argue that the requirement to produce a copy of the fraudulent document in Appendix 9 would still remain valid, but would be construed as being applicable to electronic data retrieval and evidence as necessary.

## A Paradigm Regime of Liability

The legal significance of automated passenger screening in air transport will become particularly relevant, when passengers' physical attributes and travel cards are checked both at the point of departure and the point of arrival, allowing the biometric data to be transmitted from one point to another while they are still airborne, to be verified on arrival. Although automated screening can serve as an efficient identification process and an effective security measure, there has been no documented legal study which has specifically addressed issues of admissibility of evidence and liability in relation to the use of biometric identification by automated screening.

Perhaps the only analogy is the study conducted by the United Nations Commission on International Trade Law (UNCITRAL) in 1997 on electronic commerce. This study, and the principles formulated thereby, may serve as a paradigm for biometric identification, particularly in the context of UNCITRAL's deliberations in March 1997 on 'digital signatures' in electronic commerce. At its 30th Session, held in Vienna on 12–30 May 1997, the UNCITRAL General Assembly considered the *Report of the Working Group on Electronic Commerce* in New York, 18–28 February 1997,[12] which described a digital signature that could be used to approve transnational commercial transactions conducted through electronic data interchange. The technique converts an original signature into a numerical value associated with the originator's private cryptographic key, which can be attached to a data message, making it possible to check that this numerical value has been obtained using the originator's key.[13]

If this principle is applied to a handprint, which may be encrypted dimensionally to be stored by a computer and decrypted when necessary, one could also apply by analogy the UNCITRAL recommendations that approved authorities should be able to inspect, monitor and use such electronic data. They would then be liable to any person who acts in good faith in relying on such information for any loss due to defects or technical breakdowns of the software.[14] UNCITRAL has also suggested liability based on tortious principles of negligence which could be mitigated by the contributory negligence of the aggrieved person.[15]

## Comments

Initially, automated screening of passengers using smart cards will probably be carried out by States on a regional basis, for example, so that they could be used in Europe only by European Community citizens. With the further development of technology and evolution of air transport throughout the world, it is possible to envisage a stage at which this process of passenger clearance would be used on a wider scale. Sooner or later, therefore, the users and service providers of this technology will have to address the legal consequences of this process which may arise in certain circumstances.

One of the inherent dangers of the use of biometric identification and automated passenger screening lies in the aftermath of the discovery of an inadmissible passenger. If the travel document used is a smart card, the authorities may not have supporting documentation to explain to the passenger why they are found to be inadmissible. In particular, authorities will have to address the manner in which a person may be held under such circumstances until they are handed over to the carrier for return to the point of departure.

The restraint of a person without sufficient explanation may be tantamount to the common law notion of false imprisonment, of which arrest is a species. False imprisonment is committed where a person unlawfully, intentionally or recklessly restrains another's freedom of movement from a particular place.[16] Physical detention is an essential ingredient for grounding an action in false imprisonment. Thus if a person agrees to go to a police station voluntarily, they have not been arrested even though the person taking them would have arrested them if they had refused to go.[17]

The law provides that where an officer of a State authority, such as a police or customs officer, has reasonable grounds for suspecting that an arrestable offence has been committed, they may arrest without a warrant anyone whom they have reasonable grounds for suspecting to be guilty of that offence.[18] The offence of false imprisonment is one of 'basic intent', and despite the paucity of authority as to whether the element of *mens rea* or intention is necessary to constitute the offence of false imprisonment,[19] at least one decision has recognized the requirement.[20]

In the early case of *Christy* v. *Leachinsky*,[21] Lord Simonds, while observing that it was the right of every citizen to be free from arrest, and that they should be entitled to resist arrest unless that arrest is lawful, concluded that a person cannot be arrested unless they know why they are being arrested.[22] However, this principle has since been replaced in the United Kingdom by Section 28 of the Police and Criminal Evidence Act 1984, which provides that where a person is arrested, otherwise than being informed that they are under arrest, they must be informed of the reasons why as soon as practicable afterwards. While this provision does not deny that a person who is arrested must be informed of the grounds for arrest, it dispenses with the exclusive need to inform the person at the time of arrest.[23]

In the more recent case of *Murray* v. *Ministry of Defence*,[24] the plaintiff sued the Crown for false imprisonment on the ground that she had been detained and questioned by members of the armed forces for thirty minutes before they indicated to her that she was under arrest. She claimed that her arrest took place only when she was informed that she was under arrest, and that the preceding detention was therefore unlawful. The House of Lords at appeal held that where a person was detained or restrained by a police officer and knew that they were being detained or restrained, such detention amounted to an arrest even though no formal words of arrest were spoken by the officer. Since the plaintiff had been under restraint from the moment she was identified, and must have realized that she was under restraint, she was deemed to have been under arrest from that moment, notwithstanding that the formal arrest took place half an hour later.

Lord Griffiths, quoting an earlier decision,[25] endorsed the principle that arrest did not depend merely on the legality of the act but on the fact whether the person arrested had been deprived of their liberty. His Lordship went on address the decision in *Christy* v. *Leachinsky*,[26] and noted:

> There can be no doubt that in ordinary circumstances, police should tell a person the reason for his arrest at the time they make the arrest. If a person's liberty is being restrained he is entitled to know the reason. If the police fail to inform him, the arrest will be unlawful with the consequence that if police are assaulted as the suspect resists arrest, he commits no offence. Therefore, if he is taken to custody, he

> will have action for wrongful imprisonment. However, *Christy* v. *Leachinsky* made it clear that there are exceptions to this rule.[27]

The exceptions that Lord Griffiths referred to were those expressed by Viscount Simon, where, when circumstances were such that the person detained knew the general nature of the alleged offence, the requirement for informing them of the fact and grounds for their arrest did not arise. Viscount Simon held that technical or precise language need not be used, and since any person is entitled to their freedom, if restraint was used and they knew the reason for such restraint, that was enough.[28]

In the light of the above *cursus curiae*, it is evident that immigration authorities may have to address the potential danger of restraining seemingly inadmissible passengers who are rejected by the automatic screening process at the point of entry into their country. Therefore, at least initially, when the automatic screening process has yet to be widely used and tested, immigration authorities will indeed have to tread with abundant caution.

One way to circumvent this potential problem may be to incorporate the biometric information in a machine-readable passport[29] which has already been developed by ICAO and is in wide use, so that passengers can swipe the document as they place their hand on the biometric scanner. If the turnstile fails to open, the State authorities will have a much more substantial document to examine, and forgery may be easier to detect on a document than on a mere plastic card.

## Notes

1 *Convention on International Civil Aviation*, signed Chicago, 7 December 1944, ICAO Doc. 7300/6 (1980).
2 Annex 9 to the *Convention on International Civil Aviation* (10th edn), April 1997 (Facilitation), Standard 3.38.
3 Id., Standard 3.40.3.
4 Id., Standard 3.41.
5 Ibid.
6 786 SW 2d 427 Texas Ct App. 1990.
7 421 NYS 2d 328 (Ct Cl. 1979).
8 11 F 3d 641 (6th Cir. 1993).
9 3 *Computer Law Serv. Rep.*, 138, at 139 (D Minn. 1971).
10 494 F Supp. 1,262.
11 Id., at 1,275.
12 A/CN.9/437, 12 March 1997.
13 Id., at 10, Draft Article A.
14 Id., para. 51, Draft Article H, at 17.
15 Ibid.

16 Smith and Hogan, *Criminal Law* (7th edn), London: Butterworths, 1992, at 431. See also *Rahman* v. *Queen* (1985) 81 Cr. App. Rep. 349, at 353.
17 *Campbell* v. *Tormey* (1969) 1 All ER 961, cited in Smith and Hogan, op. cit., at 432.
18 Police and Criminal Evidence Act 1984, Section 24 (6).
19 False imprisonment is generally considered under civil actions where the element of *mens rea* is not relevant.
20 *Re Hutchins* (1988) Crim. LR 379.
21 (1947) 1 All ER 567.
22 Id., at 575.
23 Smith and Hogan, op. cit., at 438.
24 (1988) 2 All ER 521.
25 *Spicer* v. *Holt* (1976) 3 All ER 71, at 79.
26 Ibid.
27 Id., 526.
28 *Christy* v. *Leachinsky,* (1947) 1 All ER 567, at 572–3.
29 For a detailed account of the machine-readable passport, see R.I.R. Abeyratne, 'The Development of the Machine Readable Passport and Visa and the Legal Rights of the Data Subject', *Annals of Air & Space Law*, 1992, Vol. XVII, Part II, at 1–31.

# PART II
# SAFETY AND
# AIR CARRIER LIABILITY

# 10 Safety in International Aviation

## Introduction

In 1995, 19 Western-built jet aircraft were totally destroyed in air crashes which killed 383 passengers and 39 crew members.[1] Although this rate of loss has been steady for the past decade, there were three major losses in 1996 – the famous Valujet and TWA aircraft in the United States, and the world's worst mid-air collision ever over new New Delhi, India, where a Saudia Boeing 747 with 312 persons aboard collided with a Kazak aircraft carrying 37 passengers and crew. All on board were killed.

At the time of writing the Council of the International Civil Aviation Organization had decided to convene an international conference for Directors General of Civil Aviation to review the ICAO Safety Oversight Programme and to consider its expansion in Montreal, from 10 to 12 November 1999.[2] ICAO released its preliminary accident and security statistics for 1996, which show that scheduled air carriers from the 185 ICAO Contracting States reported 23 fatal aircraft accidents in 1996, compared with 26 in the previous year.[3] Although the incident rate declined in 1996, the number of passenger deaths reported rose dramatically in 1996, to 1,135, compared with 710 in 1995.

Safety is the primary concern of the world aviation community, not only because the fundamental postulates of the Chicago Convention of 1944[4] call for the safe and orderly development of international civil aviation[5] and mandate ICAO to ensure the safe and orderly growth of international civil aviation throughout the world,[6] but also because the aviation world faces a critical era where, in the words of Dr Assad Kotaite, President of the ICAO Council:

> ... the international aviation community cannot afford to relax its vigilance ... ICAO would continue to take timely action to ensure safety and security standards are in effect, and that deficiencies are properly and efficiently addressed.[7]

The compelling need for higher standards in aviation safety was formally recognized when the ICAO Council adopted ICAO's Strategic Action Plan on 7 February 1997. The basic strategic objective of the plan is to further the safety, security and efficiency of international civil aviation. ICAO seeks to accomplish this task by assisting States in identifying deficiencies in the implementation of Annexes to the Chicago Convention, in particular provisions which ensure safety in aviation.

One of the core elements of ICAO activity on safety, according to its Strategic Action Plan, is assessment by teams of experts of the capacity of participating States to control the level of safety for which they have responsibility. ICAO's Safety Oversight Programme, which would implement this activity, extends to personnel licensing, operation of aircraft and aircraft airworthiness, and may in the foreseeable future extend to areas such as air traffic control and the operation of airports.

Taking a cue from ICAO, several regional aviation organizations have formally incorporated safety provisions in their documentation. The African Civil Aviation Commission (AFCAC), at its 13th Plenary Session in Abuja, 11–18 May 1995, discussed the matter of safety oversight in Africa, which led to the Commission adopting Decision S13-3 on Safety Oversight.[8] This decision recognizes that States must take appropriate measures to ensure compliance with international safety standards contained in the relevant Annexes to the Chicago Convention, and that most African States may not have the necessary infrastructure to fully implement such standards. The Commission refers to the ICAO Safety Oversight Programme in Decision S13-3, and instructs the AFCAC Bureau to improve safety oversight in AFCAC activities and promote co-operation among African States in the field of safety oversight. Through the decision, AFCAC has also requested ICAO to assist African States in introducing the Safety Oversight Programme in Africa.

At its 100th Meeting of Directors General of Civil Aviation in Paris, 14–15 May 1997, the European Civil Aviation Conference (ECAC) discussed an ECAC Recommendation on Safety of Foreign Aircraft[9] which calls for increased ramp checks on aircraft, and rigid adherence, on a bilateral basis, by States to the provisions of the Chicago Convention on licensing of personnel and certification of aircraft.[10]

The ECAC bilateral safety clause calls *in limine* for consultations to be called for at any stage where they would relate to safety standards of aircrew, aircraft or the operation of aircraft. The provision allows for the revocation of the clause if one party to the agreement finds that the other does not maintain minimum ICAO Standards. The clause also allows her random ramp checks so that one party can determine whether aircraft conform to Article 33 of the Chicago Convention, which relates to certification of airworthiness.

At the same meeting, ECAC also discussed a recommendation on leasing of aircraft and safety,[11] which calls for standards as prescribed in Annex 6 (Operation of Aircraft) to the Chicago Convention and minimum conditions on the use of leased aircraft, to ensure that they are maintained in accordance with ICAO standards of safety.

It must be noted that safety regulations of the European Community are generally stringent on product liability,[12] stipulating that any person who imports into the community a product for leasing is considered a manufacturer of that product for purposes of product liability.

Another regional organization which has recognized the compelling need for the implementation of safety oversight in its region is the Latin American Civil Aviation Commission (LACAC). At LACAC's 11th Assembly in Manaus, 7–10 November 1994, some LACAC member States adopted the Manaus Declaration, which expressed support for the role of the ICAO Council in establishing a safety oversight programme, and requested ICAO to implement the programme as quickly as possible.[13]

Both ICAO and regional aviation organizations have focused their attention on the air navigational aspects of safety oversight but the safety of civil aviation does not simply depend on safe air navigation. There are other factors, such as human conduct in the aircraft and air traffic controller liability.

Although this chapter will primarily address safety oversight of civil aviation in the field of air navigation, it will also address legal issues relating to the other areas mentioned above which affect the safety of international civil aviation.

## ICAO's Safety Oversight Programme

### *Regulatory Framework*

Three provisions of the Chicago Convention deal with the subject of safety. Primarily, Article 12 requires each contracting State to maintain uniform aviation regulations in conformity, to the greatest possible extent, with those established under the Convention. Article 31 stipulates that every aircraft engaged in international aviation shall be provided with a certificate of airworthiness issued or rendered valid by the State in which it is registered, and Article 32 requires the pilot and other members of the operating crew of every aircraft engaged in international navigation to be provided with certificates of competency. More importantly, Article 32 (b) empowers States to refuse to recognize, for the purposes of flight above their own territories, certificates of competency and licences granted to any of its nationals by another contracting State.

All these provisions really mean one thing – maintain uniform standards in certification so that safety of civil aviation can be ensured. The question is whether such uniformity is ensured in the scenario of an airline which uses large numbers of leased aircraft, or a virtual airline where most services are outsourced and largely unsupervised by the airline itself. There is also the question of whether some airlines may be tempted to accept the lowest cost in terms of contracted-out engineering and maintenance services. The solution is to ensure that regulation in the area of safety is uniform.

Incontrovertibly, responsibility for this should fall on the entire world civil aviation community. The structure required is already in place, enshrined in the ICAO Standards and Recommended Practices (SARPs), but ICAO SARPs do not have absolute powers of enforceability under international law.

Basically, ICAO promulgates its SARPs through its 18 Annexes to the Chicago Convention. Article 54(l) of the Chicago Convention prescribes the adoption of international Standards and Recommended Practices and their designation in Annexes to the Convention, while notifying all contracting States of the action taken. The fundamental question which has to be addressed *in limine*, in considering the effectiveness of ICAO's SARPs, is whether SARPs are legislative in character. If the answer is 'yes', then at least theoretically, one can insist that States adhere to SARPs.

The adoption of SARPS was considered a priority by the ICAO Council in its 2nd Session on 2 September–12 December 1947,[14] which attempted to obviate any delays in the adoption of SARPs on air navigation as required by the 1st ICAO Assembly.[15] SARPs inevitably take two forms: a negative form – such as that States shall not impose more than certain maximum requirements – and a positive form – such as that States shall take certain steps, as prescribed by the ICAO Annexes.[16]

Article 37 of the Convention obtains the undertaking of each contracting State to collaborate in securing the highest practical degree of uniformity in regulations, standards, procedures and organization in relation to international civil aviation in all matters in which such uniformity will facilitate and improve air navigation. Article 38 obliges all contracting States to the Convention to inform ICAO immediately if they are unable to comply with any such international standard or procedure, and to notify differences between their own practices and those prescribed by ICAO. In the case of amendments to international standards, any State which does not make the appropriate amendment to its own regulations or practices shall give notice to the Council of ICAO within 60 days of the adoption of the said amendment to the international standard, or indicate the action which it proposes to take.

There is no room for doubt that the Annexes to the Convention, or parts thereof, lay down rules of conduct both directly and analogically. In fact, although there is a conception based on a foundation of practicality that ICAO's international standards, identified by the phrase 'contracting States shall' have a mandatory flavour (imputed by the word 'shall'), while recommended practices, identified by the phrase 'contracting States may', have only an advisory and recommendatory connotation (imputed by the word 'may'), it is interesting that at least one ICAO document requires States under Article 38 of the Convention, to notify ICAO of all significant differences from both standards and recommended practices, thus making all SARPS regulatory in nature.[17]

Another strong factor that reflects the overall ability and power of the Council to prescribe civil rules of conduct (and therefore legislate) on a strict interpretation of the word is that in Article 22 of the Convention each contracting State agrees to adopt all practical measures through the issuance of special regulations or otherwise, to facilitate and expedite air navigation. It is clear that this provision can be regarded as an incontrovertible rule of conduct that responds to the requirement in Article 54(l) of the Convention. Furthermore, the mandatory nature of Article 90 of the Convention – that an Annex or amendment thereto shall become effective within three months after it is submitted by the ICAO Council to contracting States – is yet another pronouncement on the power of the Council to prescribe rules of State conduct in matters of international civil aviation. *A fortiori*, it is arguable that the ICAO Council is seen not only to possess the attribute of the term jurisfaction (the power to make rules of conduct), but also the term jurisaction (the power to enforce its own rules of conduct). The latter attribute can be seen where the Convention obtains the undertaking of contracting States not to allow airlines to operate through their airspace if the Council decides that the airline concerned is not conforming to a final decision rendered by the Council on a matter that concerns the operation of an international airline.[18] This is particularly applicable when such airline is found not to conform to the provisions of Annex 2 to the Convention, which derives its validity from Article 12 of the Convention relating to rules of the air.[19] In fact, it is relevant that Annex 2, the responsibility for whose promulgation devolves upon the Council by virtue of Article 54(l), sets mandatory rules of the air, making the existence of the legislative powers of the Council an unequivocal and irrefutable fact.

Academic and professional opinion also favours the view that, in a practical sense, the ICAO Council does have legislative powers. Milde says:

> The Chicago Convention, as any other legal instrument, provides only a general legal framework which is given true life only in the practical implementation of its provisions. Thus, for example, Article 37 of the Convention relating to the adoption of international standards and recommended procedures would be a very hollow and meaningless provision without active involvement of all contracting States, Panels, Regional and Divisional Meetings, deliberations in the Air Navigation Commission and final adoption of the standards by the Council. Similarly, provisions of Article 12 relating to the rules of the air applicable over the high seas, Articles 17 to 20 on the nationality of aircraft, Article 22 on facilitation, Article 26 on the investigation of accidents, etc., would be meaningless without appropriate implementation in the respective Annexes. On the same level is the provision of the last sentence of Article 77 relating to the determination by the Council in what manner the provisions of the Convention relating to nationality of aircraft shall apply to aircraft operated by international operating agencies.[20]

Milde concludes that ICAO has regulatory and quasi-legislative functions in the technical field, and plays a consultative and advisory role in the economic sphere.[21] A similar view had earlier been expressed by Buergenthal, who states:

> ... the manner in which the International Civil Aviation organization has exercised its regulatory functions in matters relating to the safety of international air navigation and the facilitation of international air transport provides a fascinating example of international law making ... the Organization has consequently not had to contend with any of the post war ideological differences that have impeded international law making on politically sensitive issues.[22]

Dempsey endorses, in a somewhat conservative manner, the view that ICAO has the ability to make regulations when he states:

> In addition to the comprehensive, but largely dormant adjudicative enforcement held by ICAO under Articles 84–88 of the Chicago Convention, the Agency also has a solid foundation for enhanced participation in economic regulatory aspects of international aviation in Article 44, as well as the Convention's Preamble.[23]

One of the issues that is being addressed by ICAO is the need for it to formulate a comprehensive response to Resolution A29-3, taking into account the related tasks planned or already in hand by the subsidiary bodies. Therefore, one of the main goals of ICAO at present is to find ways to elicit greater interest and participation in the formulation of SARPs by States, and to strengthen its capacity to monitor differences from or compliance with Standards on the basis of its own findings. The latter element is especially important, as differences filed by States do not always appear to represent reality.

ICAO believes that there are a number of reasons that prevent States from indicating their compliance, or otherwise, with ICAO SARPs. These may include:

- insufficient communication between ICAO and recipient States; loss of documentation by recipients, and delays in delivering the documentation to the responsible party beyond the target date for replies; organizational structures of civil aviation authorities which lead to difficulties in identification of, and routing to, the responsible party;
- insufficient resources within States to consider expeditiously and process ICAO documentation, and to implement the relevant standards in their national legislation;
- difficulty in comprehending and interpreting Annex material, as well as subject matter which is beyond the level of expertise of the recipient administration;
- possible lack of understanding about the role of States in the consultation phase of the development of ICAO standards.[24]

More fundamentally, it is possible that States may have insufficient resources either to implement standards or to advise ICAO of non-compliance with the relevant standards. It should be noted in this context that recent initiatives by States to address the concerns raised by the 29th Session of the Assembly and to ensure the safety of their citizens have raised fundamental questions about the effectiveness of the multilateral safety assurance afforded by the Chicago Convention.

ICAO feels that reminding contracting States continually of their obligation to notify the ICAO of any differences to the standards in the Annexes to the Convention remains a critical factor in its advances towards more State participation in its regulatory process. Furthermore, the level of implementation of those standards by States in their national legislation and procedures must be improved. These two elements complement each other: if too many States simply notify ICAO of their non-implementation of the safety standards, States could no longer assume a mutual level of minimum safety standards, and would have to resort to a bilateral or regional approach in order to ensure acceptable safety oversight.

Some catalysts for the global implementation of standards and the harmonization of national rules have been identified in bilateral and multilateral co-operation between States. As was discussed earlier, organizations such as the European Civil Aviation Conference and the African and Latin American Civil Aviation Commissions have already taken initiatives on this matter. Other organizations, such as the Conference of Directors General of Civil Aviation of the Asia and Pacific Regions, the Commonwealth of Independent States and other groups, including trading blocs, may be considered effective vehicles for the promulgation and adoption of agreements and understandings in this regard.

Another significant issue is that there is an increasing need for co-operation in the regulatory field between States in a particular geographic setting and with certain common regulatory needs which are dictated by technical, operational and environmental needs and motives. Recent years have witnessed the growing significance of regional organizations that are addressing traditional ICAO activities such as technical harmonization, standardization and regulatory matters. These activities are likely to intensify in the near future, and may well affect the role of ICAO as the principal intergovernmental organization responsible for the regulation and co-ordination of international civil aviation.

ICAO's strategy for the development and implementation of ICAO standards and recommended practices seeks to make use of modern technological tools but at the same time aim at more basic issues, such as:

- ascertaining and documenting the actual status of implementation of ICAO SARPs and the extent of differences to standards, improving communication channels amongst headquarters, regional offices and States to facilitate this objective;
- improving States' awareness of the vital role they play in the multilateral safety assurance provided for in the Chicago Convention, which is founded upon the effective implementation of ICAO SARPs;
- similarly, creating or improving States' awareness of their role in the development of ICAO SARPs, with a view of encouraging more States to be actively involved in the formulation process;
- pursuing systematic analysis of the reasons for any non-implementation of SARPs and differences to Standards;
- developing realistic programmes, including the ICAO Technical Co-operation Programmes, and their funding, to assist States in implementing SARPs, where necessary;
- establishing adequate co-ordination and co-operation between States in a regional context in the fields of rule-harmonization and the implementation of standards.

ICAO is a UN agency, and the United Nations was created during the Second World War. Although the international community originally questioned whether this wartime union of States could be converted into a peacetime organization for international co-operation, this was resolved by the creation within the Economic and Social Council (ECOSOC) of the United Nations of various specialized agencies – ICAO being one – which were brought into relationship with the United Nations.[25] The ECOSOC may enter into agreements with any of these specialized agencies, co-ordinate the agencies' activities through consultation, and define terms on which the agency concerned would be brought into relationship with the United Nations.[26]

Therefore, ICAO conceptually shares the same international status as the United Nations, while members of the ICAO Secretariat are international civil servants. The establishment of ICAO as the specialized agency of the United Nations responsible for regulating international civil aviation begs the question as to why such specialized agencies are created, instead of conferring the functions which are to be performed by them upon the United Nations itself. One of the reasons that has been adduced is that the general organization of the United Nations and its personnel could not take on all the activities that are handled by the various specialized agencies. Another is that a single organization with a greatly increased administrative personnel would have been too cumbersome and bureaucratic.

Be that as it may, the question of what status ICAO holds in the international community – which in turn would shed some light on the status of its regulations – largely lies in the definition of the word 'agency'. On the term, 'specialized agency', one commentator has observed:

> [T]hey are Specialized as to subject-matter, of course, but the implications of the second term may not be so clear. These Agencies are in fact, as the general UN is not, examples of international administrative agencies ... whose chief function is the administrative one, although the conference or representative organs associated with them (or with which they are associated), and the legislative or policy determining activities of the latter, are not to be disregarded ...
>
> The relationships to be developed between Specialized Agencies and the UN constitutes a major problem of international statesmanship. As in the case of regional organizations, whatever the value of the special institutions the situation would be difficult and dangerous unless adequate measures for coordination of the various elements could be worked out. This is a problem for searching analysis in principle and for careful application in practice. If the Specialized Agencies are created by the UN suitable co-ordination should be possible, but if it be a question of coordinating with the UN an Agency created independently the task is more difficult.[27]

This comment supports the view that a certain co-ordination exists between specialized agencies and the United Nations on the basis of their relationship *ipso facto*. Hence, it may be inferred by this argument that the regulations promulgated by a specialized agency should have similar status and leverage to any created by the parent United Nations.

Over the years, ICAO has played a seminal and alert role in monitoring safety in civil aviation, and has diligently endeavoured to enhance ICAO SARPs and obtain State compliance with these provisions.

At the 31st Session of the ICAO Assembly, held in Montreal on 19 September–4 October 1995, ICAO contracting States adopted Resolution A31-2 on increasing the effectiveness of ICAO.[28] The resolution recognizes the new and rapidly evolving technological, social, economic and legal challenges in the field of civil aviation, and directs the ICAO Council and Secretary General, within their respective competencies, to intensify efforts to develop a Strategic Action Plan for the organization. The plan is required to be implemented by a systematic process governing the financial progress and utilization of the organization. It also directs the Council to ensure the effectiveness of the ICAO safety oversight mechanism.

On 22 May 1997, ICAO officially launched its Strategic Action Plan in accordance with the directives of the Assembly in Resolution A31-2. At the launch, the President of the ICAO Council, Dr Assad Kotaite, renewed calls for increasing powers which would enable ICAO to oversee the implementation of aviation safety and security standards world-wide.[29] Dr Kotaite identified ICAO's role in the present context succinctly when he said:

> Never has there been a greater need for a strong and active ICAO … In civil aviation, globalization, commercialization of government service providers, liberalization of economic regulation, increasing environmental controls and the emergence of new technologies all have significant implications for safety and security. Addressing these issues effectively requires an unprecedented level of co-operation among countries and a corresponding level of global co-ordination which extends beyond borders.[30]

The President of the Council concluded by suggesting that ICAO's goal should be to become the recognized world-wide auditor of safety and security standards for international civil aviation.

The message of the ICAO Council's President echoes the fundamental truth that nothing in international civil aviation is parochial and disconnected.

*Concrete Action Taken by ICAO in the Field of Air Navigation*

The ICAO Safety Oversight Programme's implementation process has its genesis in a Council decision taken on 25 October 1994. The main thrust of the programme was to be the conduct of safety oversight audits by an ICAO team, upon request by the State concerned. On the following day, the Council pronounced that the programme would depend on its success at a multilateral level, and such multilateral assurance of safety would be entirely dependent upon the implementation of ICAO standards and/or filing of differences in accordance with Articles 37 and 38 of the Chicago Convention.[31] Therefore, the Council recognized the signal service rendered by Article 38, which calls for notification by States of their inability to conform to ICAO Standards, as a pivotal point in the Safety Oversight Programme, which was approved by the Council on 7 June 1995. One of the practical advantages offered by the programme to ICAO member States is the voluntary offer by ICAO of follow-up advice and technical assistance as necessary, following a safety audit.

The effective management of airspace is a subject directly related to the ICAO Safety Oversight Programme. On 27 November 1996, the Council addressed the various shortcomings in the air navigation field, and at its 150th Session in April 1997 considered a report by the Air Navigation Commission (ANC) of ICAO which identified the shortcomings.[32] The report consolidates details of progress attenuated from the respective planning and implementation groups (PIRGS) of ICAO regions. A number of shortcomings were identified in the report in the Africa-Indian Ocean Region (AFI), the Caribbean/South American Regions (CAR/SAM) and the Middle East Region (MID).[33]

Based on facts reported by the ANC to Council, the ANC discussed an action plan to address shortcomings and deficiencies in the air navigation field in June 1997, which recommended the following measures:

27. Improving collection of information by establishing non-punitive reporting mechanisms; standardizing reporting by PIRGS; drawing from incident and accident investigations; integrating user's reports; identifying and listing specific deficiencies and considering the expansion of the safety oversight programme to include all safety sensitive areas of air navigation;
28. Improving safety evaluation of reported problems by: standardizing evaluation criteria; bringing serious cases to the notice of ANC; and making a periodic co-ordinated global review of safety-related shortcomings and deficiencies;
29. Taking technical corrective and preventive actions by: determining types of remedies; implementing short-term technical

remedies; implementing long term technical remedies; and facilitating training and the use of high quality and affordable training materials;

30. Taking financial and organizational corrective actions by: improving financial management at State level; improving organizational structure at State level; promoting co-operation between States, including joint-financing agreements, international operating agencies and charges collecting agencies; facilitating a co-operative approach to air traffic management; and consolidating financial commitments and arrangements.[34]

The above general criteria can be effectively applied to specific air navigational problems such as Controlled Flight Into Terrain (CFIT) by the adoption, as recommended by ICAO, of a Minimum Safe Altitude Warning System (MSAW) for aircraft which could be applied world-wide, and a standard approach procedure design which could be used with such modern tools as Global Positioning Systems (GPS) and Flight Management Systems (FMS), which are integral recommendations of the ICAO CNS/ATM (Communication, Navigation, Surveillance and Air Traffic Management) system.

## Human Factors

The safety of civil aviation is largely dependent upon the professional conduct of the technical crew and cabin crew of the aircraft, and on interaction between the two. Whatever the relationship between the flight attendant and passenger and flight attendant and pilot, both relationships have this in common: with regard to an accident caused as a direct or indirect result of the flight attendant's conduct – be it an injury to a passenger or an aircraft accident precipitated by the conduct of the flight attendant affecting pilot performance – the legal consequences of air carrier liability would revolve round whether the act of the flight attendant or pilot, as the case may be, was tantamount to wilful misconduct on the part of the carrier. This issue is explored further in Chapter 12. To a lesser extent, safety is also affected by the conduct of airline passengers.

### *Air Crew Fatigue*

An issue which has aroused much interest is air crew fatigue, where flight safety experts have been involved in using scientific methods to study the contentious issue of pilot fatigue as a cause of incidents and accidents. Although a complete determination of fatigue-causing factors which may have an adverse effect on performance of technical crew on a flight has yet to be made, the limited information and data currently available are being used by the experts to establish a system of working guidelines and rules.

Sleep deprivation is considered a major factor in air crew fatigue, which can produce loss of concentration, slow reaction time, and produce visual illusions, disorientation and, more seriously, misinterpretation of flight instrument information. Fatigue may cause loss of interest in pilots, making them neglect the tasks of completing flight procedures and other necessary routines in flight.[35] Useful countermeasures to combat pilot fatigue have been identified recently by Airbus Industrie, which recommended that airlines take measures such as monitoring cockpit workload, flight crew alertness, sleep loss, and the snoozing habits of crew.[26] Another study by Boeing, which followed an 'alertness management' philosophy, identifies preplanned cockpit naps, assigning relief crew members to a flight, electronic crew activity monitors and scheduled interaction with cabin crew as effective measures in combating crew fatigue.[37]

Analyses of confidential reports to NASA's Aviation Safety Reporting System reflect that approximately 21 per cent of all reported aircraft accidents are related to fatigue.[38] From a legal perspective, this means that fatigue could be a serious factor for consideration on the issue of wilful misconduct, particularly if it can be shown that the defendant airline did not make any serious attempts to address the problem. Legal connotations of fatigue as an identifiable element of wilful misconduct may possibly emerge, particularly in instances relating to ultra-long-haul flights, where flight duty of a technical crew member in charge of a flight exceeds 16 hours. Dr Michael Bagshaw, Senior Aviation Physician of British Airways, has observed:

> As soon as we fly, we are venturing beyond our natural environment and compromising our health and safety, so it is a question of minimizing risks by maintaining a sense of proportion. The whole of aviation is based on a risk benefit analysis, and ultra long-haul flying is no exception.[39]

From a regulatory standpoint, ICAO has made provision for flight time and flight duty period limitations in Annex 6 to the Chicago Convention, for the sole purpose of reducing the probability of fatigue of flight crew members which may adversely affect the safety of flight.[40] The Annex identifies types of fatigue that may affect the performance of technical crew on a flight, and defines flight duty periods.[41] The definition of 'flight duty period' in the Annex is intended to cover a continuous period of duty which inevitably includes a flight or a series of flights. The period of duty is calculated to include all duties flight crew members may be required to carry out from the moment they report at their place of employment on the day of a flight until they are relieved of duties after they complete their flight or series of flights.[42] The Annex specifies that rest periods are intended to allow air crew to recover from fatigue, and the way this recovery is achieved is the responsibility of the individual.[43] The most salutary provision in the Annex relates to guidelines in the formulation of regulations or rules governing flight time limitations, which provide that the number of crew and the extent to which the various tasks to be performed can be divided among the members should be taken into account. The provision further calls for adequate horizontal rest periods to be indulged in by air crew if duty time is to be extended. Some of the critical factors identified as affecting crew performance are traffic density, navigational and communication facilities, rhythm of the work/sleep cycle, the number of landings and take-offs, aircraft handling, performance characteristics and weather patterns.[44] Similar provisions are contained in Part III of Annex 6 in regard to helicopter performance and operating limitations.[45]

In 1994, the Air Navigation Commission of ICAO considered a review of proposed amendments to Parts I and III of Annex 6 in the light of comments by States and international organizations[46] received as a result of a survey conducted by ICAO.[47] The overall comments of States were tantamount to recognizing the importance of setting universal regulatory standards on flight crew duty time.[48]

With the rapid progress in medical knowledge over the years, it would seem that carriers must recognize the effect of fatigue on air crew as a potential element of liability. It is now known that symptoms of jet lag (which the air crew is constantly subject to) are very similar to fatigue. Furthermore, the length of the trip, crossing of time zones and disruption of sleep cycles lead to excessive fatigue, and the pilot may well show signs of disorientation, irritability and confusion, and exhibit severe physical symptoms such as constipation and aches and pains.[49] In this respect, air carriers may obviate culpability by following some guidelines which have already been suggested, such as: stringent pre-planned cockpit rest periods, strategic flight crew scheduling, and more importantly, flight deck automation which may assist in ensuring more expedient cockpit management.[50]

### *Substance Abuse in the Workplace*

Although the use of drugs, psychotropic substances and alcohol in the workplace is collectively perceived as substance abuse in the workplace, alcohol abuse is a major source of concern in the area of flight safety. The increasing awareness and steady development of statistics and data on this subject make it increasingly difficult for carriers to ignore the problem. Moreover, in an instance where an accident occurs as a result of substance abuse by the air crew, the carrier would probably be a prime target as a defendant. In fact, the carrier itself may even be found accountable under Article 25(1), for failing to take adequate precautions to prevent substance abuse in the workplace in certain circumstances.

The abuse of alcohol by air crew is a general aviation problem and, admittedly, the reported role of alcohol in fatal aviation accidents has decreased consistently from the 1960s to the present.[57] Nevertheless, carriers must take adequate precautions to ensure that no incidents related to alcohol consumption by their air crew result in claims under the notion of wilful misconduct. In the United States, pilots were included in the 7,460,000 transport workers who became subject to the Alcohol Misuse Prevention Programme which commenced on 1 January 1995. The US Department of Transportation inaugurated new rules along with this programme, which prohibit any person acting or attempting to act as a crew member of a civil aircraft within eight hours of consuming any alcoholic beverage or while having a blood alcohol concentration of 0.04 per cent.[52]

On a global scale, on 11 March 1994, the United Nations General Assembly adopted Resolution 48/112 on International Action to Combat Drug Abuse and Illicit Production of Trafficking.[53] This resolution addresses the problem on a general basis, and seemingly relates to narcotic drugs and psychotropic substances. However, on a more specific scale, ICAO, at its 27th Session of the Assembly in 1989, adopted Resolution A27-12[54] (Role of ICAO in the Suppression of Illicit Transport of Narcotic Drugs by Air), which urges the ICAO Council to elaborate with a high degree of priority concrete measures in order to prevent and to eliminate possible use of illicit drugs and abuse of other drugs or substances by crew members, air traffic controllers, mechanics and other international civil aviation staff. The ICAO Assembly followed its action by adopting, at its 29th Session in 1992, Resolution A29-16[55] (Role of ICAO in the Prevention of Substance Abuse in the Workplace), whereby, having mentioned Resolution A27-12, the Assembly expressed its grave concern that substance abuse by civil aviation employees may seriously compromise aviation safety and urged the Council to maintain its vigilance over the problem of substance abuse.

As a result of the above action by the ICAO Assembly, ICAO has produced its manual on the prevention of problematic use of substances in the aviation workplace,[56] which has been developed by the Aviation Medicine Section of ICAO Secretariat. The purpose of the document, as stated in its Foreword, is to 'provide States with a tool for decision-making to use when deciding on the best policy for user States and for State licensing authorities when planning national strategies'.[57] The manual also suggests that it can be used by airlines and other employers to implement, on a practical level, established policies and strategies in a cost-effective way, with due regard for aviation safety and employees' personal welfare.

The manual consists of five chapters, cohesively woven together to give the reader a detailed account of substance abuse and its consequences. Its main thrust and strength lie in Chapter 1 which is dedicated to education of the aviation workforce, and Chapter 2, which identifies the problems and recommends suitable treatment and rehabilitation. The document also contains some useful information on strategic planning and testing.

The legal significance of this document and its relation to Article 25 of the Warsaw Convention is apparent. Air carriers can no longer plead lack of guidance or ignorance of the problem of substance abuse in the workplace in the face of such a development in the regulatory field of civil aviation; nor can they ignore the recommendations of the document in terms of training programmes and strategic planning. The existence of such guidance and regulatory material would provide persuasive evidence of law of an air carrier's wilful misconduct in the case of an adjudication of a plaintiff's rights.

*Medical Emergencies on Board*

The notion of safety on board has frequently been associated with the inability of the carrier to provide medical assistance in an emergency, and, *a fortiori*, the failure on the part of the carrier to take adequate measures to ensure that such emergencies are handled diligently and professionally. A recent development in the field of aviation medicine introduced in the summer of 1996 indicates a seminal development in this area, when United Airlines announced the fitting of a telemedicine unit on one of its commercial aircraft. The unit, which is the size of a large briefcase, is called Telemedic Systems Equipment, and was fitted in one of the carrier's Boeing 767 aircraft on a three-month trial basis.[58] It is designed to improve the crew's response to a medical emergency by measuring a number of the patient's vital signs, including ECG, blood pressure and heart rate, and transmitting them, in real time, to a doctor on the ground.

The implications of this development could be far-reaching at law. If air carriers equip their aircraft with such telemedicine facilities this would effectively preclude the allegation by an aggrieved passenger or his representative of neglect on the part of the carrier, if such measures are taken, or are perceived to be taken, as a genuine attempt by the carrier to ensure that a medical emergency could be diligently handled through such means. It must be emphasized, however, that simply installing sophisticated technical equipment would be insufficient to convince a court that the carrier had taken all necessary precautions and measures to treat a medical emergency; the carrier would have to show that it trained its personnel to use the equipment properly and, more importantly, that it instilled in its employees the significance of medical assistance on board a flight.

*Passenger Conduct*

Numerous incidents have been reported in recent times of offensive passenger conduct towards air crew and other passengers.[59] In response, the US Department of Transport and the Federal Aviation Administration have jointly released a circular advising airlines of the problems which may be caused by unruly passengers, and giving guidance to air crew on how to deal with the problem. The United Kingdom has taken concrete legal action against offensive conduct by airline passengers by making effective as from 1 July 1996 a Private Member's Bill in Parliament which gives the courts of the United Kingdom jurisdiction over foreign aircraft similar to the jurisdiction exercised over UK-registered aircraft. This new legislative measure means that offenders whose conduct on board any aircraft – whether it be foreign-registered or UK-registered – amounts to a crime in the United Kingdom and the country in which the aircraft is registered can be prosecuted in the UK courts once the aircraft lands, provided the United Kingdom is the first place of landing after the offence was committed.

US legislation on the subject of airline passenger conduct appears in the form of a regulation which provides that no person may assault, threaten, intimidate or interfere with a crew member's duties on board an aircraft.[60] There are also regulations which prohibit the boarding of international passengers who may be construed as a threat to the safety of a flight, and the serving of excessive quantities of alcohol on board. These same regulations make it mandatory for passengers to obey seat belt signs and no smoking signs.

For the airlines' part, some major carriers – notably British Airways and Virgin Atlantic in the United Kingdom and Continental Airlines in the United States – have already taken steps to ensure punitive action against offensive passengers.[61] Airline cabin crew training departments are placing more emphasis on programmes which train cabin crew to cope with problems caused onboard by offensive passengers, and to prepare themselves for the emotional strain which may result from abusive and violent behaviour by passengers.

*Air Traffic Control*

Air traffic control is not regulated internationally, it is governed, for the most part, by national laws. Attempts to encompass air traffic control within the international regulatory umbrella have failed, initially because it was considered that there were very few aircraft accidents which could be attributed to air traffic control. Later, several States developed improved and enhanced levels of safety within air traffic control, and consequently, the aviation community did not consider that it posed a serious threat to aviation safety. However, a 1994 survey has revealed that the enhancement of safety measures in air traffic control has resulted in increased congestion and delay, causing the completion of a full cycle, where safety has again become an issue for consideration within the parameters of air traffic control.[62]

Six provisions of the Chicago Convention[63] address requirements for the provision of air traffic control. In addition, three technical Annexes to the Convention[64] and a technical manual on Procedures for Air Navigation Services and Rules of the Air and Air Traffic Services[65] specify in detail the standards required for technical efficacy in air traffic control. Article 28 of the Convention lays the fundamental basis for the requirement of air traffic services by stating that each contracting State must provide airports, radio services, meteorological services and air navigational facilities to facilitate international air navigation over its territory.

One of the seminal problems in global regulation of air traffic control activities is the very complex nature of these activities and control measures. In most instances, air traffic control services are provided by instrumentalities of States, and legal liability for such activities is therefore mostly governed by municipal law. In many instances, municipal laws of States granted immunity to the State from civil or criminal liability. As a result, attempts to regulate this area of activity have consistently failed, from the very first attempt of the Comité International Technique d'Experts Juridiques Aériens (CITEJA) in 1930 to that made in 1983 by the Legal Committee of ICAO. However, it is somewhat encouraging to note that in 1983, participating States unanimously agreed at the Legal Committee that ICAO should pursue research and further study on the matter. As a result, a Rapporteur was appointed and a report prepared by him was expected to be presented at a subsequent Session of the Legal Committee. Based on the report, the ICAO Council requested the Legal Committee to decide on a future course of action.

Whatever future course of action the world aviation community decides to take on air traffic control, it is incontrovertible that this vital area of activity needs to be effectively regulated. Argentina, which is a strong proponent of this concept, put forward a draft convention in the early 1970s, which was vigorously debated at the VIth National Conference on Air and Space Law in Buenos Aires and the 25th Session of the ICAO Legal Committee. It suggested that an air traffic control agency should be *prima facie* liable for the fault of its officials, employees and agents which may result in injury or damage to persons and property. The Argentine proposal was based on the tortious principle of negligence, and contained exculpatory provisions in favour of the air traffic control agency in instances where the agency could show absence of negligence on its part.

In 1976, the International Federation of Air Traffic Controllers Association (IFATCA) in 1976 proposed a convention for air traffic control which extended to analogous technical services such as meteorology and mobile aeronautical services. The IFATCA draft convention was consistent in approach with the Argentine proposal for fault liability, but insisted on such liability being established beyond all reasonable doubt, rather than on the civil liability criterion of balance of probability.

## Comments

There is no doubt that the work being carried out by ICAO in the technical field of aviation safety oversight is both prolific and effective. It is also comforting to note that ICAO has initiated the extension of its safety oversight programme to areas other than those affected by technical factors, such as human conduct, both on the ground and in the air. The latter requires careful consideration of the development of regulation in such areas as aircraft communications and the optimum use of air crew. Globalized standards for cabin crew training and the establishment of a world-wide standard for crew conduct are also broad areas of regulation which need careful and collective consideration by States. Such a philosophy would necessarily involve a change in attitude, from treating cabin attendants as mere stewards, who serve comestibles and beverages, to considering them as crew who must ensure security and safety in the cabin.

As for air traffic control, it is time to consider a global regulation umbrella which sets basic parameters for the conduct of air traffic controllers. National legislation may still regulate this activity individually, provided certain irreducible minima are observed, such as the provision of insurance or some other form of compensation in instances of blatant negligence or fault of the air traffic control agency. Overall global standards for air crew and air traffic controllers should include measures for the prevention of fatigue and the periodic testing of mental and physical agility.

With regard to ensuring acceptable levels of passenger conduct in the aircraft, it is unfortunate that the airline industry has no unified system for collecting information on abusive or disruptive passenger incidents, but it is comforting that attention is now being devoted to this issue. At the International Conference on Disruptive Airline Passengers, held in April 1997 in Washington, USA, it was suggested that airlines develop a comprehensive data collection system relating to instances of flight disruption by passengers. The conference noted that, in North America it was generally considered that 25 per cent of instances were caused by alcohol abuse, 16 per cent by problems related to the assignment of passenger seats, 12 per cent due to various undetermined causes, 10 per cent due to prohibition of smoking in the cabin, 9 per cent were due to carry-on luggage, and the rest were the result of passengers' perception of the conduct of cabin crew.[66]

Another activity in civil aviation which requires careful safety oversight is in the maintenance of aircraft. Maintenance error is now known to cause 15 per cent of aircraft accidents.[67] The consideration of human factors in engineering and maintenance as a recognizable cause of accidents emerged only recently, but is now well established. It would therefore be prudent to monitor human conduct and impose stringent training standards among maintenance crew. Integral to such training would be attempts to improve cross-culture communications and literacy in common languages used in maintenance areas.

In the final analysis, therefore, civil aviation safety regulations should be introduced on the fundamental basis that air transport is now a high-technology industry, and any regulation promulgated must be focused on a proactive, not a reactive, approach. Aviation management must seek to regulate such aspects as cross-culture communications in the cockpit and cabin, enhanced automation in the cockpit, and a common policy on crew conduct based on available statistics on disruptive passenger conduct. For the last measure to attain fruition, a unified system of collecting information on disruptive behaviour must be implemented. The most important step at this juncture is for the world aviation community to support studies which may be initiated by ICAO in areas related to the overall issue of aviation safety.

## Notes

1 *1997 Britannica Book of the Year*, Chicago: Encyclopaedia Britannica, Inc., 1997, at 372 and 58.
2 ICAO Doc. P10 16/97, at 1.
3 ITA Press Release 284, 1–5 April 1997, at 10.
4 *Convention on International Civil Aviation*, signed Chicago, 7 December 1944. See ICAO Doc. 7300/6 (6th edn), 1980.
5 Id., Preamble, at 1.
6 Id., Article 44(a).
7 ITA Press Release 284, at p. 10.

8 Decision S13-3: Safety Oversight. See African Civil Aviation Commission, Thirteenth Plenary Session, Abuja 11–18 May 1995, AFCAC/13 Report, at 25.
9 DGCA/100-DP/7, 21/4/97, Appendix.
10 Article 31 provides that every aircraft engaged in international navigation shall be provided with a certificate of airworthiness issued or rendered valid by the State in which it is registered. Article 32 provides for the issuance of certificates of competency to technical crew of aircraft and prescribes minimum standards. Article 33 stipulates that certificates of airworthiness issued to aircraft by one State should be acceptable by another, provided certain minimum standards are followed.
11 DGCA/100-DP/8, 28/4/97, Appendix.
12 EU Council Directive 85/374/EEC of 25 July 1985.
13 ICAO Doc. 9637, *Annual Report of the Council 1994*, Montreal: ICAO, Chapter III, at 45–6.
14 *Proceedings of the Council, 2nd Session, 2 September–12 December 1947*, Doc. 7248, C/839, at 44–5.
15 ICAO Resolutions A-13 and A-33, which resolved that SARPS relating to the efficient and safe regulation of international air navigation be adopted.
16 ICAO Annex 9, 'Facilitation' (9th edn), July 1990, Foreword.
17 *Aeronautical Information Services Manual*, ICAO Doc. 8126, 0 AN/872/3. ICAO Resolution A 1-31 defines a standard as 'any specification for physical characteristics ... the uniform application of which is recognized as necessary ... and one that States will conform to'. The same resolution describes a recommended practice as 'any specification for physical characteristics ... which is recognized as desirable ... and one that member States will endeavour to conform to'. T. Buergenthal, *Law Making in the International Civil Aviation Organization*, 1969, at 10, also cites the definitions given in ICAO's Annex 9 of SARPS.
18 Article 86 of the Convention.
19 Article 12 stipulates that, over the high seas, the rules in force shall be those established under the Convention, and each contracting State undertakes to ensure the prosecution of all persons violating the applicable regulations.
20 Michael Milde, 'The Chicago Convention – After Forty Years', *Annals Air & Space Law*, Vol. IX, No. 119, at 126. See also Jacob Schenkman, *International Civil Aviation Organization*, Geneva, 1955, at 163.
21 Milde, op. cit., at 122.
22 Buergenthal, op. cit., at 9.
23 Paul Stephen Dempsey, *Law and Foreign Policy in International Aviation*, New York: Transnational Publishers, 1987, at 302.
24 Id., at 5.
25 Charter of the United Nations and Statute of the International Court of Justice, Article 57.
26 Id., Article 63(1) and (2).
27 Pitman B. Potter, *An Introduction to the Study of International Organization* (5th edn), New York and London: Appleton Century-Crofts, 1935, at 273–4.
28 See *Resolutions Adopted by the Assembly, 31st Session, Montreal, 19 September–4 October 1995*, Montreal: ICAO, 1995, at 2.
29 See *ICAO Releases Strategic Action Plan, President Renews Call for Empowerment*, ICAO News Release PIO 10/97, at 1.
30 Ibid.
31 C-WP/10066.
32 *2217th Report to the Council by the President of the Air Navigation Commission*, C-WP/10559, 3/3/97.
33 Id., at 2–4.

34 *Action Plan to Address Shortcomings and Deficiencies in the Air Navigation Field,* AN-WP/7228, 27/5/97.
35 Pierre Sparaco, 'Combating Fatigue to Enhance Safety', *Aviation Week & Space Technology,* 4 November 1996, at 49.
36 Ibid.
37 Id., at 54.
38 See Phillippa H. Gander et al., 'A NASA Study Shows How Age and Circadian Rhythm Affect Sleep Loss', *Airline Pilot,* April 1995, at 20.
39 'Sleepless Flights: Report of the Royal Aeronautical Society Aviation Medicine Group Conference "Aeromedical Aspects of Ultra Long-Haul Operations"', *Aerospace,* September 1994, at 22.
40 Annex 6 to the *Convention on International Civil Aviation (Operation of Aircraft) Part 1* (5th edn), July 1990, Attachment A, 1.1.
41 Id., at 1.2.
42 Id., at 2.2.1.
43 Id., at 2.3.
44 Id., at 3.2.
45 Annex 6 to the *Convention on International Civil Aviation, Part III* (2nd edn), July 1990, Attachment C, at 3 and 4.
46 AN-WP/6888, 28/2/94.
47 Id., Appendix A. See also State Letter AN 11/9-93/77.
48 AN-WP/6888, 28/2/94, Appendices B and C.
49 See 'Out of Synch: Jet Lag', *Airworthy Aviator,* August 1992, at 1. See also David F. Dingles, 'Crew Rest and Sleep Deprivation', Flight Safety Foundation, 35th Corporate Aviation Seminar, 18–20 April 1990, Montreal; Leonard J. Thompson, 'Disorders of Circadian Rhythm with Air Travel', *Patient Management,* December 1986, at 13; Davenport and Jensen, 'Fatigue Factors on Two Man Crews', *Pilot,* December 1989, at 23.
50 Curtis Graeber, 'Fatigue in Long Haul Operations – Sources and Solutions', Part 2, *U.K. Flight Safety Focus,* Spring 1992, Part 2, at 1.
51 See J.R. Dille and E.W. Morris, 'Human Factors in General Aviation Accidents', *Aerospace Medicine,* 1967, No. 38, at 1,063–6. See also H.L. Gibbons, 'Alcohol, Aviation and Safety Revisited: A Historical Review and a Suggestion', *Aviation Space Environmental Medicine,* 1988, No. 59, at 657–60; C.C. Ryan and S.R. Mohler, 'Intoxicating Liquor and the General Aviation Pilot in 1971', *Aerospace Medicine,* 1972, No. 43, at 1,024–6.
52 Suzanne L. Kalfus, 'Alcohol Testing Begins', *Airline Pilot,* October 1994, at 16.
53 A/RES/48/112, 11 March 1994.
54 Doc. 9662, *Assembly Resolutions in Force* (as of 4 October 1995), 1-36, at 1-37.
55 Id., at 11–24.
56 Doc. 9654-AN/945 (1st edn), 1995.
57 Id., at iii.
58 'Doctor on Board', *Aeronautical Satellite News,* October–November 1996, at 5. Although telemedicine has been used for a considerable time, this is the first known instance of its use in flight. 'Telemedicine' has been defined by the European Commission as: 'rapid access to shared and remote medical expertise by means of telecommunications and information technologies, no matter where the patient or relevant information is located'.
59 'Unruly Passengers', *Aviation Security International,* June 1997, Vol. 2, No. 2, at 4.
60 Ibid., at 6.
61 Ibid.
62 *Increasing Europe's Air Traffic Control Capacity,* European Air Traffic Control

Harmonization and Integration Programme (EATCHIP), Olsen International at EUROCONTROL Headquarters, April 1994, at 4.

63 Articles 11, 12, 15, 28, 69 and 70.

64 Annexes 2, 11 and 14.

65 ICAO Doc. 4444 (PANS-RAC).

66 Teresa Mattrick, 'International Conference on Disruptive Airline Passengers', *Airline Pilot*, June/July 1997, 24, at 26.

67 'To Err is Human', *Aerospace*, March 1997, at 16.

# 11 Liability for Personal Injury and Death

## Introduction

It is an ineluctable principle of tort law that tortious liability exists primarily to compensate the victim by compelling the wrongdoer to pay for the damage done.[1] The 2nd International Conference on Private International Law[2] which led to the introduction of the Warsaw Convention[3] obviously followed this basic principle but deviated to align the provisions of the Warsaw Convention to existing exigencies of civil aviation. The conference based its approach towards air carrier liability on the fault theory of tort, which has its genesis in the Industrial Revolution, where common law adopted the principle that a wrongdoer or tortfeasor must be at fault for them to be compelled to compensate the injured. The fault theory was introduced as a solution to the problems caused by injury to persons by the proliferation of machinery during the Industrial Revolution, on the basis that those responsible for introducing faulty machinery should pay those who are injured by it.

One of the fundamental deviations from the fault liability principle in the context of the Warsaw Conference was that, instead of retaining the basic premise that the person who alleges injury must prove that the injury was caused by the alleged wrongdoer, the conference recognized the obligation of the carrier to assume the burden of proof, presumably to obviate the inherent difficulties posed by air carriage, where it would be difficult, if not impossible, to determine fault from evidence which is reduced to debris and wreckage after an aircraft accident.

The conference succinctly subsumed its views on liability through the words of its Reporter:

> These rules sprang from the fault theory of the liability of the carrier toward passengers and goods, and from the obligation of the carrier to assume the burden of proof. The presumption of fault on the shoulders of the carrier was, however, limited by the nature itself of the

> carriage in question, carriage whose risks are known by the passenger and consignor. The Conference had agreed that the carrier would be absolved from all liability when he had taken reasonable and ordinary measures to avoid the damage ... one restriction on this liability had been agreed upon. If for commercial transactions one could concede the liability of the carrier, it did not seem logical to maintain this liability for the navigational errors of his servants, if he proves that he himself took proper measures to avoid a damage.[4]

The conference went on to suggest that if the damage arises from an 'intentional illicit act' for which the carrier was liable, it should not have the right to avail itself of the provisions of the Convention.[5] The words 'intentional illicit act' were later changed to 'wilful misconduct' by the conference, at the request of the UK delegate, Sir Alfred Dennis, and the Greek delegate, Mr Youpis.[6]

Deeming that it was not equitable to impose absolute liability upon the carrier, the conference admitted that the carrier's liability would be limited in monetary value and, furthermore, it could be freed of all liability if it had taken reasonable and normal measures to avoid the damage.[7]

The conference obviously based the Warsaw Convention on tort law principles of liability, where tort duties are primarily fixed by law, in contrast to contractual obligations, which can arise only from voluntary agreement.[8] Seventy years after the Warsaw Convention was introduced, however, there has been a palpable shift towards introducing a contractual element by the 1995 IATA Inter-carrier Agreement, which, although it does not have the legal status of a convention, since it is an agreement among air carriers, retains the basic presumption of air carrier liability of the Convention, but rejects the liability limitations of the Warsaw Convention and its Protocols by recognizing that the compensatory amount that a carrier should pay for personal injury or death may be contractually agreed upon by the carrier and claimant according to the law of the domicile of the claimant.

Admittedly, this is not what the conference envisaged. However, it must be borne in mind that the conference recognized that the Warsaw Convention applied only to the unification of 'certain' rules, as proposed by the delegate of Czechoslovakia. Also, the underlying purpose of the IATA initiative – to allow for greater flexibility for insurance underwriters on the one hand, and more leverage for airlines in their risk management on the other – is fundamentally consistent with the views of the Warsaw Conference. At the same time, the Convention does not preclude the right of a carrier to enter into agreement with a claimant on the issue of compensation. The Warsaw Conference itself recognized that:

> ... in reality, this Convention creates against the air carrier an exceptional system, because in the majority of the countries of the world, contracts of carriage are concluded under a system of free contract. The carrier is free to insert in the contract clauses which exclude or reduce his liability, as much as for goods as for travellers ...[9]

The Inter-carrier Agreement, which was approved by IATA carriers at their Annual General Meeting in Kuala Lumpur in October 1995, claims to preserve the Warsaw Convention, but carriers agree to take action to waive the limitation of liability on recoverable compensatory damages in claims for death, wounding or other bodily injury, so that recoverable compensatory damages may be determined and awarded by reference to the law of the domicile of the passenger. This provision in effect introduces a contractual element to an otherwise pure tortious liability regime. The agreement attacks the monetary limits of liability of the Convention, and retains all other provisions of liability – which are essentially the presumption of liability of the carrier, and its defences against such a presumption.

With the rejection of the liability limits, the provision relating to breaking such limits in instances where the carrier is guilty of wilful misconduct has also been rejected. Therefore, effectively, certain elements of tortious liability under the Convention have been expunged. In the final analysis, the principle of fault which the architects of the Warsaw Convention entrenched into the Convention has been rejected by the IATA agreement. Lee Kreindler observes:

> The fault system is extremely important to the public. It is a public protection. It has improved aviation safety and security. While I don't profess to understand what the international airlines are now up to, it is clear to me that one of their purposes is to put an end to the tort system, in international airline transportation, at least as between the passenger and the airline, and that I oppose.[10]

Kreindler points out the ambivalence of the IATA Agreement in designating the law of the domicile of the passenger as being applicable for the award of compensatory damages, while it retains the provision of the Warsaw Convention which designates jurisdictions.[11] Sean Gates picks up the issue of 'domicile', and observes that the IATA Agreement refers to Article 28 of the Warsaw Convention which it claims relates to 'domicile', whereas in fact it does not. Gates questions whether 'domicile' would refer to personal or corporate domicile, and holds that this is another area where the IATA Agreement has not shown clarity.[12]

This chapter will discuss the historical evolution of tort liability applicable to the Warsaw Convention, and examine the incursion of the notion of contract into a regime of pure tortious liability based on fault which was envisaged by the framers of the Warsaw Convention. It will also determine the reasons why a system of liability which is essentially based on tort law has veered towards being based on contractual agreement, where the claimant and the insurer of the airline concerned can negotiate a settlement based on the claimant's domicile.

## Historical Perspectives of Tortious Liability and Fault

The progenitor of tortious liability in the modern meaning of the term is the *Lex Aquilia,* as handed down to us in its late stage of development in Justinian's *Digest.* The *Lex Aquilia,* which had already been entrenched in the later history of Roman law, underwent yet another phase of development in the course of its reception into the European legal systems when its scope of application came to be extended to the ultimate boundaries of legal principles and propositions related to tortious liability. Finally, however, when the independent claim to compensation for delictual losses could stand on its own, natural law discarded the *Lex Aquilia.* Therefore, the growth of the *Lex Aquilia* over the centuries, which has been a field for investigation since the birth of Roman law, can offer only indirect lessons to modern law. These lessons are not destitute of interest, however: in fact, in the context of modern tortious liability, the *Lex Aquilia,* has been shaken to its foundations. Following the development of the *Lex Aquilia,* it can be noted that the relationship of liability and the distribution of loss are the principal issues of the crisis.

In its original form, the *Lex Aquilia* was one of the rules relating to private torts, a rule which superseded earlier enactments of a similar nature (among them a provision in the Law of Twelve Tables), and introduced the innovation which equalized conduct that caused losses by fire, smashing or wrecking with the notion of *damnum,* and inflicted on these acts, as well as on the killing of slaves or cattle, the punishment of paying the highest value of the chattel within thirty days and, in the event of the killing of a slave, the payment of the highest value within a year, instead of the payment of the earlier fines in a fixed amount. The liability of the tortfeasor was objectively assessed.

From the first century BC onwards,[13] jurisprudence began to widen – by way of extensive interpretation – the scope of application of the *Lex Aquilia.* In the course of this process, the sphere of losses to be made good expanded. First, the perpetrator's type of conduct became a matter of indifference, then the loss occurring to the chattel itself came to be disregarded, and finally an *actio utilis* came to be extended to losses caused to the property of a freeman owing to bodily harm befallen him. Loss caused through omission also had to be made good. In Justinian law – particularly the *Corpus Juris Civilis* – the rate of the compensation became the *interesse*, instead of the value of the chattel. Another interesting line of development was that instead of the *injuria* being assessed in an objective sense, the concept of *culpa* became the basis of liability. In addition to wilful misconduct, which was common to all private torts, the *Lex Aquilia* was solely to apply to all manner of negligence. This was the genesis of the principles of culpability, and the point of time when the *Lex Aquilia* reached codification. It must be borne in mind that, together with civil law elements which had reached a high degree of development, the *Lex Aquilia* also preserved features of criminal law on an equal basis.

There are some scholars who assume yet another stage of development, according to which, in Byzantine theory and practice, an *in factum generalis actio* which was granted by virtue of the *Lex Aquilia* would have served subsidiarily for the compensation of any culpably caused loss (including pure loss in property). Whether or not such a theory and practice had in fact become established is arguable, and since in Justinian law there was no mention of their existence, none can be adduced as having an effect on Justinian-based Western European legal development.

From the difference between the original state of the *actio legis Aquiliae* and its Justinian form – which established *culpa* as an element of liability – jurisprudence infers general trends of development in delictual liability that appear to have been confirmed by the analogous development of other legal systems, notably the bifurcation of criminal and civil law liability, and the triumph of the fault principle. In Jhering's doctrine, the two areas coincide:

> At the beginning of the law the notion of punishment dominates, the element of punishment permeates the entire law ... The development of the law manifests itself in the increasingly narrowing down of the scope of punishment and the yet higher degree of the clarity of its formulation.[14]

In connection with liability that exclusively appraises the injury caused to the injured party, Jhering does not merely emphasize the 'low cultural level' of law and civilization, but also observes that this outlook cannot be consistent with compensation for the loss. He states that 'the satisfaction of the appetite for revenge, the chastisement of the opponent' requires more: punishment – multiplying sanctions. According to Jhering, therefore, in the last stage of development it is the culpability of the tortfeasor, and not the result of their action, that binds them to compensation. This is true especially of private law, which provides for the gradual withering away of the idea of punishment. Punishment in civil law is superseded by compensation of damages – which, in its most developed form, is adjusted to the weight of the fault.[15]

Ferenc Madl comes to a similar conclusion in the course of his analysis, which embraced the whole of legal development in Antiquity. He showed that the notion of unlawfulness was generalized, that the criminal and civil law sanctions were separated (though not completely), and explained the emergence of the 'appraisal of the conduct' and the subjectivization of delictual liability. As a pioneer work and a modern synthesis, these theses of development may justly be accepted as a *communis opinio doctorum.*

For the purpose of addressing early liability concepts with a view to drawing a link to 'liability' as envisaged and applied by the Warsaw Conference, it will be useful to note that the parallel trends of development present a rather characteristic contradiction in its evolution: the civil law outlook – the emancipation of the compensation from punishment – coincides with an anti-civil law outlook: the birth of fault liability. It is fair to assume that even in the early stages of development, traces of strict liability mingled with fault liability principles.

It is the development of tortious liability, which throughout Antiquity discharged both criminal and civil law functions, that shows clearly the fundamentally divergent nature of the two considerations, compensation and liability. The abandonment of liability for the result, and the subjectivization of liability are the general characteristics and important landmarks of the development of the law as a whole. Although several attempts have been made, it is impossible to offer an explanation of this process, or even of its private law portion, as rooted in the conditions of life regulated by private law: commodity relations. The subjectivization of liability does not run parallel to the segregation of punishment and compensation but, rather, it is due to the confluence of criminal law and civil law that this subjectivization finds a way into tortious liability. At the same time as the civil law outlook makes headway, a break takes place in the process of subjectivization of liability. The common view errs when it identifies the line of development with the historical process that in the domain of torts the more and more subjectively conceived *dolus* rejects result liability, and on the grounds of *culpa* (in the narrower meaning of the term and standing for negligence) establishes liability whereupon the degrees of *culpa* begin to unfold. This error derives from the misconception that the categories of culpability tend to become more and more subtle. The actual process is not only not the development of the subjectivization of liability, but the reverse of this. In Antiquity, legal liability with the *dolus* ties liability to the most subjective condition. Strict liability swings over to the diametrically opposite. The only functionally common trait that remains is the fact that fault liability is also of a very narrow sphere.[16] In the field of private torts, Roman law adhered to liability for *dolus* only, except for the *Lex Aquilia*, however, which espoused the element of *culpa*. Liability for *culpa* would be a step backwards towards objective or strict liability. There was no straight development of the liability for *dolus*,[17] the extension of fault liability, but a completely different sphere, namely the appearance of considerations in tort law imposed by civil law contracts and loss bearing, as dictated by them. The consequences of this process also connect delictual compensation to civil law in the domain of sanctions.

The *dolus* implying fraud is one of the few fundamental concepts whose definition the otherwise extremely reserved jurisprudence of the republican era dared to attempt. On the other hand, the abstract definition of *culpa*, relying on foreseeability, is by general opinion the product of post-Classical law.[18] The applicability and credibility of the antecedents, however – both the genesis of the technical notion of *culpa* and the stages of the development of its contents – are arguable, and the theories in general conform to the state of the art of interpretation at a given time.

The term *culpa*, when it began to obtain credibility through the *Lex Aquilia* in the Classical age, stood both for unlawfulness and culpability in the wider sense of the term. Subjective culpability, however, was in the law of private torts known only as *dolus*. Even in the *Lex Aquilia*, liability for negligence turned up only later. The question that one may address is whether this definition was tied to wilfulness or not, and if so, to what extent. It may be assumed that originally it was not, since when liability came to be extended beyond *dolus*, there was no example in the law of torts whence such an extension could have been derived. It was the later development of loss and causation of loss, and not the foundations of liability, that permitted raising the question of the causes of the extension of liability: the defence against losses, which had been kept within narrow bounds by the original objective basis, or the requirement of *dolus*. Wilful damage to chattels is a far rarer occurrence than causing loss through negligence.

Fragments from the Classical period bear upon the particular cases, and still affect decisions on the definite, objective outer circumstances of each case of liability. They circumscribe cases as the basis of liability, and do not refer to a measure of liability which could be comparable to the negligence of later times. In a well-known example, the liability of a worker sawing off a branch from a tree depends on whether there was a beaten path there, and whether in this case he uttered a warning cry before dropping the branch, in instances of damage caused by his throwing away the branch, provided he did not throw it away wilfully. A rule known already from the Classical age, however, reflects more of the content of the *culpa*. In medical negligence, it is not the professional inexperience of the doctor that is by itself culpable, but that he has undertaken a treatment with which he is not familiar. In the same way it is not his 'weakness' with which a mule-driver who is unable to bridle his beast has to concern himself, but his undertaking a trade for which he ought to have known he lacked the physical strengths. One of the most significant aspects of Roman law principles regarding professional negligence is the maxim *imperitia culpae adnumeratur,* which establishes that negligence is not determined by the lack of skill of the tortfeasor, but in his undertaking work without skill. Therefore, where a person engages in a profession or occupation which calls for special skill, the degree of skill which is required is that reasonably to be expected of a person engaged in such profession or occupation. Behind the rule of *imperitia or infirmitas culpae adnumeratur,* there are considerations which are very much reconcilable with the practical causes of the extension of *Aquilian* liability. Here the content of culpability is defined by considerations of the security of trade: anyone failing to meet the requirements of a definite activity can pursue it only at the risk of compensation. As later discussions on cases in Warsaw litigation will reflect, some courts have imputed to the carrier knowledge of the fact that damage would have occurred by the carrier's undertaking a certain responsibility, such as serving liquor on board, thus reflecting the *infirmitas* principle.

This principle is, however, valid not only in the context of the *Lex Aquilia,* but also in contractual liability. Under this principle, a debtor, notwithstanding their efforts, will rightly be held liable in default. Everyone is presumed to be aware of their limits, and should therefore not undertake any activity that exceeds them. The *culpa,* thus interpreted, does not merely interconnect the two kinds of liability; it is at the same time the bridge over which further considerations of the world of contracts find access to delictual liability. It is often impossible to cite direct evidence determining whether the development of the *culpa* had taken place within the *Lex Aquilia* and then found its way from there into the law of contracts, or vice versa, but circumstantial evidence would favour the latter view. It should be kept in mind that development occurred within the frame of issues, torts and the few contracts, which were all of narrow scope and not sustained in general abstract categories. Apparently the content of the term *culpa* thus derived is tied more solidly to legal philosophy concerning commerce (as it reflects the contractual commodity relations) than to the considerations of liability of the *dolus,* with which it will share a place in the same system only after undergoing subjectivization in the law of a later age. It is characteristic that Jhering, although he conceives development as a whole as the more perfect realization of the idea of fault relying on volitional accountability in civil law (an idea which sets out from the torts and penetrates into the law on contracts), nevertheless finds the explanation for the Roman theory in the sphere of contract. He begins expanding the idea that anybody coming into a profit or desirous of profit must show diligence and care, on the basis that business presupposes the care of the businessman.

In the liability system of Classical law, it is also apparent that the foundations of liability for other than the *dolus* are not moral ones.[19] For *dolus*, everyone is responsible, irrespective of whether the contract is an onerous one, for example in the event of a gratuity. For *culpa*, however, only the one deriving a gain from the contract will be responsible.

Analysis of early liability principles reveals that social demands for legal protection (action under criminal law) against the causation of damage and for compensation could not be ignored, and *dolus* as underlying liability was ineluctable. Apparently, Classical law did not want to avoid it. The 'restoration' of strict liability would at that time have been incompatible with either the existing notion of torts or the prevalent concept of compensation. As has been seen, contractual liability affected the interest of both parties. In hindsight, it was by recourse to casuistry that Roman law tried to stem the spread of strict liability. Nevertheless, it could have been seen earlier that, as a general criterion, considerations of safety of trade of a more general nature were relevant in cases where the conduct expected from the tortfeasor already had a model: where it was attached to concrete contractual obligations. Even if the narrowly defined facts of the *Lex Aquilia* were present, Classical law immediately recognized delictual criminal action in addition to contractual compensation against the physician and leaseholder, as well as against the lienor or depositary. The assumption appears to be justified that, through this connection, the considerations of the contractual *culpa* might have found their way into the *Lex Aquilia* and brought about an extension of liability, though the *Lex Aquilia* remained void of a general formulation. The definition of the *culpa* at that time involved the requirement of safe performance of the activities in question (without loss), and this was sufficiently objective to provide a basis for framing the province of strict liability beyond the *dolus*.

As soon as the notion of the *culpa* had come to be applied in tort law, its natural background disintegrated.[20] The notion of *culpa* gradually went on to become more abstract, and was separated from its origins in contracts and began to form a general guarantee for the safety of commerce. Tortious *culpa* is absolute, and is devoid of grades.[21]

The practical requirements of the *Lex Aquilia* were the granting of actions within a wide scope yet on uniform considerations, and such requirements could be fulfilled in tort by the notion of *culpa* without the support of a contractual theory. One has to remember that Classical jurisprudence was averse to the definition and formulation of the law, and this is why theoretical works dealt with model cases. Although the rule finds expression in the totality of the partially overlapping facts at issue, no jurist has cast it into a form. The archaic principle of authority still surviving in Classical law – that authority and not the *ratio*, reason, sanctions the decision – is a valid criterion in this consideration. Thus, in the Classical wording of the *Lex Aquilia*, one does not find more of the *culpa* than the mere mention of the known rules of the republican era,[22] where these are derived from the contractual relationship, and remain immature in the use of the notions of the *culpa* and *injuria*.

In the ancillary explanation of the decision of the particular cases, the notion of *culpa* is often unuttered, and unnoticed, but it becomes strong in associating analogies.[23] In addition to what has been set forth above, one cannot ignore the fact that the genesis of the *culpa* was in contractual liability, not in the *Lex Aquilia*.

The definition of *culpa* which has become the basis of present-day liability law owes its origin to the post-Classical age. This 'bureaucratic period' in the development of Roman law expressly strived toward the creation of abstract formulae, owing to its fundamental objective of stabilizing and simplifying the law, and the substantial intensification of the influence of Greek (Hellenistic) philosophy. Casuistry was not replaced by a genuine theoretical system, however, so it was only in the case (in analogy) of the labourer dropping branches which were sawed off the tree that the *culpa* received a generalized formulation. The abstract concept is of significance because it proves, with general validity, the existence of a process – the subjectivization of the notion of negligence – which could be assumed even on the basis of the later adaptation of the particular sources. The relief of 'external causality' by 'the act attributable to the will', which Jhering celebrates as a Classical achievement, became a reality: imputing to fault a failure to foresee something that a careful man would have foreseen.

In this definition, the subjective element lies in the shift of the psychic element of foresight to the focal point. The measure, the requirement, the careful *paterfamilias*, is by its nature objective: it cannot be otherwise. Justinian law, however, does emphasize the genuine wilful fault, and so occasionally makes the standard a relative one (*Diligentia quam in suis*). Motive and decision relating to a particular act remain mutually exclusive. The worker throwing away the branch on a private plot where there was no path would be responsible only if he had seen the injured party come along. This was also a Classical concept, on the grounds of there being an objective distinction between the beaten and unbeaten path, begging the question as to what the injured was doing where there was no path. The *Digest*, however, found it necessary to adduce a subjective reason to substantiate why the worker was not liable. The tortfeasor would be found free of culpability as he could not know that somebody was passing by. The subjective outlook here prevailing was the purview of neither delictual nor contractual liability, however. It did not even originate in these concepts. The subjective motives permeate Justinian law as a whole: firstly the equitable consideration of the will, and secondly, of the individual capacities or abilities.

In a process of gradual evolution, the relaxation of the severity and formal rigidity of the law as a natural process, and as a step towards equity, made its appearance in the law of societies in later years. In Roman law, this process manifested itself in the growing influence of the idea of *humanitas*. The respect of the one for the other, the idea of the assistance extended to the poor and weak, which in combination with Christianity became particularly intense in civil law, produced equitable decisions to replace the earlier severity of the Classics.

This general subjectivization and morality found its way naturally to the law of private torts because, as discussed above, the realm of tortious liability for negligence lacked the approved motive which in the law of contracts supported the classification of the entire system of liability: the cross-referencing of responsibility and interestedness. The emphasis laid on the volitional motive in the *Lex Aquilia* is important not because of its role in concrete legal cases, but because of its influence on later European jurisprudence as it created its own dogmatic system. It is a natural corollary, therefore, that in a trend of this kind, the ideology of the decisions gains independence: the considerations of liability offering an explanation for the delictual *culpa* inseparably link it up with the liability for wilfulness resting not only for its motive but also for its essence, on the attributable will.[24]

Justinian ensured that subjectivity was firmly entrenched as the overriding principle in tortious liability, thus establishing that fault on an objective basis could no longer be retained as the pure concept of tortious liability.

Seventy years ago, the Warsaw Conference, in its wisdom, had seemingly followed the above philosophy in its evolutionary process by recognizing the need to compensate the injured in all situations, as establishment by the plaintiff of the carrier's fault in every single instance of litigation would have been impracticable. The limitation of carrier liability was an appropriate and visionary 'safety net' at least at that time and during the decades that followed. Breaking the limit by introducing fault liability was the final ingenuity of the conference, where a wilfully negligent act of the carrier would not go unnoticed, and adequate compensation for the injured was thus guaranteed.

In applying the evolutionary process of Classical Roman law to the Warsaw system, it is incontrovertible that the very nature of tort law does not admit of evolved principles of tort law going unexamined *ad infinitum*. Modern exigencies and commercial aviation demand that they be examined, not merely to raise the limits of liability, but also to provide adequately for all classes of passengers carried by air.

## Liability Under the Warsaw Convention

### *General Principles*

Generally, in law, an accusation has to be proved by the person who alleges it. Therefore, a presumption of innocence applies to an accused person until they are proven guilty. However, in the instance of carriage by air of passengers, the airline is presumed liable if a passenger alleges personal injury or if their dependants allege their death as having been caused by the airline.[25] Of course, the airline can show in its defence that it had taken all necessary measures to avoid the damage,[26] or that there was contributory negligence, [27]and obviate or vitiate its liability. This curious anomaly of the law imposing on the airline a presumption of liability is contained in the Warsaw Convention, Article 17 of which states:

> The carrier shall be liable for damage sustained in the event of the death or wounding of a passenger, if the accident which caused the damage so sustained took place on board the aircraft or in the course of any of the operations of embarking or disembarking.

To control the floodgates of litigation and discourage spurious claimants, the Convention admits of certain defences the airline may invoke, and above all limits the liability of the airline to passengers and dependants of deceased passengers in monetary terms. The Warsaw system therefore presents to the lawyer an interesting and different area of the law which is worthy of discussion.

Article 17 of the Warsaw Convention needs analysis in some detail in order to identify clearly the circumstances in which a claim may be sustained against an airline for passenger injury or death. Further, the defences available to the airline and the monetary limits of liability also warrant discussion.

### *'Accident' Generally Defined*

The Warsaw Convention stipulates that an 'accident' must cause injury or death to a passenger if it is to be considered for liability.[28]

Halsbury states:

> [T]he word accident (or its adjective accidental) is no doubt used with the intention of excluding the operation of natural causes such as old age, congenital or insidious disease, or the natural progression of some constitutional, physical or mental defect, but the ambit of what is included by the word is not entirely clear ... What is postulated is the intervention of some cause ... so as to be fairly describable as fortuitous ... it covers any un-looked for mishap or an untoward event which is not expected or designed ...[29]

Perhaps the first known attempt at definition was in a case reported in England in 1900,[30] where a man, in the course of lifting heavy machinery, vomited blood due to an abnormality of his internal organs. Smith LJ, interpreting Section 1(1) of the Workmen's Compensation Act of 1897 under which the action was brought for compensation under a personal accident insurance policy, held that the death of the man was due to disease and therefore did not accord with the true sense of the word 'accident'.[31] Collins LJ, agreeing with the view expressed by Smith LJ, decided that an accident should be fortuitous and unexpected, and in this case the event which led to the death of the worker was not fortuitous.[32] In a case which followed,[33] where a workman had to balance a beam in such a way as to avoid falling, and in the course of this precarious exercise he strained the muscles of his back, Collins MR held that an accident, to be compensated, should be fortuitous and unexpected,[34] to which Matthew LJ added that the criterion should be to determine what was likely to happen within the course of employment and what was not.

Both the cases cited seem to accord with Halsbury's inclination to treat accident as a fortuitous event. Analogically, the approach of the judges to an accident caused to an airline passenger would seemingly have included the dual criteria of there being an unexpected or fortuitous event not contributed to by the inherent ill health of the passenger and which should have occurred within the course of thier carriage by air. The later case of *Fenton* v. *Thorley and Co. Limited*[35] qualified the somewhat restrictive definition of the word 'accident' adopted in the earlier cases. Lord Macnaughten, while recognizing that an accident should be an unlooked for mishap or an untoward event which is not expected or designed,[36] observed that the earlier definition could even make a stupid act performed by a person compensable, if such was fortuitous. In this case, an appeal of an apparently healthy man who ruptured himself by an act of overexertion during employment was deemed by the House of Lords to have qualified to be allowed compensation under the rubric of 'accident'. Perhaps the most significant statement on the applicant's position was by Lord Robertson, who said:

> No one out of a law court would ever hesitate to say that this man met with an accident ... the word 'accident' is not made inappropriate by the fact that the man hurt himself.[37]

Lord Lindley, dealing with the term 'accident' in the same case, held that:

> The word 'accident' is not a technical legal term with a clearly defined meaning. Speaking generally, but with reference to legal liabilities, an accident means any unintended occurrence which produces hurt or loss.[38]

His Lordship went on to say:

> ... every injury must have a cause. The proximate cause may be an internal strain; but if, as in this case, the strain is occasioned by an effect to overcome an obstacle accidentally presented to a workman in the course of his employment I am not prepared to say that the Act[39] does not apply.[40]

Viscount Haldane LC, in a later case,[41] while agreeing with Lord Macnaughten's view in *Fenton* v. *Thorley*[42] qualified the decisions further by stating that Lord Macnaughten did not exclude intentional acts of third parties from the purview of the term 'accident'. In this case, where a schoolmaster was killed by a premeditated assault by two schoolboys, the assault was considered an accident, and compensation was allowed.

In *R.* v. *Morris*, a more recent case decided in 1972, the term 'accident' was interpreted to mean in the broadest possible terms, 'any unintended occurrence'. This was a case where two cars became locked together while the driver of one vehicle was pushing the other car, which had refused to start. Lord Widgery CJ, in examining the word 'accident', has seemingly depended upon the quantum of damage[43] more than on anything else to determine whether an accident had occurred. If this approach were to be followed, English law would show a decided inconsistency with the more laudable approach taken in the *Fenton* case.

A valid criticism which may be levelled against English common law is that at no point has there been an attempt to define the term 'accident' in concrete terms. The only positive step seems to have been that which was taken by Lord Lindley in the *Fenton* case,[44] where his Lordship stated that although there is no technical definition of the term itself, an occurrence may be considered accidental in the case of a workman if an obstacle presents itself within the course of the activity which led to the occurrence. In assessing the term 'accident', American law is not as explicit as English law, although it is noteworthy that US courts have excluded unforeseen and unexpected incidents from the purview of the word 'accident'. In *Kinavey v. Prudential Insurance Co. of America*[45] where the deceased fell from a bridge after intoxicating himself and placing himself in a position of grave risk on a railway bridge, the court held that nothing unusual or unforeseen occurred, as the risk was extremely likely to have been realized under the circumstances. Accordingly, compensation was not required to be paid to the deceased's dependants by the insurance company that had covered the deceased's life.

In a later case,[46] decided in 1957, the principles applied by the court were substantially the same as in the *Kinavey* case, where the operative criterion applied was that any act of the deceased or wounded in which he voluntarily undertook a grave risk would effectively preclude the dependants of the deceased from invoking the word 'accident' in their claim. In this case, the deceased had lain down on a busy highway and been killed by a vehicle. He was of sound mind, and had been warned by his companions of the grave danger of his act. The court held that death was due to the voluntary assumption of risk by the deceased, and that the incident did not occur accidentally.

Voluntary assumption of risk appears to be the prominent factor which excludes compensation in the United States for claims relating to death or injury by accident. In a 1951 case,[47] this principle was expressly laid down when a court refused the award of compensation in an instance where the insured died as a result of participating in 'Russian Roulette'. Similarly, in a case decided earlier,[48] the courts had held that even if a person was not aware of a particular susceptibility to risk, no award of compensation would be available to the injured person by the person who allegedly causes the injury. It therefore appears to be clear that American law seems to run parallel to English common law in insisting that only unexpected events be classified as accidental. The heavy reliance on voluntary assumption of risk underscores this fact.

The common law of Canada has, in more than one instance, expressly recognized the principle enunciated by Lord Macnaughten in the *Fenton* case, that the word 'accident' can be attributed to an unexpected incident or one which is undesigned. In a 1940 decision,[49] Crocket J spelt out the fact that an accident is an untoward event.[50] In this case, a worker incurred internal injury in the course of her duties while operating a new hand embossing machine. The decision is very clear, in that, as in the *Fenton* case, the claim was found to be compensable notwithstanding the risk, since the employee had to take the risk involved to perform her duties. Courts in Canada have refused compensation in instances where consequential damage is caused by a person's voluntary behaviour which leads to the injury. In *Travellers' Insurance Company* v. *Elder*,[51] where a customer in a restaurant used abusive language and was assaulted as a result, the court held that the injuries were effected directly and independently of causes other than through accidental means.

A noteworthy feature in the *Travellers' Insurance Company* case is that the court had relied upon the fault of the claimant as a basis for rejecting his claim,[52] and on the fact that the claimant had placed himself in a position that would objectively be considered to have brought about an assault upon himself. This approach was seen in another case,[53] where a deer poacher shot at another while poaching, which invited retaliation, resulting in the death of the poacher. The Nova Scotia Supreme Court held that death had not been caused accidentally, since the deceased, by his act of firing at the other, had invited the retaliatory shot. The rationale in the case appears to be that if the injury caused is judged to be foreseeable by the injured, such injury would not be considered accidental.

The test of foreseeability has been strongly applied in the case of *Candler* v. *London and Lancashire Guarantee and Accident Company of Canada et al.*,[54] where the court had pronounced that an injury which is the reasonable consequence of a voluntary act of the injured cannot be considered as having been caused by accidental means. In this case, the deceased met with his death by falling from the twelfth floor of a hotel. The insurance company with whom the deceased had held a life insurance policy denied compensation on the grounds that the deceased had been in an advanced state of intoxication. Grant J stated:

> The purpose of his [the deceased's] action to show his friend that he had sufficient nerve to take the risk of falling, that was obviously associated with his actions, was so evident to Simmonds [the friend] that, to use his words, he was petrified at the display. His efforts to dissuade Candler from engaging in such an act consisted partly in telling him that he need not so act … His statement that he would show he still had nerve is the conclusive evidence that he appreciated the risk involved.[55] His acts on the night in question in assuming the dangerous position he did on the top of the coping could have no useful purpose whatever except the obvious opportunity to convince Simmonds that he possessed sufficient nerve to accept the challenge that was associated therewith … His conduct was foolhardy and attended with the most obvious danger … I therefore hold that Candler's death was not caused either by accidental means or by accident …[56]

Grant J seems to have assiduously followed the objective test of foreseeability and attributed the cause of death to consequential injury arising from the initial act of intoxication of the deceased. This interpretation has precluded the death of the deceased from being considered an accident.

Two assumptions emerge from the decision in the *Candler* case. One is that in determining the occurrence of an 'accident', the courts in Canada would inevitably consider the cause of the accident as a relevant fact. The other is the incontrovertible assumption that if the incident arises out of the foreseeable consequences of an act of the deceased or injured person, the incident itself would not be considered for compensation.

It is very clear that the three jurisdictions of the United Kingdom, United States and Canada recognize at common law certain basic facts in determining whether a given incident can be termed an 'accident'. The incident should constitute the following:

- it should be an unexpected, fortuitous or untoward happening;
- it should not be a consequence of irrational conduct of the deceased or injured person;
- it should be one which is not reasonably foreseeable by the deceased or injured.

Perhaps the only exception is *Fenton* v. *Thorley*,[57] where it was recognized that an injury may be compensable even if caused with foreseeability if the risk was foreseen but was inevitable. Be that as it may, the most critical problem in this area where all three jurisdictions are concerned is that the common law has not offered an acceptable definition of the word 'accident'.

### *'Accident' in Air Law*

In commercial aviation, the word 'accident' is sometimes given as broad a definition as those just considered. The Chicago Convention of 1944 defines an accident as an 'occurrence associated with the operation of an aircraft'.[58] In Article 17, the Warsaw Convention speaks of 'the accident which caused the damage', reducing the accident to the cause, rather than to the death or injury.[59] The US Supreme Court has held that *in limine* an accident must be unexpected and external to the passenger.[60] It is not sufficient that the plaintiff suffers injury as a result of their own internal reaction to the usual, normal and expected operation of the aircraft.[61] Such incidents as hijackings, terrorist attacks and bomb threats have been considered to be accidents, together with aircraft crashes.[62] An accident could even involve such lesser incidents as tyre failure on take-off,[63] and the supply of infected food causing food poisoning of passengers.[64]

In 1982, a passenger travelling from New York to Manila suffered a massive coronary seizure in flight. The allegation against the airline was that as a result of the failure of the airline employees to render medical assistance, the patient's condition suffered irreparable deterioration, resulting in death. Responsibility devolved upon the court to fit this incident to that of an 'accident' within the meaning of the Warsaw Convention. The court readily did this by deeming that the word 'accident' in air law in this instance was not the heart attack itself, but the failure on the part of the airline to render medical assistance in flight. The court said:

> After all, it is no different from an airline's liability in a hijacking incident where the accident is not the acts of the hijackers but the alleged failure on the part of the carrier to provide adequate security.[65]

The airline was accordingly found liable for damage so sustained by the deceased passenger.

In a contemporaneous case, a passenger brought action in the US District Court of Puerto Rico for a hernia sustained by lifting a heavy suitcase from the air terminal conveyor belt. A baggage handler of the defendant airline had refused to carry the suitcase, and the plaintiff had solicited aid from her relatives, who were prevented from entering the baggage area by a guard on duty. The action against the airline was dismissed by the court, primarily on the grounds that the plaintiff did not suffer an unexpected injury, as she had previously undergone a gall bladder operation and would have known her condition to be delicate.[66]

In 1983, a medical practitioner suffering from a head cold and respiratory infection boarded an aircraft. He disembarked completely deaf. The plaintiff averred that he suffered discomfort in his ears at descent, probably due to sudden pressure changes that may have occurred. He alleged that the airline knew, or ought to have known, that passengers suffering from head colds would risk losing their hearing. In addition, it was alleged that the airline owed a duty to warn the passenger that it was dangerous to travel with a head cold. The airline denied the existence of such a duty. The US District Court for the Southern District of New York reasoned that it would be incongruous to impose a duty on an airline to envisage all possible human afflictions, assess their effect on air travel and warn passengers accordingly. In any event, the airline was in this instance not aware that the passenger was suffering from a head cold. In this decision, the court clearly indicated that the presumption of liability imposed by the Warsaw Convention on airlines, and the 'highest degree of care' doctrine applicable thereto, should not be taken advantage of by plaintiffs.[67] Similarly, there would be no cause of action against an airline where a passenger's ill health is aggravated due to acceleration at take-off or deceleration at landing.[68]

In April 1984, an intermediate Appellate Court in New York was faced with the task of deciding whether an airline can be held liable for the death of a passenger who chokes to death owing to their own intoxication. The decision was in the affirmative, and the court, in enforcing judgment against the airline, drew the analogy between a dispensing druggist and an airline. The airline serves its passengers with drink, and thus undertakes the responsibility not to serve in excess, and to exercise reasonable care for the safety of passengers. In addition, in the event of excessive intoxication of a passenger, the airline is under a legal duty to render such medical assistance as is necessary to revive the passenger, or in any event to keep them out of danger. In the light of this principle, the airline has a further duty to protect others from a drunken passenger who gets out of control.[69]

In *Air France* v. *Saks*,[70] the US Supreme Court interpreted the word 'accident' in the context of the Warsaw Convention to mean an occurrence whereby a passenger is injured owing to an unexpected or unusual event or happening that is external to the passenger,[71] and that where the injury results from the passenger's own internal reaction to the normal exigencies of air travel, such injury would not be construed as having resulted from an accident. In this case, the plaintiff was a passenger on an Air France flight from Paris to Los Angeles. During the descent, the plaintiff suffered severe pain in her left ear, which was aggravated thereafter. The plaintiff – who consulted a doctor after the plane landed – was informed that she was rendered completely deaf in her left ear. The plaintiff brought an action in a California state court on the grounds that her hearing loss was due to the negligent maintenance by the airline of the pressurization system of the aircraft which transported her. Air France moved that the allegation of the plaintiff could not be sustained, since the meaning of the word 'accident' in Article 17 of the Warsaw Convention was meant to be an unusual and unexpected happening. Further, the airline alleged that at all times the pressurization system of the aircraft had been normal. The District Court granted summary judgment to the plaintiff on the basis that 'accident' in Article 17 was meant to be an unusual and unexpected happening. The Supreme Court rejected the rationale adopted by the lower court on the ground that Article 17 refers to an accident which causes an injury, and therefore it is the cause and not the effect that is the determinant. Accordingly, the Supreme Court held that air carriers would be liable only if an accident caused the passenger injury. Thus an injury that was in itself an accident was insufficient to satisfy the requirements of Article 17 of the Warsaw Convention.

There will be no accident if, in a normal flight free of turbulence, a passenger suffers discomfort from a condition such as a hiatus hernia[72] or thrombophlebitis.[73] In *Abramson* v. *Japan Airlines*, an airline passenger suffered aggravation of a pre-existing hiatal hernia shortly after take-off from Anchorage on a flight to Tokyo. The passenger, who had been under medication for his condition for six years, had not informed the carrier prior to boarding, but claimed that had he been given occupancy of a few empty seats, he could have massaged his stomach to normalcy. The airline had claimed that there were no empty seats in the flight, contrary to the passenger's claim that there were in fact nine empty seats in the first class section of the aircraft. The passenger claimed that his hernia attack constituted an 'accident' within the provisions of Article 17 of the Convention. The court rejected this claim, and held that the plaintiff's difficulty was not in any way related to his transportation by air and, accordingly, there was no accident under Article 17.

It would have been interesting if the court had applied the principle of the *Seguritan* case,[74] where failure to render medical assistance by the airline was construed as falling within the purview of the word 'accident'. After all, the airline did not make any attempt to render assistance to the passenger in the *Abramson* case. The court's reasoning in the latter case contradicts the earlier decision, and leads to a logical absurdity. The intention of the Convention was seemingly to provide a uniform system of compensation for passengers who brought claims against airlines operating international air services. To suggest that the failure of an airline to render required assistance is excusable under the Convention is completely at odds with earlier decisions, and also arguably contrary to the intention and purpose of the Convention itself.

In so far as the word 'wounding' of a passenger in Article 17 is concerned, courts have initially held that such would only be in instances of 'bodily injury', and consequently would be palpably conspicuous physical injury.[75] This excluded mental injury. However, a later decision[76] held that the types of injury enumerated should be construed expansively to encompass as many as fall within the ambit of the enumerated types, including mental and psychosomatic injuries. This decision has been followed consistently in a strong line of cases.[77] In the United States mental injury is now entrenched in most jurisdictions as an independently compensable head of damages.[78] As Burnett CJ said in *Medlin* v. *Allied Investment Co.*[79]

> Memory and empathy tells us that 'hurt' perceived through sensory media other than that of touch may be just as painful if not more than the hurt perceived by the tactile sense. Moreover, physicians tell us that the consequences of invasion of the person accomplished through the perceptory media of sight and sound may be also as damaging if not more damaging than invasions of the persons accomplished through the sense of touch.[80]

Therefore, mental anguish or injury would now be recognized by most jurisdictions as falling within the purview of 'wounding' of a passenger under Article 17 of the Warsaw Convention.

It is apparent from the *cursus curiae* that a stringent standard of proof of the nature of the occurrence is insisted upon by the courts if liability of the carrier is to be established under Article 17 of the Warsaw Convention. In *Salce* v. *Aer Lingus Airlines*,[81] the District Court for the Southern District of New York required that the plaintiff show that the landing of the aircraft in which the plaintiff travelled was anything other than a normal landing. The plaintiff averred that he had sustained personal injuries due to the hard landing of the aircraft. In the absence of clear evidence of a hard landing, the court would presume that the landing performed by the aircraft in this instance was not an unexpected or unusual event that would satisfy the requirements of an 'accident' under the Warsaw Convention.

However, when facts are self-evident, as in the case of *Salerno* v. *Pan American World Airways*,[82] the courts would not hesitate to award damages to a plaintiff passenger. In this case, the District Court for the Southern District of New York held that knowledge of a bomb threat which subsequently caused a miscarriage to a passenger came within the meaning and scope of the word 'accident'. The plaintiff, together with her two children, were passengers aboard a PanAm flight from Miami to Uruguay. After take-off, the cockpit crew instructed the cabin crew to look for a bomb which air traffic control had informed them was on board. The crew notified the passengers, including the plaintiff. She suffered a miscarriage 24 hours after having been informed of the alleged bomb on board, and having watched the cabin crew looking for the object. The court held that an 'accident' within the meaning of the Warsaw Convention caused the plaintiff's injuries, because a bomb threat is 'external to the passenger' and is an unexpected and unusual event outside the usual, normal and expected operation of the aircraft.[83]

The above discussion reveals the salutary principle that the word 'accident' is considered far more liberally in modern air law than under other areas of common law. It also underscores the fact that courts are now more inclined to treat an act of omission on the part of an airline as an 'accident', as was shown in the *Seguritan* case.[84] The airline is presumed liable for an 'accident' where a drunken passenger assaults another, or where a passenger suffers a heart attack and is not given the necessary medical attention in flight, just to name two instances. Of course, the claimant has to adduce clear evidence of the event and the ensuing injury.

*Embarking and Disembarking*

Article 17 further provides that the accident which causes the damage should take place on board the aircraft or in the course of any of the operations of embarking or disembarking. The first alternative – being on board – is self-explanatory and does not require discussion, but the second, which involves the operations of embarking or disembarking has been subject to sustained judicial discussion and analysis. Although, *ex facie*, the words 'on board the aircraft' are not problematical, the phrase has been interpreted at least once to encompass time spent by passengers in a hotel as the result of a hijacking.[85] The argument in this case was that the passengers would have been on board if not for the hijacking. This is an extreme interpretation which seems to say that the airline is liable for all accidents within the period of time from the start of the embarkation process to the end of disembarkation.

Current law on the subject seems to favour the Day-Evangelinos test, which was developed as a consequence of a series of terrorist acts on passengers in airport departure lounges. This test considers three elements: the location of the passenger, the nature of their activity at the time of the accident, and the degree of control exercised by the airline at the relevant time. A number of US cases have accepted this test,[86] and it clearly establishes the fact that unless the passenger is under the control or direction of the airline at the terminal, there is no liability for injury or death caused to the passenger under the provisions of the Warsaw Convention. A case which brings out the significance of this test is *Adler* v. *Austrian Airlines*, where a passenger slipped on some ice and fell between the terminal building and the aircraft bus operated by the airport staff, not by the airline. A Brussels court, applying a test similar to the Day-Evangelinos test, held that the passenger was not under the control of the airline, and was thereby precluded from invoking the provisions of Article 17 of the Convention.

The test itself obviates the need to painstakingly go through every possible exigency in the light of the requirement that the accident should occur during the process of embarkation or disembarkation. Prior to the adoption of this test, there was no uniformity in the judicial reasoning behind the definition of embarkation and disembarkation. It was left to each individual court to determine whether a given situation would fall within the scope of chronology of these two extremities. Now, the Day-Evangelinos test has made the task of the courts much easier.

*Liability Limits*

Article 22 of the Warsaw Convention states:

> In the transportation of passengers the liability of the carrier for each passenger shall be limited to the sum of 125,000 francs. Where, in accordance with the law of the court to which the case is submitted, damages may be awarded in the form of periodic payments, the equivalent capital value of such payments shall not exceed 125,000 francs. Nevertheless by special contract, the carrier and the passenger may agree to a higher limit of liability.

'Franc' here refers to the French franc, consisting of 65.5 milligrams of gold at the standard of fineness of nine hundred thousandths. These sums may be converted into any national currency in round figures.[87] At the time the Convention was signed in 1929, there were 12.5 French francs to the US dollar, which makes the airline liability for passenger death or injury a maximum of US $20,000. The question arises today as to what conversion rate applies to the French franc as stipulated at the Warsaw Convention. The fact that currency fluctuations would not make the old conversion standards practicable has given rise to much debate, particularly in the United States.

In 1982, the Supreme Court of Puerto Rico held that the limits of liability of the Warsaw Convention should be converted from francs to dollars by reference to the last official price of gold in the United States, as set forth in the last CAB order dealing with the dollar equivalents of the Warsaw Convention limits of liability.[88] The most significant recent development on this point is seen in the 1984 case of *Trans World Airlines Inc.* v. *Franklin Mint Corp*,[89] where the US Supreme Court held that the limits of liability under Article 22 of the Warsaw Convention which are expressed in French gold francs are to be converted into US currency by using the last official price of gold.[90] The facts of the case were that Franklin Mint paid for the transportation of certain numismatic material by TWA from Philadelphia to London. The cargo was lost, and Franklin Mint sought US$ 250,000 as damages from the defendant airline.

The Court of Appeal for the Second Circuit somewhat unexpectedly pronounced that TWA's liability was limited under Article 22 of the Warsaw Convention, but the liability limits were unenforceable owing to the inapplicability of the Convention and impracticability of converting currency as envisaged by the Convention in 1929.[91] The Supreme Court found the limits enforceable, and cited with approval the decision of the Civil Aeronautics Board of the United States to use the last official price of gold as the basis for conversion within the authority of that agency and consistent with the US Constitution.[92]

The *Franklin Mint* case concerned the carriage of cargo, and the question arose whether the decision would apply to passenger liability as well, in terms of the applicability of the provisions of the Warsaw Convention to cases of passenger liability. In 1984, this problem was solved when the US District Court for the Central District of California held that the principal of the *Franklin Mint* decision shall apply to personal injury and wrongful death claims.[93] The *Franklin Mint* standards are not absolute and static, however. In other words, the US Supreme Court considered that the use of a limit based on gold was designed to deal with the fluctuations of inflation, and in an inflationary economic environment a fixed limit in national currency might fail to meet the desired result as envisaged by the Convention. To give effect to the objective of Article 22 and the envisaged economic uniformity, the court recognized that it may be necessary for periodic adjustments of the limit as converted into dollars. The CAB was charged with making such adjustments to accord with values of other Western currencies and changes in conversion rates of currencies of Warsaw Convention signatories. Since the US Supreme Court took into account the last valuation of the CAB in 1978 for its decision in the *Franklin Mint* case, this was taken to apply at the time the case was adjudicated in 1984.

It has also been suggested that a successful solution to the problem of matching the franc with the dollar would be to seek parity of the US dollar with special drawing rights (SDR) – a basket of currencies which would adjust themselves according to currency fluctuations in different countries. This, it is argued, would also allow a ready conversion of the SDR to any currency of any jurisdiction hearing a case of passenger death or injury under the Warsaw Convention. There is no logically compelling argument for either the *Franklin Mint* principle or the SDR principle. In most jurisdictions, courts may have to interpret the Convention on this point as best as they can, particularly in the absence of specific legislation.

### *Defences Available to the Airlines*

The discussion above covered two key factors which govern the civil liability of airlines: the presumption of liability that is imposed upon the airline, and the liability limits that apply to protect the airline from unlimited liability and spurious claimants. There are two other factors which operate as adjuncts to the initial concepts: that the airline may show certain facts in its defence to rebut the presumption, and that if the airline is found to be guilty of wilful misconduct it is precluded from invoking the liability limits under the Warsaw Convention. On the surface, these four concepts seem to group into two sets of balancing measures. The end result is that whilst on the one hand the airline is subject to stringent standards of liability, on the other it is protected by two provisions which limit its liability in monetary terms and allow a complete or partial defence in rebuttal of the presumption.

Article 20(1) of the Warsaw Convention provides that the airline shall not be liable if it proves that the airline and its agents had taken all necessary measures to avoid the damage, or that it was impossible for the airline and its agent to take such measures. Shawcross and Beaumont are of the view that the phrase 'all necessary measures' is an unhappy one, in that the mere happening of the passenger injury or death presupposes the fact that the airline or its agents had not taken all necessary measures to prevent the occurrence.[94] The airline usually takes such precautions as making regular announcements to passengers regarding the status of a flight, starting with instructions on security and safety measures that are available in the aircraft. The airline does this to conform to the requirements of the Warsaw Convention that it must take all necessary measures to prevent an accident in order to rebut the presumption of liability. Thus, in a case decided in 1963,[98] it was held that a passenger who left her seat when the aircraft went through turbulent atmosphere was barred from claiming under the Warsaw Convention for personal injury. Here it was held that an admonition of the airline that the passengers were to remain seated with their seat belts fastened during the time in question was proof of the airline having taken the necessary measures as envisaged in the Warsaw Convention.[96] This case also established the fact that 'all necessary measures' was too wide in scope, and that a proper interpretation of the intention of the Warsaw Convention would be to consider the airline to require taking all 'reasonably necessary measures'. In a more recent case, Chapman J imputed objectivity to the phrase 'reasonably necessary measures' by declaring that such measures should be considered necessary by 'the reasonable man'.[97] A similar approach was taken in a subsequent case, where the court held that the airline should show more than the fact that it was not negligent in order to invoke Article 20(1) of the Warsaw Convention.[98] The United States also follows this approach of objectivity. In *Manufacturers Hanover Trust Co. v. Alitalia Airlines*,[99] it was emphasized that the airline must show that all reasonable measures had been taken from an objective standpoint in order that the benefit of the defence be accrued to the airline. Some French decisions have also approached this defence on similar lines, and required a stringent test of generality in order that the criteria for allowing the defence be approved.[100]

The airline, which has the burden of proof, cannot seek refuge in showing that normal precautions were taken. For example, normal precautions in attending to the safety of the passengers prior to a flight are not sufficient. If the airline cannot adduce a reasonable explanation of why the accident occurred despite the reasonably necessary precautions being taken, it is unlikely to succeed in its defence.[101] In so far as the requirement of impossibility to take precautions is concerned, the courts have required clear evidence of the difficulties faced by the airline in avoiding the disaster. In one case of a crash landing, the court held that it was insufficient for the airline to show that the aircraft was in perfect condition and that the pilot took all steps to effect a good landing; the airline had to show that the weather conditions were so bad that the aircraft could not land in another airport.[102] In *Haddad* v. *Cie Air France*,[103] where an airline had to accept suspicious passengers who later perpetrated a hijacking, the court held that the airline could not deny boarding to the passengers who later proved to be hijackers. In that instance, the airline had found it impossible to take all necessary precautions, and was considered sound in defence under Article 20(1). A similar approach was taken in the case of *Barboni* v. *Cie Air France*,[104] where the court held that when an airline receives a bomb threat while in flight and performs an emergency evacuation, a passenger who is injured by evacuation through the escape chute cannot claim liability of the airline, since it would have been impossible for the airline to take any other measure.

If the airline proves that the damage was caused by or contributed to by the negligence of the injured person, the court may, in accordance with the provisions of its own law, exonerate the carrier wholly or partly from liability.[105] Contributory negligence under the Warsaw Convention has been treated subjectively as and when cases are adjudicated. The courts have not set an objective standard, as in the earlier defence. For instance, in *Goldman* v. *Thai Airways International Ltd*,[106] it was held that passengers are not guilty of contributory negligence if they keep their seat belt unfastened during the flight and suffer injury when no sign is given by the aircraft control panel to keep the seat belt on. However, if a passenger removes a bandage or brace that they are required to wear to treat an existing injury and suffer injury in flight due to the removal of the support, they would be found to have contributed to the negligence resulting in their injuries.[107]

Article 25(1) of the Warsaw Convention states that the airline shall not be entitled to avail itself of the provisions of the Warsaw Convention which excludes or limits its liability if the damage is caused by the wilful misconduct or by such default on the part of the airline as, in accordance with the law of the court to which the case is submitted, is considered to be equivalent to wilful misconduct. Article 25(1) extends this liability to acts of the agent of the airline acting within the scope of its employment, and attributes such wilful misconduct to the airline. Such action as the failure of the technical crew of the aircraft to monitor weather conditions and the failure to execute a proper approach during adverse weather conditions are examples of wilful misconduct of the airline.[108] Similarly, the failure of a crew which is going off duty to inform the incoming crew of a defect in the aircraft or any such relevant issue which would affect the safety of the aircraft could be construed as an act of wilful misconduct on the part of the airline.[109]

The effect of Article 25 is that the plaintiff becomes entitled to lift the limit of liability of the airline as prescribed in Article 22 of the Warsaw Convention if they prove that the airline was guilty of wilful misconduct. Thus the burden of proof falls on the plaintiff, and if they succeed they may claim an amount over and above the prescribed limits of airline liability.

The limitation of liability of the carrier imposed by the Warsaw Convention could be circumvented by the plaintiff proving that the carrier was guilty of wilful misconduct in causing the injury (see Chapter 12).

The question of air carrier liability and the approach taken in this context by the Warsaw Convention has seen the emergence of the scholarly analysis of two issues: should liability of the carrier be based on fault, and consequently on the principles of negligence and limited liability, or should liability be based on strict liability? Drion, in his 1954 treatise on liability,[110] enquires into the various rationales and scenarios that may arise from an intellectual extrapolation of the subject. He examines the fact that an insurance system for liability, which would inextricably be linked to a strict liability concept, would be desirable, as a plaintiff would be able to claim compensation from an impecunious defendant through the latter's insurer, on the deep pocket theory,[111] and that insurance underwriters may, in their own interest, be impelled to formulate aviation accident prevention schemes, furthuring this cause.[112] Drion proposes eight rationales for the rebuttable limitation of liability presumption that appears in Article 17, quantified by Article 22 of the Convention:

1 maritime principles carry a limitation policy;
2 the protection of the financially weak aviation industry;
3 the risks should be borne by aviation alone;
4 the existence of back-up insurance;
5 the possibility of the claimants obtaining insurance;
6 limitation of liability being imposed on a *quid pro quo* basis on both the carrier and operator;
7 the possibility of quick settlement under a liability limitation n regime;
8 the ability to unify the law regarding damages.[113]

These rationales, and whatever others form considerations of policy in the assessment of whether a liability system should be based on negligence or strict liability, should be addressed with the conscious awareness that while the Convention imposes a rebuttable presumption of limited liability on the carrier, the contributory negligence of the plaintiff can exculpate the carrier and obviate or apportion compensation. More importantly, wilful misconduct of the carrier transcends liability limits and makes the liability of the carrier unlimited. Strict liability, on the other hand, as proposed in Montreal Protocols 3 and 4, does not admit of breaking liability limits, sets a maximum limit of compensation that the carrier has to pay, and makes this limit unbreakable by such extraneous factors as the carrier's wilful misconduct.

The ultimate question is therefore whether to keep the Warsaw-Hague concept of fault and limited liability, or to embrace a system of strict liability which assures the aggrieved party of pecuniary or reipersecutory recompense, while obviating the need for lengthy determinations of who was at fault after the fact. In other words, does one point a finger at the carrier in the first instance, then limit its liability and again break the limit if it is at fault, or make the carrier pay a sum of money, the maximum limits of which have been set, with the assurance that such limits would not be raised unreasonably if the carrier was negligent?

The Convention unified legal principles relating to air carrier liability, thus precluding the application of many differing domestic laws.[114] However, it did not succeed in presenting to the world unequivocally objective and quantified rules of liability. This means that plaintiffs cannot know whether they will be compensated if injured in an air accident, since the Convention admits of challenge on the grounds of the plaintiff's conduct before, during or after the accident. The strict liability principle introduced by the Guatemala City Protocol and carried through by the Montreal protocols, on the other hand, has been applauded on the grounds that:

> First, it gets money into the hands of the passengers much more quickly. Second, it saves transaction expenses which includes legal fees and other substantial litigation costs. Third, it provides compensation to passengers in those factual situations where no responsible party is at fault, such as in an act of terrorism.[115]

Alexander Tobolewski points out very validly that actual aviation practice in terms of aviation insurance by the airlines has nothing to do with limitation of liability and claims, since airlines insure their fleets and liabilities for colossal amounts in the insurance market.[116] He therefore suggests the harmonization of the law and actual practice (presumably by infusing more specific quanta in damages), and simplification of the system of recovery, both of which strongly suggests a regime such as the one envisaged in the Montreal Protocols.[117] Werner Guldimann concludes:

> The most important and urgent matter in the present decade is the continuation of the efforts undertaken by ICAO to re-establish the former universality and uniformity of the Warsaw system by having the Montreal Protocols No 3 and 4 rapidly ratified by the greatest possible number of contracting States.[118]

Although Professor Bin Cheng holds the view that the Montreal Protocols are heavily weighted towards the carrier, inadequate set limits and that the unbreakable limit on the SDR value is undesirable,[119] the view that strict liability should be embraced seems more sensible, in view of the enormous number of passengers carried every year by air, the possible eradication of legal contingency fees, and above all, to give teeth to the meaning and purpose of law – that it should be an instrument of solace, not an opportunity for debate.

In an evaluation of the Warsaw system,[120] it has been said in 1979 that during the first 25 years of the existence of the Warsaw Convention, it had served the aviation community satisfactorily.[121] Peter Martin bases this observation on the argument that when the Hague Protocol was being drafted in 1955, it was recorded that only 55 Warsaw cases had been adjudicated, and that is a very small number of cases for an instrument of the stature of the Warsaw Convention.[122] The process of unifying air carrier liability, started by the Warsaw Convention, dealt with liability concepts, quanta of compensation, exceptions on liability, jurisdictional issues and prescription of action. It is sad, however, that together with the original Warsaw Convention, there are now seven other international agreements, few of which have ever seen the light of day. This means that the unification process started by the Warsaw Convention had been criticized and found wanting at various stages of its chequered history. The original document has been excoriated many times, prompting Professor Cheng to call it the 'Warsaw shambles',[123] although it has remained the most widely implemented private international law convention.[124]

*Ex facie*, from a strictly practical standpoint, it would appear that many facets of unification of the Warsaw Convention have come under interpretation by different philosophies, presumably due to the lack of specificity of the principles of unification and *a fortiori* the language used. For instance, the delivery of the passenger ticket and the attendant carrier liability came under a series of confounding judicial thought processes, where in two cases,[125] the courts decided that the ticket had to be delivered in such a manner as to afford the passenger a reasonable opportunity to take measures to protect against liability insurance, only to decide in *Chan* v. *Korean Airlines*[126] that the only requirement of Article 3 of the Convention was that a ticket be delivered. *Goldman* v. *Thai Airways International Limited*[127] was another case where two confusing issues were decided. The first involved the question of whether the concept of 'wilful misconduct', as reflected in Article 25 of the Convention, was to be interpreted objectively or subjectively. The second issue concerned compensatory limits which were so confusing to both the courts and the parties to litigation that an outside settlement was effected on a mutually acceptable basis.[128] The issue regarding compensatory limits for death or personal injury has had a consistent evolution, starting from the Warsaw Convention at approximately US$ 8,300, increasing twofold under the Hague Protocol of 1955, increasing again by the Guatemala City Protocol to 100,000 Special Drawing Rights (SDR) (about US$ 130,000), with the Montreal Protocols going even higher. The currency conversion to gold value has been another contentious issue for many parties to litigation, and the case of *Franklin Mint* v. *TWA*[129] left the situation in fiscal anarchy by deciding that, in the United States, the Poincaré gold franc has to be converted to the last official price of gold before the US left the gold market, not the free market price of gold. This not only reversed the overall American attitude towards seeking enhanced compensation through 360 degrees, it also awarded un–realistically low compensation to the plaintiff. Further, a case in Australia has given a new interpretation to the notion of carrier negligence in the carriage of cargo[130] and a New Zealand case has decided that any interested party can now claim compensation under a cargo claim.[131]

The Montreal Agreement of 1966 – a private agreement between carriers plying the United States – was also the result of failure by contracting States to reach an international solution to the problem of unifying principles of liability, particularly in so far as the quantum of damages was concerned. The Montreal Agreement amply demonstrates, as an ICAO document[132] points out, that a private agreement between air carriers sponsored by IATA can unhinge and question the credibility of a multilateral international treaty between sovereign States. Mankiewicz attributes this chaotic state of disagreement to the stand taken by the United States when he states:

> Indeed, there is real irony in the history of the Warsaw Convention. For more than thirty years, the United States of America have steadily and successfully fought for, and obtained and signed six protocols to amend the Warsaw Convention as well as a 'Convention Supplementary to the Warsaw Convention.' But they have ratified not one of these Warsaw instruments. In spite of the huge amounts of time and

> money spent all these years by ICAO and its member States, the US judiciary is still saddled with the awkward task of applying, construing constructively or destructively, misinterpreting and circumventing a convention which is now 60 years old ...[133]

There is only one viable alternative towards rectifying this anomaly and preserving the unification efforts of the Warsaw Convention, and that comes in the nature of ratifying the Montreal Protocols 3 and 4. As Professor Michael Milde states :

> There is hardly any viable alternative to a determined effort to bring the Montreal Protocols Nos 3 and 4 into force. If that aim is not accomplished in the very near future, we may witness a trend to denunciation of the Warsaw System by several States with the ensuing chaotic conflicts of laws, conflicts of jurisdiction, unpredictably high compensation claims and skyrocketing increase in insurance premiums.[134]

The civil liability of an airline for causing death or injury to passengers has been established by international treaty and entrenched in law by judicial interpretation. The courts have attempted to balance the interests of both the airline and the passenger, as was the perceived intention of the Warsaw Convention. The predominant feature of this area of civil liability is that air transport in terms of the commercial transportation of passengers is incontrovertibly the mode of transport that involves the highest levels of technology. Therefore, courts may find difficulty in ascertaining negligence, wilful misconduct and the overall liability of the airline in the face of complex technical arguments and defences. However, this reason alone should not justify obviating the tortious element that has so carefully been entrenched in the Warsaw Convention by its founders and used by courts over the last seventy years. As the foregoing discussions reflect, liability issues under the Warsaw Convention have been consistently addressed by the courts on the basis of their interpretation of negligence, wilful misconduct and contributory negligence, all of which are exclusively issues involving principles of tort law.

*Comments*

It is clear that the conventional interpretation of the term 'accident' in tort liability has been extended in aviation cases under Article 17 of the Warsaw Convention, where the courts have imputed intention to the carrier in certain instances. To this extent, as the *Seguritan* case,[135] which addressed the issue of the carrier's liability in not being able to regular medical assistance when necessary, and the *O'Leary* case,[136] in which a passenger was served excessive liquor in flight, prove, the courts have interpreted the Warsaw Convention to enforce liability of the carrier on the principles of intention. Wilful misconduct has therefore played an important role in establishing that, in certain circumstances at least, courts would be justified in considering that the extent of the carrier's fault is a valid consideration in the award of damages.

Fault liability, as enforced by the Warsaw Convention, may also be adequately reflected in intentional negligence, where the carrier intentionally breaches the duty of care owed to the passenger. Determination of a breach of a duty or care as a distinct evidentiary tool by the courts would act towards accident prevention, in that instances of carrier liability which emerge from accident investigations could then be used as admissible evidence.

The new trend of doing away with fault liability and introducing a system of liability that may apply irrespective of fault but aligned to monetary compensation based upon subjective assessments of jurisdictional liability has its genesis in the 1960s. During this period, civil law liability in tort entered a new phase, effectively replacing the existing system of liability with a system of liability insurance. Tortious liability was no longer considered cost-effective, and was no match for less expensive insurance. Jurists thought it more equitable – and above all, practical – to embrace a legal system that espoused loss distribution, which acted as the national precursor to liability insurance. This system of liability was assisted by three reasons which militated against fault liability and acted as catalysts towards the successful launch of liability insurance. First, a tort system based upon fault was expensive to administer compared to any system of insurance; second, litigation was fraught with delay, which a plaintiff could often ill afford; third, the unpredictable results of cases based upon fault liability often put plaintiffs under pressure to settle their claims for amounts less than they would receive if their claims were successful at trial.

The question that now arises is whether the international aviation community should retain fault liability, or embrace strict liability which is designed to obviate adjudication for tortious liability and settle claims on a subjective basis.

The task which now has to be accomplished is to inquire whether private air law needs the concept of limited liability, or whether another system could be recommended. The most compelling arguments for the limitation of liability in private air law are that it protects the financially weak aviation industry, unifies private air law against draconian domestic laws, and expedites the payment of compensation. It is interesting to analyse these concepts in today's aviation context. We live in a world where complex litigation issues emerge, carefully thought out by contingency-fee lawyers who have an inexplicable capacity to produce a variety of defendants out of a hat. For instance, there is now an awareness that there are co-liable parties – manufacturers of component parts, air traffic controllers, and even government agencies such as airports authorities. Would it be fair to limit the liability of the carrier while exposing these three categories of defendants to unlimited liability? There may also be instances where the deceased or injured may have had enormous capacity to earn during their working life, which would be interrupted or terminated by an air accident.

It is prudent to approach this question by laying due emphasis on the economic ramifications of this strictly legal consideration, since, at its core, the question addresses not principles of legal rectitude, nor issues of justice, but matters of financial interest to the parties concerned. It is therefore essential to consider the effects of limitation of liability compared to unlimited liability, and to rationalize between the two and arrive at a synthesis of the concepts, or, if possible, a totally new concept. To determine this situation, it is necessary to assess the Warsaw Convention, its principles of limitation of liability coupled with unlimited liability in the event of gross negligence of the carrier, the Montreal Protocols with their strict liability and higher limits of liability with no possibility of accommodating unlimited liability under any circumstances, and a pure instance of general liability with no inhibitions whatever. Of course, these three alternatives must be viewed from the standpoints of the plaintiff passenger or their dependants and the defendant airline. The operative theme of this inquiry would be money, not complex legal issues, since it is money that both parties are ultimately interested in.

It is incontrovertible that aviation insurers, when faced with increasing levels of claims and declining premium income, would naturally increase their policy disclaimers and seek to incorporate exclusions of cover. The aviation insurance market increasingly feels that there is no closeness at all between the underwriters and brokers on the one hand and the insured airline on the other.[137] One commentator recommends either a substantial increase in voluntary limits of liability, or total abandonment of limiting air carrier liability, implying that either would benefit both the plaintiff and the defendant.[138] Peter Martin suggests that the best prospect for the Warsaw system would be to abandon limitations.[139] He states:

> There are very good reasons for imposing on carriers at least a very high standard of care, and even strict liability. Strict liability without limitations already applies in many States to third party liability to persons other than passengers and that is generally believed to be right ... why should a passenger, therefore, be in a worse position than a person or owners of property on the ground?[140]

The insurance lawyers obviously need higher liability limits and specificity in this area. The steady disintegration of the Warsaw system, which is mainly attributable to its incompetence in providing for satisfactory compensation limits, has been proved by figures which were released by the Rand Corporation, showing that in a cross-section of cases studied, Warsaw–Montreal tickets obtained a per capita compensation of US$184,000, while non-Warsaw–Montreal tickets had received double this amount. This amount has further increased over the years, demonstrating that the Warsaw limits are being left behind rapidly.[141] It is clear that one of the viable alternatives to the IATA Inter-carrier Agreement's strict liability and private contract proposal is to consider the extension of the Warsaw limits, and the first step towards this goal is the ratification by States of the Montreal Protocols. If such a measure is accepted, it is also imperative that the scope of the Convention be extended to third parties such as air traffic controllers and manufacturers of component parts of aircraft, to seek consistency and to give the insurance market a more accurate assessment of the picture. By bringing these parties under the Warsaw umbrella, both the plaintiff and the defendant would be well served, in that the plaintiff would be assured of quick settlement, and the defendant would be comfortable with the thought that the liability is limited. This could also preclude contingency-fee appearances by lawyers.

At the same time one must not lose sight of the importance of insurance to liability under the Warsaw Convention. It must be noted that when the subject of insurance was addressed at the Warsaw Conference, the President of the drafting committee, Mr Gianini, observed:

> I may remind you that, under present conditions of air navigation, we have arrived at the conclusion that the problem is not yet ripe. But, given the importance of the problem, given that no one is disposed to consider the work already done as an end, we have expressed, on my proposal, wishes by which we indicate that the study of the problem deserves to be pursued. That is to say that we leave the door open for later discussions. In order to advance the solution of this problem, we have also expressed a wish, signed by all governments, by which we ask the governments to bring insurance into practice as much as possible. It is only then that one will be able to envisage the possibility of setting up an international rule.[142]

These prescient words of seventy years ago, which show vision and deep understanding of the future of civil aviation, should not be disregarded. It is time that the international aviation community looked hard at emerging trends relating to the Warsaw Convention, and attempted to find a balanced and workable solution.

## Emerging Trends

Of the two instances in which the Warsaw Convention provides that the carrier's liability is unlimited, one relates to the absence of documentation (absence of the passenger ticket and baggage check or air waybill), on the grounds that the document of carriage evidences the special regime of limited liability as prescribed in the Warsaw Convention; the other, which has turned out to be contentious, deals with instances where the damage is caused by the carrier's wilful misconduct, or such default on its part as, in accordance with the law of the court which exercises jurisdiction in the case, is considered to be the equivalent of wilful misconduct. Article 25 of the Warsaw Convention provides:

> The carrier shall not be entitled to avail himself of the provisions of this Convention or exclude or limit his liability, if the damage is caused by his wilful misconduct or by such default on his part as, in accordance with the law of the Court seised of the case, is considered to be equivalent to wilful misconduct.[143]

The provision further stipulates that the carrier shall not be entitled to avail it of the above provisions if the damage is caused as aforesaid by any agent of the carrier acting within the scope of its employment.[144]

The primary significance of Article 25 is that it addresses both wilful misconduct and the *equivalent* of wilful misconduct. The authentic and original text of the Warsaw Convention, which is in the French language, uses the words *dol* and *faute ... equivalente au dol.* There is a palpable inconsistency between English translation of the original text and the original text itself, in that the French word *dol* personifies the intention to inflict an injury on a person, whereas the English words 'wilful misconduct' require the defendant carrier to be aware of both its conduct and the reasonable and probable consequences of its conduct, in the nature of the damage which may ensue from the carrier's act. Wilful misconduct, therefore, may not necessarily involve the intention of the carrier, its servants or agents, and remains wider in scope as a ground of liability.

Most civil law jurisdictions have equated *dol* with 'gross negligence'. Drion[145] dismisses the element of intention by citing examples such as the theft or pilferage of goods or baggage (which are more frequent occurrences than aircraft accidents), which may not necessarily always occur with the concurrence or knowledge of the carrier, and cites a list of possible instances where gross negligence would form more justification for the invocation of Article 25. Notable examples are assault or indecent behaviour by carrier personnel, accidents caused by the conduct of personnel, serving bad food, bumpy rides causing passenger injury, and failure to inform passengers of rough weather.[146] Drion also makes the valid point of citing delay in carriage as having many dimensions which may be accommodated within the purview of Article 25 without warranting the consideration of intention.[143]

Common law jurisdictions, on the other hand, have separated 'wilful misconduct' from 'negligence', and insisted that the conduct of the carrier has to be 'wilful' or intentional for a successful case to be grounded on Article 25 of the Warsaw Convention. This approach is consistent with the original contention of the British delegate to the Warsaw Conference, who claimed that wilful misconduct should pertain to 'acts committed deliberately or acts of carelessness without any regard for the consequences'.[148] In the 1952 British case of *Horabin* v. *British Overseas Airways Corporation*, the court held:

> To be guilty of wilful misconduct the person concerned must appreciate that he is acting wrongfully, or is wrongfully omitting to act and yet persists in so acting or omitting to act regardless of the consequences, or acts or omits to act with reckless indifference as to what the result may be.[149]

In the same year, in the United States, the New York Supreme Court Appellate Division held that wilful misconduct was:

> ... dependent upon the facts of a particular case, but in order that acts may be characterized as wilful there must be on the part of the person or persons sought to be charged, a conscious intent to do or to omit doing the act from which harm results to another, or an intentional omission of a manifest duty. There must be a realization of the probability of injury from the conduct and a disregard of the probable consequences of such conduct.[150]

The above approach has been followed by subsequent US decisions, which have classified wilful misconduct as requiring 'conscious intent to do or omit doing an act from which harm results to another',[151] and 'wilful performance of an act that is likely to result in damage or wilful action with a reckless disregard of the probable consequences'.[152]

As to the provision of Article 25(1) that the equivalent of wilful misconduct would suffice to impose liability, the Convention leaves its scope wide open, including such topical issues as substance abuse in the workplace and air crew fatigue (see Chapter 10).

*Recent Judicial Decisions on Wilful Misconduct*

Arguably, the watershed decision on the notion of wilful misconduct in recent times was contained in the case *In re Korean Airlines Disaster of September 1, 1983,*[153] where the trial court considered wilful misconduct to be:

> ... the performance of an act with knowledge that the act will probably result in an injury or damage, or in some manner as to imply reckless disregard for the consequences of its performance.

The above pronouncement was used by the US courts in the 1994 decision of *Pasinato* v. *American Airlines Inc.,*[154] which concluded that the act in question of a flight attendant did not constitute wilful misconduct within the purview of Article 25(2) of the Warsaw Convention. In the *Pasinato* case, a passenger of an American Airlines flight which was bound for Chicago from Italy was struck on the head when a heavy tote bag fell from an overhead bin in the cabin. The incident was the outcome of an initial request by the passenger for a pillow immediately after take off, where the flight attendant, in a bid to open the overhead bin above the passenger to retrieve the pillow, was unable to prevent a tote bag falling from the bin on to the passenger's head. The passenger and her husband sued American Airlines under Article 25 on the grounds of wilful misconduct. The trial court was of the view:

> There is no dispute that the flight attendant opened the overhead bin to get a pillow for another passenger. The flight attendant's deposition indicates that she opened the bin with one hand, in her customary manner, with the other hand placed defensively above her head near the bin to prevent an object from falling upon her or a passenger sitting below. Further, the flight attendant stated that she tried to catch the tote bag that fell from the bin (and may have touched it as it fell), but that it fell too quickly.[155]

The court took cognizance of the contention of American Airlines that the technical and cabin crews give repeated warnings to passengers of the dangers of opening overhead bins, both over the aircraft public address system and by personal messages. The evidence of the flight attendant – that incidents of objects falling from overhead bins were infrequent and generally harmless – based on her experience, was also considered relevant. The court found difficulty in applying the criterion of the *Korean Airlines Disaster* case,[156] in that it was difficult, if not impossible, for the Court to envision how the flight attendant's actions could amount to wilful misconduct. It was of the view that the pivotal criterion for determining the existence of wilful misconduct – knowledge that the act would probably result in an injury or damage – was absent. *A fortiori*, the court observed that the other criterion established in the *Korean Airlines* case – that of an act which is performed in a manner indicating reckless disregard for the consequences – was also missing in the *Pasinato* case.

In the 1994 case of *Saba* v. *Compagnie Nationale Air France*,[157] involving damage to cargo, a federal trial court in Washington found for the plaintiff and awarded damages against the act of the defendant carrier for improperly packing and storing hand-woven Persian carpets, as a result of which some of the carpets were damaged owing to the seepage of rain water when the carpets were kept outside by the carrier pending their loading onto the aircraft. The court in this instance followed the bench in *Pasinato* by reiterating the criteria for the proof of wilful misconduct as established by the *Korean Airlines* litigation. A compelling piece of evidence which enabled the court to arrive at its conclusion in the *Saba* case was the fact that the air carrier had disregarded its own cargo handling regulations in storing the carpets outdoors, in the rain. In its findings, the court held:

> In short, through a series of acts, the performance of which were intentional, the carrier has demonstrated a reckless disregard of the consequences of its performance, This disregard is emphasized by the fact that no damage report was ever produced.[158]

The court, while waiving the liability limits of the Warsaw Convention in the *Saba* case, noted that a combination of facts can, taken together, amount to wilful misconduct. It was sufficient, in the court's view, for an act to be intended, and not necessary for the resulting injury or wrongfulness of the act to reflect intention or knowledge. It was also significant that the court further observed that a finding of wilful misconduct was appropriate when the act or omission constituted a violation of a rule or regulation of the defendant carrier itself.

Courts in the United States have been cautious to determine the parameters of 'scope of employment' as envisaged in Article 25(2) of the Warsaw convention, which imputes liability to the carrier with regard to acts of its employees acting within the scope of their employment. In the 1995 case of *Uzochukwu* v. *Air Express International Ltd*,[159] where a New York federal trial court had to decide on a case of theft by two airline employees of cargo of the two carriers, it was held that the fact that the employees had used forged documents to perpetrate the offence of theft was sufficient to conclude that the act was outside the scope of employment, and that the carrier could not be held liable under Article 25(2). It is arguable that the conclusion of the court was based on the fact that generally, in the United States, 'wilful misconduct' is regarded as the intentional performance of an act with knowledge that the performance of that act would probably result in injury or damage, or the intentional performance of an act in such a manner as to imply reckless disregard of the probable consequences.

In *Robinson* v. *Northwest Airlines Inc.*,[160] a case decided in March 1996 involving circumstances similar to the *Pasinato* case, the US Court of Appeals dismissed the appeal of the plaintiff who had lost judgment in the trial court against the carrier. The trial court had allowed a motion of the carrier that the plaintiff's claim in relation to her being injured by a piece of hand luggage falling from an overhead bin while the plane was taxiing, and additional injuries caused to her by a passenger striking her on the head with baggage, were valid at law.

The Court of Appeals, in affirming the dismissal of the action of the plaintiff, noted that while a common carrier (a carrier which opens itself to the world to conduct business in the carriage by air of passengers, baggage and goods) owes a high degree of care to its passengers, it cannot be considered an insurer of the passenger's safety. The court found that the plaintiff failed to raise an issue of fact regarding the carrier's breach of duty towards her. The court was of the view:

> Short of physical constraint of each passenger until each is individually escorted off the plane, we fail to see what Northwest could have done to prevent this accident. At best, that is precisely what the plaintiff has established; the fact that an accident occurred. However, as noted above, common carriers are not insurers of their passenger safety.[161]

A similar approach can be seen in the contemporaneous case of *Bell* v. *Swiss Air Transport Co. Ltd*,[162] where an Intermediate Appellate Court in New York State refused to allow the plaintiff's claim that the loss of his laptop computer during a security check by the airline was due to the airline's wilful misconduct. In the court's view, the plaintiff had failed to prove that the airline intentionally mishandled his baggage with knowledge or reckless disregard for the probable consequences of its conduct. The court also noted that it was the local police, not the airline, which had required the carrying out of the security check.

The case of *Singh* v. *Pan American World Airways*,[163] decided in May 1996, offers a helpful insight into the rationale for determination of wilful misconduct. In wrongful death and personal injury actions arising out of the 1995 hijacking of a PanAm flight between Bombay and New York, the jury concluded that the carrier had been guilty of wilful misconduct, on the reasoning that the management of the carrier knew, or ought to have known, of serious lapses in its security programme. In fact, representations had been made by the carrier's staff to management on several occasions prior to the hijacking. Furthermore, the jury was influenced in its conclusion by the fact that the carrier was aware of terrorist activity at European, Middle Eastern and Asian high-risk airports, and that very little had been done by the carrier to provide enhanced security at these airports.

In the case of the crash of Thai Airways Flight TG-311 near Katmandu, Nepal, in July 1992,[164] the question at issue was whether the air crew had been guilty of wilful misconduct in flying into terrain. The fatal crash occurred during the approach to Katmandu airport – known to be one of the most difficult airports in the world at which to land.[165] Evidence had revealed that the captain had given the bearings of the aircraft to the control tower shortly before the crash, and these were inconsistent with instructions previously given by the tower to the crew in the cockpit of the aircraft. The court concluded that the plane had veered towards terrain surrounding the airport due to the crew's conscious failure to monitor their navigational instruments. The court held:

> ... the captain and the first officer knew or should have known that failing to perform their duty to continuously monitor the aircraft's navigational instruments would create a grave danger under the circumstances ... both the captain and the first officer were well aware that their duty to consciously monitor navigational instruments was an act *necessary for safety* ... their duty to perform this crucial act was so obvious under the circumstances that failing to perform it was *reckless in the extreme* ...[166]

The *Thai Airways* case therefore marks an instance where the elements of wilful misconduct were imputed to the crew on the basis that, due to their expertise, they knew, or ought to have known, the reasonable and probable consequences of their act.

A further dimension to the notion of wilful misconduct was added in the *Northwest Airlines Air Crash Case*[168] of August 1996, where the Court of Appeals of the Sixth Circuit added that a finding of wilful misconduct may be based upon consideration of a series of actions or inactions. The court was of the view that since many complex safety systems interact during an airplane flight, an air disaster would usually require multiple acts. In other words, the court held that it was permissible for a jury to consider an airline's individual errors or a series of errors, and not restrict itself to the sole act which seemingly caused an accident.

If one were to analyse the rationale of wilful misconduct in the light of the *cursus curiae* so far discussed, one would conclude that wilful misconduct hinges on knowledge of the perpetrator that damage would result, or reckless disregard for consequences of an act on the part of the perpetrator. The question which then arises is whether such issues as substance abuse in the workplace and air crew fatigue would subscribe to the notion of wilful misconduct as it is currently perceived.

*Air Crew Fatigue*

Another issue which has aroused much interest is air crew fatigue, where flight safety experts have been involved in using scientific methods to study the contentious issue of pilot fatigue as a cause of incidents and accidents. Although a complete determination of fatigue-causing factors which may have an adverse effect on performance of technical crew on a flight has yet to be made, the limited information and data which is currently available is being used by the experts to establish a system of working guidelines and rules (see Chapter 10).

*Should Wilful Misconduct be Expunged from a New Liability Regime?*

From the above discussion, it may seem that the conduct of an air carrier may be *prima facie* brought into question under any of the four elements, should the carrier overtly disregard or ignore the inherent dangers presented by each individual element. The inevitable question that would arise then would be: 'Should wilful misconduct be removed from a new liability regime under such compelling emergent factors?' If the answer to this question is in the affirmative, the question would then arise: 'Would a realm of strict liability give carriers the independence to conduct themselves as they please, knowing that they are covered for all acts, whatever be their nature, by a preconceived and established scheme of insurance?' In other words, should carriers be held accountable for their acts when they wilfully and with knowledge cause damage, or should they be absolved from accountability as to their fault under all circumstances?

As discussed earlier, Lee Kreindler offers a direct response to the above questions by saying that the fault system is important to the public, and that it is a public protection. He maintains that it has improved aviation safety and security.

On the other hand, it has been contended that Article 25 is a provision which provokes litigation, and that it should be removed and replaced by a system which automatically guarantees a certain negotiable guarantee of compensation.[168]

A pre-funded system of injury compensation may tend to disregard the role played by and contribution made by a person who causes injury to another. In direct contrast to this approach, a sustained body of judicial thought has established a group of basic concepts and terms, which consist of theories of culpability and defence on the premise of responsibility of the individual. Called tort law, this thought process reflects a judicial desire to reduce the number and severity of accidents. Often called 'deterrence', this approach is best illustrated in the case of *Brizendine* v. *Visador Co.*,[169] where the court held that tort law should provide 'a healthy incentive to manufacturers to make their products safe'.[170] To this principle, courts have also added the requirement that any person who causes an accident should show that they took 'all possible means' and every precaution to prevent the accident from occurring. *Taylor* v. *Superior Court*[171] addressed the deterrence rationale that drunk driving may constitute 'malice' if performed under circumstances which disclose a conscious disregard of the possible dangerous circumstances.[172] In a previous case[173] the court stressed the need for all possible means of deterring persons from driving automobiles after drinking.

The pervasive reliance of common law on the paradigm of reciprocity, whereby a person who injures another knowing the consequences the act may cause is called upon to compensate for the damage caused, is grounded in its very fundamental sense in Aristotelian corrective justice. In Book V, Chapter 4 of his *Nicomachean Ethics*, Aristotle advocates a justice in the distribution by the State of mores, honours and other items of value on the basic postulate of merit. According to Aristotle, it made no difference if a good man defrauded a bad man, or a bad man a good one – the law should only look to the distinctive character of the injury and treat the parties as equal. The judge would, in the Aristotelian sense, attempt to equalize things by means of the penalty, taking away from the gain of the assailant or wrongdoer. The term 'gain' is applied in a general sense where suffering is estimated as loss. The duty to rectify under corrective justice is based not on the fact of injury, but on the conjunction of injury and wrongdoing. The person who injures must do wrong as well as do harm, and the person who is injured must be wronged as well as harmed. For example, someone who drives a bad bargain has no access to corrective justice, since they have been harmed but not wronged.

The system of corrective justice propounded by Aristotle and used by common law courts is compatible with the economic theory of law that it is a means of bringing about an efficient allocation of resources by correcting externalities and other distortions of the market's allocation of resources. It holds that if the person who injures does not pay, they will have no incentive to take precautions in the future, and there would be more accidents.

Judge Learned Hand, in 1947, addressed the social function of liability for wrongful acts and adumbrated an economic meaning of a wrongful act. In *United States* v. *Carroll Towing Co.*,[174] Judge Hand identified three issues: the magnitude of the loss where an accident occurs; the probability of the accident occurring; the burden of taking precautions that would avert it. According to His Honour, if the product of the first two issues exceeded the third one, the failure to take precautions would be a wrongful act. There is therefore a certain moral disapproval, and even indignation, attached to a wrongful act.

### Comments

It is not the intention of this book to offer a solution for the most suitable manner of compensation under the Warsaw system,[175] but to assess the role of tort law under the system of liability at private air law as a means of shaping the conduct of social elements. In the ultimate analysis, what matters is that the law in this area of commercial aviation must ensure that its role of administering fair and equitable justice encompasses the safety and protection of the public it serves. If liability laws in commercial aviation are to accomplish that objective, it is prudent to consider carefully the role played by the element of aviation safety in the wider context.

On behalf of the proponents of unlimited strict liability as a replacement for fault liability under the Warsaw system, one commentator recommends either a substantial increase in voluntary limits of liability, or total abandonment of limiting air carrier liability, implying that either would benefit both the plaintiff and the defendant.[176] In 1979, Peter Martin suggested that the best future for the Warsaw system would be the abandonment of limitations[177] He stated:

> There are very good reasons for imposing on carriers at least a very high standard of care, and even strict liability. Strict liability without limitations already applies in many States to third party liability to persons other than passengers and that is generally believed to be right ... why should a passenger, therefore, be in a worse position than a person or owners of property on the ground?[178]

The insurance lawyers obviously need higher liability limits and specificity in this area. The steady disintegration of the Warsaw system, which is mainly attributable to its incompetence in providing for satisfactory compensatory limits, has been proven by figures released some years ago by the Rand Corporation that, in a cross-section of cases studied, Warsaw–Montreal tickets obtained a per capita compensation of US$ 184,000 while non-Warsaw–Montreal tickets had received double this. This amount has further increased over the years, demonstrating that the Warsaw limits are being left behind rapidly.[179] It is clear therefore that if the Warsaw limits are to be retained, they must be extended, and the first step towards this goal is the ratification by States of the Montreal Protocols. It is also imperative that the scope of the Convention be extended to third parties such as air traffic controllers and manufacturers of component parts of aircraft, to seek consistency and to give the insurance market a more accurate assessment of the risks. By bringing these parties under the Warsaw umbrella, both the plaintiff and the defendant would be well served, in that plaintiffs would be assured of quick settlement, and defendants would be comfortable with the thought that their liability is limited. This could also preclude contingency-fee appearances by lawyers.

While it is conceivable that financial interests of the parties concerned would form a core issue in the aftermath of an accident, the principal driving force – aviation safety – should take precedence. Although it is necessary to compare the effects of limitation of liability versus unlimited strict liability, one must not lose sight of emerging trends which emphasize that safety must be the primary consideration.

## Notes

1 John G. Fleming, *The Law of Torts* (6th edn), The Law Book Company, 1983, at 1.
2 Warsaw, 4–12 October 1929.
3 Convention on the Unification of Certain Airlines Relating to International Transportation by Air, Warsaw, 1929.
4 Robert C. Horner and Didier Legrez (trans.), *Minutes of the Second International Conference on Private International Law, October 4–12, 1929, Warsaw*, New Jersey: Fred B. Rottman & Co., 1975, at 21.
5 Id., at 58.
6 Id., at 59–66.
7 Id., at 251–2.
8 Fleming, op. cit., at 2.
9 Horner and Legrez, op. cit., at 47.
10 Lee S. Kreindler, 'The IATA Solution', *Lloyd's Aviation Law.*, 1 November 1996, Vol. 14, No. 21, 4, at 5.
11 Id., at 6.
12 Sean Gates, 'IATA Inter Carrier Agreement – The Trojan Horse for a Fifth Jurisdiction?', *Lloyd's Aviation Law*, 1 December 1995, Vol. 14, No. 23, 1, at 2.
13 The process gathered impetus from the second half of the first century BC. Its beginnings are demonstrable as early as *circa* 150 BC.
14 Jhering, 'Das Schuldmoment im romischen Privatrecht', *Vermischte Schriften juristischen Inhalts*, Leipzig, 1897, at 158.
15 Id., at 215, 223, 229 *et seq.*
16 Naturally, result liability does not become wilfulness as the foundation of the liability instantaneously. In this connection it is of importance to note that the facts creating liability had (either with an objective or subjective explanation)

been defined with utmost precision and part of them (such as, for example, *injuria* or *furtum* among the private torts) cannot even be conceived unless wilfully committed. Nor should it be ignored that originally the *dolus* meant only the consciousness of the act, not its attributability. In the law of torts it was a condition of liability that damage or killing should be inflicted *dolo sciens;* within the scope of *stricti iuris* contractual actions (for *certa res)* the debtor answered only when non-performance or faulty performance *per eum stetit.* As borne out by casuistry, conscious action *(facere)* was sufficient to establish what has been said before, and it was not necessary that the intention should embrace the damaging result. In the domain of torts, however, the *dolus* acquired the meaning of *dolus malus* at a very early stage. Similarly, a distinction was made between *dolus* and *casus* with respect to the facts at issue which could be committed other than only wilfully.

17 Civil law liability for the wilful causation of loss has to this day preserved its specific penal traits, ignoring the interests of the tortfeasor.

18 It is natural that originally subjective attributability should, even if in a vaguely delimited form, be attached to wilfulness: for the native wit it is by far easier to distinguish this from randomness than drawing the line between attributable negligence and randomness in the domain of non-wilful results. For such a distinction to be made, extremely differentiated and socially established norms of conduct are required.

19 'Business morals' at most. *Here* the contents of *bona fides* are defined by the peculiarities of the legal relationship and the interestedness of the parties. In juxtaposition to the *dolus,* however, *bona fides* is more general and nearer to genuine morals.

20 Even where the actions cumulated. Classical law views the result of the actions wholly independently.

21 The principle that *in lege Aquilia el levissima culpa venit* merely indicates the extremely rigorous requirement of care. This is again a sign of the demand for the extension of the action.

22 *Infirmitas culpae adnumeratur.* The rules and definition from the republican era, when the penetration of dialectics into legal thinking had raised jurisprudence to a genuine discipline and made it capable of grasping legal problems in a manner abstracted from the concrete case. The *dolus* naturally survived in Classical law, but still their continued development cannot be deemed a success.

23 A similar development may be traced in the extension of the notion of 'killing'. That for killing (direct bodily impact) a direct, and for the 'procurement of the cause of death' an analogous action should be admitted, follows from the casuistry going into the minutest detail.

24 There was always a certain connection with the category of the violation of *bona fides* and the boundaries between *dolus* and the morally also attributable *culpa lata.*

25 Shawcross and Beaumont, *Air Law* (4th edn), Vol. VII, London: Butterworths, 1988, at 152.

26 Id., VII (116).

27 Id., VII (117).

28 Id., Article 17.

29 See Halsbury, *Laws of England* (3rd edn), Vol. 22, para. 585, at 293.

30 *Hensey* v. *White,* 1900 1 KB 481.

31 Id., at 484.

32 Id., at 485.

33 *Boardman* v. *Scott and Witworth* (1902) 1 KB 43.

34 Id., at 46.

35 (1903) AC 433.
36 Id., at 446–7.
37 Id., at 452.
38 Id., at 453.
39 Workmen's Compensation Act of 1897.
40 (1903) AC 443, at 455. See also *Trim Joint District School Board of Management* v. *Kelly* (1914) AC 667, at 669, and generally *Anderson* v. *Balfour* (1910) 2 IR 497 and *Nisbett* v. *Rayne* (1910) 2 KB 689.
41 *Trim Joint School Board of Management* v. *Kelly*, op. cit.
42 (1903) AC 433.
43 Id., at 231.
44 (1903) AC 433.
45 (1942) 27 A 2d 286.
46 *Allred* v. *Prudential Insurance Co. of America*, 100 SE 2d 226.
47 *Thompson* v. *Prudential Insurance Co.*, 66 SE 2d 119.
48 *Evans* v. *Metropolitan Life Insurance Co.*, 174 P 2d 961.
49 *Workmen's Compensation Board* v. *Theed* (1940) 3 DLR 561.
50 Id., at 557.
51 (1940) 2 DLR 444.
52 Id., at 448 and 449.
53 *Turner* v. *Northern Life Assurance Co.* (1953) 1 DLR 427.
54 (1963) 40 DLR 408.
55 Id., at 422.
56 Id., at 423.
57 (1903) AC 433.
58 *Convention on International Civil Aviation*, signed Chicago, 1944, Annex 13.
59 Shawcross and Beaumont, op. cit., Vol. VII, at 153.
60 *Air France* v. *Saks*, 105 S Ct 1,338 (1985).
61 Ibid.
62 *Husserl* v. *Swiss Air Transport Co. Ltd*, 485 F 2d 1,240 (2nd Cir. 1975); *Day* v. *Trans World Airlines, Inc.*, 528 F 2d 31 (2nd Cir. 1975); *Evangelinos* v. *Trans World Airlines, Inc.*, 550 F 2d 152 (3rd Cir. 1976). See also *Salerno* v. *Pan American World Airways*, 19 Avi. Cas. 17,705. (SDNY 1985).
63 *Arkin* v. *Trans International Airlines Inc.*, 19 Avi. Cas. 18, 311 (EDNY 1985).
64 *Abdulrahman Al-Zamil* v. *British Airways Inc.*, 770 F 2d 3 (2nd Cir. 1985).
65 *Seguritan* v. *Northwest Airlines, Inc.*, 86 AD 2d 658 (2nd Dept 1982). See also *Lloyd's Aviation Law*, 1 August 1982, Vol. 1, No. 4, at 1.
66 *Vincenty* v. *Eastern Airlines*, 528 F Supp. 171 (DPR 1982). See also *Lloyd's Aviation Law*, 15 July 1982, Vol. 1, No. 3, at 2.
67 *Sprayregen* v. *American Airlines Inc.*, 570 F Supp. 16 (SDNY 1983). See also *Warshaw* v. *Trans World Airlines Inc.*, 443 F Supp. 400 (ED Pa 1977); *Pironneau* v. *Cie Air-Inter* (Pan CA 3 July 1986). Cf. *De Marines* v. *KLM Royal Dutch Airlines*, 586 F 2d 1193 (3rd Cir. 1978).
68 See *Warshaw* v. *Trans World Airlines Inc.*, op. cit., at 408.
69 *O'Leary* v. *American Airlines*, 475 NYS 2d 285 (AD 2nd Dept 1984).
70 105 S Ct 1,338 (1985).
71 Id., at 1,345.
72 *Abramson* v. *Japan Airlines Company Ltd*, 739 F 2d 130 (3rd Cir. 1984).
73 *Scherer* v. *Pan American World Airways Inc.*, 387 NYS 2d 581 (1976).
74 Op. cit., n. 65.
75 *Rosman* v. *Trans World Airlines Inc.*, 34 NY 2d 385 (1974).
76 *Husserl* v. *Swiss Air Transport Co. Ltd*, 388 F Supp. 1238 (SDNY 1975).
77 *Krystal* v. *BOAC* 403, F Supp. 1332 (DC Cal. 1975). *Karfunkel* v. *Cie Nationale Air*

*France*, 427 F Supp. 971 (SDNY 977). *Borham* v. *Pan American World Airways, Inc.*, Avi. Cas. 18, 236 (SDNY 1977).

78 See R.I.R. Abeyratne, 'The Human Stress Factor and Mental Injury in American Tort Law – A Patchwork Quilt?', *The Anglo American Law Review*, 1986, Vol. 15, No. 4, at 338–60.

79 398 SW 2d 170.

80 Id., at 273–4.

81 19 Avi. Cas. (CCH) 17, 377 (SDNY 1985).

82 606 F Supp. 656 (SDNY 1985).

83 Ibid.

84 Op. cit., n. 65.

85 *Husserl* v. *Swiss Air transport Co. Ltd*, op. cit.. See also *People of the State of Illinois* v. *Gilberto*, 383 NE 2d 977.

86 *Day* v. *Trans World Airlines Inc.*, 528 F 2d 31 (2nd Cir. 1975); *Evangelinos* v. *Trans World Airlines Inc.*, 550 F 2d 152 (2nd Circ. 1977); *Leppo* v. *Trans World Airlines Inc.*, 392 NYS 2d 660 (AD 1977); *Rolnick* v. *El Al Israel Airlines Ltd*, 551 Supp. 261 (EDNY 1982).

87 Id., Article 22(4).

88 *Delgado* v. *Pan American World Airways, Inc.*, Nos R-81-12, R-80-318 (Sup. Ct PR 18 March 1982).

89 104 S Ct 1776 (1984).

90 Id., at 1,784–9.

91 *Franklin Mint Corp* v. *Trans World Airlines, Inc.*, 690 F 2d 303, 304 (2nd Cir. 2982).

92 104 S Ct, at 1,784–9.

93 In *re Aircraft at Kimpo International Airport, Korea, on November 18 1980*, MDL-482 (DC Ca. 1984), reversing the court's earlier decision at 558 F Supp. 72 (CD Cal. 1983).

94 Shawcross and Beaumont, op. cit., Vol. VII, at 116.

95 *Chisholm* v. *British European Airways* (1963) 1 *Lloyd's Report* 626. See also *Grein* v. *Imperial Airways Ltd* (1937) 1 KB 50 CA, 69–71, per Greer LJ.

96 See *Chisholm* v. *British European Airways*, op. cit., at 629.

97 *Goldman* v. *Thai Airways International Ltd* (1981) 125 *Sol. Jo.* 413 (High Ct), also in (1983) 1 All ER 693.

98 (1986) 2 All ER 188.

99 429 F Supp. 964 (SDNY 1977).

100 *Preyvel* v. *Cie Air France* (1973) 27 RFDA 198. See also *Riviere-Girret* v. *Ste-Aer-Inter* (1979) Uniform LR 173.

101 *Panalpina International Transport Ltd* v. *Densil Underwear Ltd* (1981) 1 *Lloyd's Report* 187.

102 *Mandreoli* v. *Cie Belge d'Assurance Aviation*, Milan 1972 (1974) Dir. Mar. 157.

103 (1982) 36 RFDA 342.

104 (1982) 36 RFDA 355.

105 Warsaw Convention, Article 21.

106 (1983) 3 All ER 693.

107 *Bradfield* v. *Trans World Airlines, Inc.*, 152 Cal. Rptr 172 (Ca CA 1972).

108 *Butler* v. *Aeromexico*, 774 F 2d 499. (11th Cir. 1985).

109 *Piano Remittance Corp.* v. *Varig Brazilian Airlines, Inc.*, 18 Avi. Cas. (CCH) 18, 381 (SDNY 1984).

110 Drion, op. cit., at 7.

111 Id., at 8.

112 Ibid.

113 Id., at 12–13.

114 *Reed* v. *Wiser*, 555 F 2d 1,079 (2nd Cir.), at 1,090.

115 Nicholas Mateesco Matte, 'The Warsaw System and the Hesitation of the United States Senate', *Annals of Air & Space Law*, 1983, Vol. VIII, 151, at 164.
116 Alexander Tobolewski, 'Against Limitation of Liability: A Radical Proposal', *Annals of Air & Space Law*, 1978, Vol. III, 261, at 263.
117 Id., at 266.
118 Werner Guldimann, 'A Future System of Liability in Air Carriage', *Annals of Air & Space Law*, 1991, Vol. XVI, 93, at 104.
119 Bin Cheng, 'What is Wrong with the Montreal Additional Protocol No. 3?', *Air Law*, 1989, Vol. XIV, No. 6, 220, at 232.
120 The Warsaw Convention of 1929 was amended by: The Hague Protocol 1955, the Guadalajara Convention 1961, The Guatemala City Protocol, 1971, and the Montreal Protocols 1, 2, 3, 4, of varying dates. It should also be noted that the Montreal Agreement of 1966, a private arrangement between air carriers, also purported to amend the Warsaw Convention. Hereafter, joint references to all these instruments shall be referred to as the 'Warsaw system'.
121 Peter Martin, '50 Years of the Warsaw Convention: A Practical Man's Guide', *Annals of Air & Space Law*, 1979, Vol. IV, 233, at 234.
122 Ibid.
123 Bin Cheng, 'Wilful Misconduct: From Warsaw to the Hague and from Brussels to Paris', *Annals of Air & Space* Law, 1997, Vol II, 55, at 55. Rene Mankiewicz also uses the word 'shambles' when he describes the Warsaw Convention. See, Rene H. Mankiewicz, 'From Warsaw to Montreal With Certain Intermediate Stops ...', *Air Law*, 1989, Vol. XIV, at 26.
124 Martin, op. cit., at 239.
125 *Warren* v. *Flying Tiger Line, Inc.*, 352 F 2d 494 (CA9 1965); *Mertens* v. *Flying Tiger Line, Inc.* 341 F 2d 841 (CA2 1965).
126 21 Avi. 18,228 (1989).
127 1983 3 All ER 693.
128 D.A. Kilbride, 'Six Decades of Insuring Liability Under Warsaw', *Air Law*, Vol. XIV, Nos 4/5, 183, at 187.
129 18 Avi. 17,778 (1984).
130 *SS Pharmaceutical Co. Ltd* v. *Qantas Airways Ltd* (1988) 1 *Lloyd's Law Reports* 319.
131 *Tasman Pulp and Paper Co. Ltd* v. *Pan American World Airways, Inc. and others*; see *Annals of Air & Space Law*, 1987, Vol. XI, at 323 for a detailed account.
132 Ref. LE 3/27, 3/28–91/3, at 5.
133 Mankiewicz, op. cit., at 259.
134 Michael Milde, 'ICAO Work on the Modernization of the Warsaw System', *Air Law*, 1989, Vol. XIV, Nos 4/5, 193, at 206.
135 Op. cit., n. 65.
136 Op. cit., n. 69.
137 D.A. Kilbride, 'Six Decades of Insuring Liability Under Warsaw', *Air Law*, 1989, Vol. XIV, Nos 4/5, 183, at 191.
138 Id., at 192.
139 Martin, op. cit., at 248.
140 Ibid.
141 Werner Guldimann, 'A Future System of Liability in Air Carriage', *Annals of Air & Space Law*, 1991, Vol. XVI, 93, at 96.
142 Horner and Legrez, op. cit., at 183.
143 See Convention for the Unification of Certain Rules Relating to International Carriage by Air, signed Warsaw, 12 October 1929, reproduced in *Annals of Air & Space Law*, 1993, Vol. XVIII, Part II, 323, at 339.
144 Id., Article 25, 2.
145 Drion, op. cit., para. 181, at 212.

146 Id., para. 181.2, at 213.
147 Id., para. 181.4 and 5, at 213.
148 Horner and Legrez, op. cit., at 42.
149 (1952) 2 All ER 1,016, at 1,022.
150 *Goepp* v. *American Overseas Airlines*, New York Supreme Court, Appellate Division (1st Dept) 16 December 1952; [1952] US Av. R 486; IATA ACLR, No. 12.
151 *Grey* v. *American Airline Inc.*, 4 Avi. 17, 811 (2nd Cir. 1955).
152 *Wing Hang Bank Ltd* v. *Japan Air Lines Co.* 12 Avi. 17,884 (SDNY 1973).
153 932 F 2d 1475, 1479 (DC Cis), cert. denied, 1125 Ct 616 (1991).
154 No. 93 C 1510, 1994 Westlaw 17 1522 (ND Ill. 2 May 1994).
155 Ibid.
156 *In re Korean Airlines Disaster of September 1983*, 932 F 2d 1,475 (DC Cir.) cert. denied, 112 S Ct 616 (1991).
157 866 F Supp. 588 (DDC 1994).
158 Ibid.
159 1995 Westlaw 151 793 (EDNY 27 March 1995).
160 No. 94-2392 (6th Cir. 15 March 1996).
161 Ibid.
162 25 Avi. Cas. (CCH) 17, 259 (Sup. Ct App. Tm. NY 1st Dept 1996).
163 920 F Supp. 408 SPNY (1996).
164 See *Koirola* v. *Thai Airways International*, 1996 Westlaw 402403 (ND Ca. 26 January 1996).
165 See Article 25, 'Thai Airways found guilty of Wilful Misconduct in 1992 Kathmandu Crash Litigation', *Lloyd's Aviation Law*, 15 March 1996, Vol. 15, No. 6, at 1.
166 Id., at 2–3.
167 86 F 3d 498 (6th Cir. 1996).
168 Gerald M. Mayo, 'Implementation of the IATA Intercarrier Agreement', *Lloyd's Aviation Law*, 1 April 1996, Vol. 15, No. 7, at 2.
169 305 & Supp. 157 (D Or. 1969).
170 Id., at 160.
171 24 Cal. 3d 890 (1979).
172 D 892.
173 *Harrell* v. *Ames*, 265 Or. 183 at 190 (1973).
174 159 F 2d 169 (2nd Cir. 1947).
175 For a detailed discussion and analysis of the various initiatives taken recently by Japan, the International Air Transport Association (IATA) and the International Civil Aviation Organization (ICAO) in seeking a new regulatory system of private air carrier liability, see R.I.R. Abeyratne, 'Regulatory Management of the Warsaw System of Air Carrier Liability', *Journal of Air Transport Management*, 1997, Vol. 3, No. 1, at 37–45.
176 Bin Cheng, 'What is Wrong with the Montreal Additional Protocol No. 3?', *Air Law*, 1989, Vol. XIV, No. 6, 220, at 232.
177 Peter Martin, '50 Years of the Warsaw Convention: A Practical Man's Guide', *Annals of Air & Space Law*, 1979, Vol. IV, 233, at 248.
178 Ibid.
179 Werner Guldimann, 'A Future System of Liability in Air Carriage', *Annals of Air & Space Law*, 1991, Vol. XVI, 93, at 96.

# 12 Air Carrier Liability for Negligent Acts of Cabin Crew Members

## Introduction

The notion of vicarious liability in the common law of tort – whereby employers are held liable for the negligent acts of their servants if such acts are performed within the scope of their employment – also applies to private international air law aspects of liability. Therefore, a negligent act of an airline crew member, whether technical crew (such as pilots and first officers) or cabin crew (cabin attendants), would directly impute liability to the airline which employs the crew member concerned. However, principles of air carrier liability part company with general tort law principles of vicarious liability and negligence at this point, and enter the realm of the Warsaw Convention, which sets unique rules of liability. This chapter will examine these rules of liability within the context of the professional conduct of airline cabin crew members, and analyse principles of law that govern this specific area of liability.

There is no doubt that cabin crew are essential to commercial aviation, and that they should also be subject to standardized training methods and codes of conduct, as are pilots, mechanics, aeronautical engineers and other professionals who are involved with the successful operation of a commercial flight. There is a compelling need for the international aviation community to conduct an in-depth study of the feasibility of introducing a unified system of rules relating to the conduct of cabin crew, which could include principles of protection of cabin crew and provide for compensation in case of injury since cabin crew deal with the 'human factor' of a flight, which can be most unpredictable at the best of times.

The perceived lack of attention paid by the aviation community to the importance of the flight attendant's safety role on commercial flights may pose serious problems in the area of air carrier liability, but it is heartening to note that there is now a growing awareness of the importance of cabin crews. For instance, in 1994, the United States officially recognized that flight attendants play a critical role in the safety of passengers by limiting the length of their duty times and introducing mandatory rest periods under federal law. Under Federal Aviation Administration (FAA) regulations, flight attendants must be given at least 9 hours' rest for duty periods lasting up to 14 hours in any 24-hour period. For longer periods, the FAA prescribes specific rest periods and larger cabin crews. The rules also give flight attendants a full 24 hours' rest for every seven calendar days. Federal law had previously mandated minimum rest periods for air traffic controllers and technical crew.[1]

There have been innumerable complaints in the past by technical crew (pilots and flight engineers), alleging that unacceptable cabin crew conduct has jeopardized flight safety. A commentary published in March 1995 reported that during a hectic night approach to a busy US airport, a flight attendant opened the door to the flight deck to remove dinner trays, flooding the cockpit with light and distracting the flight crew. The flight attendant had refused the captain's earlier request to bring meals forward early in the flight, and the food was brought in only after the descent had begun.[2] In his report, the captain wrote that 'the approach was unsafe', and described a serious breakdown in communication between the cockpit crew and the cabin crew. Confirming a near miss with a smaller aircraft which the captain blamed on the commotion caused by the unfortunate entry of the flight attendant to the cockpit, he wrote:

> The captain is helpless to plan the approach any more. The flight attendants ignore requests and directions from the captain. They work for the marketing department and don't hesitate to tell pilots they don't have to listen to them. On this flight, the flight attendant's blatant disregard of the captain's request resulted in an unsafe approach. If the flight attendant had listened to the captain's request to bring meals up, she would not have been in the cockpit at low altitude causing a distraction.[3]

There have also been instances where cabin crew members have been instrumental in causing involuntary injury to passengers. One such instance occured when a passenger on board an American Airlines flight from Italy to Chicago was injured when a heavy tote bag fell on him from the overhead luggage rack in the aircraft when a flight attendant opened it to retrieve a pillow for him. One of the considerations the court had to decide upon was the plaintiff's contention that American Airlines had failed to provide adequate instructions to its crew on the operation of aircraft apparatus.[4]

Clearly, the conduct of cabin crew members during the course of their employment affects two classes of persons – passengers in the cabin and technical crew in the cockpit. In both instances, any adverse conduct on the part of cabin crew which results in claims for damages would affect the employer airline adversely, bringing to bear the intrinsic and incontrovertible link between the airline and its cabin crew members. Also, any liability that arose out of the conduct of cabin crew would involve air carrier liability on principles of vicarious liability at tort. This chapter will therefore examine the role of the flight attendant in air carrier liability, emphasizing general principles of air carrier liability as they revolve round the conduct of the flight attendant. There will also be a discussion of the relationship of the flight attendant with the passenger on the one hand and the pilot on the other, with a view to eliciting principles of air carrier liability in both instances where the conduct of the flight attendant precipitates a claim by a passenger or the representative of the passenger for injury by the air carrier.

## Air Carrier Liability

### *General Principles*

The Warsaw Convention of 1929[5] provides that, for the transportation of passengers, the carrier must deliver a passenger ticket which shall carry certain details.[6] The Convention also says that the absence, irregularity or loss of the passenger ticket shall not affect the existence of the validity of the contract of transportation, which shall none the less be subject to the rules of the Convention. Nevertheless, if the carrier accepts a passenger without a passenger ticket having been delivered, the carrier shall not be entitled to avail itself of those provisions of the Convention that exclude its liability.[7]

The Warsaw Convention imposes a presumption of liability on the carrier in the case of death or injury caused to a passenger. As a precaution against the possible floodgates of litigation that this presumption could give rise to, the Convention limits liability of a carrier to specified sums of money, unless it could be proved that the carrier did not take necessary precautions to avoid death or injury to its passengers or was guilty of wilful misconduct. Damage for death or injury under the Convention is linked to an 'accident'. An accident as envisaged in Article 17 of the Warsaw Convention has sometimes been given a broader definition than in ordinary legal parlance. While in ordinary common law usage an accident is an event which, under the circumstances, is unusual and unexpected,[8] the Chicago Convention of 1944 defines an 'accident' as an occurrence connected with the operation of an aircraft.[9] Article 17 of the Warsaw Convention speaks of liability of a carrier in the event of an accident which caused damage, reducing the accident to the cause rather than to the death or injury.[10] The United States Supreme Court has held in *Air France* v. *Saks*[11] that an accident must be unexpected and external to the passenger. It is not sufficient that the plaintiff suffers injury as a result of their own internal reaction to the usual, normal and expected operation of the aircraft.[12] In *De Marines* v. *KLM Royal Dutch Airlines*[13] – a case with identical facts to the *Saks* case – the court reasoned that:

> An accident is an event, a physical circumstance, which unexpectedly takes place not according to the usual course of things. If the event on board the airplane is an ordinary, expected and usual occurrence, then it cannot be termed an accident. To constitute an accident, the occurrence on board the aircraft must be unusual, an unexpected happening.[14]

At air law, therefore, it is clear that an accident has to be an unexpected event, as at common law. The distinction lies in the cause, and the attendant circumstances thereupon that regard such incidents as bombings, hijacking, terrorist attacks to be considered as accidents, together with aircraft crashes,[15] more on the grounds of the conduct of the airline based on the cause of the 'accident' rather than on an incident itself. Arguably, the case which clearly and unequivocally brings out the contextual juridical application of the word 'accident' in air carrier liability is *Seguritan* v. *Northwest Airlines,*[16] where, in an instance where a passenger suffered a massive coronary seizure in flight, the court held that the accident was not the seizure itself but the failure on the part of the carrier to render medical assistance. The carrier's failure to render medical assistance was the accident 'which caused the damage' inasmuch as, according to the court, a carrier's failure to provide adequate security to passengers in an instance of a terrorist attack.

The Day-Evangelinos test[17] (or as it is sometimes called, the tripartite test) evolved with the emerging difficulties of judicial interpretation of Article 17 of the Warsaw Convention.[18] The provision admits of compensation being awarded only if an accident takes place 'on board the aircraft or in the course of any of the operations of embarking or disembarking'.[19] The arcane precision with which many accidents have occurred after the enactment of this provision, and their varied nature, has given rise to notable judicial fecundity in the interpretation of the words 'embarking' and 'disembarking'. Although the words 'on board the aircraft' do not present complex issues *in limine,* there has been at least one instance where the time spent by passengers in a hotel consequent to a hijacking has been interpreted as time spent 'on board', on the basis that if not for the *novus actus interveniens* of a hijacking that impelled the passengers to seek solace in a hotel room, they would have been on board the aircraft anyway.[20]

One can therefore imagine the degree of concern the words 'embarking and disembarking' would cause the fertile judicial mind. The words clearly meant the period of time during which the passenger ascends the steps of the aircraft or descends the aircraft after a flight.[21] The words 'any of the operations', however, extend the scope of this fundamental act, and could well mean the time of check-in at the terminal, the period before or after security screening, and the time spent in the 'sterile' area. Courts have wavered between views, however, and have finally accepted the Day-Evangelinos test, which was developed as a consequence of a series of terrorist acts on passengers in airport lounges. This is, for all purposes, an objective tripartite test, so called because it takes into account three key factors when considering whether a plaintiff was 'embarking' or 'disembarking'. The three factors are:

1 the location of the passenger;
2 the nature of their activity at the time of their accident;
3 the degree of control exercised by the airline at the relevant time.

The test, while clearly establishing that unless the passenger is under the control or direction of the airline there is no liability for the death or injury to a passenger, also demonstrates through a cogently analysed *cursus curiae* that there is a real danger of the test being applied subjectively in many circumstances. To illustrate this, a Brussels court brought in the application of a test analogous to the tripartite test, and held that a passenger who slipped on some ice and fell between the terminal building and the aircraft bus was not under the control of the airline, since the bus was operated by airport staff. No question was asked whether the airport staff were the agents of the airline, or whether the bus service was part of the contract of carriage between the airline and the passenger.[22]

The significance of this test to the aviation lawyer is in an acquisition of a clear view of what 'location', 'activity' and 'control' really mean. On the subject of 'location', in the recent decision of *Buonocore* v. *Trans World Airlines*,[23] the court held that TWA was not liable for the murder of a passenger by terrorists while waiting in the public area of da Vinci airport in Rome, since the murder did not come within the terms 'embarkation' or 'disembarkation' under Article 17. The deceased had checked in and approached a snack cart in the main concourse area of the airport when he was struck down by terrorist fire. The main criterion on which the courts anchored their decision was that although Buanocore had checked in and received his seat assignment, he had not gone through security inspection. In the earlier case of *De La Cruz* v. *Domincana de Aviacion*,[24] the court had held that a plaintiff who slipped and fell while on the way to a baggage claim area was not in the disembarkation process. He had descended a flight of steps from the aircraft to the ramp and entered the arrivals building, passed through immigration control, and while walking down the hallway, had slipped and fallen.

The position of the courts on the other two elements has also been somewhat inconsistent. In the case of *Seidenfaden* v. *British Airways*,[25] the courts expressed the need for there to be a 'clear manifestation of control'[26] for compensation to be awarded. In another case,[27] the court held that an airline passenger could not claim when she fell at the immigration area, which was just 300 yards away from the arrival gate. The rationale adopted by the court was that the area was not leased or under the control of the carrier, and therefore the passenger was out of the carrier's control. As for the activity of the passenger at the time of the accident, it is a fairly straightforward proposition that almost any activity that a passenger would usually be involved in would be related to their travel under the circumstances.

The ambiguities of the tripartite test can be attributed to the original case of *Day* v. *Trans World Airlines*,[28] where the court considered the activity of the passenger, the restrictions placed on the passenger's movement, the imminence of actual boarding, and the physical proximity of the passenger to the gate as criteria for establishing the test.[29] It is time that a more realistic approach was taken by the courts, while taking into consideration the involvement of the airlines in today's security, the steps taken by airlines in securing their passengers, and the spirit of the Convention in introducing a rebuttable presumption of carrier liability and attendant limitation of liability.

The more recent case of *Craig* v. *Compagnie Nationale Air France*,[30] demonstrates that courts are now likely to interpret the word 'accident' in the Warsaw Convention so as to prevent the likelihood of claims being brought for any injury that may seem to be an accident at first glance. In the *Craig* case, the US Court of Appeal considered the claim for damages brought by a passenger who had tripped over a pair of shoes of the passenger seated next to her while returning to her seat. The neighbour, who was fast asleep, had removed his shoes and had placed them in front of him. The plaintiff had been to the toilet, and was returning to her seat at a time when the cabin crew had finished serving a meal and the main lights in the cabin had been switched off to allow the passengers to sleep. The court observed:

> It was the plaintiff's burden to demonstrate that the presence of shoes on the floor between two seats was unexpected or unusual event ... Plaintiff did not submit or point to any evidence (such as an affidavit from a flight attendant) that finding shoes on the floor between two seats was unusual or unexpected. Nor did the plaintiff ask for a trial or further discovery to establish anything more than her own declaration.[31]

In a case decided in Canada, where a 72-year-old woman who suffered from severe osteoporosis claimed that she had suffered injury as a result of the aircraft in which she was travelling going through 'expected' turbulence,[32] Sutherland J of the Ontario Court in Canada (General Division), dismissing the action, observed:

> Air turbulence itself is not unexpected or unusual. Up to some level of severity it is a commonplace of air travel ... I find as fact that the turbulence encountered here on the flight in question, while greater than that previously experienced ... did not amount to an 'accident' within the meaning of Article 17 of the Warsaw Convention as the term accident is defined in *Air France* v. *Saks*. The degree of turbulence encountered on the flight cannot be said to have been unusual or unexpected.[33]

This decision adds to the thrust of the recent trend adopted by courts, where 'accident' under the Warsaw Convention is interpreted in order to effectively preclude frivolous claims based on a loose interpretation of the word.

## Conduct of the Flight Attendant Affecting the Passenger

In the 1994 case of *Pasinato* v. *American Airlines*,[34] where the plaintiff alleged wilful misconduct on the part of the carrier when the act of opening an overhead bin by a flight attendant resulted in a tote bag falling on the plaintiff and injuring him as a result, the trial court accepted a definition of 'wilful misconduct' of a previous case which identified it as:

> The performance of an act with knowledge that the act will probably result in an injury or damage, or in some manner as to imply reckless disregard for the consequences of its performance.[35]

The court applied the above definition to the facts of the case and arrived at the conclusion that the American Airlines flight attendant's actions in no way constituted 'wilful misconduct'. The court explained:

> There is no dispute that the flight attendant opened the overhead bin to get a pillow for another passenger. The flight attendant's deposition indicates that she opened the bin with one hand, in her customary manner, with the other placed defensively above her head near the bin to prevent an object from falling upon her or a passenger sitting below. Further, the flight attendant stated that she tried to catch the tote bag that fell from the bin (and may have touched it as it fell), but that it fell too quickly.[36]

The plaintiffs claimed that repeated warnings were given over the public address system of the aircraft as to the innate hazardousness of the act of opening the overhead bins, which reminded passengers of the dangers of baggage shifting in the bins during flight. The plaintiffs further claimed that the flight attendant should have known, the nature of the contents of the baggage in the bin in question. However, the court was more inclined to accept the fact that incidents of objects falling from overhead bins were rare and that the flight attendant in question had been involved only in six such incidents during her seventeen years of tenure as a flight attendant, none of which had resulted in injury or inconvenience to passengers.

The court was also concerned with the formulation of an adequate and suitable definition of 'wilful misconduct' which was basically known to be the quality of behaviour resulting in an act committed with the knowledge that such act will 'probably result in an injury or damage'.[37] Another interpretation of 'wilful misconduct' recognized an act performed in a manner indicating reckless disregard for the consequences of the act as reflecting wilful misconduct on the part of the person committing such act. Applying the second criterion to the case in issue, the court recognized the act of the flight attendant in placing her hand in a defensive posture and nearly catching the article of baggage as it fell to be one which indicated the taking of sufficient care and precaution to preclude an accident from occurring.

Owing to the nature of cabin baggage which is now carried by passengers, courts place more stringent emphasis on the degree of care owed by the airline to passengers in warning them of the inherent danger of injury from falling overhead baggage. In *Andrews* v. *United Airlines*,[38] where upon arrival of the aircraft in which he was travelling, a passenger was hit by a piece of baggage descending from an overhead bin, it was the general view of the US Court of Appeals for the Ninth Circuit, that airlines in the modern-day context had a more onerous responsibility than their counterparts of the past to warn passengers of the increasing hazards of baggage falling from overhead baggage compartments. The court anchored its view on the fact that, nowadays, passengers hand-carry much larger cabin baggage, such as computers and musical instruments, which barely fit in the overhead bins. Therefore, the court held that the airline's duty of care in cautioning passengers and taking adequate care against the cause of accidents relating to falling overhead baggage was of a higher standard than that which had been expected in the past. However, the storage and retrieval of overhead cabin baggage is not always the sole responsibility of the flight attendant. Courts have held that a negligent passenger who stores his baggage carelessly is also responsible for overhead baggage. In *USAir Inc.* v. *United States*,[39] the US Court of Appeals for the Ninth Circuit, applying the law of California, held that a passenger who negligently stores baggage in an overhead bin must jointly share liability with the airline company if such baggage causes injury to another passenger. The court further held that regardless of whether the offending passenger sought or received assistance from a flight attendant when storing his briefcase, he had a duty to use care in placing his luggage in the overhead compartment and, in this case, he had breached that duty. As the offending passenger was travelling on the business of his employer, his negligent act occurred during the scope of his employment, and his employer was therefore responsible for the injuries caused by his negligent act. Also, although the court was able to trace the actual act of opening of the overhead bin to a flight attendant, it held that the negligent act of the flight attendant in opening the baggage compartment was not a superseding cause of the injury and did not exonerate the negligence of the passenger (and his employer) in storing the brief case in an 'unstable' manner.

*Lamkin* v. *Braniff Airlines, Inc.*,[40] is an interesting case which considered the rights of a passenger on a flight from Miami to Boston who suffered second and third degree burns when a cup of coffee spilled on to her lap. Shortly after take-off a flight attendant had served hot coffee to the passenger in a Styrofoam coffee cup. The coffee spilled when the passenger placed the cup on the seat-back tray in front of her and the passenger seated in the front moved the seat backwards. The injured passenger sued Braniff Airline, alleging negligence in the hiring and training of cabin staff, and negligence in the use of an allegedly defective coffee maker, seats, cups and trays. A claim for failure to warn against the excessively high temperature of the coffee was also laid.

The Federal Trial Court in Massachusetts which examined the case dismissed all claims alleged, holding that the passenger had failed to offer any evidence of negligence on the part of the airline with respect to the serving of hot coffee or treating the passenger's injury. The court also dismissed the claim of failure to warn, on the ground that the passenger herself was aware that the coffee was hot, and therefore needed no warning as to that fact. Moreover, there was no showing that any of the airline's employees was aware that the coffee was hot enough to burn a passenger. Although the court had no difficulty in agreeing with the passenger that an airline was subject to a high degree of care and that the standard of care required may approach that of an insurer, it observed that, nevertheless, a carrier is not strictly liable for accidents which befall its passengers, and an injured person must prove negligence on the part of the carrier in order to recover.

One of the significant findings of the court in this case was that the doctrine of *res ipsa loquitur* – which permits one, on the facts of a case, to 'draw an inference of negligence' in the absence of a finding of a specific cause of the occurrence when an accident is of the kind that does not ordinarily happen unless the defendant was negligent – was inapplicable. The court found that neither the passenger's expert nor common knowledge supported a finding that the mere occurrence of the accident demonstrated negligence on the part of the carrier, particularly where the expert was not qualified to testify as to the cause of the injury and had no particular expertise regarding the proper functioning of a coffee machine.

## Conduct of the Flight Attendant Affecting the Pilot

Several dramatic accidents have emphasized certain deficiencies in cockpit–cabin co-ordination and communication. Poor communication between pilots and members of cabin crew results from historical, organizational, environmental, psycho-social and regulatory factors. The basic problem is that technical crew and cabin crew represent two distinct and separate cultures, which may often inhibit satisfactory teamwork. Although the role of the technical crew in flight safety has been well documented,[41] the flight attendant's safety role has been treated at best with ambivalence, where flight attendants are considered 'back-end crew', maintaining a fairly orderly cabin and serving refreshments. Of course, flight attendants may assist in incidents involving terrorism or emergency evacuation, but the role of the flight attendant has been trivialized. Perhaps the main reason for the perceived bifurcation of the two types of crew is their geographic locations, where the cockpit and the cabin remain two distinct geographic and social environments.[42] As there are different areas of responsibility which devolve upon technical crew members and cabin crew members, the existence of two separate cultures is inevitable. Often, through no fault of its own, and due to its particular responsibilities, the technical crew in the cockpit may isolate itself from the cabin crew, leading to serious lapses of communication between the two. Australian accident investigator David Adams observes:

> If you look at almost any [airline] company, you will usually find that the cabin attendants and the flight crew are very clearly separated. They work for different branches of the company in most cases. The culture is one of almost complete separation. Yet, the fact of the matter is, in a safety situation, these two sections of the company have to work together. And the consequences of not working together quite often means a bunch of people get killed.[43]

One commentator's study of crew members' attitudes in flight reflects significant differences between personality dimensions of US pilots and flight attendants. The study attributes these psycho-social differences to pilots being task-oriented and preferring a cognitive style of problem-solving based on logic and systems-oriented reasoning; flight attendants, on the other hand, were identified as preferring an affective cognitive style and orientation to decision-making.[44]

## Wilful Misconduct

Wilful misconduct as an exception to the 'limitation of liability' rule appears in all three air law conventions that admit of liability limitations.[45] The original French text of the Warsaw Convention provides that if the carrier causes the damage intentionally or wrongfully or by such fault as, in accordance with the court seised of the case, is equivalent thereto, it shall not be entitled to claim the limitation of liability.[46] Drion[47] maintains that the English translation inaccurately states that the liability limitations of a carrier will be obviated if the damage is caused by its 'wilful misconduct' or by such 'default'.[48] The contentious issue in this is what kind of misconduct is required? Drion is of the opinion that by approaching the issue in terms of conflicting concepts, the question whether *faute lourde* – as proposed originally in the French text and for which there was an English equivalent, gross negligence – was in fact more appropriate than the word *dol,* which is now used in the document and for which no accurate English translation exists, has emerged as a critical one which needs resolution as to what standards may be used in extrapolating the words *dol* or 'wilful misconduct'.[49] Miller[50] takes a similar view when she states that the evils of conceptualistic thinking that had pervaded the drafting of Article 25 and rendered it incoherent, has now been rectified by the Hague Convention, which has introduced the words ' done with intent to cause damage or recklessly and with knowledge that the damage would probably result'.[51]

This confusion was really the precursor to diverse interpretations and approaches to the concept of wilful misconduct under Article 25 of the Warsaw Convention. The French Government took steps by its Air Carrier Act of 1957 to rectify ambiguities in this area by interpreting *dol* in the Convention as *faute inexcusable*, or deliberate fault, which implies knowledge of the probability of damage and its reckless acceptance without valid reason,[52] making a strong analogy with the Hague Protocol's contents. This interpretation, needless to say, brought out the question whether such reckless acceptance would be viewed subjectively or objectively.

The Belgian decision of *Tondriau* v. *Air India*[53] considered the issue of Article 25 of the Convention and the Hague interpretation. The facts of the case were commonplace, involving the death of a passenger, and a consequent claim under the Convention by his dependants. The significance of the case lay, however, in the fact that the Belgian court followed the decision of *Emery and others* v. *SABENA*,[54] and held that, in the consideration of the pilot's negligence under Article 25, an objective test would apply, and the normal behaviour of a good pilot would be the applicable criterion. The court held:

> Whereas the plaintiffs need not prove, apart from the wrongful act, that the pilot of the aircraft personally had knowledge that damage would probably result from it; it is sufficient that they prove that a reasonably prudent pilot ought to have had this knowledge.[55]

The court rationalized that a good pilot ought in the circumstances to have known the existence of a risk, and no pilot of an aircraft engaged in air transport ought to take any risk needlessly. However, the Brussels Court of Appeal reversed this judgment and applied a subjective test, asserting that the Hague Protocol called for 'effective knowledge'. Professor Bin Cheng seems to prefer the objective test in the interpretation of 'wilful misconduct' in Article 25, on the grounds that a subjective test would defeat the spirit of the Convention and that judges would be 'flying in the face of justice in search of absolute equity in individual cases'.[56]

Peter Martin, analysing the Court of Appeal decision in *Goldman* v. *Thai Airways International Ltd*,[57] agrees with Bin Cheng, and criticizes the lower court decision which awarded Mr Goldman substantial damages for injuring his hip as a result of being thrown around in his seat in turbulence, in an instance where the captain had not switched on the 'fasten seat belt' sign.[58] Martin maintains that Mr Goldman failed to prove that the pilot knew that damage would probably result from his act, as envisaged in the Hague Protocol principle. Being an aviation insurance lawyer, Martin is concerned that while the English courts have a proclivity towards deciding Article 25 issues subjectively, insurance underwriters could view the breach of the limits stringently. Both on the need for objectivity and on the count of the adverse effects on insurance, it is difficult to disagree with Cheng and Martin.

In the 1994 case of *Saba* v. *Compagnie National Air France*[59] – in which the Federal Courts of Washington examined a case relating to damage caused by rain water to Persian rugs which were entrusted to a carrier for transport – the court considered evidence presented that the carrier had disregarded its own cargo handling regulations as well as plain common sense. The interpretation of wilful misconduct adopted *In re Korean Airlines Disaster of September 1 1983*,[60] established that:

> Wilful misconduct is the intentional performance of an act with knowledge that the act will probably result in an injury or damage, or in some manner as to imply reckless disregard of the consequences of its performance.[61]

The court noted that it was also clear that a combination of factors can, taken together, amount to wilful misconduct. The court further observed that only the act needs to be intended, not the resulting injury or the wrongfulness of the act. Another significant finding of the court in this case was that evidence of wilful misconduct could be drawn from the determination of whether the carrier or its servants followed regulations adopted by the carrier in performing the alleged act. If regulations of the carrier were not followed, the court concluded that *ipso facto* such would reflect wilful misconduct on the part of the carrier.

## Recent Developments on Compensable Limits

In November 1992, all international air carriers of Japan amended their conditions of carriage to accord with directives of the Japanese Ministry of Transport. These amendments waived passenger liability limits in international carriage by air as stipulated in the Warsaw Convention *per se* and as amended by the Hague Protocol of 1955. Accordingly, the Japanese carriers waived their right to invoke liability limits under the Convention's Article 20(1) for claims under 100,000 SDR for passenger injuries and deaths. In other words, the Japanese carriers waived their right under this category of claim to prove the absence of fault in order to rebut the presumption of liability imposed by the Convention under Article 17. This made the carriers of Japan strictly liable for claims under 100,000 SDR. As for claims above 100,000 SDR, the limitation of liability would be waived and fault would be presumed but rebuttable, as in the original Convention. Professor Bin Cheng has commented:

> This brave and enlightened initiative on the part of the Japanese airlines, in being the first to remove the limit on carriers' liability for passenger death or injury ... represents a historic landmark in the evolution of the Warsaw System. It provides an unmistakeable signal to all other airlines and governments that it is now time to give up the pathetic struggle to bring life to the dismal 1971 Guatemala City Protocol in the form of the Montreal Additional Protocol No. 3 (MAP3). It should also hasten the end of what is in effect an international cartel, that is already in tatters, of low compensation limits.[62]

George N. Tompkins Jr endorses the Bin Cheng view and goes a step further in examining the Japanese amendments as suitable for the United States:

> The Japanese Initiative approach presents the simple solution to the problem which has caused all of the perceived ills of the Warsaw liability system. The simplicity of the approach is emphasised by the fact that no international convention or agreement would be required to adopt and put into place the Japanese Initiative approach in the United States ... The focus of current and future attention, therefore, should be upon the Japanese Initiative approach and how to make it adaptable and acceptable in the United States and presumably thereafter, throughout the aviation world.[63]

Japan has publicly stated that it is totally dedicated to the preservation of the Warsaw system on the basis that the system eliminates 'choice of law' problems and retains unifying principles of liability. The Japanese Initiative approach complements the Warsaw system in that compensation is automatically guaranteed under the Japanese Initiative approach, without the claimant having to produce his passenger ticket. Also, compensation is assured without distinction as to origin, destination or nationality of the passenger concerned.[64]

Against the backdrop of an initiative taken by the European Civil Aviation Conference (ECAC) urging member States of ECAC to participate in a European Inter-carrier Arrangement setting up a new special contract which would contain liability limits of at least 250,000 SDR, the International Air Transport Association convened its Airline Liability Conference in Washington DC in June 1995. The conference concluded that the Warsaw Convention system must be preserved, but the existing passenger liability limits for international carriage by air are grossly inadequate in many jurisdictions, and should be improved as a matter of urgency, urging governments at the same time through the International Civil Aviation Organization, and in consultation with airlines, to act urgently to update the Warsaw system, including liability issues.

The conference also set up two working groups to assess and report on a suitable liability package and appropriate and effective measures to secure complete compensation for passengers. The findings of these working groups have resulted in agreement among IATA members to prepare a new inter-carrier agreement, to replace the Montreal Agreement of 1966, which includes the following elements:

- full compensatory damages, with no fixed liability figure;
- no explicit waiver of the carrier's defences under the Warsaw/Hague system;
- explicit reservation of the carrier's rights against third parties; and,
- promotion of widespread implementation of the Agreement by the airlines.

The IATA inter-carrier agreement therefore provides for a single universal system without specified limits, the award of recoverable compensable damages to be in accordance with the law of domicile of the passenger, and an 'umbrella accord' which gives carriers maximum flexibility to adjust their conditions of carriage, taking into account applicable government regulations.

The 31st Session of the ICAO Assembly considered the developments generated by the IATA Conference of June 1995 and observed that although in the short term new limits might be accomplished through an inter-carrier agreement, most States may need a more substantive approach such as the adoption of a new protocol under the Warsaw system. Accordingly, the Assembly decided to direct the ICAO Council to continue its efforts to modernize the Warsaw system as expeditiously as possible. The Assembly also urged States to ratify Montreal Protocol No. 4, independently of Additional Montreal Protocol No. 3.[65]

Further to its Washington meeting of June 1995, IATA held its Annual General Meeting on 31 October 1995 in Kuala Lumpur, Malaysia, where its member carriers unanimously approved and adopted an inter-carrier agreement which, when implemented, will obviate the limitation on recoverable damages for passenger injury or death provided by the Warsaw system and the Montreal Agreement of 1966 (which raised Warsaw limits applicable to air carriage from or through the United States). The inter-carrier agreement essentially preserves the Warsaw Convention against threats of denunciation by States and effectively precludes litigation under Article 25 of the Convention which may seek to overcome the limitation on recoverable damages for passenger injury or death. However, the inter-carrier agreement retains the right of the carrier to refute presumption of its liability under Article 20 of the Warsaw Convention, in the event the carrier is able to show that it took necessary precautions against the accident or that such precautions could not be taken under the circumstances. The thrust of the agreement is to enable carriers and passengers or their dependants to mutually agree limits of liability or settlement which in turn enables the carrier to agree upon a sum of liability based on a passenger's domicile rather than a flat sum that was used across the board by the Warsaw system.

## Comments

Both under the present system of liability and under the new IATA inter-carrier agreement (which has yet to be accepted by States), the role of the flight attendant in air carrier liability hinges upon whether or not the carrier could prove that it took necessary precautions to avoid causing injury or death to a passenger which may have been caused by the conduct of its cabin crew, or whether it was impossible to take such precautions. Under the present liability regime, a carrier is *prima facie* liable up to prescribed limits, and if it proves prudence in its professional conduct, it could avoid liability or seek mitigation thereof. On the other hand, if the plaintiff proves wilful misconduct, such limits could be transgressed, leading to unlimited liability of the carrier. Under the proposed unlimited liability scheme within the Japanese initiative and under the IATA umbrella, however, the question of wilful misconduct of the carrier is obviated in the context of limitation of liability, in that the latter would not exist. The liability of the carrier would then hinge on the exception to liability which is based on the principle of good conduct, which the Warsaw system identifies as the taking of due measures and precautions by the carrier to ensure the avoidance of death or injury to a passenger, or the impossibility of taking such precautions. In this sense, emerging trends in air carrier liability would hinge heavily on the specific conduct of airline crew. The conduct of flight attendants would therefore be subject to more minute judicial scrutiny under such a system.

## Notes

1 *Air Letter*, 17 August 1994, No. 13,060, at 1.
2 Rebecca D. Schute, 'On a Collision Course', *Air Line Pilot*, March 1995, at 20.
3 Ibid.
4 *Pasinato* v. *American Airlines, Inc.*, No. 93 C 1510, 1994 Westlaw 171522 (ND Ill. 2 May 1994). For a more detailed report and analysis of this case, see *Lloyd's Aviation Law*, 1 June 1994, Vol. 13, No. 11, at 4–5.

5 Convention for the Unification of Certain Rules Relating to International Carriage by Air, signed at Warsaw on 12 October 1929.
6 Id., Article 3.1.
7 Id., Article 3.2.
8 Halsbury states that the word 'accident' 'excludes the operation of natural causes such as old age, congenital diseases, or insidious diseases, or the natural progression of some constitutional, physical or mental defect', Halsbury, *Laws of England* (3rd edn), Vol. 22, para. 585, at 293. The case of *Fenton* v. *Thorley and Co. Ltd* (1903) AC 443 qualified this somewhat restrictive definition of the word 'accident' when Lord Lindley said: 'the word "accident" is not a technical legal term with a clearly defined meaning. Speaking generally, but with reference to legal liabilities, an accident means any unintended occurrence which produces hurt or loss', id., at 453. A later case, *The Board of Management of Trim Joint School* v. *Kelly* (1914) AC 667, held that an intentional act of third parties could also be considered an 'accident' at common law.
9 Annex 13, Convention on International Civil Aviation 1944.
10 Shawcross and Beaumont, *Air Law* (4th edn), Vol. VII, London: Butterworths, 1988, at 153.
11 105 S Ct 1,338 (1985).
12 Ibid.
13 580 F 2d 1,193 (3rd Cir. 1978).
14 Id., at 1,052.
15 *Husserl* v. *Swiss Air Transport Co. Ltd*, 485 F 2d 1,240 (2nd Cir. 1975); *Day* v. *Trans World Airlines, Inc.*, 528 F 2d 31 (2nd Cir. 1975); *Evangelinos* v. *Trans World Airlines, Inc.*, 550 F 2d 152 (3rd Cir. 1976), *Salerno* v. *Pan American World Airways*, 19 Avi. 17,705 (SDNY 1985).
16 86 AD 2d 658.
17 This test is the result of decisions in *Day* v. *Trans World Airlines, Inc.*, 528 F 2d 31 (2nd Cir. 1975) and *Evangelinos* v. *Trans World Airlines, Inc.*, 550 F 2d 152 (2nd Cir. 1977).
18 Article 17 of the Warsaw Convention states: 'the carrier shall be liable for damage sustained in the event of the death or wounding of a passenger, if the accident which caused the damage so sustained took place on board the aircraft or in the course of any of the operations of embarking or disembarking.'
19 Ibid.
20 *Husserl* v. *Swiss Air Transport Co. Ltd*, 388 F Supp. 1,238 (SDNY 1975).
21 *Scarf* v. *Trans World Airlines, Inc.*, 4 Avi. 17,795 (SDNY 1955). See also *Chutter* v. *K.L.M. Royal Dutch Airlines*, 132 F Supp. 611 (SDNY 1954).
22 *Adler* v. *Austrian Airlines*, 78 SC Eu. 564, at 568.
23 22 Avi. Cas. (CCH 17,731 SDNY 1990). Also cited in 900 F 2d, at 10.
24 22 Avi. Cas. (CCH 17,639 SDNY 1989).
25 No. 83-5540 (ND Cal. 1984).
26 Id., at 5,543.
27 *Knoll* v. *Trans World Airlines, Inc.*, 528 F 2d 31 (2nd Cir. 1975).
28 Op. cit., n. 17.
29 Analysed in *Buonocore*, 900 F 2d, at 10.
30 45 F 3d 435, 1995.
31 Ibid.
32 *Quinn* v. *Canadian Airlines International Ltd*, Ontario Court, General Division, 18 OR 2d 326 (rendered 30 May 1994), reported in *Lloyd's Aviation Law*, 1 September 1 1994, Vol. 13, No. 17, at 1–2.
33 Id., at 351–2.
34 Op. cit., n. 4.

35 *In re Korean Airlines Disaster of September 1 1983*, 932 F 2d 1,475 (DC Cir.), cert. denied, 112 S Ct 616 (1991).
36 Ibid.
37 Definition given in *In re Korean Airlines Disaster*, op. cit., at 1,479.
38 See *Lloyd's Aviation Law*, 1 June 1994, Vol. 13, No. 11, at 1–3.
39 14 F 3d 1,410 (9th Cir. 1994).
40 853 F Supp. 30 (D Mass. 1994).
41 See E.L. Wiener, 'Cockpit Automation', in E.L. Wiener and D.C. Nagel, *Human Factors in Aviation*, San Diego: Academic Press, 1988, at 433–59.
42 Rebecca D. Schute, 'Cockpit–cabin Communication I: A Tale of Two Cultures', *The International Journal of Aviation Psychology*, 1995, Vol. 5, No. 3, 257, at 258.
43 Cited in V.P. Moshansky, *Commission of Inquiry into the Air Ontario Crash at Dryden, Ontario*, Toronto, Canada: Minister of Supply and Services, 1992, at 1,087.
44 See M.J. Vandermark, 'Should Flight Attendants be Included in CRM Training? A Discussion of Major Air Carriers' Approach to Total Crew Training', *The International Journal of Aviation Psychology*, 1991, Vol. 1, at 87–94. See also A. Merritt, 'Human Factors on the Flight Deck: The Influence of National Culture', paper presented at the Seventh International Symposium on Aviation Psychology, Columbus, Ohio, April 1993.
45 The Convention for the Unification of Certain Rules Relating to the Assistance and Salvage of Aircraft at Sea, Brussels, 1938, The Rome Convention 1933, and the Warsaw Convention 1929.
46 Article 25.
47 H. Drion, *Limitation of Liabilities in International Air Law*, Martinus Nijhoff, 1954, at 195.
48 Ibid.
49 Id., at 200.
50 Georgette Miller, *Liability in International Air Transport*, Deventer: Kluwer, 1977, at 200.
51 Hague Protocol 1955, Article XIII.
52 Miller, op. cit., at 202.
53 *Revue Française de droit arien*, 1977, at 193.
54 5 December 1967; *Revue Française de droit arien*, at 184.
55 Transcript of judgment, at 4.
56 Bin Cheng, 'Wilful Misconduct: From Warsaw to the Hague and From Brussels to Paris', *Annals of Air & Space Law*, 1977, Vol. II, 55, at 99.
57 (1983) *Law Society's Gazette*, 8 June 1983, at 1,485.
58 Peter Martin, 'Intentional or Reckless Misconduct: From London to Bangkok and Back Again', *Annals of Air & Space Law*, 1983, Vol. VIII, at 145–9.
59 866 F Supp. 588 (DDC 1994).
60 932 F 2d 1,475, at 1,479 (DC Cir. 1991).
61 Ibid.
62 Bin Cheng, 'Limit on Air Carriers' Liability for Passenger Injury or Death: The Rising Sun Eclipses Guatemala City and Montreal – USA, Quo Vadis?', *Lloyd's Aviation Law*, 15 May 1994, Vol. 13, No. 10.
63 George N. Tompkins Jr, 'The Case for the Japanese Initiative Approach in the United States', *Lloyd's Aviation Law*, 1 December 1994, Vol. 13, No. 23, at 4–5. See also generally Koichi Abe, 'The Warsaw Convention and the Waiver of Limitations of Liability by the Airlines of Japan', *Lloyd's Aviation Law*, 15 June 1993, Vol. 12, No. 12, at 1.
64 Opening Statement of Japan Airlines Delivered by Koichi Abe, Vice President, Legal Affairs, at the International Air Transport Association, Airline Liability

Conference, 19–27 June 1995, Washington, DC. See ALC-Item 7, WP 21-Doc. II, at 2–4.

65 See ICAO papers, A31-WP/224, P/57, *Report on Agenda Item* 36.2, at 36.2-3.

# 13 Exposure of Air Crew to Cosmic Radiation

## Introduction

This chapter will discuss the impact of certain scientific studies into the effects of cosmic radiation on air crew, and legal issues that may arise as a consequence.

Cosmic radiation is composed of high-energy subatomic particles and photons, and is mainly generated by sources outside the solar system, gaining in intensity as altitude above the ground increases. This phenomenon has been subject to attention from the scientific community since 1907, and has been recognized as a hazard to air crew and any others who spend part of their working life at high altitudes.[1] Although all life is exposed to ionizing radiation[2] to some degree, it is an incontrovertible fact that technical and cabin crew members of air carriers are exposed to more cosmic radiation than most of the general population who spend their working hours on the ground.

Despite the fact that the human body is able to tolerate being bombarded by low-level ionizing radiation, and the effects of such radiation are not significant, further exposure beyond a certain threshold is reported to increase health risks, including the risk of contracting cancer. Other afflictions which have been identified are genetic mutations in human egg cells and sperm cells, and irreparable damage to a developing embryo or foetus.[3]

## Radiation at High Altitude

In recent times, several separate studies have been carried out to determine the effects of cosmic radiation on air crew. A common trend in all these studies is the considerable risk to prostatic cancer and acute myeloid leukaemia, and its link to cosmic radiation. In a 1992 review of acute leukaemia,[4] the risk factors of the disease have been identified as exposure to ionizing and non-ionizing radiation, and to benzene. Of these, benzene, which is a known leukaemia-causing agent, is present only in negligible concentration in jet fuel and jet fuel vapours, and its potency in jet fuel as a leukaemia-causing agent was tested in 1991,[5] when it was shown that a cohort of workers (a group of workers whose behaviour was followed over a period after exposure to the test substances) who were exposed to jet fuel did not show any increased leukaemia risk. Therefore, the cause for acute myeloid leukaemia may be deduced to be exposure to ionizing radiation. A Canadian Pacific Airlines Study in 1990[6] and a British Airways study conducted in 1992[7] both concluded that the cohorts of airline crew tested revealed that acute myeloid leukaemia was the main type of non-chronic lymphoid leukaemia found among them.

In the development of the Anglo-French Concorde aircraft, which introduced regular civil air transport at supersonic speed for the first time, a joint Anglo-French aeromedical group identified cabin pressure, oxygen equipment and ionizing radiation as the most critical medical issues at Concorde's cruising altitude. The team was of the view that solar cosmic radiation (which consists of low-energy particles which are produced at high intensity) can penetrate the upper layers of the atmosphere and reach Concorde's cruising altitude. The team therefore recommended the installation in the aircraft of an in-flight radiation dosimeter mounted in the forward passenger cabin. This device is designed to alert the crew to levels of radiation from solar flares and other causes which are injurious. In such instances, the aircraft would be requested to descend to a safer altitude.[8]

At the Human Performance (HUPER) Committee meeting of the International Federation of Airline Pilots' Association (IFALPA) held in Oslo in June 1996, a discussion on cosmic radiation involved a paper which concluded that air crew are one of the most highly exposed occupational groups. This conclusion was allegedly based on the fact that five to ten times more chromosome aberrations are found in air crew in Germany and Italy than in the normal population, and that there was strong evidence of significantly increased cancer rates among air crew – a finding which was particularly reflected in epidemiological studies conducted in Canada, the United Kingdom, United States, Japan and Finland.[9]

At its Autumn Council in October 1992 in Frankfurt and in November 1992 in Athens, the same HUPER Committee of IFALPA identified the main health risks for air crew resulting from exposure to cosmic radiation as the possibility of contracting cancer, several hereditary defects and damage to the unborn child.[10] The IFALPA paper opined that 300 cabin crew members out of every 100,000 would die of radiation-induced cancer and lose approximately fifteen years of their life expectancy. Also, the paper estimated that one miscarriage per 1,000 pregnancies would result from exposure to cosmic radiation usually experienced at high altitudes by air crew during pregnancy. The main risk in this regard, the paper submitted, was solar flares.[11]

However, in 1992, the Director of Health Services of British Airways concluded in a research paper that, at that time, the existing limitations on exposure to radiation by air crew, as imposed by the International Commission on Radiology Protection (ICRP), had no serious implications for commercial aviation and that, with airline schedules at that time, it was practically impossible for individual air crew members to approach the occupational exposure limit.[12]

This view appears to be diametrically opposed to the conclusions of a significant study[13] released in Canada in 1996 by Canadian medical specialist Pierre Band, who published his findings after conducting research between 1989 and 1992 on all male pilots employed for one year or more since 1 January 1950 (women pilots were excluded from the study due to their small numbers). A total of 2,740 eligible pilots were identified, of whom 2,680 (97.8 per cent) were successfully traced on a comparison between standardized mortality ratios and standardized cancer incidence. As Band concludes:

> Our study found no statistically significant excess for non-chronic lymphoid leukemia and not all subtypes of leukemias associated with radiation exposure were observed. However, the incidence rate for acute myeloid leukemia (AML), exceeded the expected number; it is of interest to note that acute myeloid leukemia (AML) was also the main type of non-chronic lymphoid leukemia found among British Airways and Canadian Pacific Airlines pilots.[14] No definite explanation for this excess risk can be provided at this time. Although a chance occurrence cannot be excluded, a synergistic effect between known or suspected leukemia risk factors remains a possibility. Monitoring of in-flight radiation exposure as well as long term follow-up of cohorts of civil aviation crew members is needed to further assess cancer incidence, particularly brain cancer and leukemia risk.

## Air Carrier Liability

Three primary considerations apply in instances of employment which expose employees to the risk of exposure to radiation:

1 justification – all exposure to radiation must be *justified;*
2 exposure must be *as low as reasonably achievable;*
3 *dose limits* set for individuals must be observed.[15]

In 1990, the ICRP published its recommendations on radiological protection, which define occupational exposure to radiation as 'exposures incurred at work as the result of situations that can reasonably be regarded as being the responsibility of the operating management'.[16] The ICRP further recommends that there should be a requirement to include exposure to natural radiation sources as part of occupational exposure only in instances where use or production of radon warrants attention in the workplace; operations with and storage of materials in the workplace would involve the emission of significant traces of radioactive material, operation of jet aircraft; and spaceflight.[17] It is worthy of note that the ICRP, in its reference to operation of jet aircraft, makes mention primarily of air crew, but also mentions couriers, who may fly more frequently than other passengers.[18]

According to the ICRP, the consequences of gradual exposure to radiation include:

- the probability of a person dying from a radiation-induced cancer;
- the weighted probability of a person suffering from a radiation-induced non-fatal cancer, or a severe hereditary disease occurring in the children of irradiated parents.

The ICRP also holds that a consideration of the time of appearance of these detrimental effects relative to exposure is relevant in determining causation. In relation to the above consequences, the ICRP has set a threshold limit of radiation[19] and recommends that any intervening practice to obviate the production of radiation or minimize exposure of humans to radiation should do more good than harm, and that such a protective system must be optimized to maximize the net benefit, while providing adequate protection for the individuals exposed. Above all, the ICRP's recommendations underscore the need for preventive measures to preclude seriously detrimental effects on any individual.

With regard to the sustenance and continued success of a preventive programme, the ICRP recommends that an overall assessment of its effectiveness should be conducted regularly.

There are two categories of persons who may be affected by continual exposure to radiation in the course of air transportation: those affected by direct exposure, such as air crew and couriers, and the offspring of such persons, who may be exposed to radiation in the foetal stage through exposure of their parent.

## Bodily Integrity of Air Crew

The main legal issue to be considered in this context – whether an airline would be liable for injuries or death suffered by air crew or their progeny as a result of sustained exposure to radiation – originates from a person's right to 'bodily integrity'. A person has a legal right in almost any jurisdiction of the world to know of and determine risks which may adversely affect their body through a process introduced by another. Airlines may arguably have a duty (particularly in the light of compelling facts now emerging through several studies on exposure of air crew to radiation) to apprise their crews of the risk involved, and to obtain their consent that such a risk would be an acceptable factor in the course of their employment. It is arguable that an analogy to the situation of air crew in this regard is the voluntary exposure of persons to radiation for purposes of medical research.

The seminal principle of 'bodily integrity' as a person's legal right is reflected in the Nuremberg Code which was formulated by the Nuremberg Trial after the Second World War. The Code was articulated in a court opinion judging 23 Nazi physicians guilty of 'crimes against humanity' for their experimentation on humans during the war. Although admittedly the Nuremberg situation – which involved medical experimentation on individuals – is different from the situation of air crew who are exposed to radiation in the course of their official duty, it is logical to consider that the underlying principle of 'bodily integrity' applies in both situations, where a person's knowledge and consent becomes necessary prior to exposure to risk.

The first provision in the Nuremberg Code stipulates:

> The voluntary consent of the human subject is absolutely essential. This means that the person involved should have legal capacity to give consent; should be situated as to be able to exercise free power of choice, without the intervention of any element of force, fraud, deceit, duress, over-reaching or other ulterior form of constraint or coercion; and should have sufficient knowledge and comprehension of the elements of the subject matter involved as to enable him to make an understanding and enlightened decision ...

The US Supreme Court recognized the above provision as a cognizable factor in determining liability for radiation exposure in the 1994 case *In Re Cincinnati Radiation Litigation*,[20] citing as persuasive authority the dissenting judgment of Judge O'Connor in *United States* v. *Stanley*,[21] where Her Honor underscored the fact that the US Constitution ensured an individual's right to receive the protection of the Nuremberg Code. Justice O'Connor refused to accept the majority decision in the *Stanley* case that injuries arising out of the injection of drugs during the course of a person's employment were not compensable. It would therefore seem that the *Cincinnati Radiation* case has established that, in the United States, exposure to radiation and injury therefrom which can be related to a person's employment can be compensable.

The *Cincinnati Radiation* case, which involved radiation treatment on an experimental basis on several patients who were diagnosed with terminal cancer at the Cincinnati General Hospital from 1960 to 1971, left the courts to consider the liability of the hospital, particularly in the circumstances where the patients had not been informed of the risk of death from the radiation experiments. In its analysis of applicable law the court anchored itself on the case of *Washington* v. *Harper*,[22] where the Supreme Court had held that state prison officials could administer anti-psychotic drugs to a prisoner against his will or without his knowledge and consent only if the prisoner was dangerous, the treatments were justified in the medical interest and the prisoner received adequate protection and procedural safeguards.

Those three criteria can be analogically applied to the instance of air crew members being exposed to scientifically known levels of radiation at high altitudes without their knowledge or consent. The last criterion – that of ensuring protective safeguards – would act as an essential supplement to obtaining the consent of the air crew for exposure to the risk, since it is an essential prerequisite for an employer to take adequate precautions against a danger in the workplace, whether or not the consent of the employee is obtained.

## Safeguards and Precautions to be Taken by the Carrier

Whatever technological measures may help alleviate the adverse effects of exposure to radiation, the air carrier's liability, if it fails to take precautionary measures, is based on the fundamental tort law principle that the carrier owes a duty of care not to cause harm or injury to others who use the carrier's services, whether for purposes of employment or otherwise. If one were to consider cases regarding injury caused by tobacco smoking to passengers while in flight as an analogy, then the 1980 decision of *Ravreby* v. *United Airlines Inc.*[23] would take a prominent place as persuasive authority. The Iowa Supreme Court in *Ravreby* implicitly recognized that air carriers owe a duty of care to non-smoking passengers, and that care should be taken, to the extent possible, by the carrier not to expose non-smokers to tobacco smoke in the cabin.[24] The court observed:

> The carrier's duty stops just short of insuring the safety of the passenger, and the common expressions of the law on this subject are that the

carrier is bound to protect the passenger as far as human care and foresight will go, and that the carrier is liable for slight negligence.[25]

The significance of the *Ravreby* decision as an analogy to legal considerations with regard to exposure to radiation in aircraft at high altitude also lies in the fact that the court balanced the interest of the passenger with the advantage of expedience inherent in air transport. It was the court's view that the carrier would be liable for damage caused by dangers which are reasonably and naturally anticipated, and the required care on the part of the carrier must be such as not to prevent the practical performance of the carrier's duty to transport with expedition in accordance with the usual requirements of the business. Accordingly, a court adjudicating on a case which involves a claim of a person against exposure to cosmic radiation while in flight may consider the justification for flight at high altitudes (greater speed and decreased fuel consumption) as a criterion which may mitigate a carrier's liability without totally exculpating the carrier from liability. In any event, it is incontrovertible that the carrier has to take reasonable measures to protect its employees and passengers from injury, whatever the justification.

Given the compelling nature of the scientific data available on the extent of injury which may be caused to a person by cosmic radiation at high altitudes, a court may well consider the cause of such exposure as a tort – a private offence which is generally wrong at civil law and committed to the harm of a person's self or property by another person.[26] The exposure of air crew by an air carrier to cosmic radiation without the consent of the crew would therefore amount to the tort of battery, which has been defined as the intentional and direct application of force to another person,[27] or unjustified intentional physical interference with a person.[28] To preclude such an inference by the courts, air carriers may have to show every evidence of there having been adequate measures taken to prevent or at least minimize the dangers of exposing their air crew to cosmic radiation.

## Rights of the Unborn Child

As scientific evidence has shown, exposure to cosmic radiation at high altitudes could seriously damage a foetus, resulting in the birth of a physically malformed and grievously ill child. It is therefore ineluctable to conclude that the liability of the air carrier would be extended to the unborn child on the legal basis of foreseeability, as enunciated by Lord Atkin in the seminal case of *Donaghue* v. *Stevenson*,[29] where His Lordship said:

> You must take reasonable care to avoid acts or omissions which you can reasonably foresee would be likely to injure your neighbours. Who, then, in law is my neighbour? The answer seems to be – persons who are so closely and directly affected by my act that I ought reasonably to have them in contemplation as being so affected when I am directing my mind to the acts or omissions which are called in question.[30]

The primary test of liability therefore lies in the reasonable foreseeability that your careless conduct will cause injury. In this case, since the scientific world has already identified the unborn child as vulnerable to exposure to cosmic radiation, it cannot be doubted that this category of person is included within the parameters of foreseeability envisaged by the *Donaghue* case.

Although some jurisdictions do not recognize the rights of the unborn child *en ventre de sa mère*, the horrendous outcome of the administration of the drug Thalidomide several decades ago brought out an outpouring of powerful feeling across several jurisdictions. The 1963 South African case of *Pinchin* v. *Santam*[31] is a good example, where Justice Hiemstra observed of a child born with cerebral palsy caused by injury to the pregnant mother:

> If one can visualize a mind so evil as to allow the intentional administration of a drug like Thalidomide, in order to produce a misshapen infant, our law would be archaic and inflexible if it should refuse an action.[32]

Even in jurisdictions which do not recognize that the foetus itself has a legal personality, and on that basis refuse to award compensation to a child for ante-natal injuries, it is logical to argue that the right of action would belong to a child, and would crystallize at their birth. The enlightened Australian case in 1972 of *Watt* v. *Rama*[33] recognized that the criterion for the award of compensation for ante-natal injury should lie on the fact that the injury is reasonably foreseeable to the pregnant woman such that the child would be born in an injured condition.

Although laws of some jurisdictions in North America do not admit of awarding compensation to a foetus if the foetus was not viable or capable of independent life at the time of injury, it is heartening that a 1974 report stated:

> It is highly probable that the common law would, in appropriate circumstances, provide a remedy for a plaintiff suffering from a prenatal injury caused by another's fault.[34]

In 1976, a right of action for ante-natal injuries was established in the United States when a Private Member's Bill became the Congenital

Disabilities (Civil Liability) Act 1976 as a result of the vast outpouring of feeling which surrounded the plight of the Thalidomide babies.

Of course, in most instances, when both mother and child sue for compensation for injury to the child, the mother's case may become stronger than that of the child. In the 1969 UK case of *S.* v. *Distillers*,[35] Hinchcliffe J stated:

> So far as Mrs. S's claim is concerned, it is plain that this lady suffered a grievous shock. For a happily married woman, it is difficult to comprehend any greater shock than seeing your child born misshapen and deformed. The fun and joy of motherhood is partially destroyed. Instead of enjoying and being able to show off the baby to your friends there is a natural reluctance to do so. This has not been the sort of shock which has worn off like so many cases of shock that come before the courts; this is permanent. Ever since the birth Mrs. S. has been depressed, anxious and worried. She is daily reminded of her handicap. There is always a cloud over her happiness. She now has to take drugs prescribed by her doctor and she has a sense of guilt which makes it harder for her to recover, although Heaven knows she has nothing to blame herself for. This unhappy lady is entitled to damages for grievous shock, for future travelling expenses quarterly, for special clothes for the boy, together with something for the loss of wages.[36]

The *Distillers* case principle would not, however, detract from the fact that many common law judicators would not hesitate to consider seriously the sensibility of *Watt* v. *Rama*[37] in considering an unborn child's trauma and injury, which continues after birth as a compensable head of liability, whether as an extension to the injuries caused to the mother or on a *sui generis* basis.

## Comments

In defence of the air carrier, the considerations of justification, exposure of crew members to minimum levels of radiation and the setting of limits for maximum dosage of radiation would be relevant. As for justification, it is clearly in the air carrier's favour, since it is indubitable that flying at high altitudes can be justified by invoking expediency and economy – two fundamental advantages inherent in air transport. As for the other two considerations, the principles of tort law would inevitably come into play, where the carrier would have to show that due care and diligence was exercised in averting or minimizing risk. It would also be incumbent upon the carrier to show the court that it acted prudently to apprise the air crew of the possibility of exposure to radiation as an occupational hazard and obtained the consent of the crew members prior to adopting such measures.

There is also the possibility that, if evidence of adverse effects on the human body by exposure to radiation at high altitudes becomes more compelling, the courts may impose strict liability without regard to negligence, on the basis that flying at high altitudes is an ultra-hazardous activity. There would be no difficulty for the courts in adopting this attitude, particularly if compelling numbers of plaintiffs of the same category seek compensation alleging similar symptoms.

## Notes

1 See Professor I.R. McAulay, 'Cosmic Radiation: Exposure of Air Crew', *IFALPA International Quarterly Review*, September 1996, at 26.

2 'Ionizing radiation comes from several sources – as terrestrial radiation from the Earth, as cosmic radiation from the solar system and as galactic radiation, which is a combination of cosmic radiation and secondary radiation. Ionizing radiation may also occur from radioactive isotopes in the human body. See Stanley R. Mohler, MD, 'Flight Crews and Cabin Crews Encouraged to Increase Awareness of Inflight Ionizing Radiation', *Human Factors & Aviation Medicine*, March–April 1996, Vol. 43, No. 2, at 32.

3 See Mohler, op. cit., at 33. See also generally W. Friedberg and E.G. Darden, 'Galactic Cosmic Radiation Exposure and Associated Health Risks for Air Carrier Crew Members', *Aviation Space and Environmental Medicine*, November 1989, at 1,104–5.

4 R.A. Cartwright and A. Staines, 'Acute Leukemias', *Baillière's Clinical Haemotology*, Vol. 5, 1992, at 1–26.

5 A. Seldén and G. Ahlborg Jr, 'Mortality and Cancer Morbidity After Exposure to Military Aircraft Fuel', *Aviation Space Environmental Medicine*, 1991, Vol. 62, at 789–94.

6 P.R. Band, J.J. Spinelli, V.T. Ng, J. Moody and R.P. Gallagher, 'Mortality and Cancer Incidence in a Cohort of Commercial Airline Pilots', *Aviation Space Environmental Medicine*, 1990, Vol. 61, at 299–302.

7 D. Irvine and D.M. Davies, 'The Mortality of British Airways Pilots, 1966–1989: A Proportional Mortality Study', *Aviation Space Environmental Medicine*, 1992, Vol. 63, at 276–8.

8 See John Ernsting and Peter King (eds), *Aviation Medicine* (2nd edn), London: Butterworths, 1990, at 477. See also H.A. Hopkins, 'Piloting Aspects of the Concorde', *Airways International*, September–October 1964, at 27–9.

9 Discussion Paper, IFALPA Human Performance Committee Meeting, Oslo, 18–20 June 1996, Agenda Item 1.7.1, Cosmic Radiation 97 HUP158, 5 June 1996, at 2.

10 IFALPA HUPER Committee, November 4 1992, Athens, Radiation Exposures of Flight Crew, *Status Report*, L93 b402, 12 November 1992, Attachment at 3.

11 Ibid. The International Commission on Radiological Protection (ICRP) has recommended that pregnant females should not exceed a dose of 2 mSv to the abdomen. The maximum exposure condition in flight implies a monthly dose of about 0.8 mSv. See *Annals of the ICRP*, 1991, ICRP Publication 60, 21, at 1–3.

12 D.M. Davies, *Cosmic Radiation and Commercial Aviation*, British Airways plc, 1992, at 7.

13 Pierre Band, *Mortality and Cancer Incidence of Air Canada Pilots*, Health Canada, 1996.
14 Band et al., op. cit.; Irvine and Davies, op. cit.
15 See McAulay, op. cit., at 30.
16 '1990 Recommendations of the International Commission on Radiological Protection', *Annals of the ICRP*, 1990, Vol. 21, Nos 1–3, Chapter 4, Section 5.1.1 (134), at 33.
17 Id., Section 5.1.1 (136).
18 Ibid.
19 7.3 × 10-2Sy-1. This coefficient is supplemented by limitations on such factors as the tissue-weighting factor and cancer specific tissue factor, which are too scientific for consideration in an article of this nature. For more information, see *Annals of the ICRP*, op. cit., at Chapters 3, 5 and 6.
20 See Morris L. Hawk, 'The Kingdom Ends: In re Cincinnati Radiation Litigation and the Right to Bodily Integrity', *Case Western Reserve Law Review*, 1995, Vol. 45, at 977–97.
21 483 US 699 (1987).
22 494 US 210 (1990).
23 15 Avi. Cas. (CCH) 18, 235 (Iowa Sup. Ct 1980).
24 In this context, it should be noted that a trial relating to a lawsuit filed by 30 non-smoking flight attendants of US airlines who had sued eight major tobacco companies for a variety of ailments caused by years of breathing tobacco smoke in aircraft commenced on 2 June 1997. See *Air Letter*, 6 January 1997, No. 13,652, at 3.
25 Id., 18,238.
26 Michael Grossman and Philip Price, *Tobacco Smoking and the Law in Canada*, 1992, at Section 16.
27 Winfield and Jolowicz, *Winfield and Jolowicz on Tort* (12th edn), 1984, at 54.
28 Ibid.
29 [1932] AC 562.
30 Id., at 580.
31 (1963) (2) SA 254 (W).
32 Id., at 259.
33 [1972] VR 353.
34 The Law Commission, *Report on Injuries to Unborn Children*, 1974, Cmnd 5709, at 3.
35 (1969) 3 All ER 1,412.
36 Id., at 1,422.
37 [1972] VR 353.

# 14 The Use of Civil Aircraft and Crew for Military Purposes

## Introduction

The question of whether civil aviation and military aviation have demarcated operational regimes or whether they can still function in symbiosis has become a debatable one, in view of developments in the air transport industry which have occurred over the years. At its incipient stage, civil aviation held closer ties with military aviation since both were the protégés of government, and were controlled by instruments of State. In recent times, however, governments are increasingly ceasing to be the principal actors of commercial aviation, thereby making at least a cosmetic deviation from civil aviation and recognizing the aspects of private enterprise (which often control civil aviation) as the real protagonists in matters pertaining to civilian air transport.

Security against aggression was naturally the paramount consideration at the end of the Second World War. It is therefore incontrovertible that considerations regarding a post-war civil aviation regime would have been bifurcated between civil and military aviation when the Chicago Convention of 1944[1] was being drafted.[2] Article 3 of the Convention, which provides that the Convention shall apply only to civil aircraft, explicitly excludes State aircraft, such as aircraft used for military, customs and police purposes, from the jurisdiction of the Convention. Furthermore, the Convention expressly prohibits aircraft of a contracting State which are used for military purposes (on the basis that aircraft used for military purposes are 'State aircraft') from flying over the territory of another State or landing thereon without authorization or by special agreement or otherwise.[3] Under Article 3(d) of the Convention, contracting States undertake to have due regard for the safety of navigation of civil aircraft when issuing regulations for the use or application of State aircraft.

Annex 2 to the Chicago Convention – pertaining to Rules of the Air – which was adopted on 15 April 1945, further protects civil aircraft by providing that interception of civil aircraft shall be governed by appropriate regulations and administrative directives issued by Contracting States in compliance with Article 3(d) of the Chicago Convention.[4]

Perhaps the most fundamental difference between the operation of civil and military aircraft lay in the fact that, although they were expected to share the same skies, the procedures by which they did this varied greatly. Civil aircraft depended entirely on predetermined flight paths and codes of commercial conduct which varied depending on aircraft type and types of traffic carried, whereas military aircraft operated in line with the exigency of a situation, and were not necessarily always guided by predetermined flight paths. This dichotomy led to the adoption of Resolution A10-19 by the 10th Session of the ICAO Assembly in 1956. The Assembly Resolution, while recognizing that the skies (airspace) as well as many other facilities and services are commonly shared between civil and military aviation, focused on ICAO's mandate to promote safety of flight,[5] and reinforced the thrust of Article 3(d) of the Chicago Convention. The Resolution called for all contracting States to co-ordinate between their various aeronautical activities in order that the common use of airspace be so arranged that safety, regularity and efficiency of international civil air navigation be safeguarded.[6]

The prioritizing of civil and military aircraft operations therefore seems to favour civil aviation, even if purely to safeguard life, limb and property. If this principle were to be extended to the use of civil aircraft for military exigency, one could arguably apply the overriding pronouncements of the Chicago Convention, its Annex 2 and ICAO Resolution A10-19 to conclude that the use of civil aircraft for military purposes – if absolutely necessary – would have to be carried out under the same principle of protection of civil aviation from the spontaneous risk that military operations carry with them.

The fact that military strategists have come to expect support services from civil aircraft and civil aviation is becoming more evident with the increasing need for military operations, both in war situations and in instances of human tragedy brought about by civil conflict or natural disaster. There have been many such instances in recent times, ranging from the use by the UK military of chartered commercial cargo aircraft in the Falklands Crisis in 1982 to earlier practices of India and Pakistan in 1971, when both countries used passenger aircraft for the transportation of their troops during the Indo-Pakistan war. More recently, there have been instances of civil passenger aircraft being used to transport terrorists under heavily armed guard.[7]

This chapter will examine the principles of international law governing the use of civil aircraft and crew for military purposes.

## Air Law Principles

The Chicago Convention is as good a starting point as any in determining the international legal principles governing the use of civil aircraft and crew for military purposes. As discussed earlier, the Convention absolves itself of its application to 'State aircraft', of which military aircraft has been identified as a species. Article 4 of the Convention recognizes that every contracting State agrees not to use civil aviation for any purpose inconsistent with the aims of the Convention. Therefore, the Convention states by implication that no country which has accepted the Convention in a manner consistent with the international recognition of a treaty would use civil aircraft for purposes that would erode the aim of the Convention – to promote the development of a safe and orderly regime of international civil aviation and air transport services which would be operated soundly and economically. By this provision, therefore, the Chicago Convention protects both the safety and economic viability of civil aviation. The *prima facie* principle which the Convention protects is that which provides for the protection of civil aviation from physical and economic risk. Based on this fundamental postulate, a commercial civil airline could object to its aircraft being used for military purposes not only on grounds of safety, but also on the ground that such use would adversely affect the economic interests of the airline concerned.

Another legal issue which may emerge from the use of civil aircraft for military purposes is that, according to Article 3 of the Convention, a legal determination of the status of the aircraft and its crew would be entirely dependent upon the use to which the aircraft is put; therefore the crew of a civil aircraft would lose the protection afforded by the Chicago Convention if they were to perform military duties in the aircraft when they are assigned such, or when they carry out a military project such as ferrying military personnel in their aircraft.

The aim of the Chicago Convention – to develop and foster safe, regular and economic civil air transport services in the world – is transferred to ICAO for action. Article 44(b) of the Convention makes it an objective of ICAO to encourage the arts of aircraft design and operation for peaceful purposes, and Article 44(d) specifies an overall objective for ICAO to meet the needs of the peoples of the world for safe, regular, efficient and economical air transport. However, ICAO's scope is circumscribed in the case of war, referring to which, the Convention provides in Article 89:

> In case of war, the provisions of this Convention shall not affect the freedom of action of any Contracting States affected, whether as belligerents or neutrals. The same principle shall apply in the case of any Contracting State which declares a state of national emergency and notifies the fact to the Council.

This provision would effectively preclude the formal application by a State of provisions of the Chicago Convention in an instance of war, or in an instance of national emergency where the ICAO Council is advised of such an emergency. However, these requirements are not applicable to Article 9(b) of the Convention, which empowers a State to temporarily restrict or prohibit flying with immediate effect of any aircraft over any part of that State's territory in exceptional circumstances or during a period of emergency or in the interest of public safety.

Of course, the absence of such a provision in the Chicago Convention would by no means have affected the overall right of a State, at international law, to take extraordinary measures temporarily to suspend provisions of a convention which prescribed rules of conduct on a general basis. As the Provisional Court of International Court of Justice pronounced in 1923:

> ... international Conventions and more particularly those relating to commerce and communications are generally conducted having regard to normal peace conditions. If, as the result of a war, a neutral or belligerent State is faced with the necessity of taking extraordinary measures temporarily affecting the application of such Conventions in order to protect its neutrality or for the purposes of national defence, it is entitled to do so even if no express reservations are made in the Convention ...[8]

Although instances such as war and national emergency are fairly straightforward to deal with, there are modern-day exigencies of civil aviation which make it difficult for one to determine the boundaries between civil and military aviation. Such problems were highlighted by the International Federation of Airline Pilots' Associations (IFALPA) at the 26th Session of the ICAO Assembly in 1986.[9] IFALPA claimed that the three uses put forth in Article 3(b) of the Chicago Convention – military, customs and police services – did not adequately address other common uses of aviation, such as the transportation of remote station supplies, emergency assistance and humanitarian missions, or the transport of State diplomatic and foreign service personnel aboard aircraft chartered by a State. IFALPA claimed that the potential problems confronting the flight crew of State aircraft which operate international civil air transportation services which involved military, police or customs services were twofold:

1 operations by such aircraft did not come under any international air law Conventions and were destitute of legal protection, thereby effectively precluding the State aircraft concerned of being protected under an applicable legal regime;
2 the ambivalence with regard to the operative legal regime that would apply in the event of an accident involving such aircraft being investigated – would a civil or military investigative and judicial process apply?

The perceived inadequacy of Article 3(b) of the Chicago Convention in addressing an instance such as the carriage of a few deportees or repatriates under guard in a civil aircraft performing scheduled airline operations bring to bear the lacuna in the Chicago Convention which caused concern to IFALPA in its submissions to the ICAO Assembly in 1986. In fact, IFALPA drew the attention of the ICAO Assembly on two successive sessions – the 27th and 29th Sessions – and the Assembly responded with a request to the Secretary General of ICAO to undertake a study on civil/State aircraft. The study was concluded in 1993, and was submitted to the ICAO Council by the Secretary General at the Council's 140th Session.[10]

The Secretariat study on civil/State aircraft focused on one broad issue – whether certain aircraft used in military, customs or police services could be considered as civil aircraft, not State aircraft, in certain circumstances. It suggested to the ICAO Council that in view of the equivocal wording of Article 3(b) of the Convention which states '[A]ircraft used in military, customs and police services *shall be deemed* [my emphasis] to be State aircraft', it may mean that the qualifier in Article 3(b) was meant to apply only in the context of the Chicago Convention. The study also suggested that in view of the dependence of the provision on the usage of aircraft as a criterion of identification of civil and State aircraft, one could take into account the following indicators:

1 *The nature of the cargo carried* – Are they supplies or equipment for the military, customs or police services of a State? Article 35 of the Convention recognizes that the mere carriage 'of munitions or implements of war' does not by itself make an aircraft a State aircraft.
2 *Ownership of the aircraft* – Is it owned privately or by the State?
3 *Operation* – What degree of control and supervision of the operation of the aircraft is carried out by the specified services?
4 *Passengers or personnel carried* – Are they military, customs or police officials, or members of the public at large? Is the particular flight open for use by members of the public?
5 *Aircraft registration and nationality markings.*

6 *Secrecy of the flight* – Will a usual civil (ICAO) flight plan be submitted and the usual air traffic clearances obtained?
7 *Nature of crew* – Are the crew civilian, or are they military, customs or police personnel, or employed by these services?
8 *Operator* – Is the operator a military, customs or police agent?
9 *Documentation* – Are the documents required by the Chicago Convention and its Annexes to be carried on civil aircraft in fact being carried (e.g. certificate of registration, certificate of airworthiness, licences for the crew, journey log book?
10 *Area of operations* – Will the aircraft fly to, or over, areas in a situation of ongoing or imminent armed conflict?
11 *Customs clearances* – Will the normal clearances be obtained?[11]

The study concluded that the manner in which Article 3(b) has been written gives rise to a multiplicity of problems regarding its interpretation, and submitted that a proper interpretation of the provision should show that no aircraft used in military, customs or police services should be considered to be a civil aircraft under the Convention.

## Legal Status of Civil Aircraft Under International Law

As discussed in Chapter 5, the nationality of aircraft is fundamental to its states under international law, and this has a profound effect on the contingency of the use of civil aircraft for military purposes. Such use would not only have an impact on States' responsibility towards the owners of aircraft, but also would affect other States which are linked to the airlines concerned by designation.

Professor Brownlie observes:

> ... today, one can regard responsibility as a general principle of international law, a concomitant of substantive rules and the supposition that acts and omissions may be categorized as illegal by reference to the rules establishing rights and duties. Shortly, the law of responsibility is concerned with the incidence and consequence of illegal acts, and particularly the payment of compensation for loss caused.[12]

International responsibility relates both to breaches of treaty provisions and other breaches of legal duty. In the *Spanish Zone of Morocco Claims* case, Justice Huber observed:

> ... responsibility is the necessary corollary of a right. All rights of an international character involve international responsibility. If the obligation in question is not met, responsibility entails the duty to make reparation.[13]

It is also now recognized as a principle of international law that the breach of a duty involves an obligation to make a reparation appropriately and adequately. This reparation is regarded as the indispensable complement of a failure to apply a convention and is applied as an inarticulate premise that need not be stated in the breached convention itself.[14] The International Court of Justice affirmed this principle in 1949 in the *Corfu Channel* case[15] by holding that Albania was responsible under international law to pay compensation to the United Kingdom for not warning that Albania had laid mines in Albanian waters which caused explosions damaging ships belonging to the United Kingdom.

## Insurance Implications

Although *ex facie* a State which leases or charters an aircraft from another State can arrogate to itself by agreement the responsibilities which accrue to the State of original registration of such aircraft, the ramifications of such an eventuality, particularly in the context of a lessee State using a leased aircraft for military use, would be unthinkable. From a purely insurance perspective, where most aircraft insurance policies contain stringent war risk insurance clauses, a civil aircraft used for any military purpose would entail cancellation of the insurance policy at short notice. An aircraft operator which obtains a civil insurance policy for its aircraft would also lose liability protections for passengers carried in a civil aircraft used for military purposes. In addition, all crew insurance covered by a policy obtained for civil aircraft would usually be rendered null and void if such crew were used to operate a civil aircraft for military purposes.

The most fundamental postulates of insurance are expectation and foreseeability or absence thereof, so that an insured is only protected under an insurance policy against events which cannot be predicted or foreseen at the time the policy is obtained. Therefore, if an airline insures its aircraft knowing or with the expectation that the aircraft would be used by its government for military purposes, the insurance contract between the insurer and the insured airline would be deemed voidable.

The seminal principle of voidability of an insurance contract for non-disclosure of material facts by the insured was emphasized in the 1928 case of *Stipcich* v. *Metropolitan Life Insurance Co.*,[16] which held:

> Insurance policies are traditionally *uberrimae fidei* [done in utmost good faith] and a failure by the insured to disclose conditions affecting the risk of which he is aware, makes the contract voidable at the insurer's option.[17]

Generally, an aviation insurance policy is no different from other policies in that there exists a relationship of *uberrimae fidei* between the insured and the insurer. This is based on the philosophy that the insured is aware of facts about the property they insure and of attendant risks such property may be exposed to, making them obligated at law to disclose such facts to the insurer.

It is only in this manner that the insurer could assess the risk to which the property is exposed and decide, *in limine,* whether to accept such a risk or not. Furthermore, such disclosure would enable the insurer to decide the terms of the contract, including the applicable insurance premiums. Rod Margo[18] points out the fundamental philosophical distinction of the practice of the principle *uberrimae fidei* when he states that the duty of good faith usually applies equally to both insurer and insured, although in the United Kingdom the principle is applied more to the actions of the latter, while in the United States the principle is applied more to the conduct of the former.

The *uberrimae fidei* principle, which requires the insured to disclose material facts which are within the purview of the insurer's knowledge and which may affect the conditions of an insurance policy, may not necessarily apply in instances where the insured airline may be unaware of a fortuitous future decision of its government to deploy aircraft operated by the airline for military purposes. Essentially, the duty of the insured to disclose material facts (facts which may affect the decision of the insurer to insure the property concerned at appropriate premium levels) ceases immediately after the insurance contract is concluded (but applies again at the time the policy comes up for renewal). The above principles also apply to instances of misrepresentation, where the insured may misrepresent facts relating, *inter alia,* to the specific use of aircraft. It must be emphasized, however, that any instance of a civil aircraft being used for military purposes could immediately expose the insurance policy covering such aircraft to be made voidable at short notice, irrespective of whether such use was disclosed or not, or whether such a contingency was envisaged or not by the insured at the time of obtaining the policy, unless such instances are already incorporated in the policy.

AVN 48B, the war risk exclusion used in the London insurance market, is based on the philosophy that war and associated risks pose the highest risk exposure to insurers. Accordingly, this exclusion primarily excludes all risks associated with war, and would be deemed to cover the use of civil aircraft for military purposes. The US insurance market uses AVN 48B and also CWEC (Common North American War Exclusion Clause). At the discretion of the insurer, and by mutual agreement between the insurer and the insured, a war risk may be included in an aircraft hull insurance policy on payment by the insured of a higher premium. Of course, such an inclusion would be cautiously worded to include only selected war risks, and it is extremely doubtful whether the use of civil aircraft for military purposes, particularly in the context of war or internal conflict in a State, would be found acceptable to the insurer.

## Legal Status of the Crew Member Under International Law

The main concern of IFALPA at the 26th Session of the ICAO Assembly was the status of the crew member of a civil aircraft when operating or working on a flight which is engaged in a military operation. In the strictest interpretation of the law, this apprehension was justified, since it is arguable whether the legal status of a crew member would automatically change from that of civilian to military personnel the moment the use of a civil aircraft is changed to perform a military function, whether it be the transport of military supplies or the carriage of soldiers. This is particularly true when the crew member serves in a country which is in military conflict.

The Geneva Convention Relative to the Protection of Civilian Persons in Time of War of 12 August 1949[19] refers to two categories of civilians. One, designated 'protected persons', consists of persons who find themselves, in the event of a conflict or occupation, in the hands of a party to the conflict or occupying power of which they are not nationals. This excludes nationals of a State not bound by the Convention, nationals of a neutral State, and nationals of a co-belligerent State having normal diplomatic representation in the State. Special safeguards for this category are laid down in Part III of the Convention. The second category, which includes the first, comprises the entire populations of countries in conflict, regardless of nationality, race, religion or political opinion, and is protected under Part II.

Article 50 of the 1977 Protocol to the Geneva Conventions of 12 August 1949 and Relating to the Protection of Victims of International Armed Conflicts (hereafter referred to as Protocol I) defines a civilian population:

1. A civilian is any person who does not belong to one of the categories of persons referred to in Article 4 A (1), (2), (3) and (b) of the third Convention and in Article 43 of this Protocol. [These consist of members of the armed forces, militias, volunteer corps, including those of organized resistance movements fulfilling certain conditions, and inhabitants who spontaneously take up arms to resist an invader.] In case of doubt whether a person is a civilian, that person shall be considered to be a civilian.
2. The civilian population comprises all persons who are civilians.

3. The presence within the civilian population of individuals who do not come within the definition of civilians does not deprive the population of its civilian character.

According to the above definition, a crew member who operates a civil aircraft for a military purpose may not perforce be considered a member of the armed forces. It is also arguable whether a crew member of a civil aircraft would cease to a civilian merely because they perform functions which assist the military. However, with no specific provision of law to interpret the particular circumstances, it would be natural for one to suggest the possibility that military service may be imputed to a crew member of a civil aircraft in such circumstances.

It may be said in brief that a civilian is a person who is not a member of the armed forces and does not belong to the militia, volunteer corps or organized resistance movement, whether or not such a movement is recognized by the adverse party. The term excludes inhabitants of a non-occupied territory who spontaneously take up arms to resist an invader. A civilian is thus a person not directly involved in hostilities, and a civilian population consists of such persons. The basic rule is that the parties to a conflict should distinguish between civilians and civilian objects on the one hand and combatants and military objects on the other, and should direct their operations against the latter. The safeguards for the former are operative whether the conflict is of an international character or not, and in whatever territory they may be, whether the war is specifically declared or not, and whether or not a party to the conflict is recognized by the adversary.

The protection of civilians in multilateral conventions dates back to the Geneva Convention for the Amelioration of the Condition of the Wounded in Armies in the Field of 22 August 1864.[20] At that time, civilians were usually at risk if they ventured near the battle fields or if combatants took shelter in their homes after a battle. The Convention therefore provided that inhabitants who brought help to the wounded 'shall be respected and shall remain free'.[21] In addition, generals of belligerent powers were to appeal to their humanity and inform them of the immunity which humane conduct conferred upon them. A civilian giving shelter to a wounded combatant was protected and exempted from billeting or from paying war contributions. The aim was to encourage the humanitarian involvement of civilians in support of wounded and sick combatants.

If one were to apply this still applicable incipient principle of the nineteenth century to the case of a crew member who operates a civil aircraft for a military purpose which is calculated to assist civilian populations, one may well argue that the crew member would not fall within the interpretive parameters of the Geneva Convention, and would remain civilian in status. However, such a conclusion is not inflexible, and would depend entirely on the exigencies of each case.

In the case of a civil aircraft which is used by the military as a medical aircraft, the status of the crew member is unequivocal and would have the protection of the status of the aircraft in terms of the purpose to which it is being put at the time. In the case of medical aircraft, whether they are operated by military or civil personnel, the following basic principles apply.

First, the crews must distinguish *three zones*, on land or sea, each of them to include the airspace above it:

1 *Zones not controlled by the enemy* – these include land or sea areas controlled by friendly forces and uncontrolled areas of the sea. Within these zones, whether in flight, on the ground or on the water, the medical aircraft is entitled to respect and protection, whether or not there has been any prior agreement with the adverse party. The State responsible for its use nevertheless possesses the option of notifying the adverse party – a precautionary measure to be recommended, especially if the aircraft is intended to be flown within the range of enemy ground-to-air weapons.
2 *Contact zones or their equivalent* – these are the areas on land where the opposing forces confront each other, especially where they are exposed to direct fire from the ground. In the parts of these zones which are physically controlled by friendly forces and in land areas where control has not been clearly established, the safety of medical aircraft can be guaranteed only by prior agreement between the military authorities of the opposing parties. Without such an agreement, the aircraft operate at their own risk, though they are not officially deprived of immunity; once their character has been recognized by the adverse party, they must be respected.
3 *Land or sea areas physically controlled by an enemy* – overflying these always presupposes prior agreement by the competent authority of the latter. However, if a navigational error or an emergency affecting the safety of the flight causes the medical aircraft to fly into such areas without or in breach of an agreement, the aircraft must make every effort to identify itself. If it succeeds in doing so, the adverse party shall refrain as far as possible from attempting an attack, either by ordering the aircraft to land or to alight on water, or by taking other measures, and allowing time for compliance with the orders given.

Crew members should recognize the fact that, like other vehicles and medical units, medical aircraft may not be used to gain military advantage or to render military objectives immune from attack. The general rule concerning weapons and ammunition which may be found in protected vessels or other forms of transport is fully applicable to medical aircraft. The use of medical aircraft to collect or transmit military intelligence data or to carry equipment for this purpose is also forbidden. Finally, only the prior consent of the enemy can permit them to search for the wounded, sick and shipwrecked in zones 2 and 3.

In overflying a zone controlled by the enemy or a zone not clearly controlled by any force, medical aircraft must comply with any order to land or to alight on water for the purposes of inspection. This operation must be carried out rapidly, without aggravating the state of the wounded and sick, removal of whom from the aircraft shall not be ordered unless unavoidable.

The purpose of the inspection is strictly limited to verifying that the aircraft:

- is in fact used exclusively for medical transport and under the authority of a party to the conflict, even if it does not belong to military aviation, or if its use as such is temporary;
- is not in violation of the general and special restrictions to be observed;
- has not flown without or in breach of a prior agreement where such agreement is required.

If the inspection shows that the conditions have been fulfilled, the aircraft may resume its flight without delay; the only passengers permitted to be retained are those belonging to the party that made the inspection or to its allies. If, on the other hand, the inspection brings to light a breach of any of the relevant rules, the aircraft may be seized by the adverse party. However, it may be used only as a medical aircraft if that was its permanent assignment. The occupants must be treated in conformity with the provisions of the Conventions and the Protocol, in particular those relating to wounded persons, prisoners of war, civilians and medical personnel.

The ILO cites the example of France, where, unless otherwise agreed by the parties, a contract of employment for a specified period may be terminated before its expiry only in the event of serious misconduct or *force majeure*. Moreover, in the event of termination for serious misconduct, the provisions governing disciplinary measures may apply – in particular the requirement of a preliminary interview.

## Comments

There are three basic situations where the possibility of civil aircraft being used for military purposes arises: international armed conflict, non-international armed conflict, and natural disasters. In all three instances, civil aircraft would rarely be used for combat purposes. Such aircraft would mostly be used for humanitarian purposes or for ferrying military personnel and medical and food supplies. It is therefore reasonable to conclude that, in all three instances, the principles of 'humanitarian law of war', as it is known today, shall apply to civil aircraft in non-combatant situations.

The entirety of humanitarian law of war is grounded on the principle that force may be employed only against those persons who themselves use or threaten to use force. In general terms, those who have immediate ability to apply force are termed belligerents or combatants. Non-combatants are usually spared attack or violence in a state of war. Non-combatant persons are generally classified into two categories:

1 medical personnel and religious personnel (such as chaplains) within the armed forces;
2 all persons who do not take up arms and do not engage in or actively assist in the use of force against the adversary.

Under these two broad headings, civil air crew operating civil aircraft for non-combatant military purposes would clearly be classified as non-combatants, and would therefore be classed as civilians. These definitions have been formalized in Article 1 of the Hague Regulations of 1907,[22] which defines belligerents, and provides that the laws, rights and duties of war apply not only to armies, but also to aviation and volunteer corps fulfilling the following conditions:

1 they are commanded by a person responsible for them and his subordinates;
2 they have a fixed, distinctive emblem recognizable at a distance;
3 they carry arms openly;
4 they conduct their operations in accordance with the laws and customs of war.

Under this definition, civil air crew may satisfy the first two criteria, but may be excluded from the category of 'belligerent' if they do not carry arms and respect the laws and customs of air, as provided for in the other two criteria. The operative definition reflects a thin line between the four criteria, under which civilian populations have been known to have come under the definition of 'belligerent' in instances where they carried arms and respected the laws and customs of war in situations of civil uprising.[23] In this context, much would depend on the particular circumstance under which civil air crew are ordered by a State to perform functions of a military nature in civil aircraft.

On the question of whether a crew member of a civil aircraft has a right to refuse to serve in that aircraft if it is used for a military purpose, much would depend on the interpretation of the basic tenet of employment enshrined in Article 23 of the Universal Declaration of Human Rights. The provision states that everyone has the right to work and to free choice of employment. On the strength of 'free choice', it is arguable whether a choice made by a crew member to serve in a civil aircraft operating scheduled air services could be disregarded by their employer in assigning them to serve in an aircraft used for military purposes.

Air crew members (particularly technical crew) are usually engaged under a contract of employment for a specified period to perform a specified task. A study conducted by the International Labour Organization (ILO) in 1995 revealed that in many countries a distinction is drawn between contracts for a specified period and those of indeterminate duration, with the general rules governing reprimand, disciplinary action or dismissal being more stringently applied to the latter.[24] In this sense, a pilot of an aircraft who is usually on a fixed-term contract is less vulnerable to disciplinary action by an airline than a colleague who is on a permanent contract.

The ILO also concluded that, during the term of their contract, workers in many countries who are engaged under a contract for a specified period are generally in a better position as regards job security than those under a contract of indeterminate duration, since the normal dismissal procedures are not applicable to fixed-term employment.

In the instance of capture of persons in a state of armed conflict, persons of doubtful status are vulnerable to the arbitrary decision-making of their captor. Therefore, Article 5 of the Geneva Prisoners of War Convention of 1949 leaves no room for doubt that, in the present context, a person of doubtful status should not be dealt with arbitrarily. Article 5 provides:

> Should any doubt arise as to whether persons, having committed a belligerent act and having fallen into the hands of the enemy, belong to any categories enumerated in Article 4, such persons shall enjoy the protection of the present Convention until such time as their status has been determined by a competent tribunal.

The 'competent tribunal' would inevitably be a civil court in the context of captured civilian air crew, as was decided in 1968 by the

Privy Council, which decided on the status of Chinese Malay nationals who had been captured along with Indonesian paratroopers.[25] In the instance of such air crew performing combative functions, they could be arraigned before a court martial or a specially constituted military tribunal.

As for the status of civil aircraft in military operations, Protocol I to the Hague Air Warfare Rules[26] contains provisions on the protection of civilian objects which are analogous to the protection offered to civilians. The Protocol stipulates:

> Insofar as objects are concerned, military objectives are limited to those objects which are by their nature, location, purpose or use make an effective contribution to military action and whose total or partial destruction, captors or neutralization, in the circumstances ruling at the time, offers a definite military advantage.[27]

According to this definition, there are three operative criteria which would determine whether a civil aircraft which is used for a military purpose is not a civilian object:

1 the nature, location, purpose or use of the aircraft;
2 whether the particular use of the aircraft makes an effective contribution to military action;
3 whether its destruction, capture, or neutralization would offer a definite military advantage.[28]

For the first criterion, consideration would focus on whether the aircraft which should have been operating outside combat zones was in a combat zone or questionable zone for any particular purpose. The second criterion would seek to establish the purpose to which the aircraft was put, and inquire whether that purpose was integral to the advancement of military operations. For example, if a civil aircraft were to be observed carrying military combat equipment, this would fulfil this criterion. The third criterion calls for a *definite* military advantage, emphasizing that a mere advantage gained in the capture of the aircraft would not satisfy the criterion. The Protocol makes the express distinction between the carriage or possession by an object (aircraft) of food and essential items needed for civilian populations in armed conflict situations and the carriage of essential food and medical items for troops, denying protection to civil aircraft in the latter contingency.

A significant development in the law of warfare which may affect the status of civil aircraft and crew performing military functions has emerged in the now all too common area of non-international armed conflicts. Until the Geneva Conventions were adopted in 1949, the popularly accepted notion at law was that internal conflicts were not subject to international regulation or legislation. The traditional view was that such conflicts fell within the parameters of domestic jurisdiction of the State in whose territory such conflicts took place. The established government of the State was accordingly expected by the international community to handle and resolve the conflict with the application of its municipal laws. Any violation by an outside State with the 'rebel' faction was deemed an act of intervention.

The above approach was gradually eroded with the rapid changes in the international context over the past thirty years and, more recently, characterized by a greater degree of stability in the global balance of power. At present, a fragile distinction exists between international and non-international armed conflicts, with the latter regarded as worthy of international recognition and intervention if the interests of the international community are affected adversely by them.

In such situations, the laws applicable to international warfare discussed above would be as valid and applicable in instances of intervention in internal armed conflicts by States other than those in whose territories such conflicts take place.

In the ultimate analysis, the responsibility for using civil aircraft and crew for military purposes rests with the State concerned. The fundamental legal premise which applies in such situations is that, in international relations, the erosion of one's legal interest by another creates the latter's responsibility. As discussed earlier, State responsibility is a recognized principle of international law in the modern context. The law of international responsibility involves the incidence and consequence of acts which are irregular and illegal at international law, leading to the payment of compensation for the loss caused. In the modern context, therefore, it may be worthwhile to examine whether Article 89 of the Chicago Convention should be reviewed and the international community and ICAO be given more control over the use of civil aircraft and crew in instances outside the purview of civil aviation.

## Notes

1 *Convention on International Civil Aviation*, signed Chicago, 7 December 1944.
2 Eugene Sochor, *The Politics of International Aviation*, London: Macmillan Press, 1991, at 86.
3 *Convention on International Civil Aviation*, Article 3 (c).
4 Annex 2 to the *Convention on International Civil Aviation, Rules of the Air* (9th edn), July 1990, Article 3.8.
5 As per Article 44 of the Chicago Convention.
6 Doc. 7707, A10-8/16, 10/8/56.

7 Sochor, op. cit., at 94–6.
8 See the *Wimbledon* case PC1J:A, 1 (1926), at 36–7, per Anzilotti and Huber JJ.
9 See Status of aircraft (civil/state) A26-WP/51, LE/2, 25/8/86.
10 See Secretariat Study on 'Civil/State Aircraft', C-WP/9835, 22/9/93.
11 Ibid., Attachment at 9–10.
12 Ian Brownlie, *Principles of Public International Law* (4th edn), Oxford: Clarendon Press, 1990, at 433.
13 1925 RIAA ii 615, at 641.
14 *In Re Chorzow Factory (Jurisdiction) Case* (1927) PCIJ, Ser. A, No. 9, at 21.
15 *ICJ Reports* (1949), 4, at 23.
16 277 US 311 (1928).
17 Ibid., at 316.
18 See Rod Margo, 'Aspects of Insurance in Aviation Finance', *Journal of Air Law & Commerce*, 1996, Vol. 62, 423, at 431.
19 United Nations Treaty Series, Vol. 75, at 287–417.
20 For the full text of Convention, see D. Schindler and J. Tomar (eds), *The Laws of Armed Conflicts: A Collection of Conventions, Resolutions and Other Documents* (3rd edn), Dordrecht: Martinus Nijhoff, 1988, at 495–556.
21 Article 5 of the *Geneva Convention of 22 August 1864, for the Amelioration of the Condition of the Wounded in Armies in the Field.*
22 See James Brown Scott (ed.), *The Hague Conventions and Declarations of 1899 and 1907* (2nd edn), New York: Carnegie Endowment for International Peace, Oxford University Press, 1915, at 107.
23 Hague Regulations, Article 2. A similar definition can be seen in Article 4, para. A(b) of the Geneva Prisoners of War Convention of 1946.
24 *Protection Against Unjust Dismissal*, Report of the 82nd Session of the International Labour Conference, 1995, Geneva: ILO, at para. 37.
25 *Public Prosecutor* v. *Oie Hee Koi* (1968) AC 829 (PC).
26 Rules of Air Warfare, drafted by a Commission of Jurists at the Hague, December 1922–February 1923.
27 Ibid., Article 52, para. 2.
28 See also the corresponding assessment of an earlier and slightly different draft by the International Committee of the Red Cross, *Draft Additional Protocols to the Geneva Conventions of August 12, 1949: Commentary*, Geneva: ICRC, 1973, at 60–1.

# 15 Management of the Warsaw System

## Introduction

The latest innovation in air carrier liability – the IATA Inter-carrier Agreement on Passenger Liability – was unanimously approved and adopted by the 51st Annual General Meeting of IATA in Kuala Lumpur on 31 October 1995. It represents an unusual form of international law-making whereby an association of private airlines is setting standards for international compliance. However, this initiative can be hailed as a courageous attempt to lead the way in modernizing the international unification of private air law, subject to approval by governments. The agreement also attempts to offer a visionary interpretation and appreciation of existing international legal instruments. Another advantage of this initiative is that it brings into focus serious weaknesses of current unified private international air law, and shows the readiness of the industry to find solutions which are calculated to be beneficial to the consumer. Although allegedly tendentious, this initiative has assisted the IATA carriers to appear willing to take an ostensibly selfless action to clarify the treaties and protocols which govern the system of private liability in aviation.

However laudable the IATA initiative is, it is incontrovertible that even if it is implemented by air carriers with the approval of respective governments, it cannot be a permanent measure towards the unification of private air law in consonance with the law of treaties. A new legal regime, or at least a suitable modification of the current one, will be reached only if States themselves revisit the Warsaw system and formally revise it or replace it with a totally new instrument. Nothing short of global unification on a broad basis could successfully establish a new system of liability in this area. Such a system should aim at effective risk management on a global and common basis, obviate complex conflict of laws issues, and harmonize, as far as possible, conflicts of jurisdiction. The management of such a system has to ensure a large degree of predictability and certainty, so that a victim will obtain just and equitable compensation for damage caused, while at the same time ensuring that the air carrier concerned will not be left at the end of the settlement with vastly increased premiums when the insurance is renewed.

Of course, any management system which is charged with introducing and implementing measures must attempt to restore as much as possible the *status quo ante* and introduce clear rules on the jurisdiction of courts of law. Jurisdictional issues bring to bear the compelling need to prevent conflicts of jurisdiction or lack of jurisdiction and settle issues related to forum shopping – which is detrimental to all parties concerned – thereby calling for the elimination of ambivalence. Besides, clear and unified rules are essential to enable the airline industry to obtain effective and economic insurance coverage.

The above features of management can only be achieved by regulatory measures. These in turn would have to be introduced by the international community through the auspices of ICAO, which is the only international body charged with responsibility for regulating matters of global civil aviation. As a first measure, the management process should commence with an in-depth review of the existing state of affairs.

## The Warsaw System

One outstanding feature of the Warsaw system in terms of management strategy is its own genesis. In 1929, the Warsaw Conference – which was the precursor to the Warsaw Convention – in a brilliant show of liability management, veered from established legal concepts of tort law to place a presumption of liability on the carrier. This reversal *prima facie* ensured the award of compensation to the claimant, and reserved the right of the carrier to rebut the presumption of liability in exceptional circumstances when the carrier takes all necessary precautions to avoid the damage or when it is impossible to take such measures. Contributory negligence of the injured or dead passenger was also a factor in favour of the carrier. The final strategy of the conference was to blend the presumption of liability of the carrier with a limitation of liability which protected the carrier against floods of litigation and the possibility of being sued for huge sums of money, while introducing a provision in the Warsaw Convention that would break the limit of liability in case of the carrier's wilful misconduct. This balanced management structure was built by the Warsaw Conference at a time when air transport was in its infancy and carriage by air was a dangerous adventure. Most airlines (with the exception of US ones) were owned by the government and operated by the public service. The limitation of liability therefore primarily served to protect not only the airlines but the governments themselves. However, now, after seventy years, the limitation of liability of the Warsaw Convention has become unrealistically low, and presumed fault of the carrier has given way to more expedient trends which ensure compensation to the claimant and protection of the carrier concerned.

After its introduction, the Warsaw Convention underwent several metamorphoses, partly due to the rapid evolution of air transport and partly due to the growing dissatisfaction of States with its liability limits. Article 41 of the Warsaw Convention vested responsibility for the amendment of the Convention in the Government of France. France transferred this responsibility on a *de facto* basis to the Legal Committee of ICAO and to a diplomatic Conference convened by the ICAO Council. The Hague Protocol of 1955 was a result of this transfer of authority. Changes made by the Hague Protocol to the Warsaw Convention were largely cosmetic – the most important being an increase in the liability limits which was thought to be inadequate even in 1955. In 1966, the United States denounced the Warsaw Convention as amended by the Hague Protocol (the United States never ratified the Hague Protocol), and management of the Warsaw System was 'taken over' by the airline industry with the adoption of the 1966 Montreal Protocol – a temporary solution, reached essentially by the airlines, to increase the limits of liability and introduce the principle of strict liability regardless of fault on the part of the carrier. The IATA-sponsored Montreal Protocol effectively precluded the Warsaw system from being denounced by the United States, but gradually paled into insignificance as its limits of liability too became hopelessly inadequate in the face of the forces of inflation.

Perhaps the most innovative management change of the system occurred in 1971, when the Guatemala City Protocol introduced the principle of strict liability irrespective of fault while at the same time increasing the limit of liability to US$ 100,000 (from US$ 20,000 in the original Warsaw Convention, and US$ 40,000 in the Hague Protocol). The Protocol also simplified requirements for documents of carriage to enable electronic data-processing and computer record maintenance of tickets. The Protocol quite cleverly linked the two elements of limits of liability and electronic ticketing by making the US$ 100,000 limit unbreakable even in the case of faulty ticketing by the carrier concerned. In other words, the carrier's wilful misconduct, even if proved, could not result in compensation over and above the limit being awarded to the claimant. The Protocol also had a provision relating to the periodic adjustment of limits of liability (set to be consonant with inflationary trends), a 'settlement inducement' clause to facilitate and expedite out-of-court settlements, and a 'personal injury' clause, compared to the purely 'bodily injury' clause of the Warsaw Convention which did not admit of claims for mental distress. In addition, the Protocol embellished the principle of contributory negligence by unifying the principles already included in the Warsaw Convention further, and introduced the principle that the jurisdiction of the courts of the injured passenger's residence would be recognized in the case of personal claims under the Warsaw system. A supplementary compensation fund was yet another management tool used by the Guatemala City Protocol, whereby provision was made for States to have flexibility in awarding compensation to victims over and above the limits of liability, by having access to the compensation fund.

Apart from the fact that, despite its many virtues, the Guatemala City Protocol has yet to enter into force, one of its inadequacies was its link to a 'gold standard' in its extrapolation of liability limits. Therefore, the entry into force of the Guatemala City Protocol was initially obstructed due to the crisis of gold as the world-wide yardstick of values, and its replacement by the SDR (Special Drawing Rights – a basket of currencies set by the International Monetary Fund) in international banking parities. More than twenty years ago – in September 1975 – ICAO held another Diplomatic Conference that adopted three 'Additional Protocols 1975' and a 'Montreal Protocol No. 4, 1975', all of which have been waiting ever since to enter into force. Protocols 1, 2 and 3 are to fulfil a minor function – to add to the Warsaw Convention, and that Convention as amended at The Hague in 1955 and in Guatemala City in 1971. They also addressed the 'gold clause' (gold francs) to express the amount of the limits in terms of Special Drawing Rights. Montreal Protocol No. 4 was a substantive amendment of the Warsaw Convention as amended at The Hague with respect to cargo. It simplified the formalities of the air waybill, allowed its replacement by a computer record, and pioneered the regime of strict liability regardless of fault in the international carriage of cargo – a vast modernization of unified law.

It is interesting to assess the failure of the Montreal Protocols and question the reasons why such numerous attempts at modernized unification of private air law are still rejected over twenty years after their proposal. As for Montreal Protocol No. 3 and Protocol No. 4 – which incorporate the Guatemala City Protocol – there is explicit provision in the Guatemala City Protocol in Article XX that they cannot enter into effect unless ratified by the United States. Although the United States, which supported the Protocols vigorously, has been keen to ratify them, many pragmatic difficulties which have emerged from these instruments have seemingly precluded the United States from recording its ratification to them.

The Warsaw system and its window of litigation on 'wilful misconduct' of the carrier has given rise to indiscreet attempts by claimants at unlimited compensation, making the system unmanageable as a whole. Some examples are the litigation in US courts on cases such as the PanAm 103 litigation (the *Lockerbie* case) and the Korean Air (KL 007) case, where the evidence points to damage being caused by unlawful action beyond the control of the carrier. The standards used by juries in these cases, which render their verdict on a preponderance of probabilities rather than on the criminal law standards of finding evidence beyond reasonable doubt, make judgments sensitive to factual and evidential interpretation which may not always necessarily admit of an equitable finding by the court concerned.

## States' Initiatives to Limit Liability

The growing dissatisfaction with the Warsaw system has led to unilateral actions by States and airlines which represent a *de facto* amendment of the system and the consequent diffusion of its homogeneity. In keeping with the flexibility afforded by the Warsaw Convention, whereby airlines may enter into contracts for higher levels of liability, many airlines of the world have unilaterally increased their liability to 100,000 SDR – about US$ 150,000 – and the available evidence does not suggest any substantial increase of the insurance premiums for such an increase in the limits. Italy has already imposed a 100,000 SDR limit on all Italian air carriers anywhere in the world, and on all foreign carriers operating to, from or through the Italian territory. Since 1992, the United Kingdom requires all carriers licensed by the Civil Aviation Authority to increase their limit of liability to 100,000 SDR. More than three years ago, in November 1992, the Japanese air carriers agreed on a new tariff provision under which they accept liability without limit. They will not use the defence under Article 20, and accept the strict liability principle up to the sum of 100,000 SDR. Above that sum, the defences under the Warsaw Convention would be available, and their liability would be based on fault with reversed burden of proof. This 'Japanese initiative' is a historic breakthrough, and so far has not been copied anywhere else in the world. In 1995, Australia enacted new legislation which will increase the carriers' liability to about 260,000 SDR (about US$ 390,000). The European Union (EU) initially proposed a regulation on air carrier liability requiring operators serving a point within the European Union to increase their liability limit to no less than 600,000 ECU (about US$ 750,000). The more broadly based European Civil Aviation Conference (ECAC) encouraged its members to require, for transportation involving ECAC territory, a limit of at least 250,000 SDR (about US$ 380,000). According to the ECAC recommendation, the limit of liability should be revised every three years. It also suggests that those who suffer damage should receive the uncontested part of the claim within three months, and an immediate payment of 5 per cent of the limit should be paid in case of injury, or 10 per cent in case of death. The most recently proposed EU Council Regulation on air carrier liability would remove any statutory limit of liability, and would introduce strict liability up to the sum of 100,000 ECU.

## IATA Initiatives

On 24 September 1993, IATA requested an authorization from the European Commission and from the US Department of Transport to initiate discussions among its member air carriers concerning the conditions and limits of liability. Such an authorization and anti-trust immunity were seemingly necessary in order to avoid falling foul of anti-trust and competition regulations. The European Commission granted such authorization in September 1993, and the US Department of Transport only issued Order DoT 95-2-44 on 22 February 1995 – some 17 months later – while still exploring a solution to implement a supplemental domestic system that would permit ratification of Montreal Protocol No. 3 (originally limited to 120 days, later extended until 31 December 1995, and then until 1 November 1996, still awaiting ratification).

The DoT order expressed conditions and expectations that in passenger claims arising from international journeys ticketed in the USA, a passenger would be entitled to prompt and complete compensation on a strict liability basis, with no passenger limits and with the measure of damages to be available in the US domestic carriage. Furthermore, the order required the coverage to extend to US citizens and permanent residents travelling internationally anywhere in the world. The DoT saw the possible results of the IATA deliberations as temporary, pending entry into force of Montreal Protocols Nos 3 and 4, and still apparently expressing hope that these instruments will enter into force, since the most current official ICAO policy still urges speedy ratification of Protocol No. 3. Although it would seem somewhat unusual that negotiations relating to a multilateral international instrument were conducted by a business association of airlines and subject to strict conditions and expectations formulated by a single government, one cannot reasonably find fault with such actions in the context of commercial exigency which have arisen through a natural breakdown of management of the Warsaw System of liability.

An IATA Committee considered the matter in Atlanta in May 1995, and from 19 to 23 June 1995 IATA convened an Airline Liability Conference in Washington. The conference was attended by 67 airlines from all parts of the world, six regional airline associations and by observers from ICAO, ECAC and the EU. The IATA Conference arrived at the following conclusions:

i) The Warsaw Convention must be preserved. However, the existing passenger liability limits for international carriage by air are grossly inadequate in many jurisdictions and should be revised as a matter of urgency;
ii) Governments, through ICAO, and in consultation with airlines, should act urgently to update the Warsaw Convention system and to address liability issues;
iii) Governments should act expeditiously to bring into force Montreal Protocol No. 4 (cargo) independently of their consideration of Montreal Additional Protocol No. 3.

The conditions and expectations for the conference set out in US DoT Order 92-2-44 of 22 February 1995 restricted the ability of participating airlines to reach agreement at this Washington session on the enhancement of compensation for passengers under the Warsaw Convention system. In particular, the conference objected to the United States' expectation that the results of the conference would ensure full compensatory damages for claims by all US citizens and permanent residents travelling between countries outside the USA, on the basis that it would discriminate between passengers' nationalities and would impose on airlines an unreasonable responsibility that should be borne by the US Government.

The IATA Conference in Washington DC in June 1995 failed to draft a text of an inter-carrier agreement similar to the 1966 Montreal Agreement due to its inability to comply with the strict conditions and expectations imposed by the US authorities. The conference established two working groups – one to study the cost impact on airlines of the enhanced liability package accepted unilaterally or recommended by different groups, and another to assess and report on appropriate and effective means to secure complete compensation for passengers, including the Japanese initiative and the US Supplemental Compensation Plan, taking particular account of the circumstances of small and medium-sized airlines. The new inter-carrier agreement was presented for the approval of the 1995 IATA Annual General Meeting on 30–31 October 1995 in Kuala Lumpur, and it had not gained governmental approval at the time of writing.

At the 30th Session of the ICAO Legal Committee held in Montreal on 28 April–9 May 1997, the Committee adopted the text of a Draft Convention for the Unification of Certain Rules for International

Carriage by Air, which was scheduled to be placed for approval of ICAO contracting States at a diplomatic conference in early 1999. This decision was endorsed at the 32nd Session of the ICAO Assembly held in Montreal on 22 September–2 October 1998.

The IATA Conference in Washington DC in June 1995 recommended that the new, enhanced liability package should be adopted by airlines as quickly as possible, to include the following:

- an updated liability limit of 250,000 SDR, taking into account the effects of inflation on the limits in the 1966 Montreal agreement, the 1971 Guatemala City Protocol and 1975 Montreal Additional Protocol No. 3, as well as limits proposed by governments;
- periodic updating of liability limits to reflect the effects of inflation;
- standards and procedures for up-front payment to meet claimants' immediate needs, in accordance with established local custom, practice and applicable local law;
- the retention of the defence under Article 21 of the instruments of the Warsaw system (contributory negligence);
- where circumstances so require, a waiver up to 250,000 SDR of the defences under Article 20, paragraph 1 of the instruments of the Warsaw system;
- where circumstances so require, recovery of proven compensatory damages beyond 250,000 SDR through appropriate and effective means;
- complete compensation, as allowed by and in accordance with applicable law.

The June 1995 IATA Airline Liability Conference was swiftly followed by two working group meetings on 25–26 July 1995 in London and 7–8 August 1995 in Washington. These meetings and their outcome had a profound impact on the approach to the possible solution of the problem. After less than two days of consultations with insurance brokers in London, it was concluded that a 'split' two-tier system of liability (up to 250,000 SDR and then above that limit through 'pooled' insurance coverage) would be unwieldy, expensive and risk-prone.

The working groups recommended as the most realistic, least complicated and most cost-effective approach a definitive merging of the previously considered 'two-tier' solution. They recommended a *complete waiver of any limits*, subject to the condition that full recoverable compensatory damages will be determined on the basis of the *law of the domicile* of the passenger, and that, in principle, the defences under the Warsaw system will remain available to the carrier. Thus, without sufficiently wide discussion and with the indirect involvement of the insurance brokers, a new inter-carrier agreement was prepared which departs substantially from all previous initiatives and eliminates completely the concept of a limit of liability which has thus far been the basic feature of unified private air law. The text has been drafted to permit maximum flexibility to the carriers in developing their individual conditions of carriage and tariff filings, taking into account applicable governmental regulations. Carriers have wide flexibility under the IATA Agreement to waive any defences up to a specified monetary amount of recoverable compensatory damages (as circumstances may warrant), which flexibility was also provided for in the Japanese initiative.

There is no doubt that throughout the history of the unification of private air law, the issue of the amount of the limit of liability has been the most controversial element. While it proved possible and desirable to unify provisions on the documents of carriage and their legal relevance, the regime of liability, provisions on successive and combined carriage and the rules relating to the jurisdiction of courts, the limitation of liability provision has escaped any efforts at satisfactory unification, due to the economic disparities of states and variations in cost of living in different parts of the world. The question that emerges now under the IATA Agreement is whether a complete removal of the limitation of liability will prove acceptable insurers of all airlines – big or small – and be conducive to more effective unification of law on a global scale. Although no economic studies have been made which have resulted in transparent data on the effect of this measure on insurance premiums, in particular for the small and medium-sized airlines, the IATA Joint Working Groups anchored their arguments for recommending the adoption of a universal waiver of limits on the fact that any numerical limit will continue to attract litigation which would be calculated to avoid its effectiveness, will become a baseline for settlement negotiations and a 'target' for claims, will need to be updated regularly to take account of inflation and will require a 'second-tier' mechanism for the USA (and probably elsewhere), thus creating implementation and harmonization difficulties. On the other hand, the working groups contended that the absence of a numerical limit will restore the 'universality' of the Warsaw limits system, promote and facilitate negotiated as opposed to court-imposed settlements in each jurisdiction in accordance with local considerations and levels of damages, and lead to insurance premium levels which will eventually reflect the actual damages paid out, rather than hypothetical concepts of risk.

### Assessment of the IATA Inter-carrier Agreement

The new IATA Inter-carrier Agreement on Passenger Liability was adopted on 31 October 1995, and was signed by 11 airlines – Air Canada, Air Mauritius, Austrian Airlines, Canadian International, Egyptair, Japan Airlines, KLM, SAS, Saudi Arabian Airlines, Swissair and TACA – reflecting the fact that all geographic regions were represented. It is interesting that no explanation is available as to why none of the major US airlines signed. Perhaps anti-trust legislation means that they prefer to wait for explicit government approval on the basis of the specific tariff clauses to be developed by the airlines for the implementation of the agreement. The agreement came into effect on 1 November 1996 between signatory airlines. The IATA Agreement, which was broader in scope than the Montreal Agreement of 1966, did not explicitly replace the Montreal Agreement since the latter agreement pertained only to a segment of air carrier liability. It also set limits of liability on carriage primarily involving travel from or to the United States. However, the IATA Inter-carrier Agreement may be lauded as a courageous and creative initiative which encouraged airlines to consider the real need for a change in liability principles calculated to accord with current exigencies.

An international agreement or treaty, to be acceptable to the international community under principles of public international law, has to be agreed between sovereign States. To that extent, the IATA Inter-carrier Agreement, which was essentially an agreement between commercial airlines, remains inapplicable to States. However, the initiative of the International Civil Aviation Organization, which culminated in the International Conference on Air Law, held in the form of a diplomatic conference in Montreal from 10 to 28 May 1999 is expected to lay the basis for a new convention to replace the Warsaw Convention in totality.

Accordingly, the Inter-carrier Agreement cannot change the mandatory provisions of the Convention. Carriers may only agree that, in the practical application of the Convention, they will not invoke the limit of liability with respect to death, wounding or other bodily injury of the passenger and, possibly, that up to a specified monetary amount they will waive the defences available under the Convention. This approach does not contribute to the evolution and modernization of unified private air law – the 'no limit' approach is by necessity attached to the antiquated body of the 1929 Convention or the 1955 Protocol; the creative development of the unified law achieved in 1971 at the Guatemala City Conference (simplification of documentation and its possible replacement by a computerized record, strict liability, settlement inducement clause, enhancement of the jurisdiction of courts to favour the claimant) is no closer to implementation than before.

The jurisdiction of courts remains mandatorily restricted to the fora enumerated in Article 28 of the Convention – place of residence of the carrier, its principal place of business, place of the carrier's establishment or the court having jurisdiction at the place of destination. It is far from clear at present how a competent court may be convinced by the private Inter-carrier Agreement to determine and award compensation by reference to the law of the domicile of the passenger. One of the drawbacks of the 'domicile' principle is that a court would readily consider the *lex fori* as overriding the domicile of the claimant. There is no *cursus curiae* relating to decisions which have judgments based on the law of the domicile of the passenger.

The reference to the law of the domicile of the passengers is undoubtedly an ingenious tool to seek a balance in the award of compensation on a global scale and to keep insurance premiums of carriers under control. According to the 'domicile' theory, passengers from countries with a low cost of living would qualify for low levels of compensation according to the law of their domicile, and passengers from countries with a high cost of living would qualify for high levels of compensations. However, the concept of 'domicile' is not a magic wand that would solve disparities in the determination and award of compensatory damages. There is no global unity in the definition of the concept of 'domicile' as jurisprudence will show. In any case, the application of the law of the domicile of the passenger has no legal basis in the face of in Articles 17 and 24(2) of the Warsaw Convention, and cannot be made binding by the terms of the carrier's tariff or the IATA Inter-carrier Agreement.

Some of the emergent problems that remain unanswered even after acceptance of the IATA Agreement are as follows:

- What will be the situation in cases of successive carriage performed by different air carriers – one of them party to the Inter-carrier Agreement and the other not – which are not governed by exactly the same terms? Similarly, what will be the problems in the ever-growing practice of code-sharing, when one carrier concludes the contract of carriage and another actually performs it, and if they are not both parties to the agreement or not governed by the same terms?
- What will be the impact of the 'no limit' approach on insurance premiums, in particular for the small and medium-sized carriers? There is no transparency in the field of specific insurance premiums, and they appear to be a closely guarded business secret, known only to the particular airline and their insurance broker. It is generally believed that major airlines with modern

fleets of aircraft and established safety records would benefit from economies of scale, and the insurance premiums would represent a smaller portion of their operating costs than would be the case of small or medium-sized airlines.

The IATA Joint Working Groups believed that insurance costs related to the new approach in the Inter-carrier Agreement may be mitigated since:

- airlines already generally face the risk of current Warsaw/Hague/Montreal Agreement/voluntary limits being broken, especially in the USA, and must insure against this risk;
- the measure of compensatory damages being calculated according to the law of the domicile of the passenger should minimize 'forum shopping', reduce the cost of claims paid, and create a more predictable environment;
- insurance brokers indicate that, in a market-driven scenario, waiver of liability limits will better reflect the real long-term costs of compensatory damages.

At least some of the logic of this evaluation sounds unconvincing. For instance, there is absolutely no guarantee that the courts will determine and award compensation by reference to the law of the domicile of the passenger. The concept of 'domicile' is not uniformly defined in law, and the 'domicile' of a passenger is a fortuitous and unpredictable element, particularly if one were to consider the multitude of international passengers the airlines carry. It is more sensible to expect that overall insurance premiums will be determined by the highest perceived risk, defined by expected claims on behalf of passengers domiciled in a country or countries with the highest level of compensation. A certain amount of 'forum shopping' cannot be prevented by the imperative provision of Article 28 of the Convention, although claimants still do not enjoy the enhanced jurisdiction which they would have benefited from under the Guatemala City Protocol and Protocol No. 3, Article 28.

The airlines' initiative in attempting to overcome the impasse which is now presented by the Warsaw system is commendable. However, it has been alleged that the airlines are not acting with an altruistic concern for the well-being of their passengers; their interest is seemingly to streamline and clarify their own risk-management problems and to avoid lengthy and costly litigation. Their action is also alleged to be motivated by an effort to pre-empt a more damaging possible action by the US and other governments – a potential denunciation of the Warsaw system that would create chaotic and unpredictable conflicts of laws and conflicts of jurisdiction issues which would benefit no one but the powerful lobbies of the trial lawyers and enhance time-consuming, costly and unpredictable litigation. It is claimed that the new Inter-carrier Agreement will expedite the settlement of claims and there will be little need for such adversary litigation under the Agreement. The claimant will only have to prove the extent of recoverable compensatory damages.

The very concept of 'recoverable compensatory damages' remains undefined in the international unification of law under the Warsaw Convention and the Hague Protocol – the only imperative sources of law in force. The Warsaw Convention, in Article 17, refers only to 'damage sustained', and in no way prescribes that such has to be determined and awarded by reference to the law of the domicile of the passenger. There still remains a vast disparity between the jurisprudence in the United States and the rest of the world as to whether only 'pecuniary' damage is to be compensated and, in particular, in the face of the US jury awards for pre-death pain and suffering, loss of consortium, loss of parental guidance, loss of enjoyment of life, etc., which often reach amounts out of any proportion with the compensation awarded anywhere else in the world. Therefore, the 'mental trauma' suffered by a passenger remains a contentious issue under the Warsaw Convention and the Hague Protocol, and is subject to different decisions before different courts of law.

Although the IATA Inter-carrier Agreement on Passenger Liability cannot amend the Warsaw instruments in force, it strongly affects their practical application and renders many of their provisions moot. For example, the penalty for defects in the documents of carriage or in the 'notice' becomes irrelevant in a 'no limit' environment. In practice, it means that the formalities of the documents of carriage prescribed by the Convention have no practical legal consequences, and they could be disregarded. A computer record could replace the formal passenger ticket and baggage check. The concept of 'wilful misconduct' in Article 25 of the Convention and the Hague Protocol also becomes irrelevant unless a claimant attempts to go beyond the 'compensatory' damages and claims punitive damages which are still technically claimable in the USA under Article 24 of the Convention.

## Regulatory Management of the Warsaw System

### *ICAO Initiatives*

On 15 November 1995, the Council of the International Civil Aviation Organization decided to establish a Secretariat Study Group to assist ICAO's Legal Bureau in developing a mechanism to accelerate the modernization of the Warsaw system. The results of the Study Group's deliberations of February 1996 are reflected in a new draft instrument which has been developed by the Legal Bureau of ICAO.

The elements of the new draft Convention are contained in a single consolidated legal instrument representing a composite text that is meant to replace the current complex system of conventions and protocols. It retains the framework of the Warsaw Convention, while at the same time including some elements of the Hague Protocol. The draft instrument has fully incorporated the cargo provisions of Montreal Protocol No. 4 and, where appropriate, has included provisions of Montreal Protocol No. 3 and the Guatemala City Protocol.

Provisions of the ICAO instrument on the issue of passenger liability are similar to the principles of the Japanese initiative. However, the ICAO instrument has retained the status quo on liability principles regarding baggage and cargo, aligning documentary requirements to facilitate the flow of passengers, baggage and cargo and to obtain the benefits of new technology in the issuance of documents of carriage.

Jurisdictional issues have been retained in the new ICAO document as they appear under the present regime, with the possibility of adding another jurisdiction along the lines of the Guatemala City Protocol. As for notice of application of the new rules, such would be given to the passenger in the same manner as prescribed in the Hague Protocol. The concept of damages, to be awarded in accordance with the law of the forum, has been left unchanged.

## Comments

As the Kuala Lumpur Agreement by no means represents a final solution, but remains only a temporary and pragmatic solution showing a possible way out of the impasse that has existed between the States for some thirty years, the current challenge for States will be to expedite studies in the framework of the ICAO Legal Committee and to finalize a new convention unifying the rules relating to international carriage by air. Introducing another Protocol may not be the right approach, as there is already a jumbled maze of legal documents that are neither self-contained nor authentic in all ICAO languages and are kept by different depositaries.

As has been demonstrated in the ICAO initiative, the best elements of the Guatemala City Protocol and the substance of Protocol No. 4, coupled with the 'no limit' concept (if widely accepted by the industry), provide a good starting point for such a new convention, provided an effective way is found to award compensation with reference to jurisdictional issues and further unify a definition of recoverable compensatory damages. It may be also desirable to consider the inclusion of a 'settlement inducement clause', forcing the air carrier or the claimant to pay the costs of litigation if they do not make or accept an offer of settlement equal to the eventual judicial award. Making payments to the claimant immediately after the accident (as recommended by ECAC and formulated in the last draft EU Council regulation) would also serve a valuable socio-economic purpose, and is therefore a worthwhile consideration, although it appears quite unrealistic to make such payments 'not later than ten days after the event' as Article 4(1) of the proposed EU Council regulation suggests. It does not take a skilled and experienced legal practitioner to figure out that more time than that is required in practice just to determine the identity of the claimant or claimants, and what their respective rights may be.

A unified law of international air transport which addresses modern, commercial exigencies of aviation must be urgently adopted in the form of an international treaty which is supported by the political will of sovereign states and which is binding on the courts of law. Montreal Protocol No. 4 of 1975 (cargo) is not an independent instrument, but only an element of the separate and distinct international instrument known as the 'Warsaw Convention as Amended at The Hague, 1955, and by Protocol No. 4 of Montreal, 1975', the result of the sequential amendment of the system by a protocol and then by a protocol to that protocol. There is no authentic, consolidated text of such an instrument, and it has to be construed by inserting it into the original Warsaw Convention of 1929 (the text of which is authentic only in French), the amending provisions of the Hague Protocol of 1955 and the amending provisions of Montreal Protocol No. 4 of 1975. The resulting instrument would contain the Warsaw/Hague provisions with respect to passengers and baggage (not so far ratified by the United States, and not acceptable to it), as well as the 'new' and acceptable provisions relating to cargo. Many States may face difficulty in ratifying, at this stage, an instrument containing what are perceived as obsolete provisions with respect to passengers. The situation is not made any easier by the fact that Montreal Protocol No. 4 would not permit a sweeping reservation that the ratification does not apply to the provisions relating to passengers. Under these circumstances, it is encouraging that the ICAO draft instrument has included the provisions of this protocol, thus obviating a further separate consideration of it by States.

Since the implementation of the IATA Inter-carrier Agreement is facing practical difficulties, it is apparent that airlines will feel compelled to implement it in different modified forms to suit their specific needs (e.g. some airlines are contemplating different conditions for different routes or not to apply the waiver of the limits or of defences with respect to claims made by public social insurance or similar bodies, whether such are used for indemnity or contribution or acquired by way of subrogation or assignment). This status quo would undoubtedly lead to further disunification of the law, and consequent disarray.

A further threat to the credibility and sustenance of the IATA Agreement is the proposal of the Commission of the European Communities for a Council regulation that would constitute valid law in respect of the 15 members of the European Union and their carriers. Of course, the regulation would have applicability only within the EU, but nevertheless, unlike the IATA Agreement, it is a valid law, albeit in a limited but regional context, which extends the jurisdictional purview of Article 28 of the Warsaw Convention to a court of a member State where the claimant has their domicile or permanent residence.

Theoretically, future regulatory management which admits of the modernization of the Warsaw system and review of the ratification of international air law instruments may take one of two directions. The international aviation community may wish to revisit Montreal Protocol No. 3 and address once again the contentious characteristic of the Protocol as reflected in its rigid and unbreakable limit of liability, with a view to obviating it in line with modern commercial exigencies. It may, on the other hand, wish to draft a new legal instrument (along the lines of the ICAO initiative), taking into account the latest developments in the international arena, as reflected by the Japanese initiative and initiatives of IATA and the European Union. The former may include consideration of a special contract which may be beneficial to the passenger, and the latter may attenuate the still useful elements of the Guatemala and Montreal instruments. In any event, management of this complex area of private liability in air law should not be undertaken without the consideration of the implications of such commercial practices as code-sharing by airlines, the use of electronic tickets in the carriage of persons by air, the use of computer reservation systems and electronic tagging of baggage. The successful management of the Warsaw system of liability or a totally new system would depend on the extent to which the international aviation community accommodates these prolific commercial practices within its regulatory umbrella.

# 16 The Millennium Bug

## Introduction

When business reopens after the weekend on Monday 3 January in the year 2000, we could be witnessing the start of a complete breakdown in any operations which are computer-driven. The reason: most computers and sites have systems that use date fields which allow only two bytes to express the year. For example, 1999 is stored as '99' and the year 2000 is stored as '00' meaning that affected computers will assume that '00' refers to the year 1900. The result may be, as aptly stated by William McDonough, President of the Federal Reserve Bank, the complete collapse of human interaction:

> The failure to get it right will affect the integrity of the payment system, financial markets, and the performance of the domestic and global economics.[1]

It would not be an exaggeration to say that such a widespread computer crash could leave us in total darkness (because of our utility company's reliance on computers), without office telephones, (because the phone network is will be computerized), and any automobiles which rely on computer chips may not run.[2]

The enormity of the problem lies in the fact that even 2000-compliant or 'millennium-proof' computer systems will malfunction if they acquire data from non-compliant systems.

The already increasing trend toward litigation as a solution to computer systems failures will accelerate, with millennium bug claims resulting in an exponential rise in litigation world-wide, filed by clients whose investments are affected, by shareholders of companies whose software does not survive the transition to the year 2000, by claimants whose relatives or dependants die as a result of the problem or those who are injured by it, and by class actions filed by various affected persons who use non-compliant computer software packages. Transportation claims brought by clients of operators which are unable to execute the contracts of transportation entered into will be high on the list. Class action suits and individual suits for death or injury caused by accident in air transportation may account for a high proportion of lawsuits if the air transport industry does not act to modify the computers and programs which control airline schedules and airline safety.

The cost to fix the millennium bug world-wide (not only for the aviation industry) is estimated at US$ 500 billion, and IATA has estimated that airlines alone will need US$ 1.6 billion.[3]

For the aviation industry, the problems will be esoteric indeed. On Monday 3 January 2000, users of aircraft hangars the world over could arrive to find that their computerized furnaces had been shut down since Friday night, the inter-office telephone system does not work, and the AOG Brake Assembly has lost its entire component database! The biggest and most ominous concern would be the aircraft themselves, where, although their auto-flight functions, EFIS and engine control would not melt down as they do not usually operate on a time and date information system given by their computers, more critical functions such as Flight Management Systems (FMS) and Integrated Flight Control Systems would collapse, as they are usually time/date-sensitive.

The millennium problem could also affect air traffic control systems run by date/time-sensitive software. In addition, owners of Global Positioning Systems (GPS) in the United States will have the more compelling problem of having to face a similar problem in advance – on 22 August 1999, when the GPS week-numbering system will reset to zero. Known as the GPS Week-Number Roll Over Date, this day has been set for the satellites to download the new almanac to the GPS to reconnect to the satellites.

It could be envisaged that much of the penal action brought against negligent businesses operators would be *ex post facto*, to claim compensation from or punish those responsible for not taking action right now to rectify the problem.

One of the measures that may act as an effective legal safeguard is to carry out a legal review of software vendor contacts to reveal the legal obligations of a vendor to help rectify the problem before it occurs in the year 2000. Another measure is for the responsible party to keep meticulous records of all efforts made to rectify the problem before the turn of the century. The inclusion of indemnities and warranties in merger contracts, for example in the instance of airline mergers which are occurring now, is advisable, together with the establishment beforehand of legal immunity from shareholder claims as a result of the millennium bug.

## The Aviation Industry and the Millennium Bug

### *Airlines*

The aviation industry is posed a unique challenge by the millennium bug. The cost of this challenge to airlines, as assessed by the International Air Transport Association (IATA), will be US$ 1.6 billion.[4] In addition, there may be costs as a result of flight delays caused by non-compliant computer systems. Civil airlines are integrated in terms of information technology with airports, ground handling, avionics and engineering, air traffic control and maintenance in their daily operations. This means that the IT requirements of each of these sectors, however varied and multifarious, have to mesh together for security and safety purposes so that airlines perform their task of carrying passengers and freight without mishap.

Having addressed the problem individually, airlines and suppliers began to realize that the scale of the millennium bug requires more concerted effort, and called upon IATA to co-ordinate a sustained effort to tackle the problem on a collective basis. Accordingly, IATA set up a dedicated working group, which commenced its research in October 1996.

The primary function of the working group is to create awareness among the aviation industry of the significance of the problem, and to create a certain commonality among the various sectors of the industry in order to handle the problem according to collective standards.

The airlines' concerns and their approach to the problem (through IATA) have been addressed mainly with regard to safety issues concerning communications with air traffic control and airport infrastructural entities. The airlines are also addressing the problems of realigning their sales and ticketing systems to accord with the upcoming Economic Monetary Union in the European Union States on 1 January 1999.

On the subject of air traffic control, in the United States alone, air traffic computers rely on programs containing have more than 23 million lines of code in 50 different computer languages distributed among 250 systems. IATA reports that the Federal Aviation Administration (FAA) is taking a two-pronged approach in tackling the millennium bug *vis-à-vis* air traffic control.[5] This approach calls for upgrading existing air traffic computers to adapt to the new millennium, and the replacement of some computers by new compliant machinery. The primary objective and mission of US air traffic control, however, is to ensure safety, even at the cost of re-routing flights and incurring flight delays if necessary.[6]

The UK's Civil Aviation Authority (CAA) has identified some 300 of the 600 computer systems it operates in order to provide air traffic control services, and has already made headway in implementing 75 new systems to cope with the problem when it arises. EUROCONTROL (the European organization for safety of air navigation), which has 27 European States as members and provides air traffic control service management for 36 of them, has begun remedial work on its mainframe computer in collaboration with neighbouring air traffic control authorities.

### *Airports*

Airports, although not beset with the magnitude of safety problems faced by airlines and air navigation systems, could none the less be affected by the millennium bug to the extent that their terminals and their reservations and display systems, gating and escalator systems could all grind to a halt if their computers are not made year 2000-compliant. An Airport Council International (ACI) spokesman has stated:

> This is a micro processing problem, and it is very diverse. Airports are going to be assessing all their older systems. Otherwise you have the potential of access traffic problems, or even disruptions with magnetic card fuelling systems.[7]

### *The Insurance Industry*

Aviation insurers will certainly be concerned about how those they insure are handling the millennium bug. Any flaw in the attempts of the insured – the airlines – to fix the problem will have direct ramifications on the insurance industry, which will have to pay claims resulting from safety-related incidents and accidents involving aircraft. The Aviation Insurance Officers Association (AIOA) and Lloyds Aviation Underwriters Association (LAUA) have drafted both a questionnaire to assess airlines' preparedness and an exclusion clause which could deny cover to insured clients if they show that they are unprepared, thus offering proof that they did not exercise due care or diligence in tackling the problem.

## Legal Liabilities

### *Due Diligence at English Tort Law*

Aviation companies will be required to show that they have exercised due diligence or, in other words, adequately dispensed with the duty of care they owed to the consumer in addressing the millennium bug and overcoming it, well before the dawn of the new millennium. *A fortiori*, in the case of airlines, air traffic control services and air navigation services, the duty of care owed is tantamount to a guarantee of safety of life and limb. In this context, airlines could be compared to other professionals with special skills, such as medical doctors, so the diligence and care required would be objectively assessed at a higher level than that which is required of the common man.

At common law, therefore, the jurisprudence related to medical malpractice would be a distinct analogy, and principles enunciated therein would serve as a yardstick in instances of claims against the aviation industry.

In English law, the burden of proving negligence rests on the plaintiff, who has to prove that the defendant was negligent and that such negligence resulted in the loss or injury alleged. English law knows no sharp categories of care, and a degree of care and diligence which a defendant must exercise corresponds to the degree of negligence for which they are responsible,[8] and the defendant must do what is reasonable in the circumstances. A good example is the case of *Marshall* v. *Lindsay*,[9] which held that a defendant who is charged with professional negligence can clear themselves if they show that they acted in accordance with general or approved practice. A 1953 decision[10] held that the competent practitioner would know when a case is beyond their skill, and thereupon it would become their duty either to call in a more skilled person or to order removal of the patient to a hospital where skilled treatment is available. The case also held that when a consultant takes over the responsibility for the treatment of a patient, it is a defence in favour of that consultant to show that they had acted on the specific instructions given by another consultant. This principle would indeed be persuasive authority in the case of computer consultants hired by the aviation industry to correct the millennium bug.

It can also be observed that, in strict legal analysis, negligence means more than heedless or careless conduct, whether in omission or commission; it properly connotes a breach of duty which causes damage to the person to whom the duty was owing. However, a doctor who fails to diagnose a disease cannot excuse themselves by showing that they acted to the best of their skill if a reasonable doctor would have diagnosed it.[11] The civil liability of medical professionals towards their patients is compendiously stated in *R.* v. *Bateman*[12] as follows:

> ... if a person holds himself out as possessing special skill and knowledge and he is consulted as possessing such skill and knowledge, by or on behalf of a patient, he owes a duty to the patient to use due

> caution in undertaking the treatment. If he accepts the responsibility and undertakes the treatment and the patient submits to his direction and treatment accordingly, he owes a duty to the patient to use diligence, care, knowledge, skill and caution in administering the treatment. No contractual relation is necessary, nor is it necessary that the service be rendered for reward ... The law requires a fair and reasonable standard of care and competence. This standard must be reached in all the matters above mentioned. If the patient's death has been caused by the defendant's indolence or carelessness, it will not avail to show that he had sufficient knowledge; nor will it avail to prove that he was diligent in attendance, if the patient has been killed by his gross ignorance and unskilfulness ... As regards cases where incompetence is alleged, it is only necessary to say that the unqualified practitioner cannot claim to be measured by any lower standard than that which is applied to a qualified man. There may be recklessness in undertaking the treatment and recklessness in the conduct of it. It is, no doubt, conceivable that a qualified man may be held liable for recklessly undertaking a case which he knew, or should have known, to be beyond his powers, or for making his patient the subject of reckless experiment. Such cases are likely to be rare.[13]

The primary question, therefore, is whether in all the circumstances the defendant acted with the skill and competence to be expected from a person undertaking the particular activity and professing that specific skill.

One of the difficulties that may be encountered in the determination of professional negligence is whether there are specific established norms within a particular jurisdiction which recognizes what constitutes established proper professional practice. The classic statement of the governing principles is to be found in the direction to the jury given by McNair J in *Bolam* v. *Friern Hospital Management Committee*:[14]

> ... where you get a situation which involves the use of some special skill or competence, then the test whether there has been negligence or not is not the test of the man on top of the Clapham omnibus, because he has not got this special skill. The test is the standard of the ordinary skilled man exercising and professing to have that special skill. A man need not possess the highest expert skill at the risk of being found negligent. It is well established law that it is sufficient if he exercises the ordinary skill of an ordinary competent man exercising that particular art ... there may be one or more perfectly proper standards; and if a medical man conforms with one of those proper standards then he is not negligent ... a mere personal belief that a particular technique is best is no defense unless that belief is based on reasonable grounds ... a doctor is not negligent if he is acting in accordance with ... a practice (accepted as proper by a responsible body of medical men skilled in that particular art), merely because there is a body of opinion that takes a contrary view. At the same time,

> that does not mean that a medical man can obstinately and pigheadedly carry on with some old technique if it has been proved to be contrary to what is really substantially the whole of informed medical opinion.[15]

The *Bolam* test has been applied to every exercise of professional skill and judgement. The courts have rejected attempts to categorize professional tasks by subdividing them for the purpose of ignoring the *Bolam* case in particular contexts.[16] The test is not merely confined to cases relating to highly technical skills.[17] The *Bolam* case has received approval in Parliament,[18] the House of Lords[19] and the Privy Council.[20]

The House of Lords, in *Whitehouse* v. *Jordan*,[21] rejected the idea that mere errors of judgement cannot amount to negligence.[22] Lord Fraser observed:

> ... merely to describe something as an error of judgement tells us nothing about whether it is negligent or not. The true position is that an error of judgement may, or may not, be negligent; it depends on the nature of the error. If it is one that would not have been made by a reasonable competent professional man professing to have the standard and type of skill that the defendant held himself out as having, and acting with ordinary care, then it is negligent.[23]

In this context, the position of English common law is of great significance to the position of the aviation industry in the context of the millennium bug.

It is generally recognized that in determinations of negligence on the part of medical practitioners, the defendant must exhibit the degree of skill which a member of the public would expect from a person in their position. Pressures on the practitioner for which they are in no way responsible will not detract from guilt for an error on their part.

Moral responsibility and incompetence are generally considered mutually exclusive from negligence. In *Wilsher* v. *Essex Area Health Authority*,[24] the medical staff of a hospital were considered negligent for making an error in administering too much oxygen to a baby who, as a result, became blind. The plaintiff was an infant who was born prematurely suffering from various illnesses, including oxygen deficiency. His prospects of survival were considered to be poor and he was placed in the 24-hour special care baby unit at the hospital where he was born. The unit was staffed by a medical team, consisting of two consultants, a senior registrar, several junior doctors and trained nurses. While the plaintiff was in the unit, a junior and inexperienced doctor monitoring the oxygen in the plaintiff's bloodstream mistakenly inserted a catheter into a vein rather than an artery, but then asked the senior registrar to check what he had done. The registrar failed to see the mistake and, some hours later, when replacing the catheter, did exactly the same thing himself. Mustill LJ observed:

> This appeal raises three questions of law relating to the allegation that the defendants are liable for breach of duty. (1) What is the nature of the cause of action on which the plaintiff relies? (2) What standard of care was demanded of those members of the medical and nursing staff who are said to have been negligent? (3) On whom rests the burden of proof in relation to the allegation of negligence?

His Lordship also quoted with approval the *Bolam* case:

> ... a doctor who adopts a practice accepted as proper by a responsible body of medical men skilled in the relevant branch of medicine is not to be taken as negligent merely because there is a contrary view. Although this principle may have some bearing on the later episodes, it can have nothing to do with the first episode, for, although there were witnesses who regarded it as excusable in a young doctor not to know about the significance of the loop and its absence, there was no body of medical opinion which could regard it as appropriate to overlook the indications given by the X-rays as to the position of the catheter. The doctors made a mistake, although not necessarily a culpable one.[25]

Errors of judgement are often the fundamental basis for negligence at English law. In *Whitehouse* v. *Jordan*,[26] the plaintiff, who was born in 1970 with severe brain damage, brought an action against, *inter alia*, the first defendant, a senior registrar at the time of his birth, and the hospital authority, claiming that the damage had been caused by the first defendant's professional negligence. The principal allegations of negligence were that in the course of carrying out a 'trial of forceps delivery', the first defendant had pulled too long and too strongly on the plaintiff's head, thereby causing the brain damage. At the trial, the mother of the plaintiff said that when the forceps had been applied, it had felt like a deadened electric shock that lifted her hips off the delivery bed. Both the first defendant and the doctor who had assisted him denied that she had been lifted off the bed or that the first defendant had pulled violently with the forceps. The first defendant denied that the plaintiff's head had been wedged or stuck. Lord Wilberforce observed:

> ... first, it is necessary, in order to establish liability of, and to obtain an award of compensation against, a doctor or a hospital that there has been negligence in law. There is in this field no liability without proof of fault. Secondly, there are strict limitations upon this power of an appeal court to reverse the decision of the judge on an issue of fact.[27]

A significant consideration relating to the plaintiff's burden of proof of the defendant's negligence is that if the evidence is equally balanced so that there is no balance of probability in favour of the plaintiff 's contention of negligence, the action fails. In other words, if it is not clear whether the injury complained of may have occurred without carelessness on the part of the defendant, the plaintiff will not be considered as having discharged the burden of proof. The 1983 case of *Ashcroft* v. *Mersey Regional Health Authority*[28] concerned a case where, on 20 January 1978, the plaintiff submitted herself to an operation on her left ear. It was performed by a surgeon of long experience, great skill and the highest reputation. The operation proved to be disastrous, for the plaintiff was left with a partial paralysis of the left side of the face, an injury for which she claimed damages, alleging that the operation was carried out negligently. The paralysis was caused by damage to the facial nerve. Kilner Brown J observed:

> Where an injury is caused which never should have been caused, common sense and natural justice indicate that some degree of compensation ought to be paid by someone. As the law stands, in order to obtain compensation an injured person is compelled to allege negligence against a surgeon who may, as in this case, be a careful, dedicated person of the highest skill and reputation. If ever there was a case in which some reasonable compromise was called for, which would provide some amount of solace for the injured person and avoid the pillorying of a distinguished surgeon, this was such a case.[29] The proposition that an error of judgement by a medical man is not negligence is an inaccurate statement of the law. It may be; it may not. The question for consideration is whether on a balance of probabilities it has been established that a professional man has failed to exercise the care required of a man possessing and professing special skill in circumstances which require the exercise of that special skill. If there is an added burden, such burden does not rest on the person alleging negligence; on the contrary, it could be said that the more skilled a person is the more the care that is expected of him.[30]

A fundamental principle in common law with regard to professional negligence is that when a professional lacks the skill and experience to deal with a particular case, or realizes the possibility of their client being adversely affected by that professional's work which should be referred to a specialist practising in the field related to that work, they should refer the matter to someone who is competent to deal with it. In the 1952 case of *Payne* v. *St. Helier Group Hospital Management Committee,*[31] Donovan J held that a medical officer who incorrectly diagnosed a disease was negligent in that he had failed to refer the patient to a consultant medical practitioner.

However, the above principle is tempered with the premise that if a professional acts in accordance with general and approved practices of their profession, that would indeed constitute a good defence to a claim in negligence. In the Canadian Case of *Vancouver General Hospital* v. *McDaniel*,[32] the Privy Council reversed the decision of the Court of Appeal of British Columbia which imputed negligence to a hospital for allowing a small group of patients to be in a room with the plaintiff – a diphtheria patient who contracted smallpox thereafter. The Privy Council held:

> ... a defendant charged with negligence can clear his name if he shows that he has acted in accordance with general and approved practice. The appellants, in his Lordship's opinion, even if the onus rested on them of doing this, have in this case done so by a weight of evidence that cannot be ignored.[33]

The 1955 case of *Hunter* v. *Hanley*[34] established three criteria which determine a doctor's deviation from normal practice. They were:

1 it must be proven that there is a usual and normal practice;
2 it must be proven that the defendant had not adopted that practice;
3 it must be established that the course the doctor adopted is one which no professional of ordinary skill would have taken if they had been acting with ordinary care.[35]

Conducting a proper examination of the patient, particularly if the patient had not been seen earlier by a doctor for the ailment complained of, is a basic responsibility which would fall in the first category of usual and normal practice.[36] A wrong diagnosis, if proved, or failure to refer a patient to another physician where necessary, would fit into the third category. Caution must be exercised, however, in determining whether the doctor could have, according to their skill, knowledge and experience, diagnosed a disease correctly, as in the case of *Sadler* v. *Henry*,[37] where Cassels J held that the defendant medical practitioner was not negligent in failing to diagnose localized meningitis, since there were no signs or symptoms which could reasonably have led him to suspect that condition.

*Due Diligence in the USA*

Of comparative interest to the legal liability of the aviation industry would be the area of tortious liability relating to medical malpractice in the United States. Malpractice is defined as bad or unskilful practice on the part of a physician or surgeon resulting in injury to a patient,[38] or the failure of a physician to exercise the required degree of care, skill and diligence; or the treatment by a surgeon or physician in a manner contrary to accepted rules and with injuries resulting to a patient. The law relating to malpractice is based on three elements:

1 the professional relationship of physician and patient;
2 departure of the physician from some professional duty owed the patient;
3 the linking of such departure of duty to the proximate cause of injury.

In an instance when the physician is a specialist, they are bound to exercise a degree of skill and knowledge which is usually possessed by similar specialists. Such skill and knowledge is expected to be of a higher level than that which is possessed by the general practitioner. Where the doctor is a specialist, they are bound to exercise that degree of skill and knowledge which is ordinarily possessed by similar specialists, and not merely the degree of skill and knowledge of a general practitioner.[39] This rule is well stated in *Corpus Juris Secundum*:[40]

> A physician holding himself out as having special knowledge and skill in the treatment of a particular organ, disease or type of injury is bound to bring to the discharge of his duty to a patient employing him as such specialist, not merely the average degree of skill possessed by general practitioners, but that special degree of skill and knowledge possessed by physicians who devote special study and attention to the treatment of such organ, disease or injury, regard being had to the state of scientific knowledge at the time.

Similarly, a general practitioner who undertakes to treat a case which clearly lies within the field of a special branch of medicine will be held liable for failure to use skill equal to that of a specialist.[41]

The fundamental principle of professional conduct obtaining in the United States is that the physician is in a position of trust and confidence as regards their patient, and it is their duty to act with the utmost good faith toward the patient. If they know that they cannot accomplish a cure, or that the treatment adopted will probably be of no benefit, it is their duty to advise the patient of these facts.[42] In *Waltuck* v. *Poushter*,[43] it was held incorrect to dismiss the complaint where the proof was that the defendant was called to the decedent's home and treated her for complaints of malaise, head pains, elevated temperature and blood in her left ear. He was called *later* that day, and advised that her condition had *worsened*. Yet he made no effort at treatment or to contact a *specialist* to evaluate her symptoms. She then died of meningitis. It was held that a jury could find that his professional knowledge should have alerted him to the possible consequences of his failure to treat the complaints, or led him to perceive the seriousness of the plaintiff's condition.

It is one of the fundamental duties of a physician to make a properly skilful and careful diagnosis of the ailment of a patient, and if they fail to bring to that diagnosis the proper degree of skill and care and make an incorrect diagnosis, they may be held liable to the patient.[44] Furthermore, the physician must inform themselves by the proper tests and examinations, of the condition of their patient to undergo a proposed treatment or operation, so that they may intelligently exercise the skill of their calling.[45] The duty of exercising reasonable skill and diligence includes not only the diagnosis and treatment, but also the giving of proper instructions to the patient in relation to conduct, exercise and the use of an injured limb.[46]

*Due Diligence under Roman Dutch Law*

Another area of common law which brings to bear an interesting analogy in the law of negligence and due diligence is the Roman Dutch law. Under Roman Dutch law, negligence falls within the purview of the ancient *Lex Aquilian* concept of *culpa,* which is established objectively. The question for the courts is not what a tortfeasor was thinking or not thinking about, expecting or not expecting, but whether their behaviour was or was not such as is demanded of a prudent person under given circumstances. Negligence, therefore, may be defined as conduct which involves an unreasonable risk of harm to others.

The notion of duty of care is essentially an English common law principle, and Roman Dutch jurist McKerron cites with approval the dictum of Lord McMillan in *Bourhill* v. *Young*:[47]

> The duty to take care is the duty to avoid doing or omitting to do anything the doing or omitting to do which may have as its reasonable and probable consequence injury to others, and the duty is owed to those to whom injury may reasonably and probably be anticipated if the duty is not observed.[48]

In the 1934 case of *Perlman* v. *Zoutendyk,*[49] Watermeyer J delivered a watershed decision which established the essence of professional negligence. The case involved an instance where a sworn appraiser had issued a certificate of valuation with the knowledge that it would be used for the purpose of inducing someone to lend money on the property valued. The court held:

> ... in Roman Dutch law the duty to exercise reasonable care arises wherever the defendant whose act is complained of should reason-

> ably have foreseen probability of harm being caused by his act to another person, except, perhaps in those cases in which the act complained of can be said to be justified or exercised.[50]

The above dictum in the *Perlman* case, when compared with that of *Bourhill* v. *Young* above, reflects that duty of care is a common feature in both the Roman Dutch law and English common law. The Roman Dutch law requires two distinct questions to be answered:

1 What was the standard of care required of the tortfeasor at the time the alleged tortious act was committed?
2 Did the conduct of the tortfeasor comply with that standard?

One of the methods the courts have employed in answering these questions is to place themselves, as nearly as they can, in the position of the tortfeasor at the time when the act was committed, and to judge whether ordinary care which can reasonably be expected from a reasonable person under all circumstances was shown by the tortfeasor.[51] It is arguable, therefore, that this fundamental premise would be extended by jurisdictions which follow the Roman Dutch law to instances of professional negligence.

One of the most significant aspects of Roman Dutch law principles regarding professional negligence is the maxim *imperitia culpae adnumeratur*, which establishes that negligence is not determined by the lack of skill of the tortfeasor, but in their *undertaking* work without skill. Therefore, where a person engages in a profession or occupation which calls for special skill, the degree of skill which is required is that reasonably to be expected of a person engaged in such profession or occupation. Innes CJ observed:

> ... the Court will have regard to the general level of skill and diligence possessed and exercised at the time by the members of the branch of the profession to which the practitioner belongs.[52]

It is arguable that the above principle, when applied to a medical practitioner who examines a patient showing symptoms of an irregularity in the brain, should require that they refer the patient to a competent neurosurgeon. Similarly, an aviation industry entity would be required by law to refer a problem such as the one posed by the millennium bug to experts or consultants if the computer experts in the industry entity concerned cannot handle the problem themselves.

Under Roman Dutch law, the burden of proving negligence – on a preponderance of probability – rests with the plaintiff. Proof must be adduced not only to show the defendant's negligence, but also to draw a link between the defendant's negligence and the harm caused.

Wherever direct evidence of the defendant's negligence is not available, negligence may be established by inference of facts. Moreover, the plaintiff need not demonstrate their case; the court is entitled to act on a balance of probabilities.

Therefore, under the Roman Dutch law, as in English law and US law, it can be said that, when considered as an objective fact, negligence may be defined as conduct which involves an unreasonable risk of harm to others. It is the failure in given circumstances to exercise that degree of care which the circumstances demand. A requisite of liability in negligence is the breach of duty to the plaintiff.

## Comments: Action Required by the Aviation Industry

In order to obviate the need to defend possible claims which aver the lack of due diligence on the part of the aviation industry with regard to the millennium bug, it needs to act immediately. Airlines, airports, aircraft manufacturers and other aviation service providers must initially carry out a technical audit to fully comprehend the scope of the problem and draw up an action plan, taking a comprehensive inventory of software and systems used, and assessing whether such material would be susceptible to problems that may be created by the millennium bug.

The assessment of the scope of the problem should not be restricted to the information technology units of the organization's concerns, but should extend to all departments in the user areas in order to collect a full inventory of computer products that need to be compliant.

The next step is to carry out a comprehensive legal audit of all agreements entered into by the organization concerned, with a view to mapping out an action plan based on the legal responsibilities that may arise with agreements already entered into and those which are yet to be concluded. Such an audit would not only give the organization considerable awareness and preparedness to negotiate its contracts, but would also fortify the organization with effective leverage to negotiate future contracts. The legal audit should be comprehensive, in that it should examine all IT-based contracts and other major non-IT contracts which may be affected by possible claims.

Risk management remains a key element in addressing the millennium problem, and preparations to counter it should include a full audit of current insurance policies, with a view to determining whether such policies cover the problems envisaged in the year 2000. All exclusion clauses which may preclude the liability of the insurer should be reviewed in the process of this audit.

In addition to the legal and insurance audits, a commercial audit of all current and future suppliers is necessary, to determine whether such suppliers have attached warranties to their products to cover the problem. *Non obstante,* the auditors should also look into the liquidity of the suppliers, to ensure that they are likely to be in business in the years to come, since warranties alone may not suffice if the suppliers concerned are extinct when the problem emerges and, consequently, claims are made against the aviation industry entity concerned.

Once the three audits are completed, it is necessary to draw up an action plan, the first step of which should be to determine whether the organization concerned has the legal right to carry out repairs to its software. Once the necessary repairs have been carried out, the most tedious and time-consuming part – testing the systems – must be completed. For example, a year 2000-compliant computer reservation system should ensure not only the correct date structure, but also the fare structure, in order to avoid charging a passenger the incorrect fare as a result of adjustments carried out to the computer software.

Once the testing is satisfactorily carried out, we enter the final phase of the programme: monitoring its efficacy. Given the enormity of the task and the complexity of the problem, it is likely that further malfunctions will arise during the months following 1 January 2000, and dealing with these needs to be considered as the final part of the rectification process.

## Notes

1 Mark Grossman, *Misery Loves Company: The Year 2000 Crisis*: <http://www.mgrossmanlaw.com/lawtips/030298.html>.
2 Ibid.
3 Patrick Garett, 'The Millennium Bug: How the Airline Industry Will Cope With This Critical Issue', *Orient Aviation,* March 1998, Vol. 5, No. 4, at 14.
4 See 'Defusing the Millennium Bug', *Airlines International,* March/April 1998, Vol. 4, No. 2, at 58.
5 Id., at 60.
6 Ibid.
7 'Countdown to 2000', *Jane's Airport Review,* April 1998, Vol. 10, No. 3, at 38.
8 *Giblin* v. *McMullen* (1869) LR2PG 317, at 337, per Law, Chelmsford.
9 1935 1 KB 516.
10 *Pudney* v. *Union Castle Mail S.S. Ltd,* 1953 *Lloyd's Reports* 73.
11 Margaret Brazer (ed.), *Street on Torts,* London: Butterworths, 1982, at 205.
12 (1925) 94 LJKB 791, see *Akerele* v. *The King* [1943] AC 255 and also Linden's article 'The Negligent Doctor', *Osgoode Hall Law Journal,* Vol. 11, at 31.
13 Id., at 798.
14 [1957] 2 All ER 118, [1957] 1 WLR 582, at 586–7.
15 Ibid.
16 *Gold* v. *Haringey Health Authority* [1988] 8 C&P 475.
17 *Alchemy (International) Ltd* v. *Tattersalls Ltd* [1985] 2 EGLR 17.

18 Congenital Disabilities (Civil Liability) Act 1976, Section 1(5).
19 *Whitehouse* v. *Jordan* [1981] 1 All ER 267, [1981] 1 WLR 246, HL; *Maynard* v. *West Midlands Regional Health Authority* [1985] 1 All ER 635, [1982] 1 All ER 634, HL; *Sidaway* v. *Bethlem Royal Hospital and the Maudsley Hospital Governors* [1985] AC 871, [1985] 1 All ER 643, HL.
20 *Chin Keow* v. *Government of Malaysia* [1967] 1 WLR 813 PC.
21 [1981] 1 All ER 267, at 276. See also [1981] 1 WLR 246, at 258.
22 An argument to this effect had been put forward by Lord Denning MR in the Court of Appeal [1980] 1 All ER 650, at 658, CA. Lord Denning was concerned that there might be an explosion of medical malpractice claims if the courts did not reduce the standard of care applicable to professional persons.
23 [1981] 1 WLR 247.
24 (1987) QB 730. See also (1986) 3 All ER 801.
25 (1986) 3 All ER 801, at 812.
26 (1981) 1 WLR 246.
27 Id., at 258.
28 [1983] 2 All ER 245 aff'd 1985 2 All ER 96.
29 Id., at 246.
30 Id., at 247.
31 [1952] CLYB 2,442.
32 [1935] 152 LTR 56.
33 Id., at 57–8.
34 1955 SC 200.
35 Id., at 206.
36 See *Barnett* v. *Chelsea & Kensington Hospital Management Committee* [1969] 1 QB 428, and *Kavanaugh* v. *Abramson* (1964) 108 SJ 320.
37 [1954] IBMJ 1,331.
38 Charles Kramer, *Medical Malpractice* (4th edn), New York: Practising Law Institute, 1976, at 6.
39 *Beach* v. *Chollet*, 120 Ohio St. 449, 166 NE 415 (1928).
40 70 CJS *Physicians and Surgeons*, para. 41.
41 Herzog, *Medical Jurisprudence*, 1931, at 157; Gordon, Turner and Price, *Medical Jurisprudence*, 1953, at 121. In *Monahan* v. *Devinny*, 223 App. Div. 547, 229 NYS 60 (3rd Dept 1928), the defendants were chiropractors who treated the plaintiff unskilfully, as a result of which he became paralysed. The court held that the defendants were illegally practising medicine in violation of the Education Law, so that 'in an action of this kind they must be held to the same standards of skill and care as prevail amongst those who are licensed'. *NY Educ. Law*, para. 6,501, subd. 4, defines the practice of medicine thus: 'A person practices medicine within the meaning of this article, except as hereinafter stated, who holds himself out as being able to diagnose, treat, operate or prescribe for any human disease, pain, injury, deformity or physical condition, and who shall either offer or undertake, by any means or method, to diagnose, treat, operate or prescribe for any human disease, pain, injury, deformity or physical condition.'
42 Regan, *Doctor, Patient and the Law*, 1950, at 34; *Benson* v. *Dean*, 232 NY 52, 133 NE 125 (1921). Stryker, *Courts and Doctors*, p. 9 states: 'The relationship of patient and physician is to the highest possible degree a fiduciary one, involving every element of trust and confidence.' The American Medical Association, *Principles of Medical Ethics*, para. 8 provides: 'A physician should seek consultation upon request, in doubtful or difficult cases, or whenever it appears that the quality of medical service may be enhanced thereby.' See also Annot, 'Duty to Send Patient to Specialist', 132 *ALR* 392 (1949).
43 42 AD 2d 673, 344 NYS 2d 369 (4th Dept 1973).

44 41 Am. Jur., *Physician and Surgeon*, para. 95 (emphasis added).
45 41 Am. Jur., *Physician and Surgeon*, para. 94 (emphasis added).
46 *Pike* v. *Honsinger*, 155 NY 201, 49 NE 760 (1898).
47 [1942] 2 All ER 396, at 402.
48 R.M. McKerron, *The Law of Delict* (7th edn), Capetown: Juta & Co., 1971, at 26.
49 1934 CPD 151.
50 Id., at 154.
51 *S.A.R.* v. *Bardekber*, 1934 AD 473, at 480, per Wessels CJ.
52 *Van Wyk* v. *Lewis*, 1924 AD 438, at 444.

# PART III
# CONCLUSION

# 17 General Conclusion

At its 32nd Session, which was conducted in Montreal from 22 September to 2 October 1998, the Assembly of the International Civil Aviation Organization endorsed the establishment of a universal Safety Oversight Programme which would comprise regular, mandatory, systematic and harmonized safety audits. These audits will be carried out by ICAO in all its 185 contracting States from 1 January 1999, with their consent and at their request, under a Memorandum of Understanding signed by and between the State concerned and ICAO.[1]

The ICAO Safety Audit is aimed at determining whether individual States have the capacity to provide safe air navigation services to aircraft which traverse their airspace. It comes at a critical time in aviation history, when international civil aviation is on the threshold of a new millennium, which in its first fifteen years portends a virtual doubling of air traffic, both in the upper and lower airspace.

In 1997, the total scheduled international flights operated by the 705 carriers of the 185 contracting States of ICAO carried a total of approximately 1,448 million passengers and 26 million tonnes of freight.[2] In the same year, there were an estimated 16,993 operational aircraft (each carrying more than a maximum take-off weight of 9,000 kg), which was a 59 per cent increase from 10,712 aircraft operating a decade earlier.[3] In 1997, 1,309 jet aircraft were ordered (as against 1,003 in 1996), and 674 were delivered in the same year.[4]

If this were not sufficient to reflect the gigantic proportions to which international air transport has grown, more daunting figures loom ahead. For instance, it is estimated that the world-wide jet transport fleet will double by 2015.[5] With the current aircraft accident rate at 1.76 accidents per million departures (the best safety record of all modes of transportation), there are aggressive calls to reduce this rate by half, to 0.88 accidents per million departures by the year 2015. Moreover, the Gore Commission of the United States has called for an 80 per cent reduction in fatal aircraft accidents.[6]

ICAO'S own figures reveal that of the world-wide airline accident data compiled by ICAO, since 1970, controlled flight into terrain (CFIT) continues to be the most serious threat to safety, accounting for 58 per cent of total fatalities.[7] This is a significant increase from 40 per cent prevailing during the period 1988–97. During the previous decade (1978–87), CFIT deaths amounted to 31.5 per cent of all fatalities.[8]

Although the above figures are certainly foreboding, the silver lining is that there is an awareness of the enormity of the problem and an effort to identify contributory factors to the aircraft accident rate, including: underdeveloped aviation infrastructure; poor airline operating practices; inadequate national aviation oversight of varying degrees; poor air traffic control capability; lack of navigational aids and radar coverage; and substandard airport equipment.[9] Unsatisfactory meteorological facilities have also been identified as possible causes of aircraft accidents.

The ICAO programme for the prevention of controlled flight into terrain commenced in 1992 and went steadily ahead with the formation of the ICAO and Industry CFIT Task Force in 1993. This task force was established in co-ordination with the Flight Safety Foundation of the United States. The pre-eminent aim of the task force was identified at ICAO's 31st Assembly in 1995 as the reduction of the global CFIT accident rate by 50 per cent by 1998. Pursuant to this aim, the ICAO Assembly adopted Resolution A31-9, by which the Assembly directed the ICAO Council to continue to develop the ICAO programme for the prevention of CFIT accidents, and urged all ICAO member States to take all necessary measures to assist in achieving the primary objective of a 50 per cent reduction in the global CFIT accident rate by 1998.

For its part, during 1995–98 ICAO, through its Air Navigation Commission, completed the development of a framework which encapsulates the seminal ICAO activities in pursuit of aviation safety. The Commission created a comprehensive document which encompassed a Global Aviation Safety Plan (GASP) which aims at giving ICAO leadership to gain a commitment from States and the industry to enhance aviation safety world-wide.

At its 32nd Session, the ICAO Assembly in October 1998 recognized that the ICAO Safety Oversight Programme has reached a saturation point in terms of policy, and sought to address this in developing the oversight programme. It was considered at this session that there were regional deficiencies and shortcomings in the field of air navigation, and that contracting States must correct such problems.

In it deliberations, the Assembly found useful the developments of the US safety programme developed in April 1998 through its Federal Aviation Administration (FAA), called 'Safer Skies', which was designed to achieve a fivefold reduction in fatal accidents. Through this programme, the FAA intends to address the CFIT issue, matters pertaining to engine failures, weather, loss of control, and so on.

Taking the above into consideration in the context of its own Global Aviation Safety Plan, the ICAO Assembly adopted Resolution A32-15, which recognized that ICAO's primary objective is to continue promoting the safety of international civil aviation, and noted that the expected increase in the volume of international civil aviation would result in an increasing number of aircraft accidents unless the accident rate was reduced. The Resolution endorses the ICAO Plan while urging contracting States to examine and revise their laws if necessary to achieve a proper balance among the various elements of accident prevention efforts and to encourage increased voluntary reporting of events that could affect aviation safety. ICAO is instructed by this resolution to develop appropriate policies and guidelines in this regard.

Whether it be the management of the upper atmosphere or controlled flight into terrain, air traffic services play an integral part in preventing collisions between aircraft and between aircraft and obstructions. The rapidity with which commercial liberalization is sweeping the evolution of commercial air transport brings to bear the real possibility of proliferation of aircraft in the skies, and air traffic services have to adapt towards managing efficiently the movement of these aircraft. It is critical, therefore, that air traffic services manage the separation between aircraft both in the air and on the ground, and professionally issue clearances to aircraft to land or take off.

Airspace management is intended to maximize the use of airspace through such tools as time- and space-sharing through appropriate segregation of these elements. The proper collection of data, evaluation of options and planning and allocating of airspace is the primary facet of airspace management. The eventual goal of efficient airspace management remains the ensuring of an optimum flow of air traffic, which could be constrained by such factors as the inadequate provision of air navigation facilities and unexpected meteorological conditions.

Current limitations in the air traffic management systems mostly stem from the inadequacy of the air traffic control system used worldwide. Mostly, the information flow between air traffic control systems and aircraft may be insufficient to sustain improvement in these services. Another shortcoming of the ground air traffic control system is that it may lack the ability to accurately assess the air traffic flow and thereby be unable to survey and optimize such traffic flows.

Air traffic ground control systems often follow data on aircraft performance and environmental factors which are not always realistic.

The realities of a global air traffic management (ATM) system have been diligently sought by ICAO and the planning and implementation of satellite-based Communication, Navigation and Surveillance (CNS) technologies are being implemented through the various ICAO regions. These CNS systems have to be fully in consonance with global air traffic management standards, in order for an internationally harmonized CNS/ATM system to prevail. Once this is achieved, a global ATM system would be able to allow flexibility to the user/operator in selecting preferred flight profiles, while retaining the advantage of the system in terms of safety. A global system would be a more efficient tool than the present ground-based, unit-by-unit system in organizing airspace and creating a single continuum of airspace. Above all, such a system would be able to service increased capacity to meet the future traffic demand of commercial aviation.

Satellite communication in CNS/ATM systems would also allow more accurate data to be available, making it possible to reduce delays and increase airspace capacity at the same time. Congestion in the lower airspace in particular would be obviated by improved flow management through satellite-based communications. Under this system, more approach streams for landing would be a definite possibility, through a global extrapolation of airspace achieved through the inflow of satellite communications.

The ICAO Global Air Navigation Plan for CNS/ATM systems, which incorporates the above philosophy and envisions the implementation of its CNS/ATM systems through its Planning and Implementation Regional Groups (PIRGs), is consistent with, and indeed would assist the concept of 'free flight' as introduced by the FAA of the United States. On 31 October 1995, a task force, initiated by the FAA, concluded the defined 'free flight' as: 'a safe and efficient flight operating capability under instrument flight rules in which the operators have the freedom to select their path and speed in real time.'[10] Air traffic restrictions are imposed only to ensure separation, to preclude exceeding airport capacity, to prevent unauthorized flights through special use of airspace, and to ensure flight safety. Restrictions are limited in extent and duration to correct the identified problem. Any activity which removes restrictions represents a move towards free flight.

The concept of 'free flight' *per se* is not new. The basic objective of prudent air traffic controllers world-wide is to manage the airspace which they oversee to offer the optimum airspace to users at a minimum level of congestion and zero risk. The communion of 'free flight' as proposed by the FAA and the global CNS/ATM system pursued through ICAO would sustain only if both have a common objective to provide more efficient services, both in the area of flight operations and supporting services. Another caveat is that 'free flight' should not be perceived to devolve upon pilots the prerogative to go and come as they please. Separation assurance provided by air traffic control is an essential and mandatory prerequisite towards ensuring safety. Collision avoidance cannot be guaranteed if aircraft operate at random on individually optimized tracks. However, the global air traffic management system could support 'free flight' if it were to set the parameters and monitor the activity within its own periphery. Therefore, there is no doubt that more work is needed in order to mesh the two concepts together.

In Europe, the Transport Ministers of the European Civil Aviation Conference (ECAC) initiated a study culminating in an Air Traffic Management Strategy for Europe for the years after 2000. This study has its genesis in the Fifth Meeting of ECAC Transport Ministers (MATSE/5) in Copenhagen on 14 February 1997, when an Institutional Strategy for Air Traffic Management was adopted and it was decided that the revised EUROCONTROL Convention would form the legal postulate for implementing ECAC Institutional Strategy.

The overall objective of the ATM strategy for Europe is that there be a uniform European ATM network for all phases of flight, to enable the safe, economic, expeditious and orderly flow of traffic through European airspace. In order to achieve this objective, the first premise of the strategy is that the airspace of ECAC States shall be considered a continuum, and shall not be constrained by national boundaries. However, the strategy reinforces and affirms the principle of State sovereignty by recognizing that every State has complete and exclusive sovereignty over the airspace above its territory. The strategy also aims to ensure that ATM operations are compliant with ICAO CNS/ATM plans and operate on the basis of uniformity throughout the ECAC area, while providing a seamless service to the user at all times.

The above initiatives by ICAO in its Global Plan for Aviation Safety and CNS/ATM systems implementation, by FAA in terms of free flight, and by EUROCONTROL in its ATM Strategy all encompass the safety of aviation and therefore are equally applicable to the management of upper airspace, lower airspace and to controlled flight into terrain. Above all, these systems have a common aim: to liberalize and develop CNS/ATM systems to ensure safety and durability. This trend transcends the currently used ground air traffic management system, which is constrained when faced with the proliferation of commercial activity in air transport, resulting in the rapid increase of aircraft movements.

Although the most compelling element of the management of airspace is to ensure safety, one cannot underestimate the importance of coping with the economic realities brought about by the proliferation of aircraft in airspace.

The projected doubling of the world aircraft fleet by the year 2015 is merely a corollary of the profound changes taking place right now in commercial aviation. As discussed earlier, at the threshold of the new millennium, the airline industry has already began to use such intrepid commercial tools as franchising and outsourcing to maximize profits. Therefore, an effective approach is now needed to face the challenge of congestion, both from a safety angle and from an economic prospective. To accomplish this task, in-depth forecasting of regional traffic movements should be carried out, and these studies should form the basis for future planning for air traffic management in the various regions of the world.

Arguably, the first assumption in such a joint study should be that the demand for air travel would be based on numerous complex variables such as governmental policy on the award of air traffic rights, liberalization/deregulation policies and the commercial profiles of their air carriers. Other factors are governmental policies on tourism, and restrictions or promotion of migration by various States. In general, the study should also address regional trends such as the formulation of trading blocs, pace of economic growth (particularly in developing countries) and the overall investments allocated by governments of a region for infrastructural development and the movement of business capital within a region.

A long-term demand for air travel in a region would presuppose that region's economic developments and its proclivity towards the growth of its income levels, as reflected and extrapolated by the demographic trends in the region and the Gross Domestic Products of its countries. The political environment of a region as well as individual countries would also play a major role in such an assessment.

## Notes

1 ICAO News Release, PIO 12/98, at 1 and 2. At the 32nd Session of the Assembly of ICAO, Contracting States adopted Resolution A32-11 which gives legal effect to the ICAO Safety Audit Programme.
2 *Annual Report of the Council 1997*, Montreal: ICAO, at 2.
3 Id., at 4.
4 Ibid.
5 See Paul Proctor, 'Accident Analysis Renews Focus on Infrastructure, Safety Issues', *Aviation Week & Space Technology*, 15 June 1998, at 49.
6 Ibid.
7 See Reinhard Menzel, 'Analysis Shows that CFIT Continues to Account for the Heaviest Loss of Life Worldwide', *ICAO Journal*, April 1998, Vol. 53, No. 3, at 5.
8 Ibid. The author states that during 1988–97, the second most serious safety problem, loss of control, accounted for 26 per cent of all fatalities. Technical malfunctions had accounted for 21 per cent of all fatalities, while fire and/or

explosion rated at 9 per cent, and collision, icing and windsheer had accounted for 6, 2 and 1 per cent respectively.

9 Proctor, op. cit. The author cites Boeing Aircraft Company, which maintains that 90 per cent of all functioning instrument landing systems (ILS) are located in North America and Europe.

10 See *Action Plan – Dynamic Air Traffic Management*, RTCA, Inc., 15 August 1996, at 1.

# Index

# Index of Cases Cited